DONEGAL

from waves to wilderness

Kate Slevin

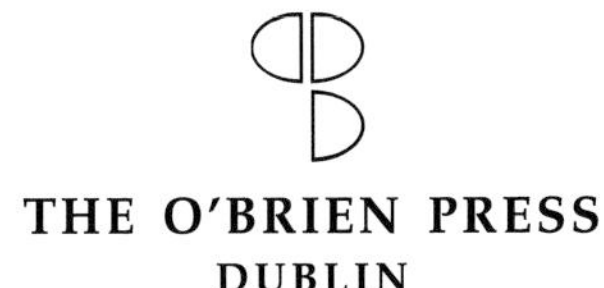

THE O'BRIEN PRESS
DUBLIN

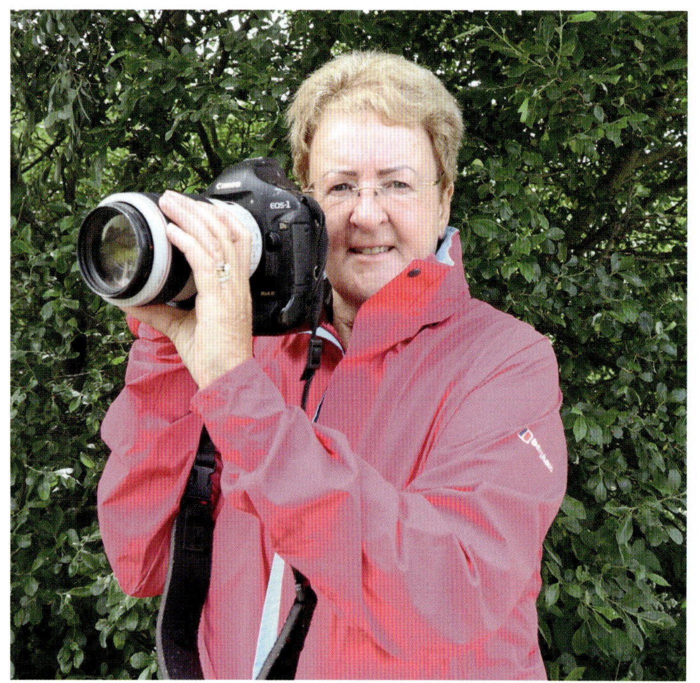

KATE SLEVIN, from southeast Donegal, grew up surrounded by the wild beauty of Ireland's most northwesterly county. When her husband, John, passed away in 2014, she turned to photography as part of her healing process, drawing inspiration from the natural, wild landscape around her.

This is her first book.

www.kateslevinphotography.com

kateslevinphotography

First published 2024 by
The O'Brien Press Ltd,
12 Terenure Road East, Rathgar,
Dublin 6, D06 HD27, Ireland.
Tel: +353 1 4923333; Fax: +353 1 4922777
E-mail: books@obrien.ie
Website: obrien.ie
The O'Brien Press is a member of Publishing Ireland.

ISBN: 978-1-78849-476-2

8 7 6 5 4 3 2 1
28 27 26 25 24

Printed and bound by Drukarnia Skleniarz, Poland.
The paper in this book is produced using pulp from managed forests.

Published in

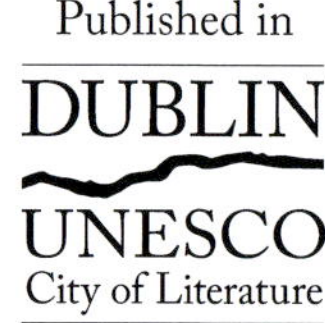

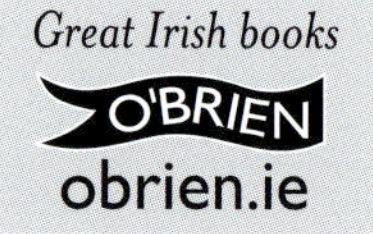

CONTENTS

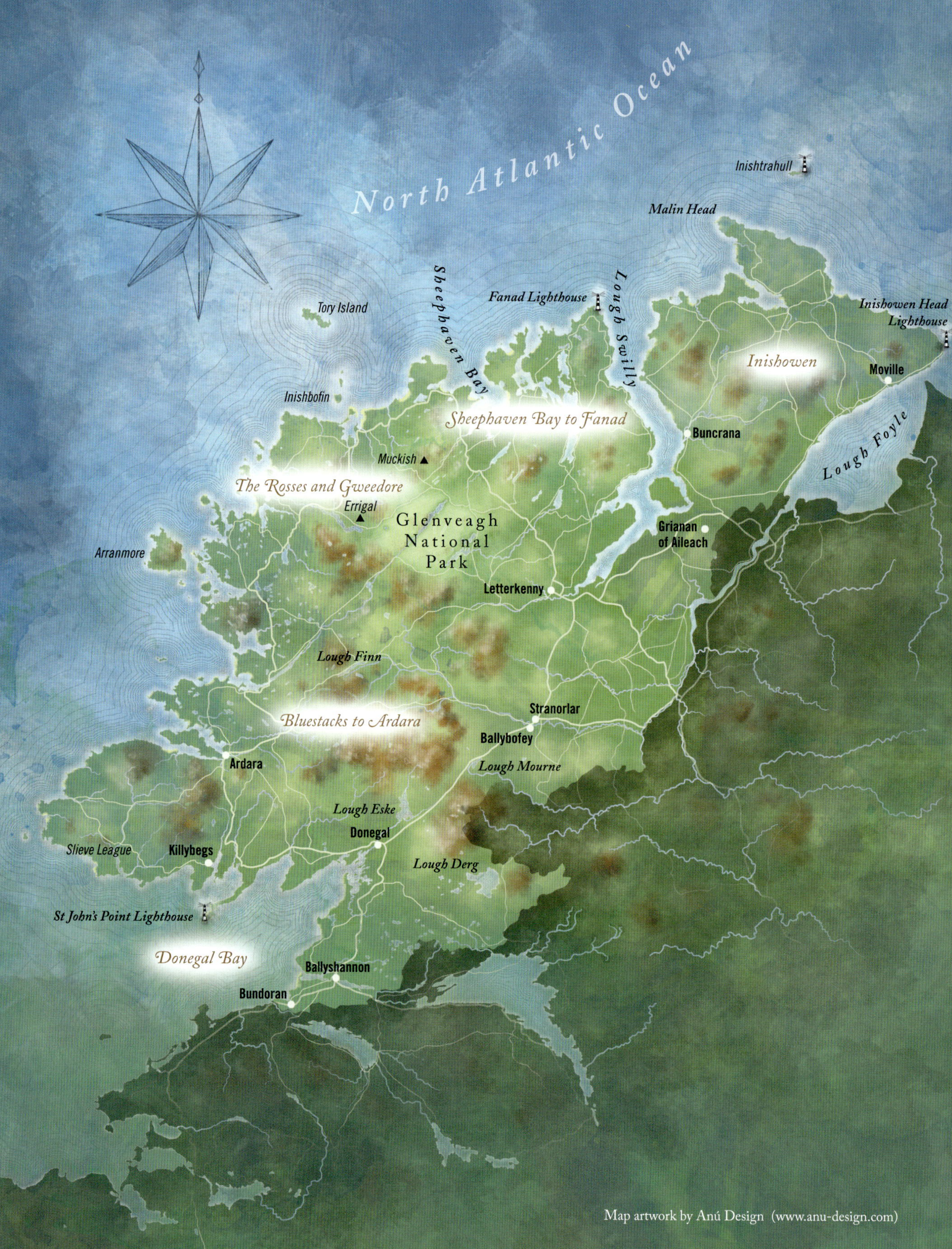

North Atlantic Ocean
Inishtrahull
Malin Head
Tory Island
Fanad Lighthouse
Loughan Swilly
Inishowen Head Lighthouse
Inishbofin
Sheephaven Bay
Inishowen
Moville
Sheephaven Bay to Fanad
Buncrana
Muckish ▲
Lough Foyle
The Rosses and Gweedore
Errigal ▲
Glenveagh National Park
Arranmore
Grianan of Aileach
Letterkenny
Lough Finn
Stranorlar
Bluestacks to Ardara
Ballybofey
Lough Mourne
Ardara
Lough Eske
Donegal
Slieve League
Killybegs
Lough Derg
St John's Point Lighthouse
Donegal Bay
Ballyshannon
Bundoran
Map artwork by Anú Design (www.anu-design.com)

INTRODUCTION

Ireland's most northwesterly county, Donegal is renowned for its untamed landscapes and its spectacular and ruggedly beautiful seascapes. It is a feast for the senses! With the longest coastline of any county in Ireland – in all, it has 1,134 kilometres to discover – Donegal boasts some of the most stunning coastal scenery and some of the finest beaches in the world.

I grew up in the countryside outside Stranorlar. In 1994, I met my husband John and we moved to Barnesmore in southwest Donegal. Our favourite way to enjoy a day off was to travel the length and breadth of the county. John passed away suddenly in 2014 and it was then that photography and its invitation to explore the raw, natural beauty around me helped clear the head and mend the heart a little bit. Somehow it rekindled my creativity and became a part of the healing process, so our journey together continues through my photographs. Bereavement became part of my life again recently with the death of my beloved nephew Stephen. Taking the images in the pages that follow was a blessing that drew me back into the creative healing journey of photography.

Exploring Donegal at different times of the day and in different seasons is what inspires me and rewards me with those special moments of being a photographer. I believe in creating photos by choice and yet there is a magic in finding a photo opportunity by chance. Add a sunrise or sunset, and the land, sea and sky collide in a kaleidoscope of colour!

Donegal people are renowned for their special warmth, friendliness and hospitality, so stop a while and have a chat.

I hope you enjoy this book as much as I have enjoyed the journey to create it.

Kate Slevin

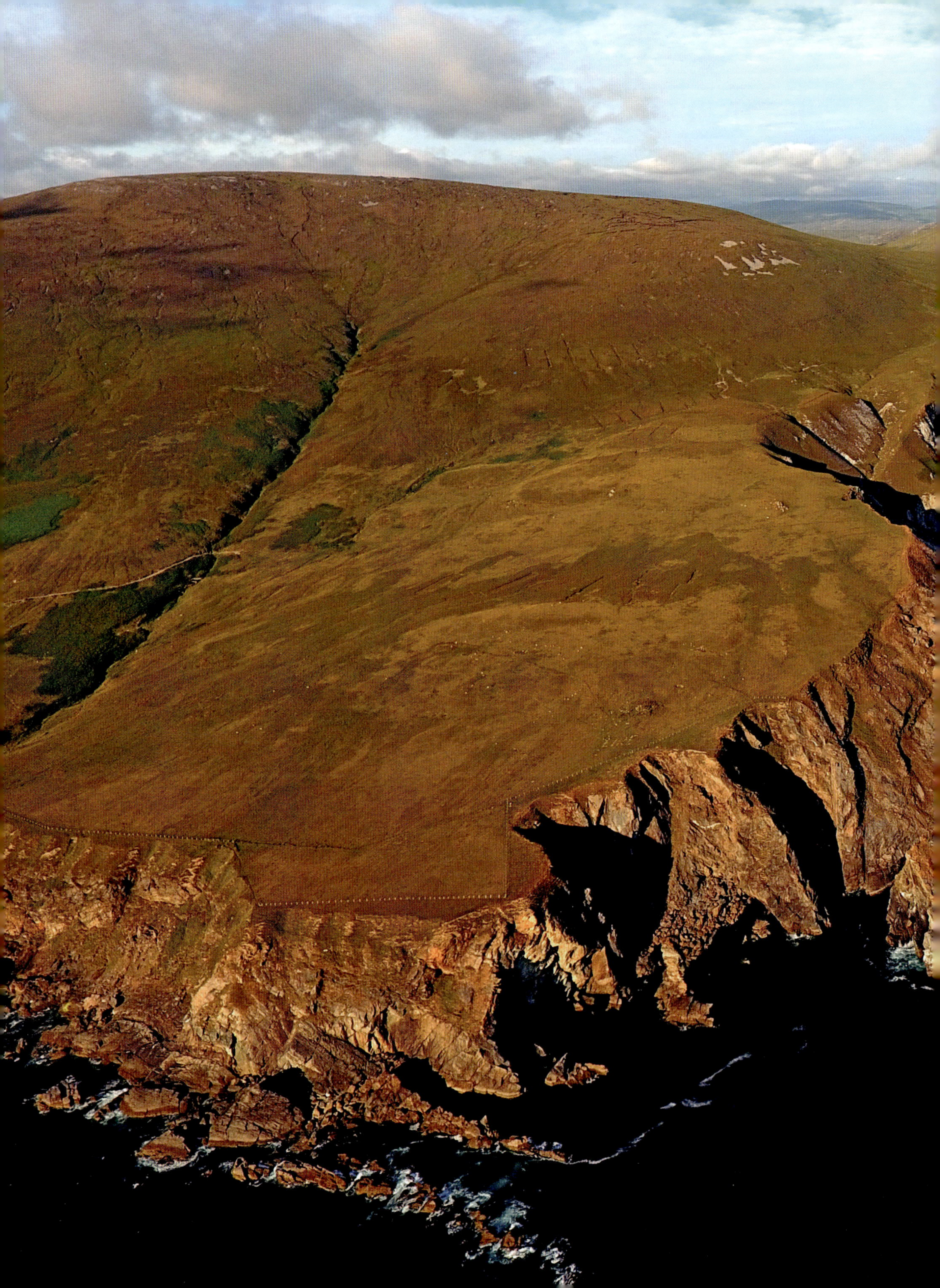

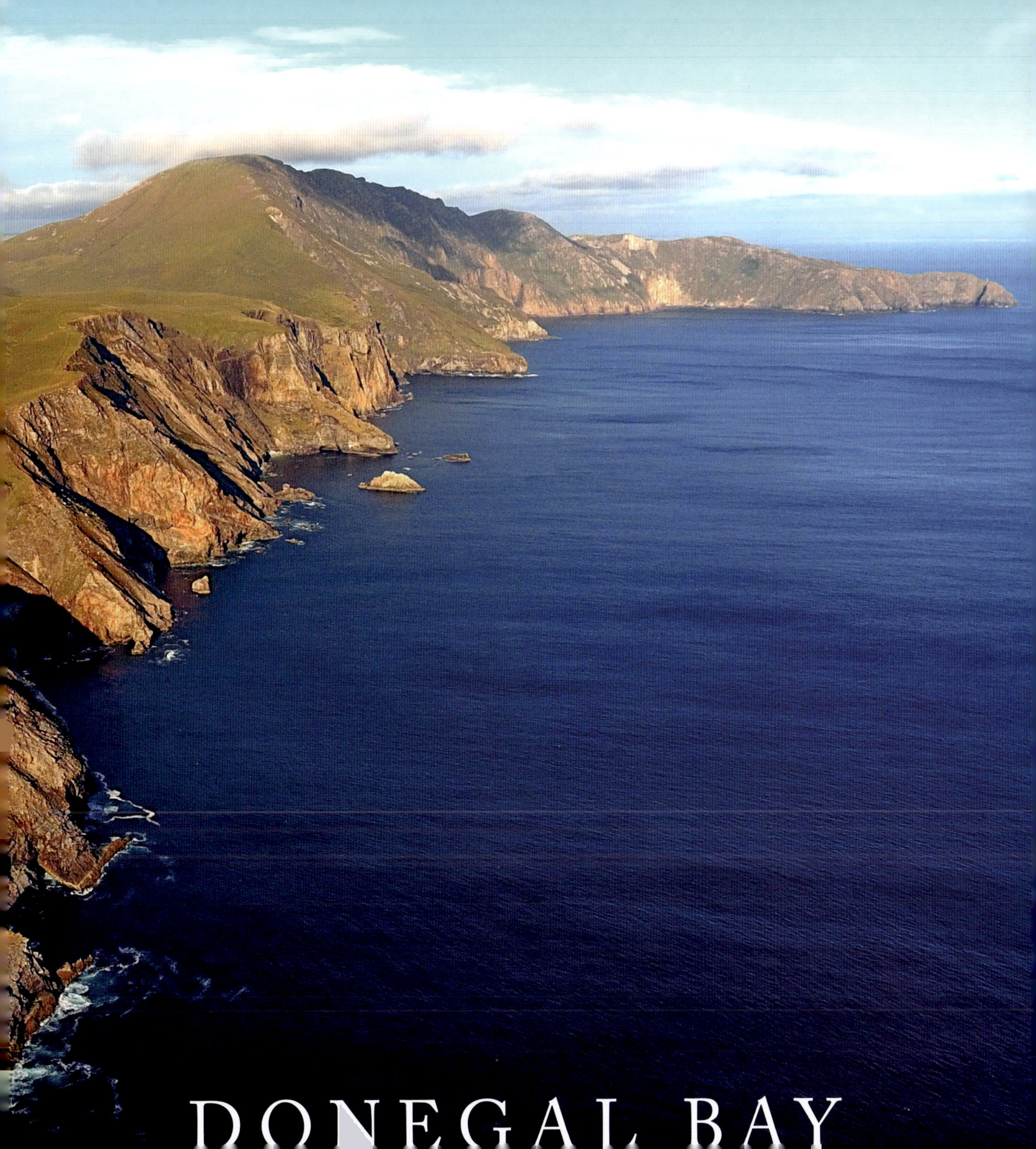

DONEGAL BAY

We follow the road most visitors take, beginning in the south of the county around Donegal Bay. A sculpted natural wonder, the Slieve League Cliffs in southwest Donegal are synonymous with the county. They are among the highest sea cliffs in Europe, and almost three times the height of the Cliffs of Moher in County Clare. Words fail to capture their sheer height and majesty.

Opposite, top: At Bundoran, the roar of the ocean whispers to surfers of all ages to accept the challenge to ride the waves, in stunning coastal scenery. The Blue Flag beach is a short walk from the town's Main Street.

Opposite, bottom: Sunset reflections seen from The Mall Quay in Ballyshannon, Ireland's oldest town. It is the birthplace of Rory Gallagher, who was one of the world's greatest rock guitarists.

Previous pages: Slieve League is often photographed from the viewpoint at Bunglass. This view, however, was taken near Glencolmcille shortly before sunset. There's little can compare with the breathtaking majesty of these sea cliffs, which rise to 601 metres (1,972 feet).

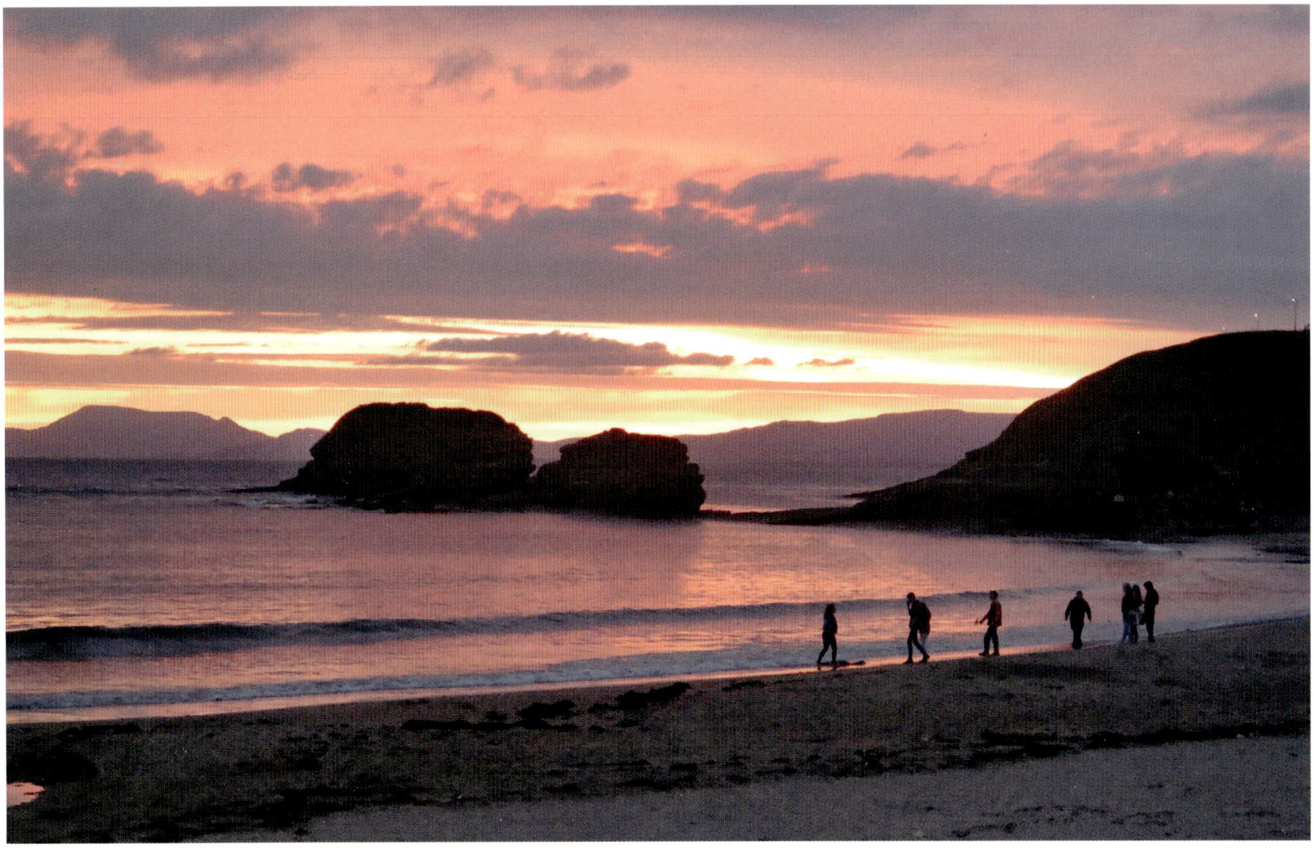

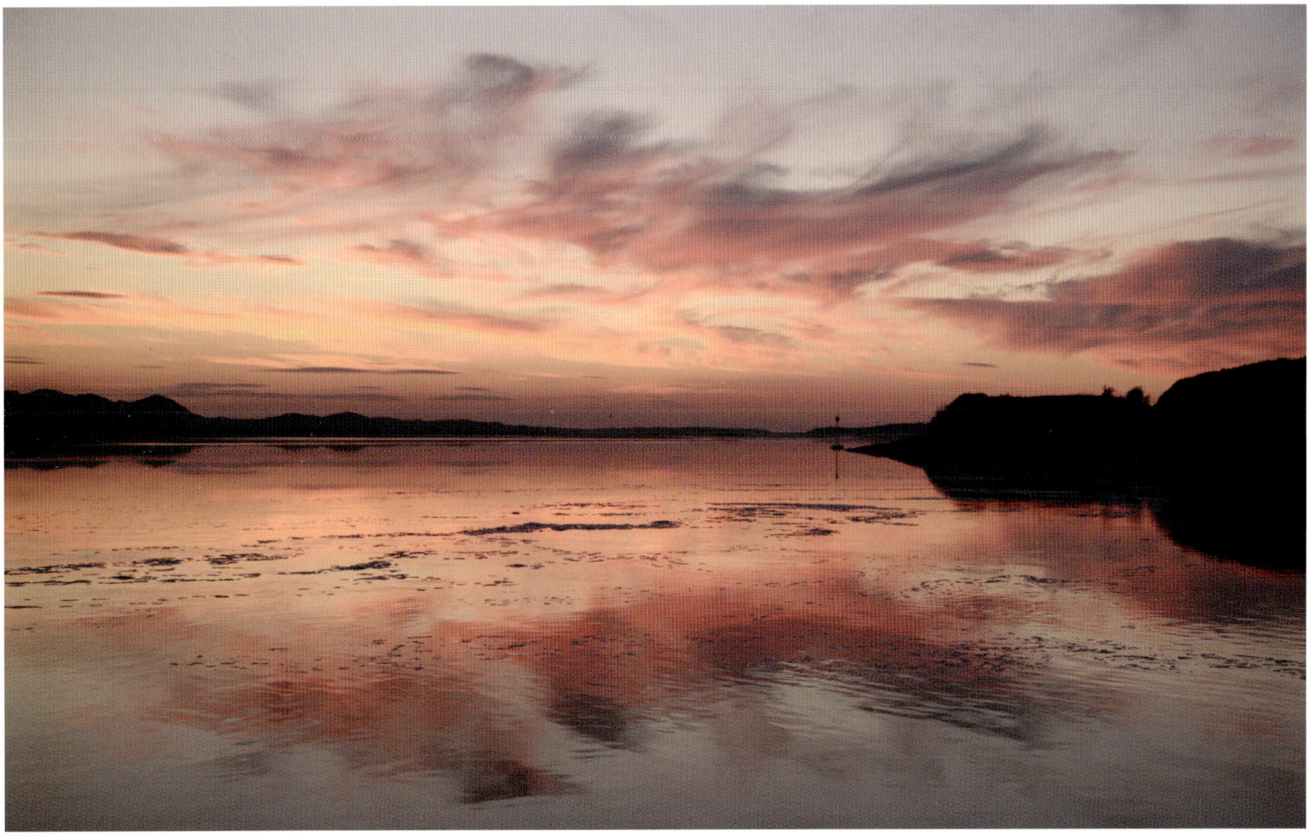

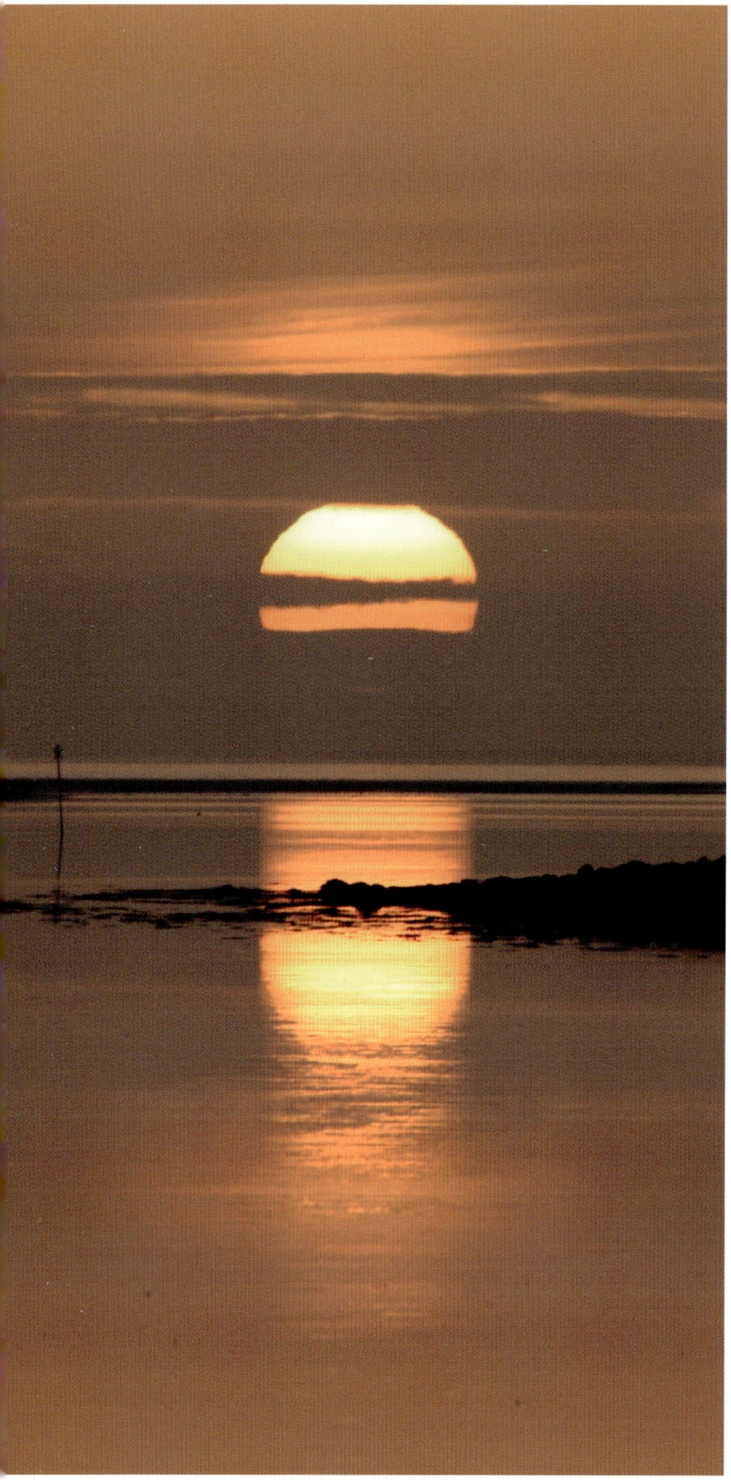

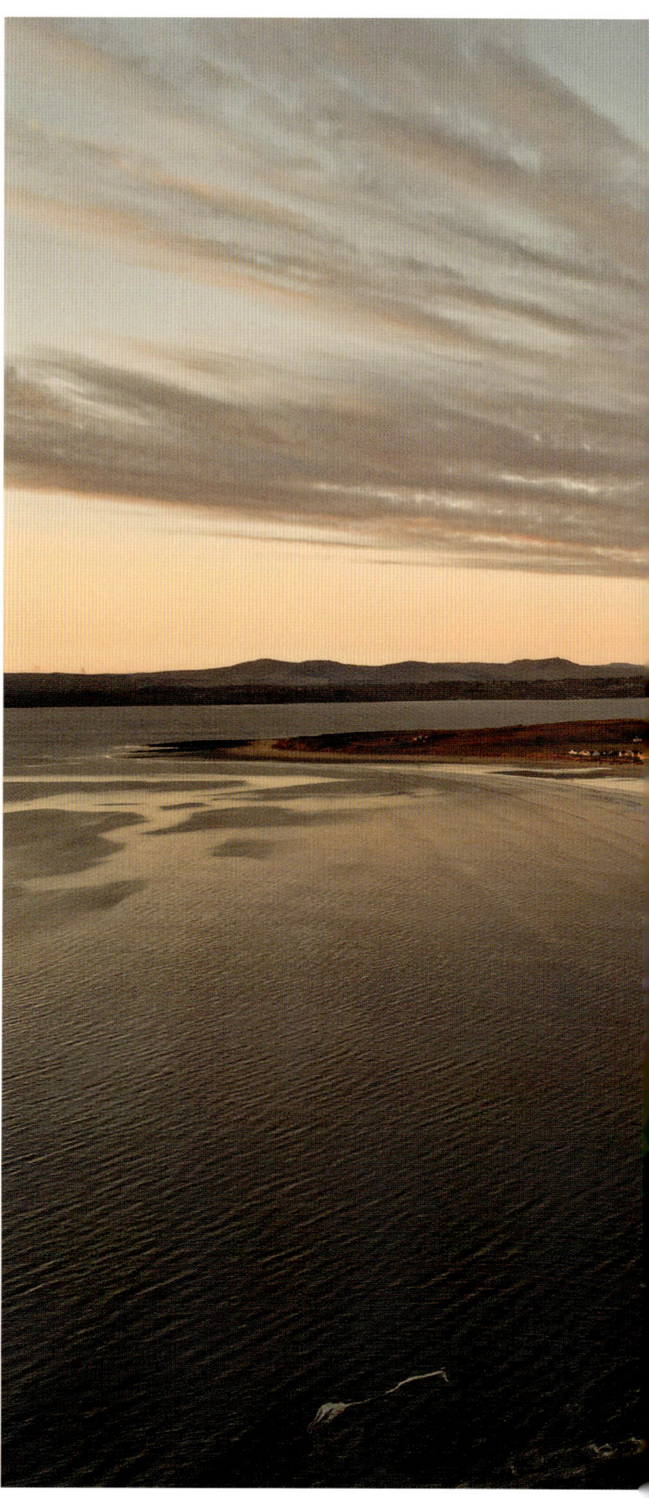

Above left: The best sunsets need cloudy skies: this was captured near St Ernan's Island, a short distance from Donegal town.

Above right: Last light at Rossnowlagh, viewed from the clifftop south of the village. When life moves too fast and you feel lost in the chaos, this beach is a great escape. Rossnowlagh (which translates from Irish, appropriately enough, as 'the heavenly cove') is a Blue Flag beach and one of Europe's best surfing sites.

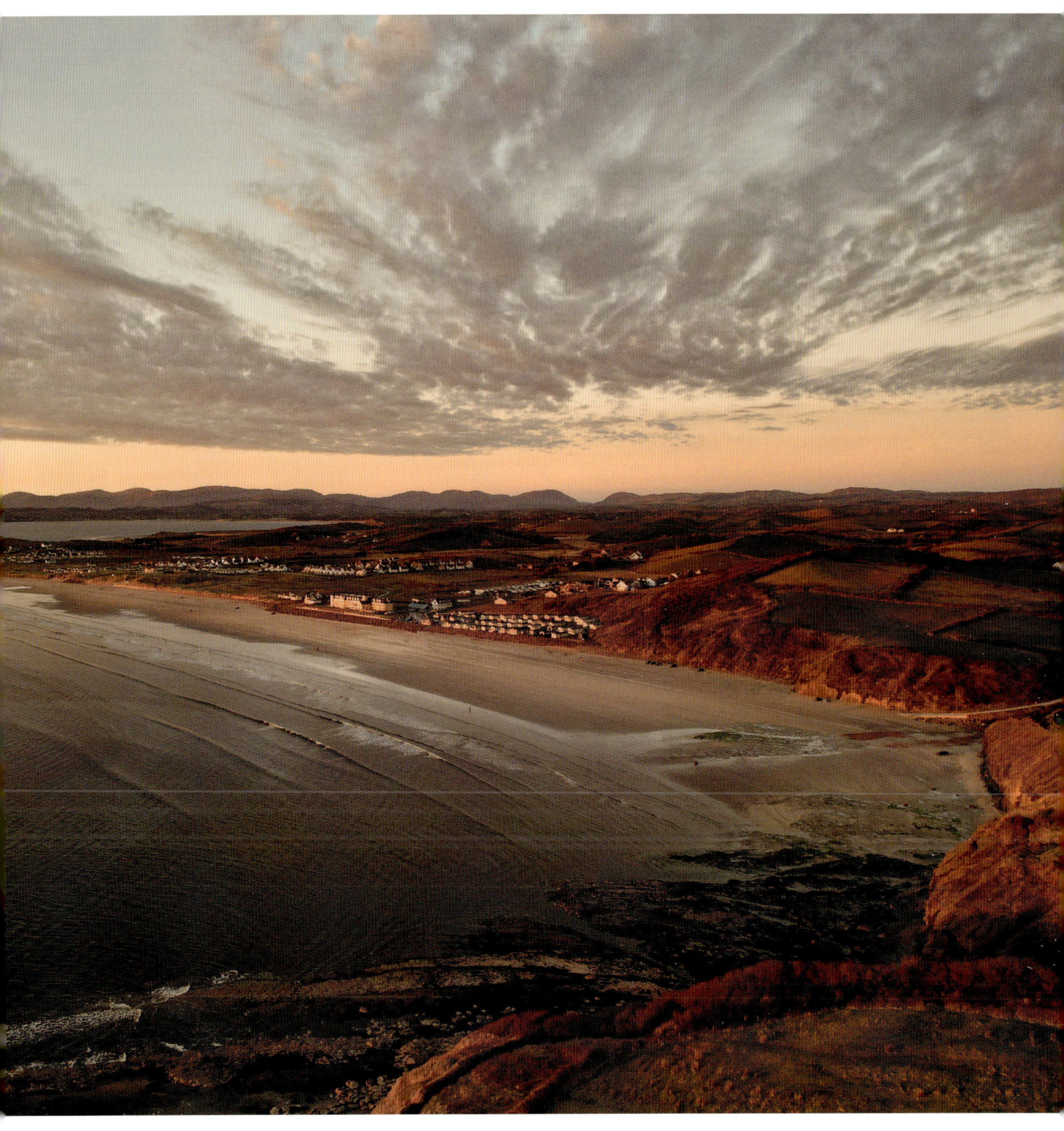

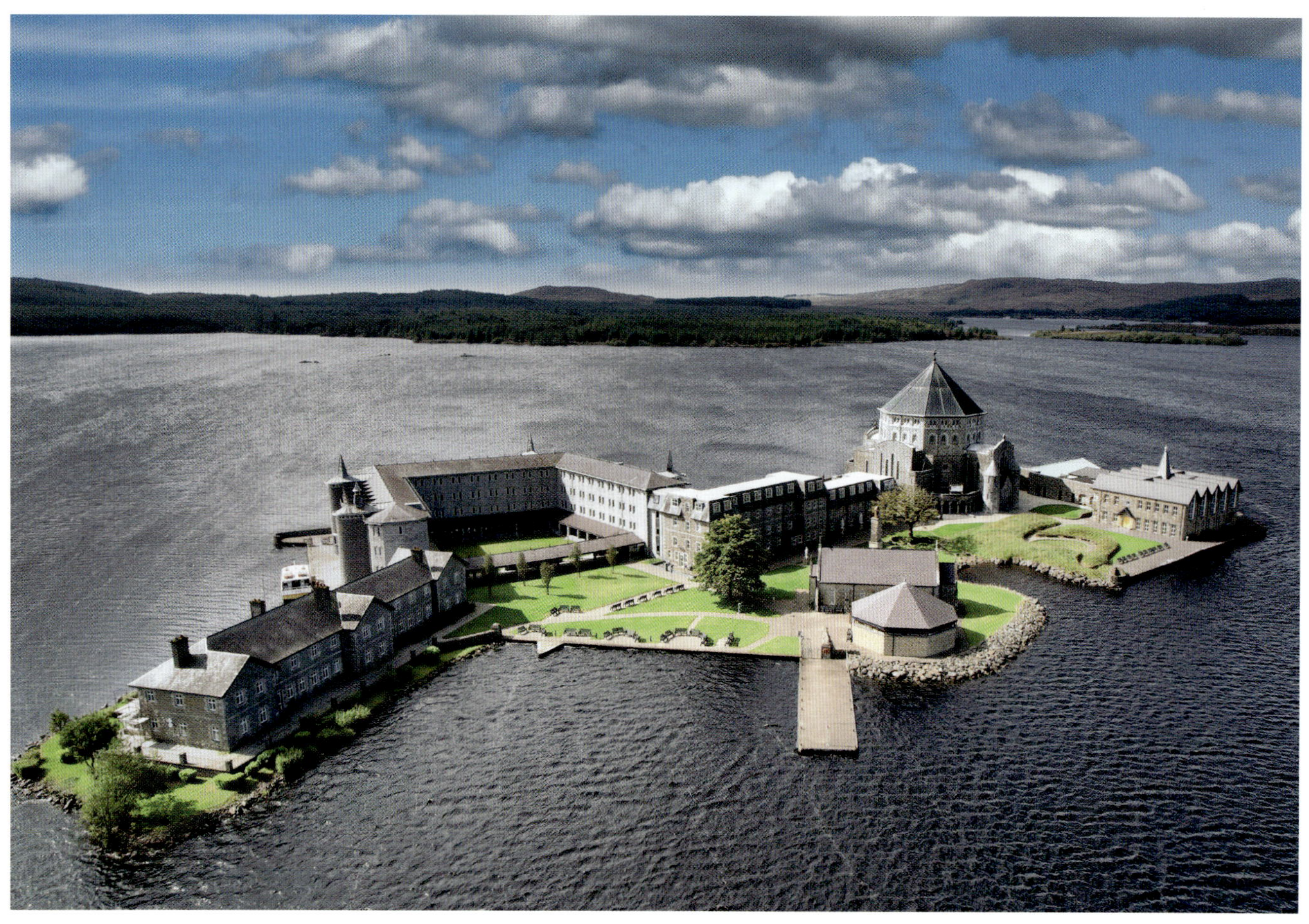

Station Island, Lough Derg. The Sanctuary of St Patrick has been a place of prayer since the foundation of a monastery there by St Davog *c*. AD 500. It became famous across Europe as St Patrick's Purgatory from AD 1170. Pilgrims have a choice of three-day and one-day retreats on the island.

Nestled at the quiet end of a country lane is Mullinasole, originally a small fishing
village, on the estuary of the River Murvagh. The beach here has exceptional sea
views with stunning reflections, especially at sunrise and sunset. The phrase 'picture
perfect' doesn't do it justice!

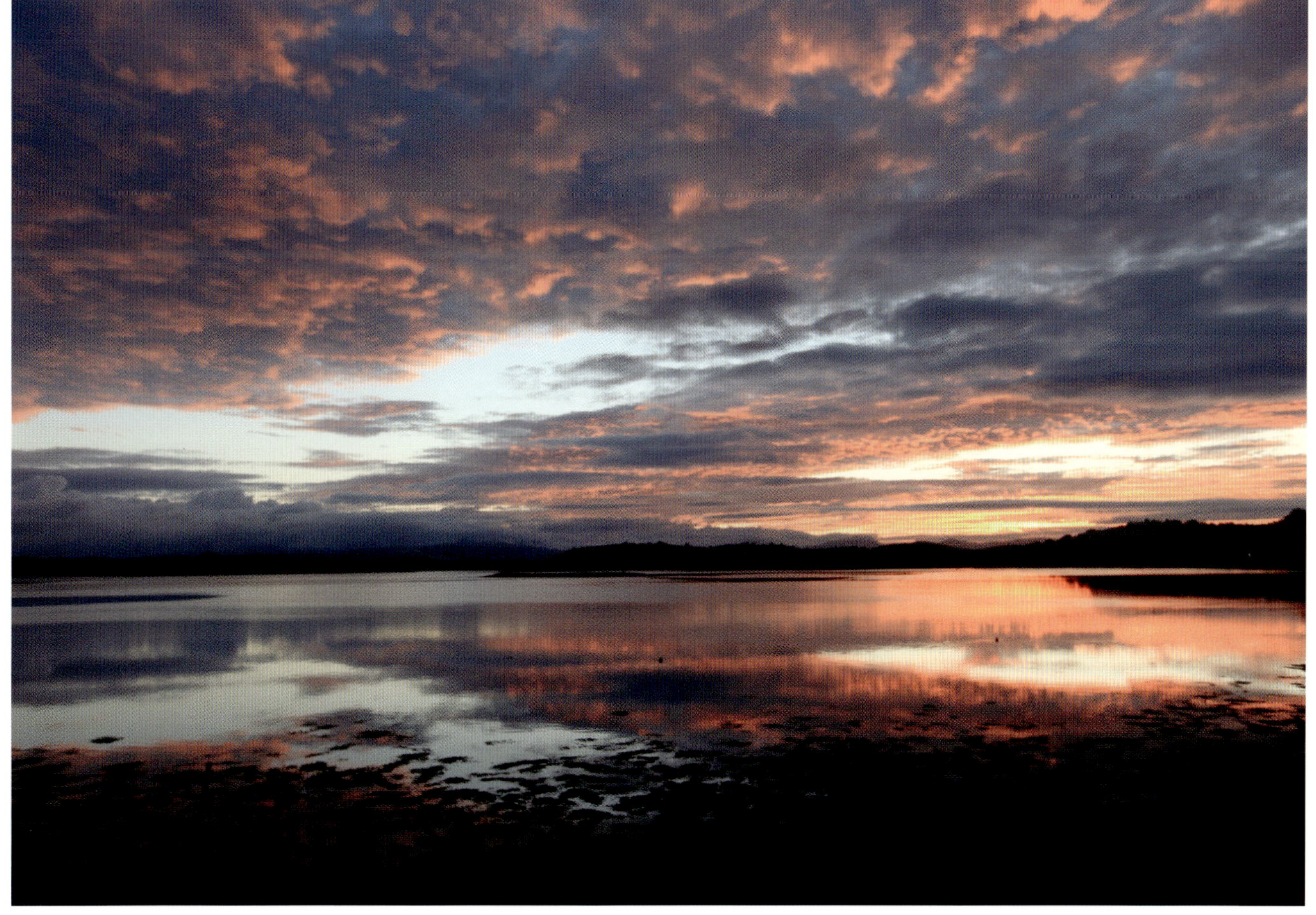

Riverside Gate Lodge at Drumbristan Glebe, Murvagh, was built *c.* 1820. Formerly the gate lodge of Murvagh House, this charming building is set in the countryside against a wooded backdrop, with the shores of Donegal Bay a short distance to the north. The triple-arch Murvagh Bridge over the Ballintra River was built *c.* 1790.

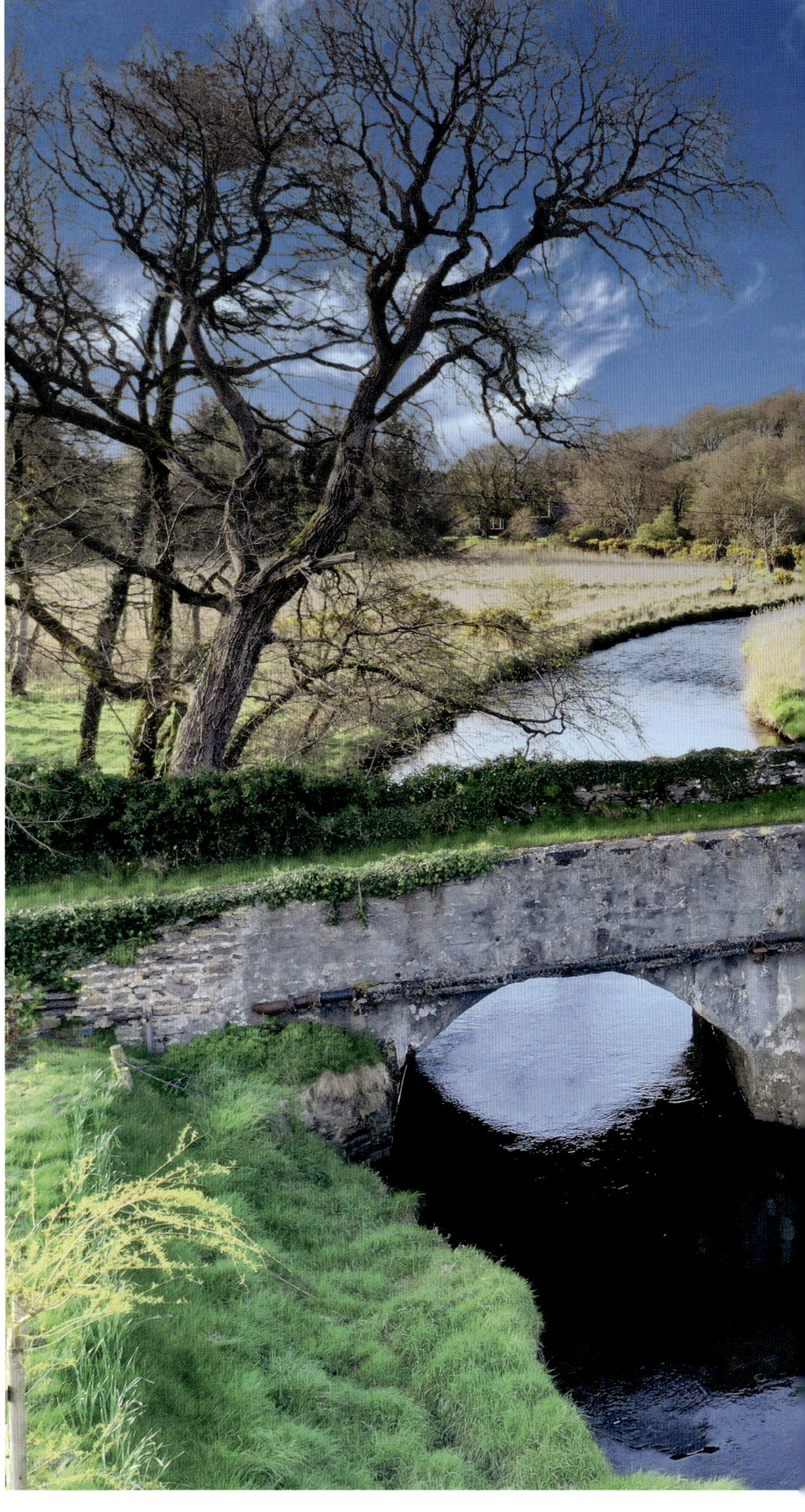

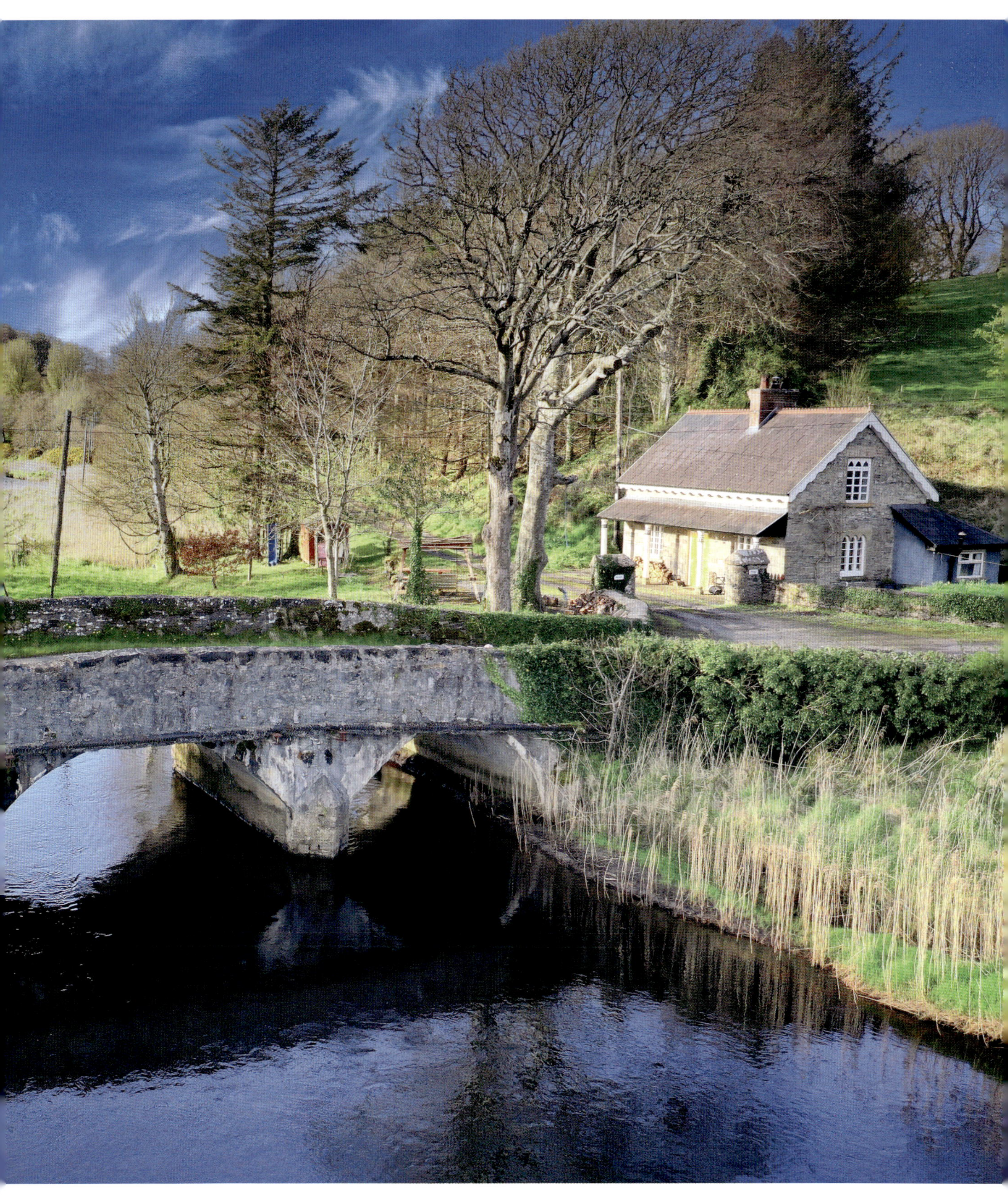

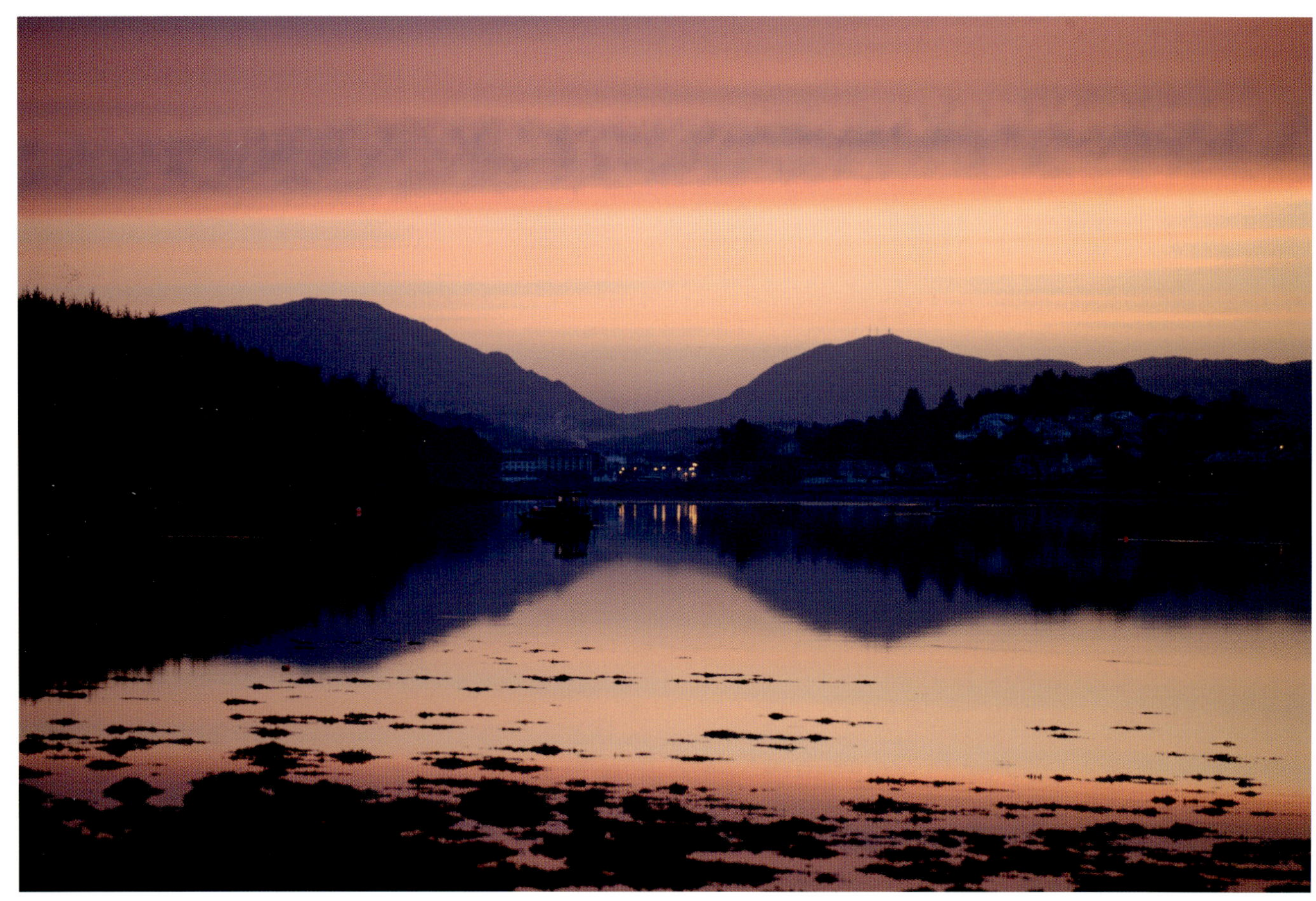

Colours of dawn at Summerhill, with Donegal town harbour and the Bluestack mountains of Croaghconnellagh (on the left) and Croaghonagh beyond in the distance.

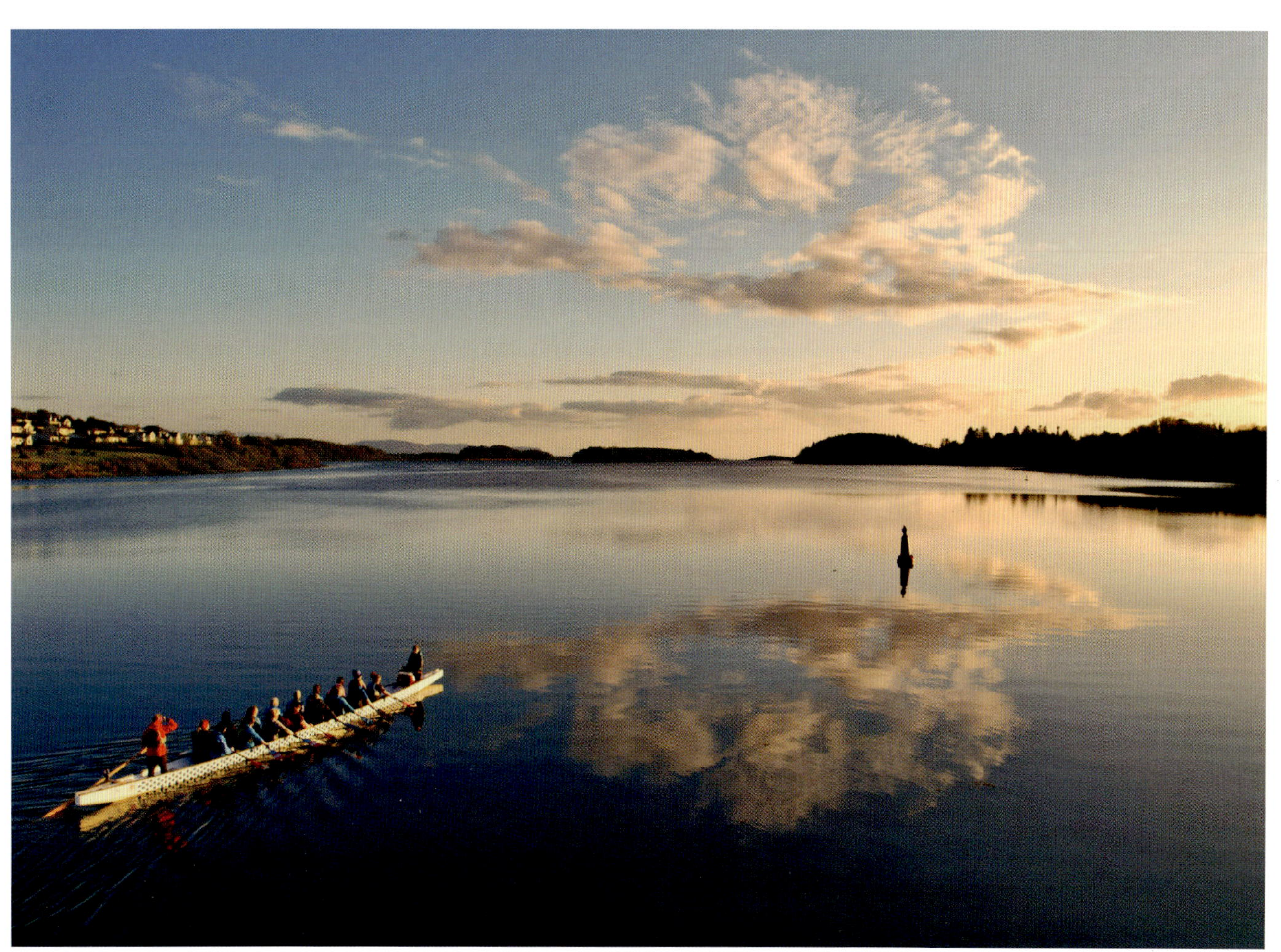

Members of Donegal Dragons, a dragon boat club formed for breast cancer survivors and supporters, enjoying sunset on Donegal Bay.

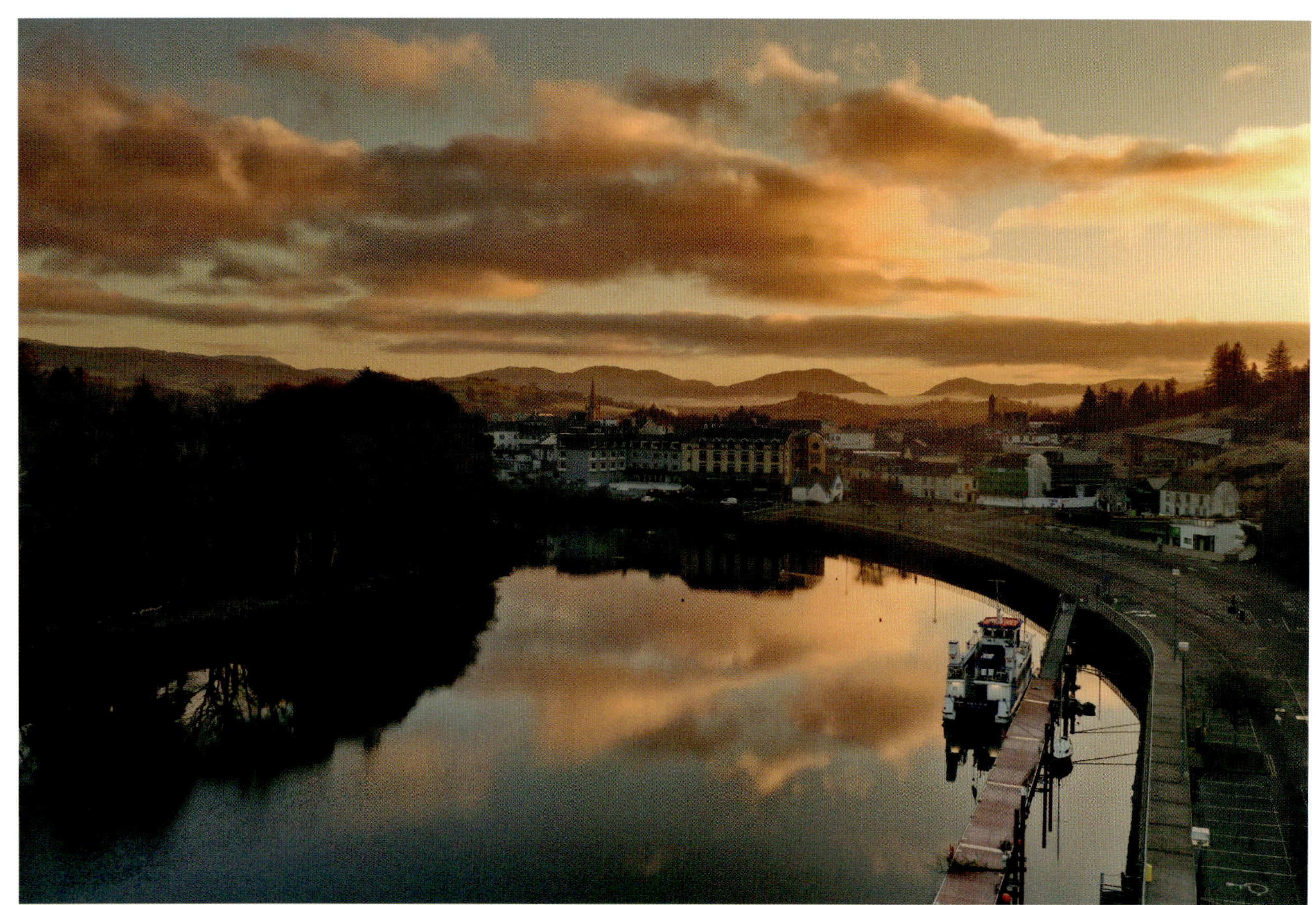

Morning reflections at sunrise on the pier in Donegal town, with not a
soul in sight, only the sound of waves lapping.

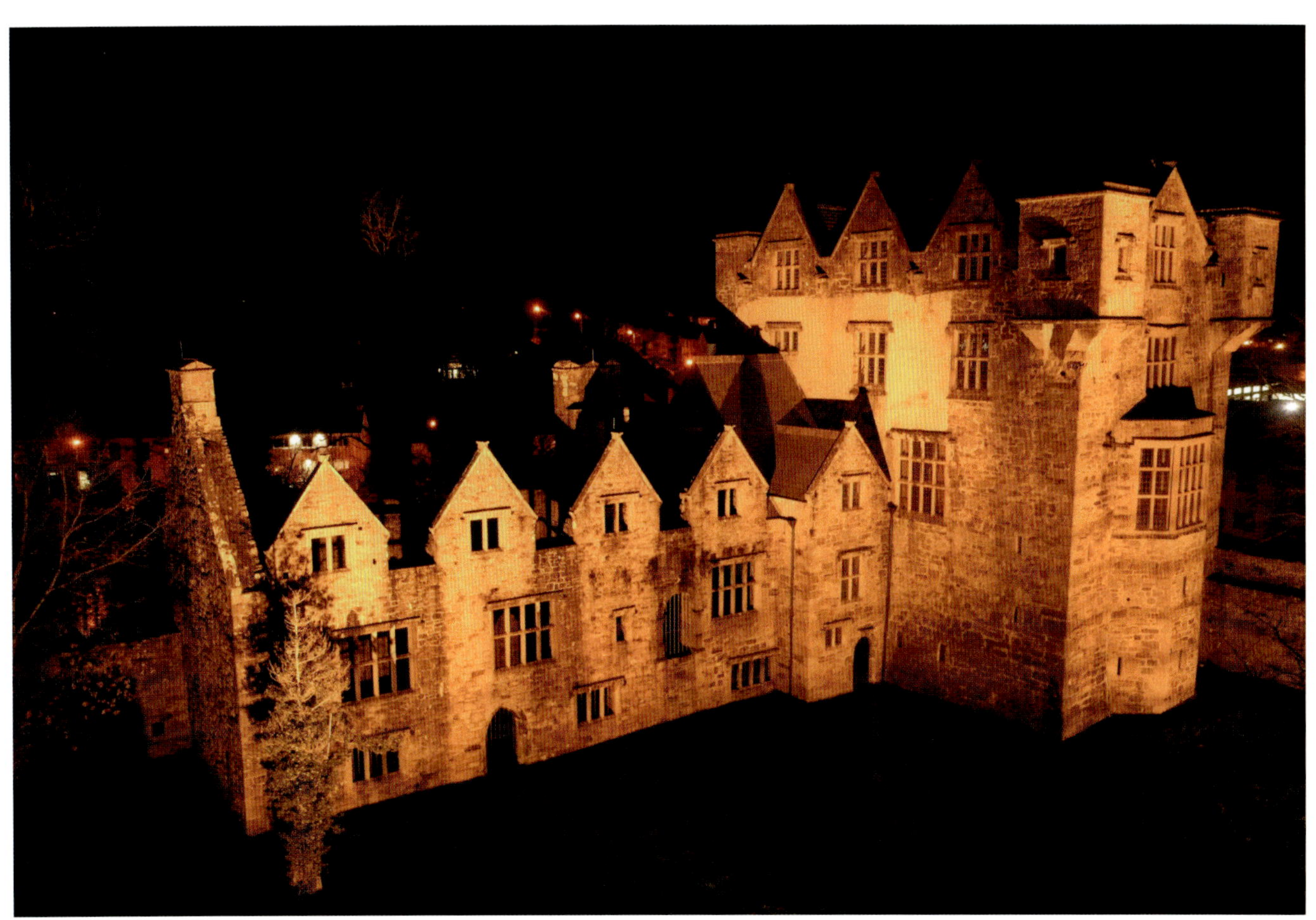

Donegal Castle in Donegal town was the stronghold of the O'Donnell clan, lords of Tír Conaill. It was built on a bend on the River Eske for defensive reasons, with the river protecting it on two sides. Before leaving Ireland in the Flight of the Earls in 1607, Red Hugh O'Donnell burnt his home to the ground in the hope of keeping it safe from enemy hands. However, it became the property of Sir Basil Brooke, an English captain, who built a manor house adjoining the original tower. It fell into ruin but was extensively restored in the 1990s.

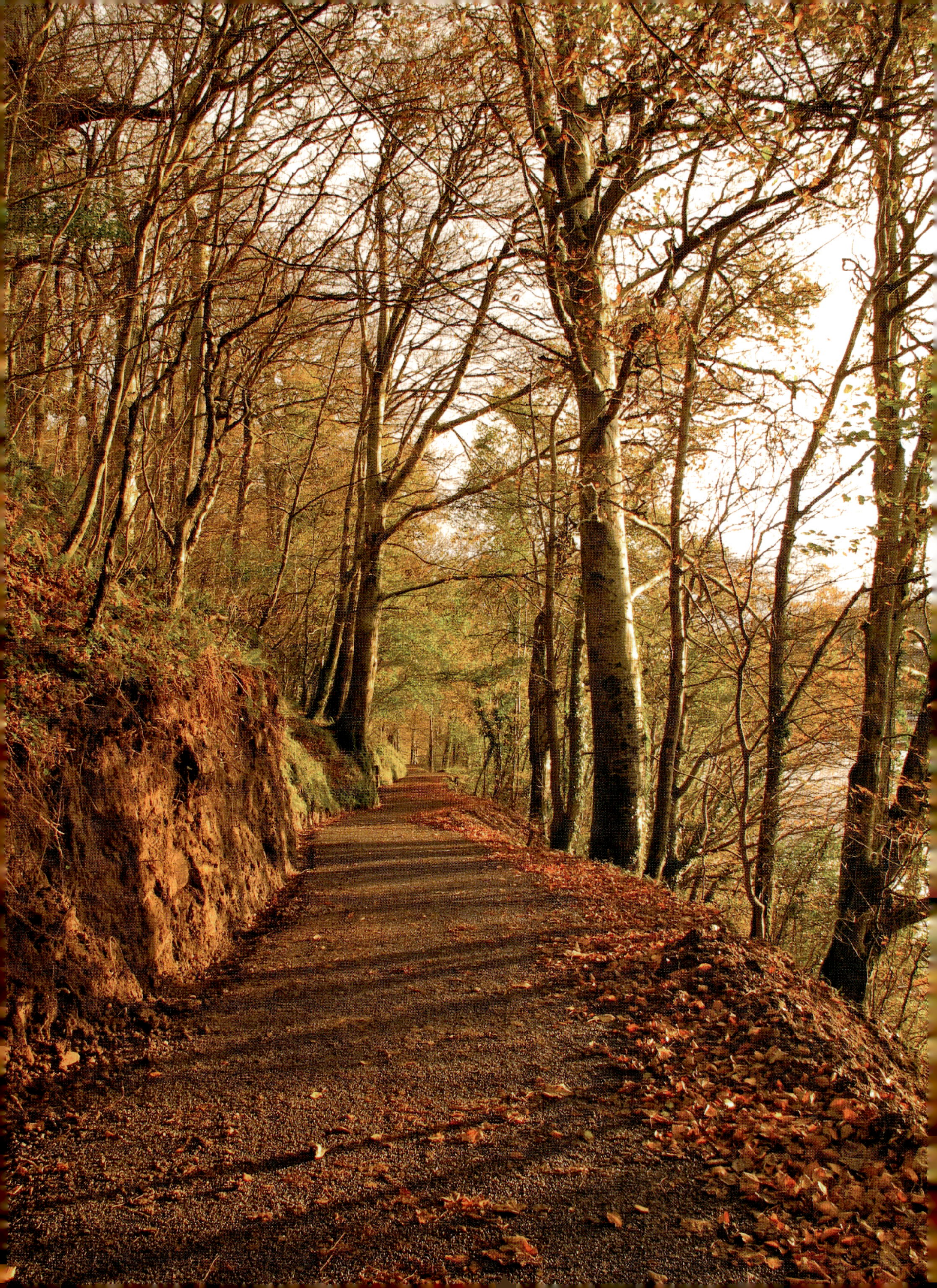

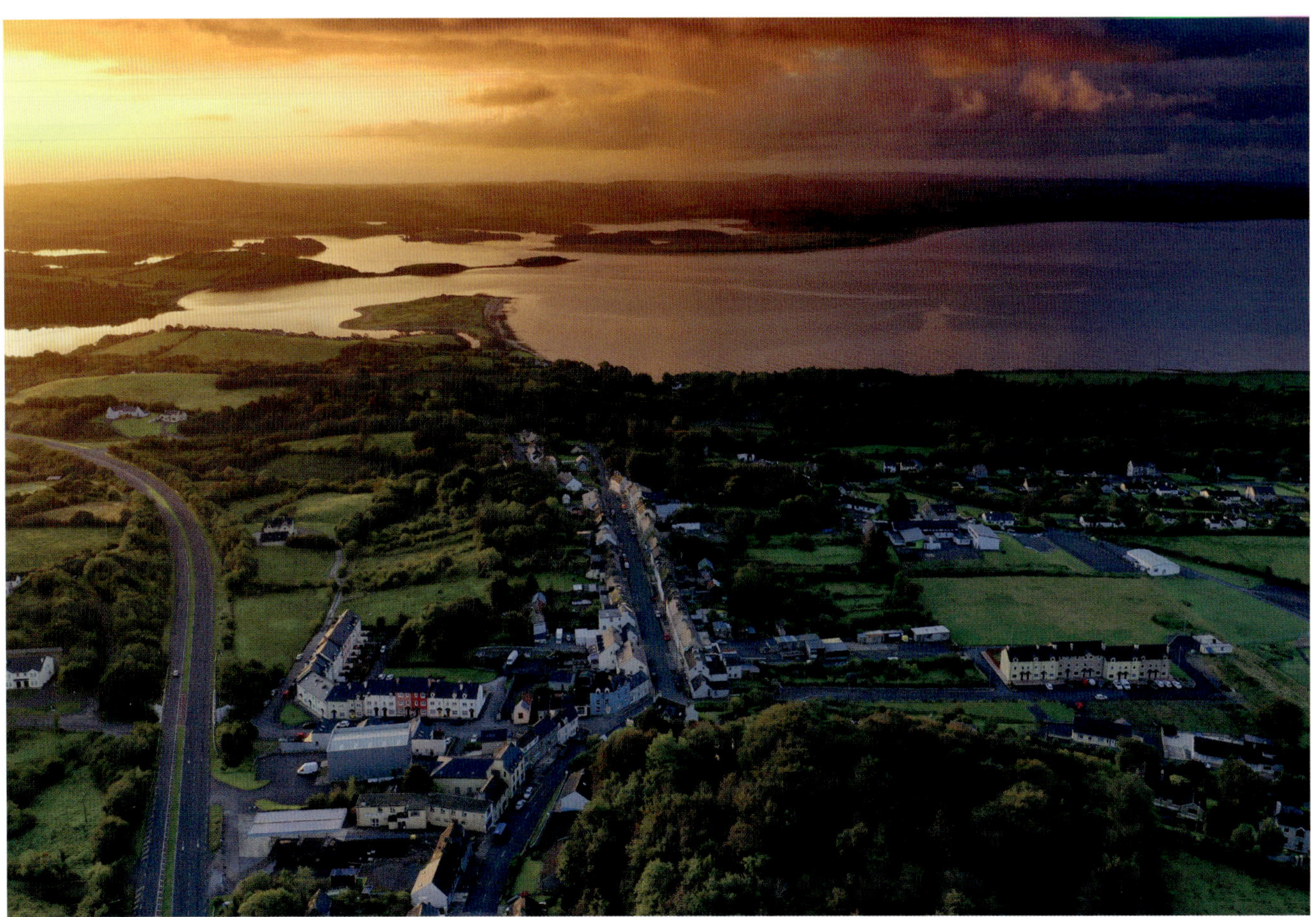

Mountcharles was originally called Tamhnach an tSalainn, meaning the 'Field of Salt' and dates back to the 1700s. Salt was extracted from seawater and used to preserve locally caught herring. The English name Mountcharles came into use after the Plantation of Ulster and is attributed to Albert Conyngham, an ancestor of Lord Henry Mountcharles of Slane Castle in County Meath. The shore has two sandy beaches, and offers exquisite panoramic views of the bay, the Bluestacks and the Sligo Mountains and has the longest stone wall in the area.

Opposite: The Bank Walk in Donegal town, a scenic looped walk set in natural woodlands, runs along the west bank of the River Eske leading to Donegal harbour.

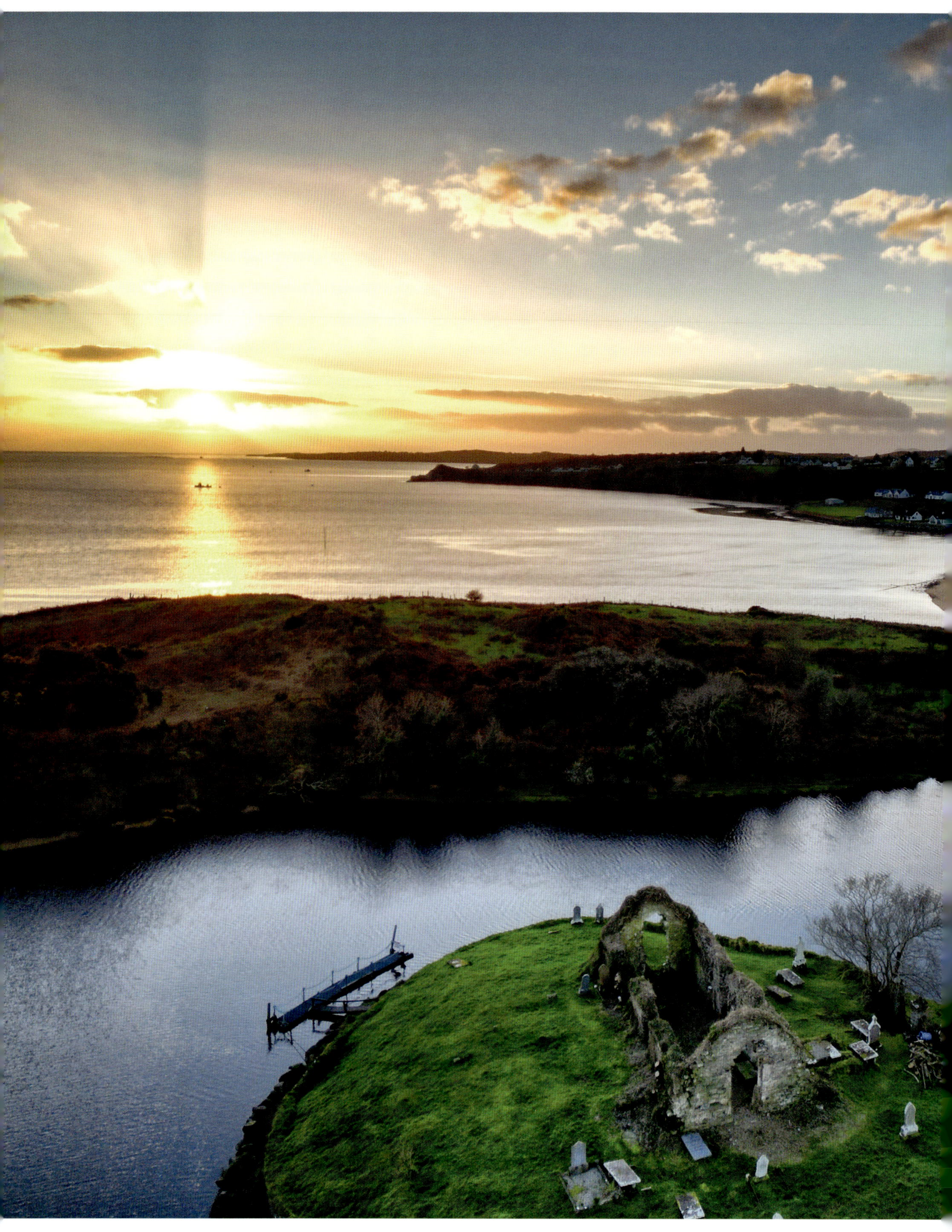

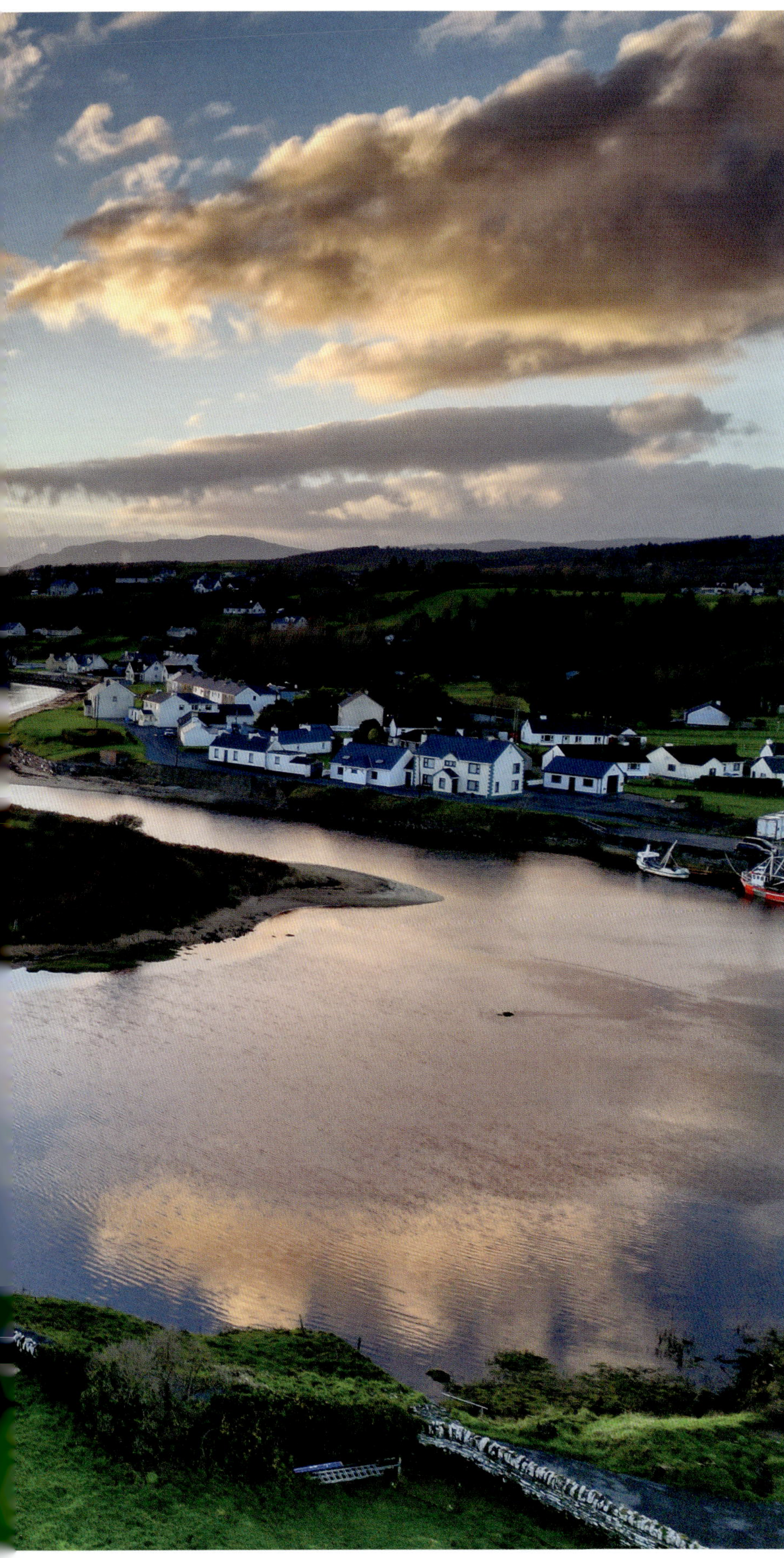

The village of Inver, at the mouth of the Eany River, is set in the midst of spectacular coastal scenery. The remains of Inver church, on a bend at the mouth of the river, mark the site of an early Christian monastery, St Naul's, which remained in use up until 1807. The church dates back to, or was modified, about 1610. It was described in 1622 as being in 'reasonably good repair' and having a thatched roof. In the graveyard is the broken tombstone of Thomas Nesbitt, the inventor of the harpoon gun for whaling. He was born in Inver in 1730.

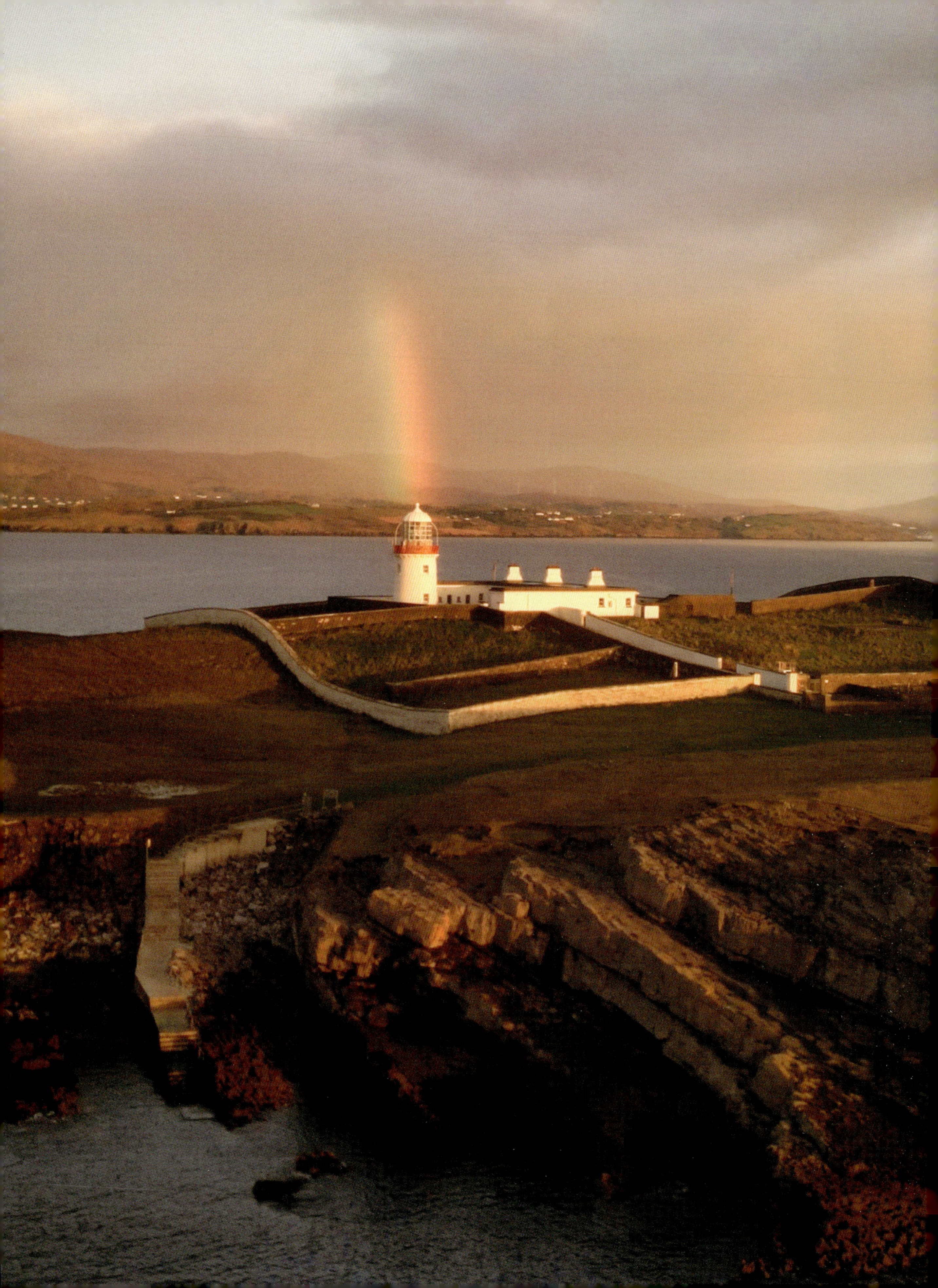

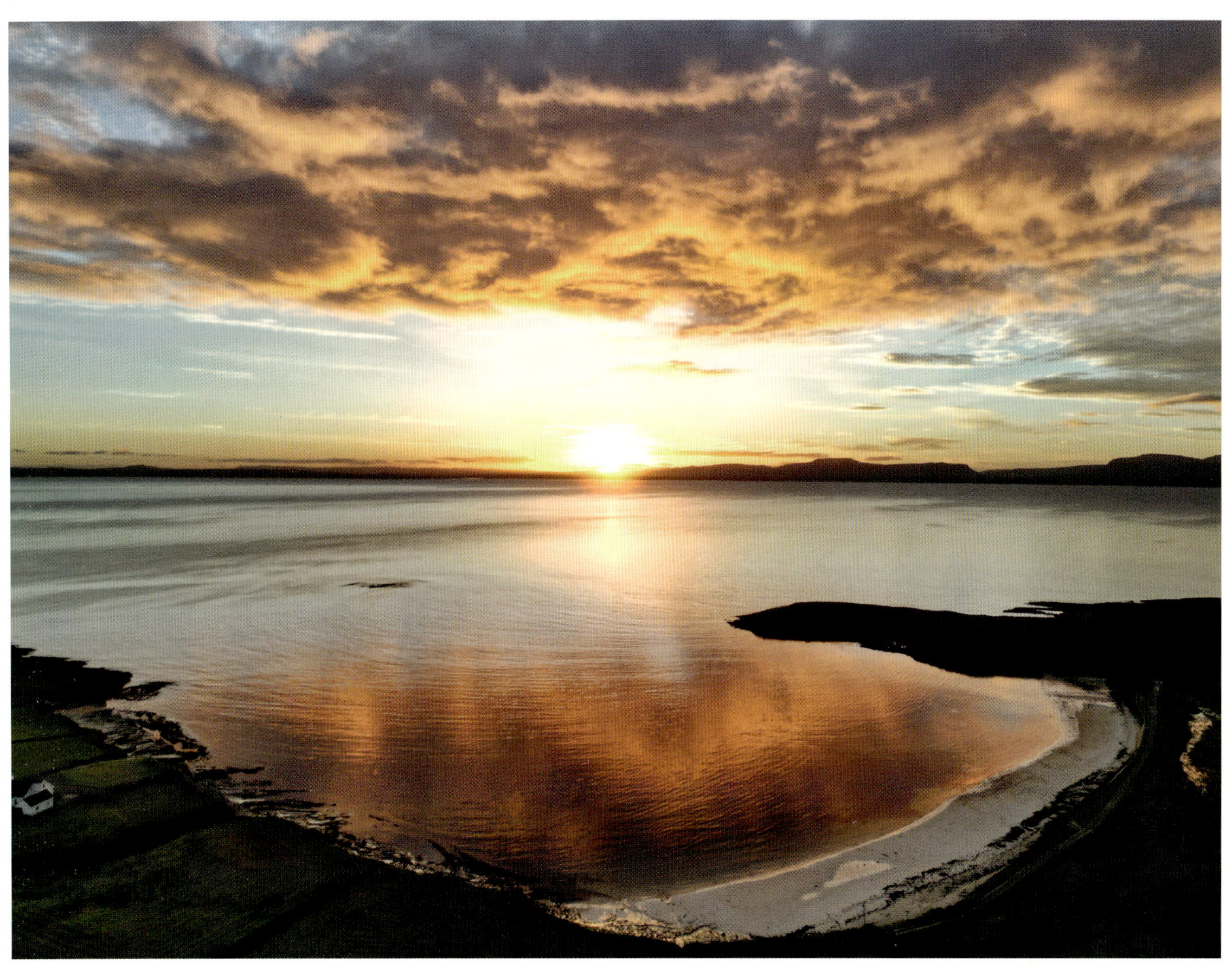

Sunrise at Coral Beach, St John's Point, Dunkineely.

Opposite: St John's Point Lighthouse sits at the end of the longest peninsula
in Ireland. It is a paradise of seclusion, with the sea on three sides.

The ruins of McSwyne's Castle on the narrow headland of St John's Point near Dunkineely. Views stretch along the Point to Killybegs and Slieve League in the distance. The castle was built in 1400 and was owned, along with the adjoining lands, by the McSwynes, who originally came from Argyll in Scotland. In the Plantation of Ulster, both the castle and lands were granted to Scotsmen, first to William Stewart and later to John Murray. Situated on the edge of McSwyne's Bay, the ruins are battered by Atlantic waves and gales, and are now in danger of falling into the sea.

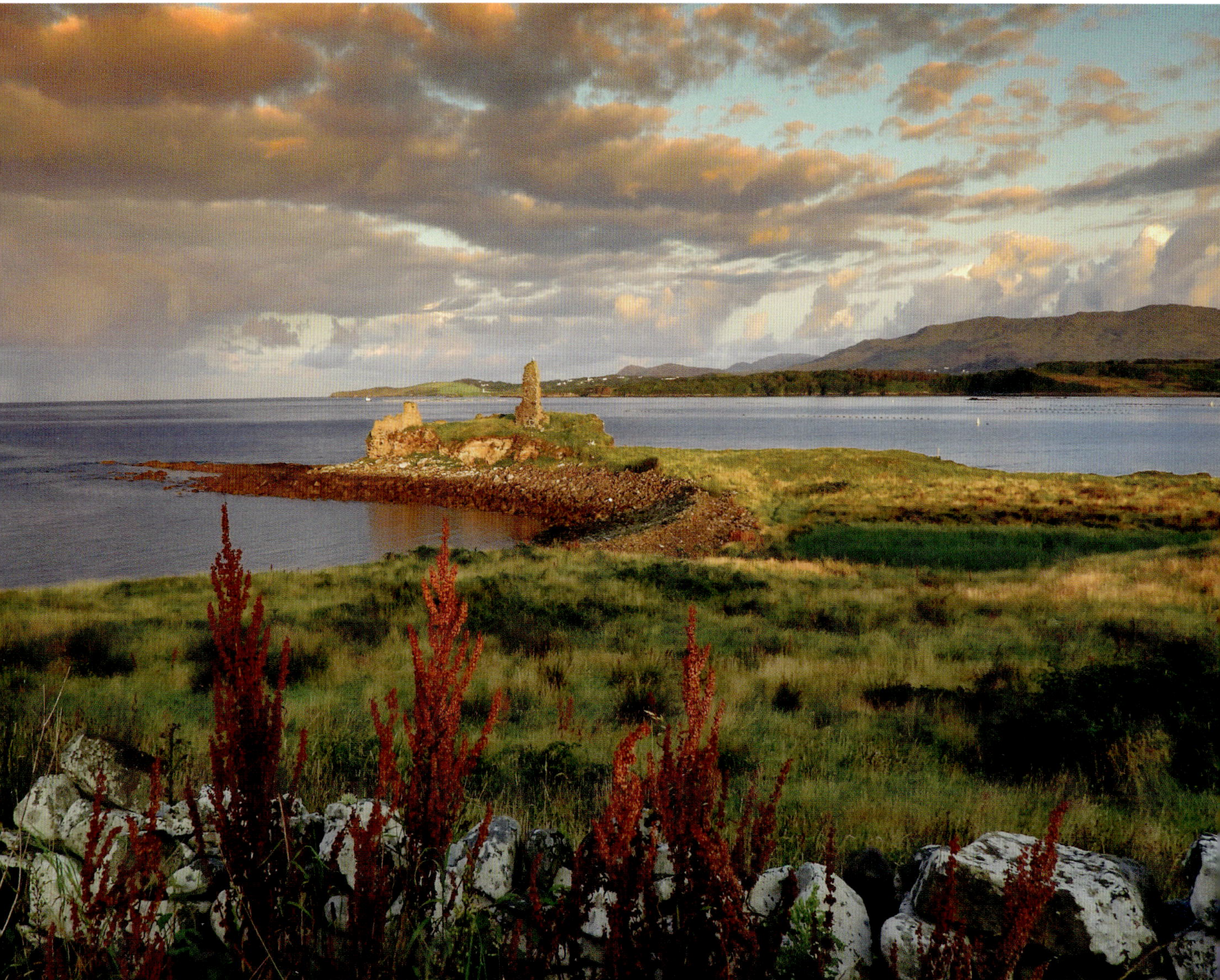

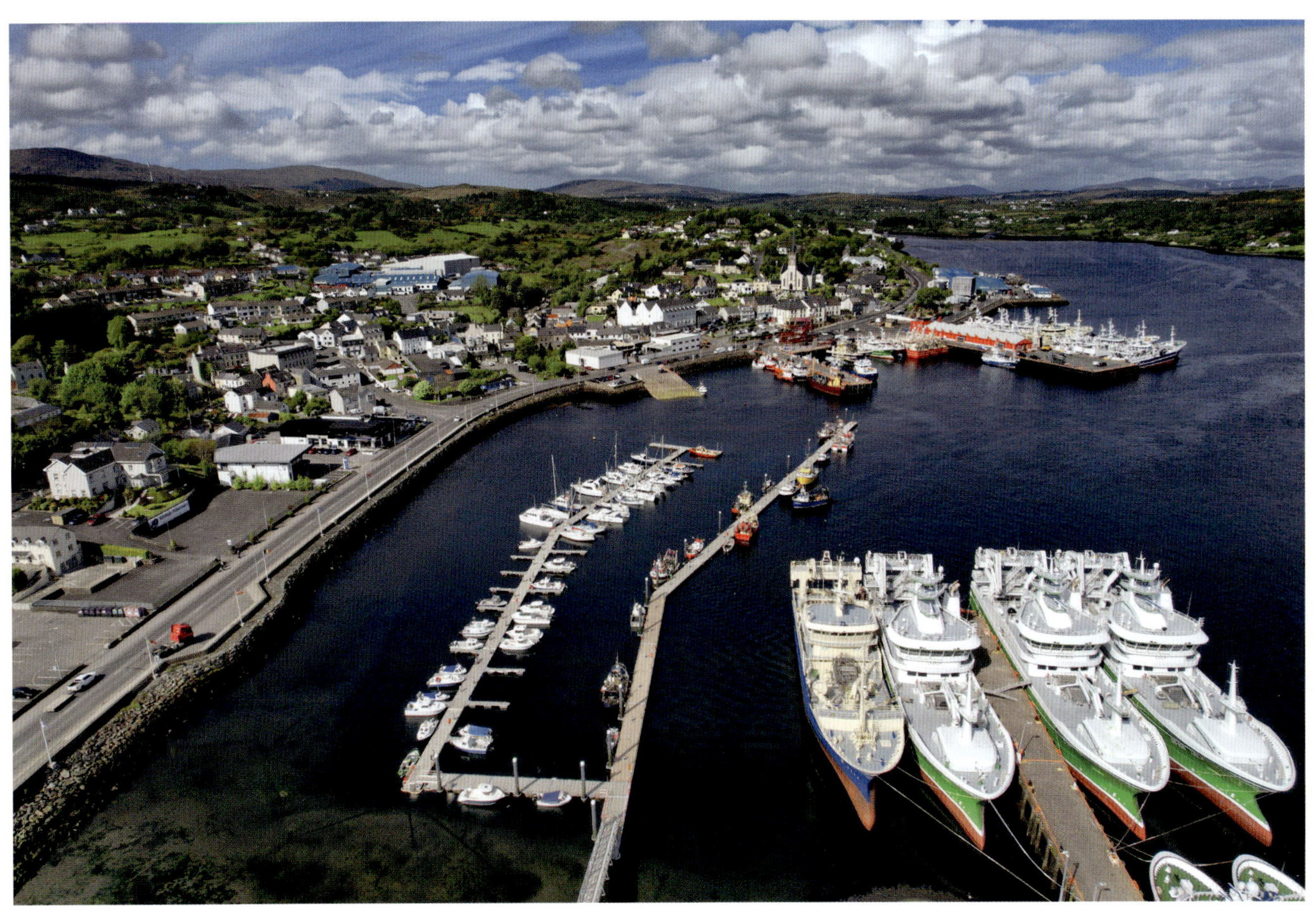

Fishing boats and trawlers moored in Ireland's largest fishing port, Killybegs.

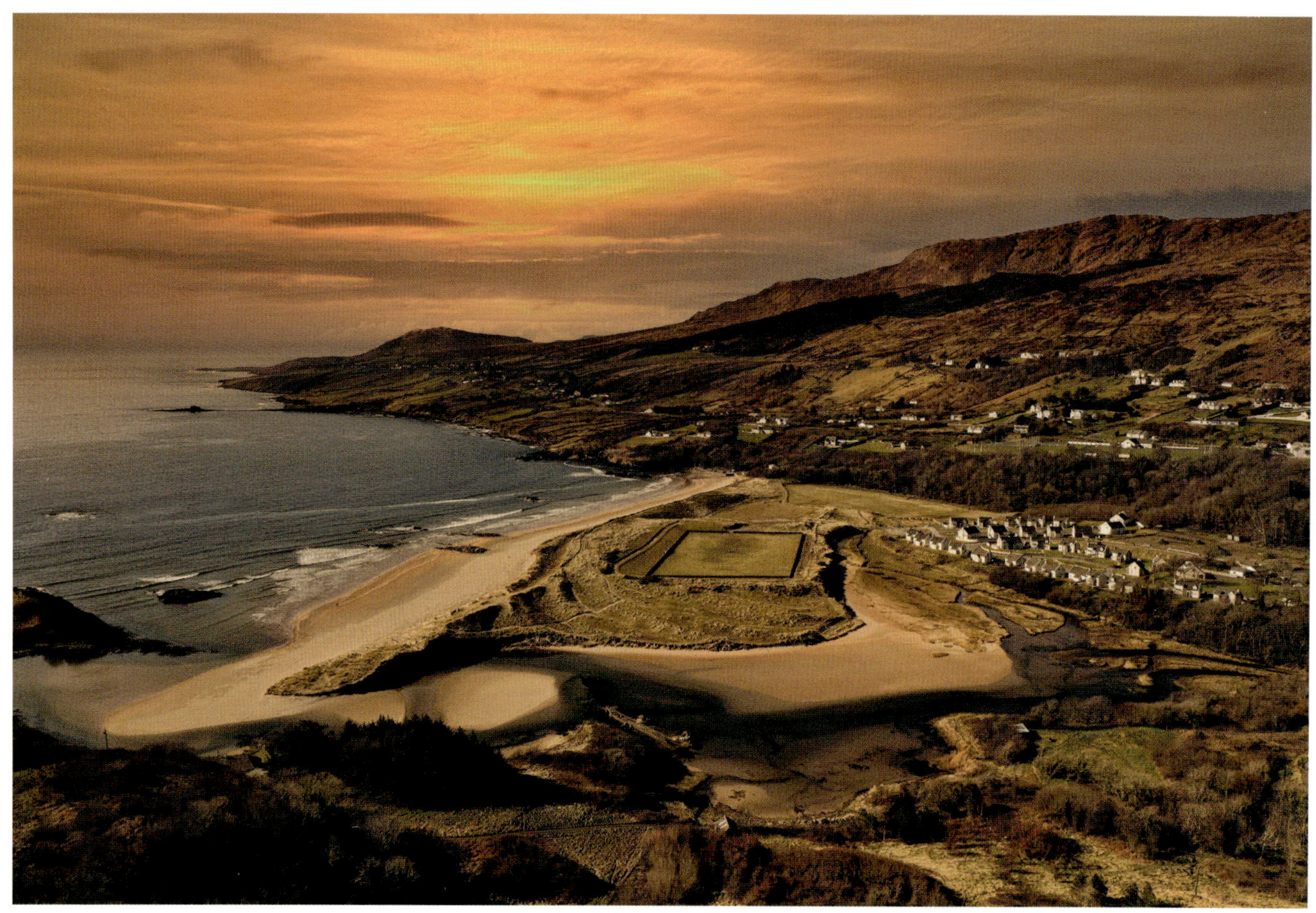

Fintragh Beach, just under three kilometres west of Killybegs, is a perfect expanse of open sea and golden sand with a backdrop of sand dunes that lead to the old Killybegs GAA pitch, with the estuary of Fintragh River to the east. An American Flying Fortress bomber, en route from Newfoundland, crash-landed on this beach on 20 February 1944, having run out of fuel. The ten crewmen were brought to Fintra House and given a warm Killybegs welcome.

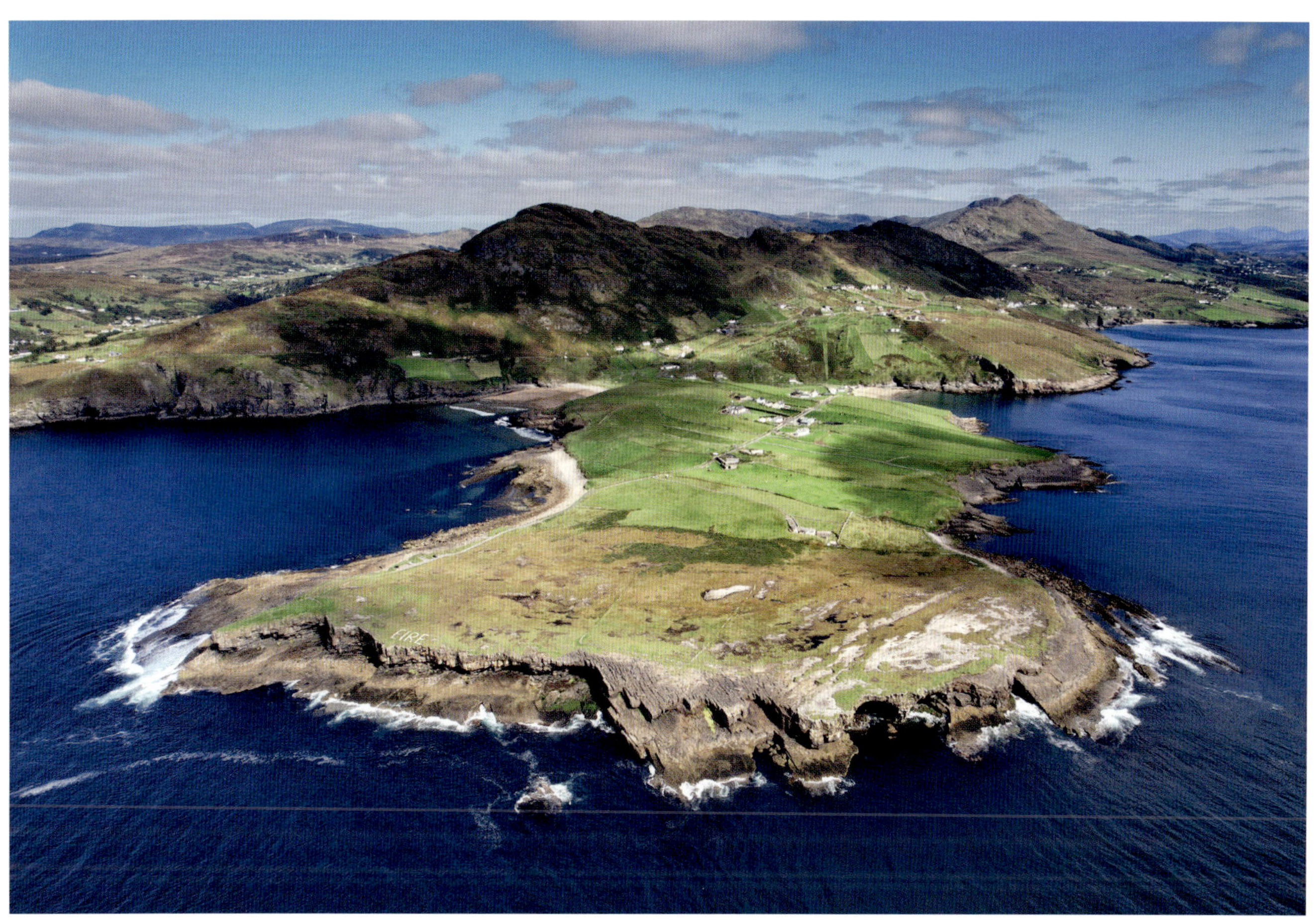

Muckross Head, situated between Killybegs and Kilcar at the base of Muckross Hill, juts into the Atlantic with a beach on either side. The impressive cliffs at the end of the peninsula are popular with rock climbers.

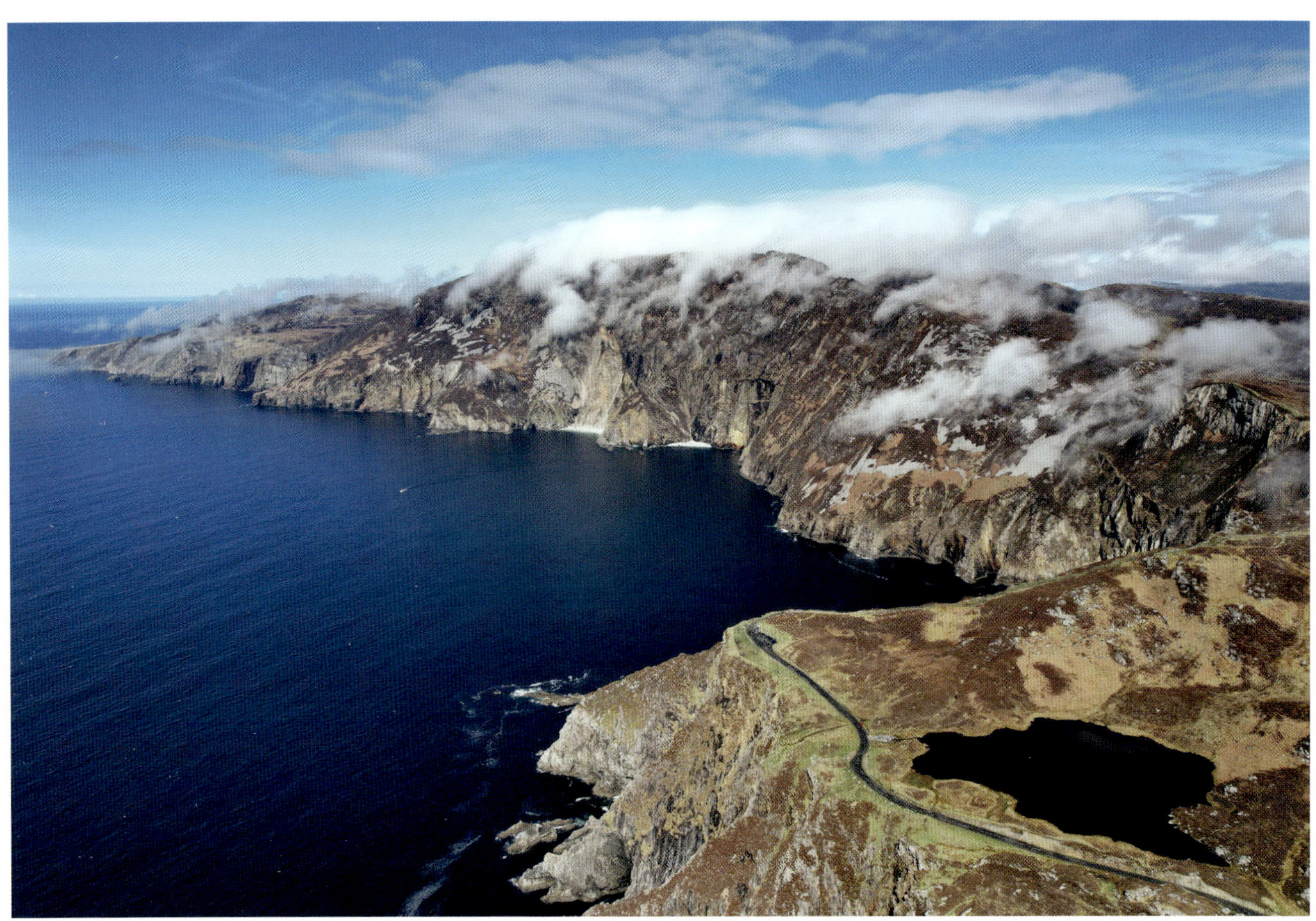

The breathtaking landscape of Slieve League as fog rolls off the top of the cliffs. This quartzite formation bears the signs of glaciation but has (so far) proved remarkably resistant to the effects of marine erosion, in spite of the constant pounding of the wild Atlantic waves.

Silver Strand at Malinbeg is surrounded by high horseshoe-shaped cliffs, which act as a giant windbreak, making this beach a natural sun trap. Also known as Trabane, Malainn Bhig and Malinbeg, Silver Strand is seven kilometres from Glencolmcille. The bay is accessed by a steeply sloping series of steps (over 165 of them: easy on way down but not so easy going back up!).

Following pages: Glen Head and the Sturrall Ridge is a place of tremendous natural beauty and changing colours, whatever the weather.

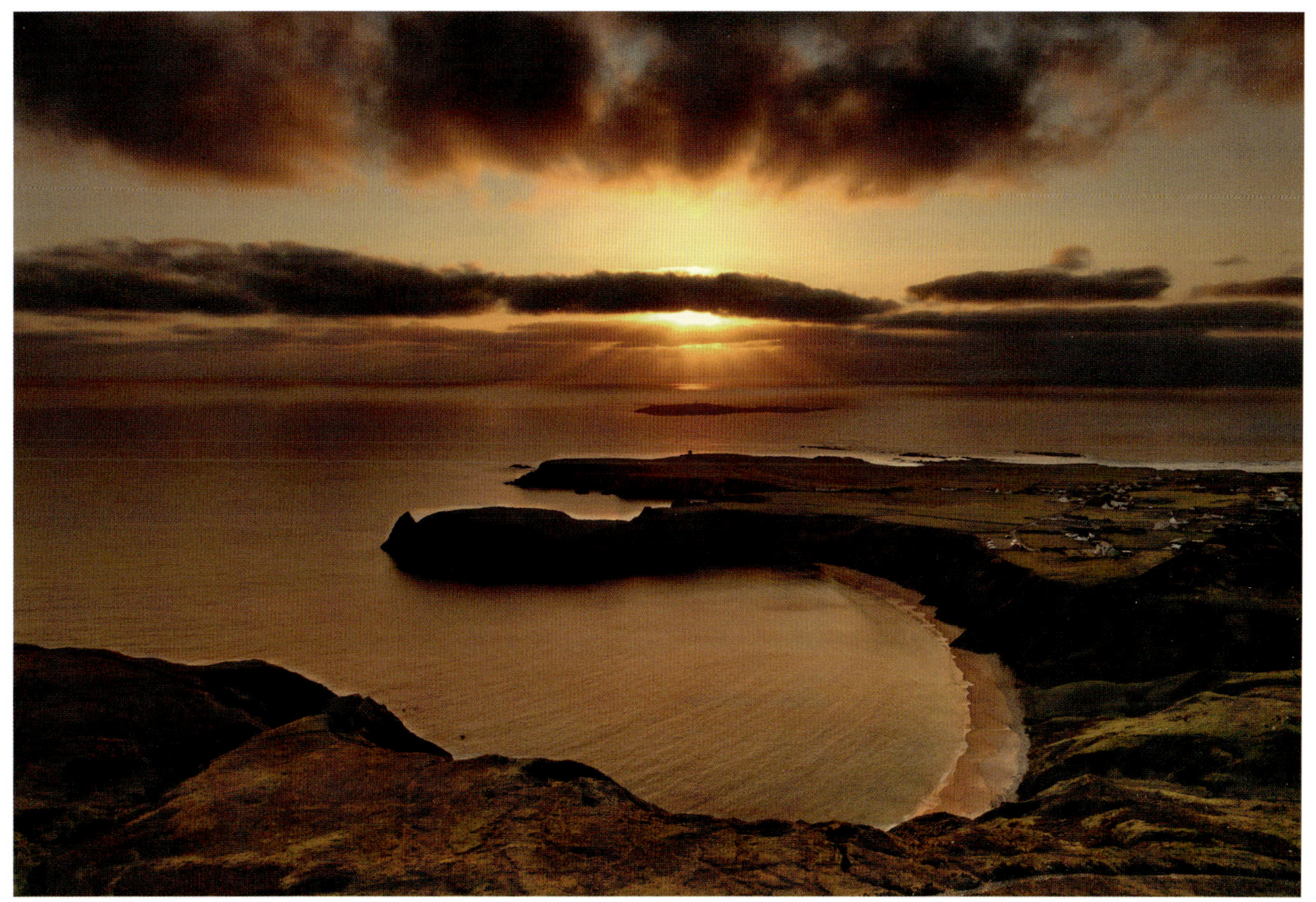

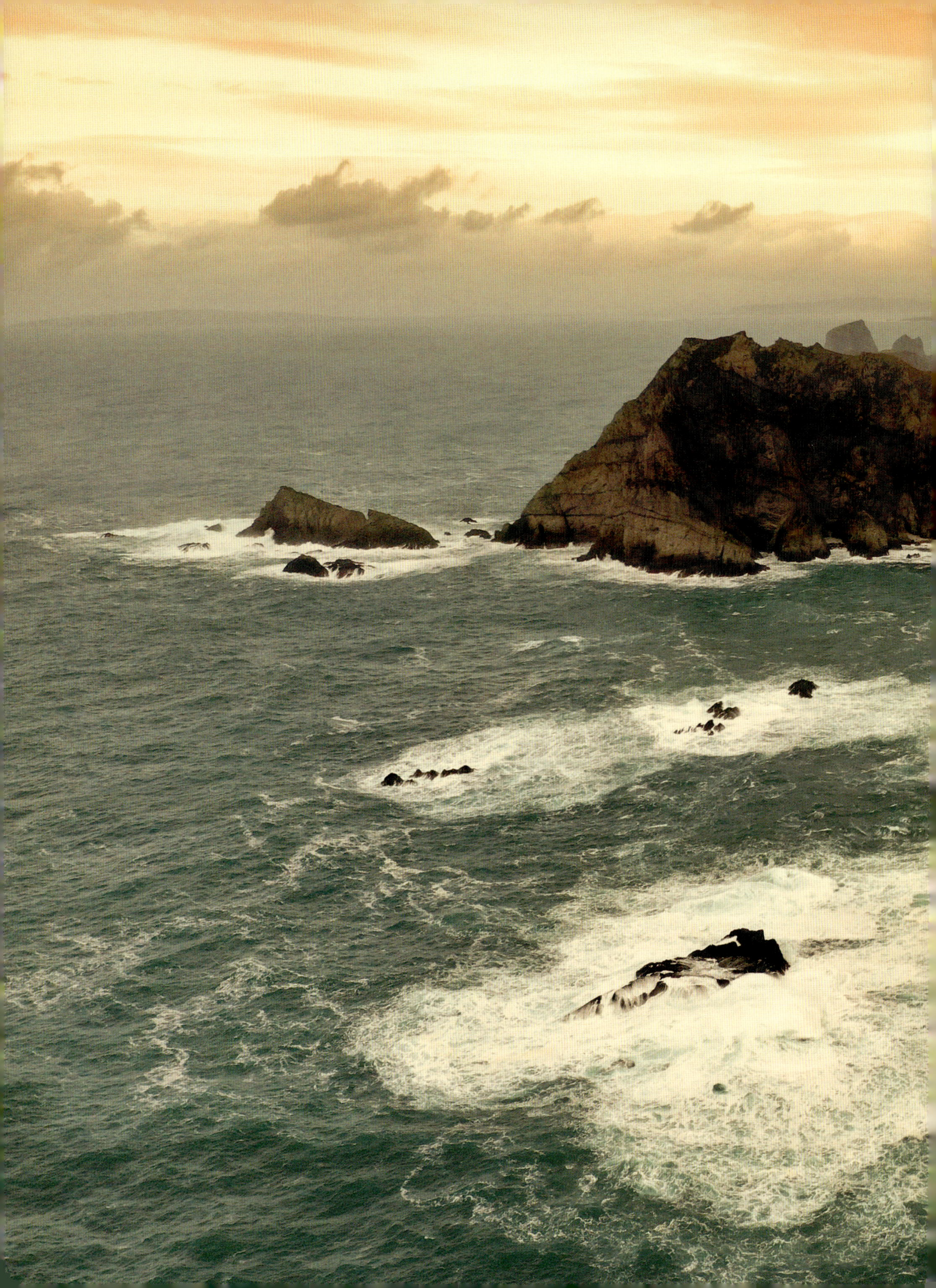

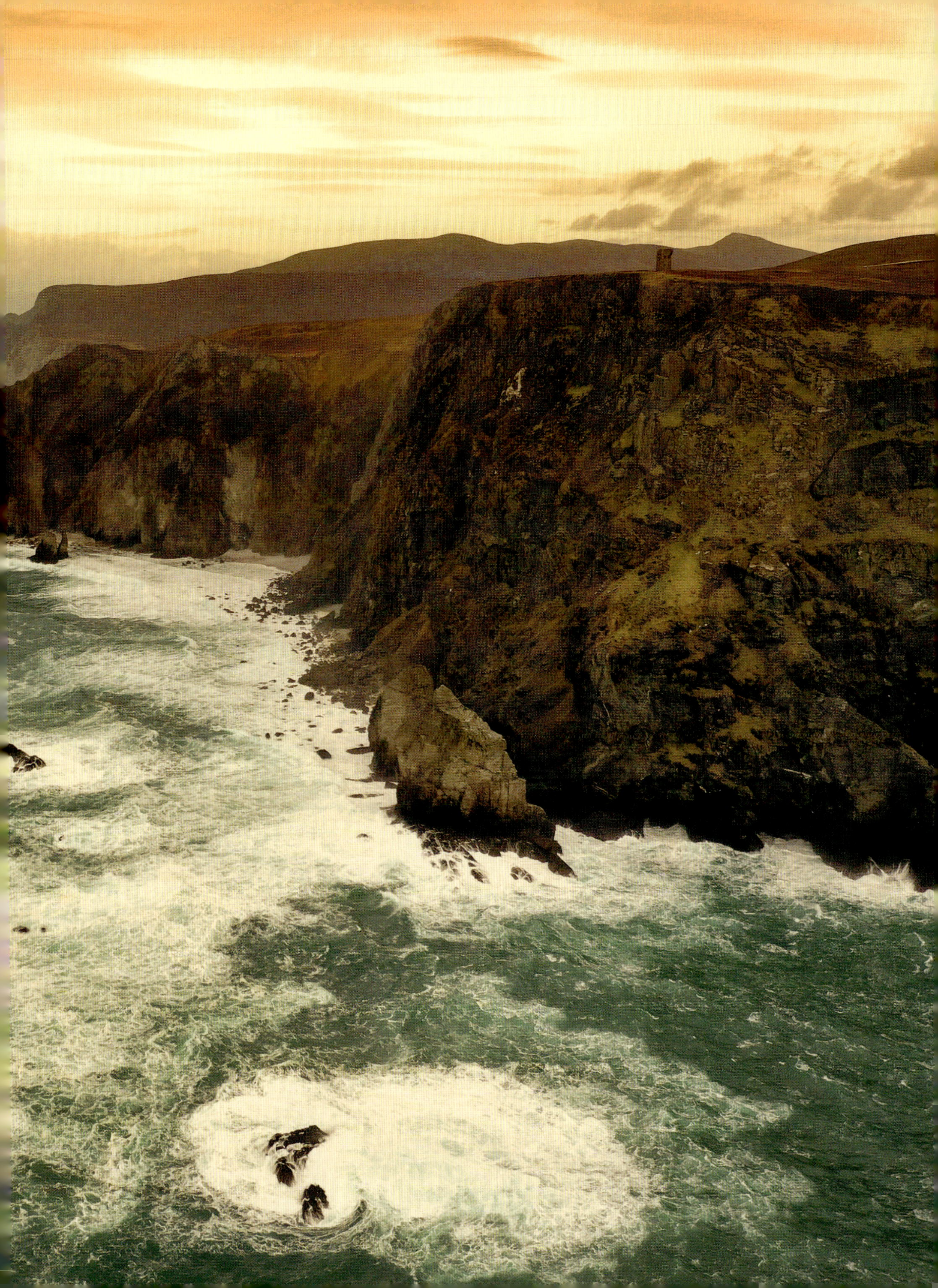

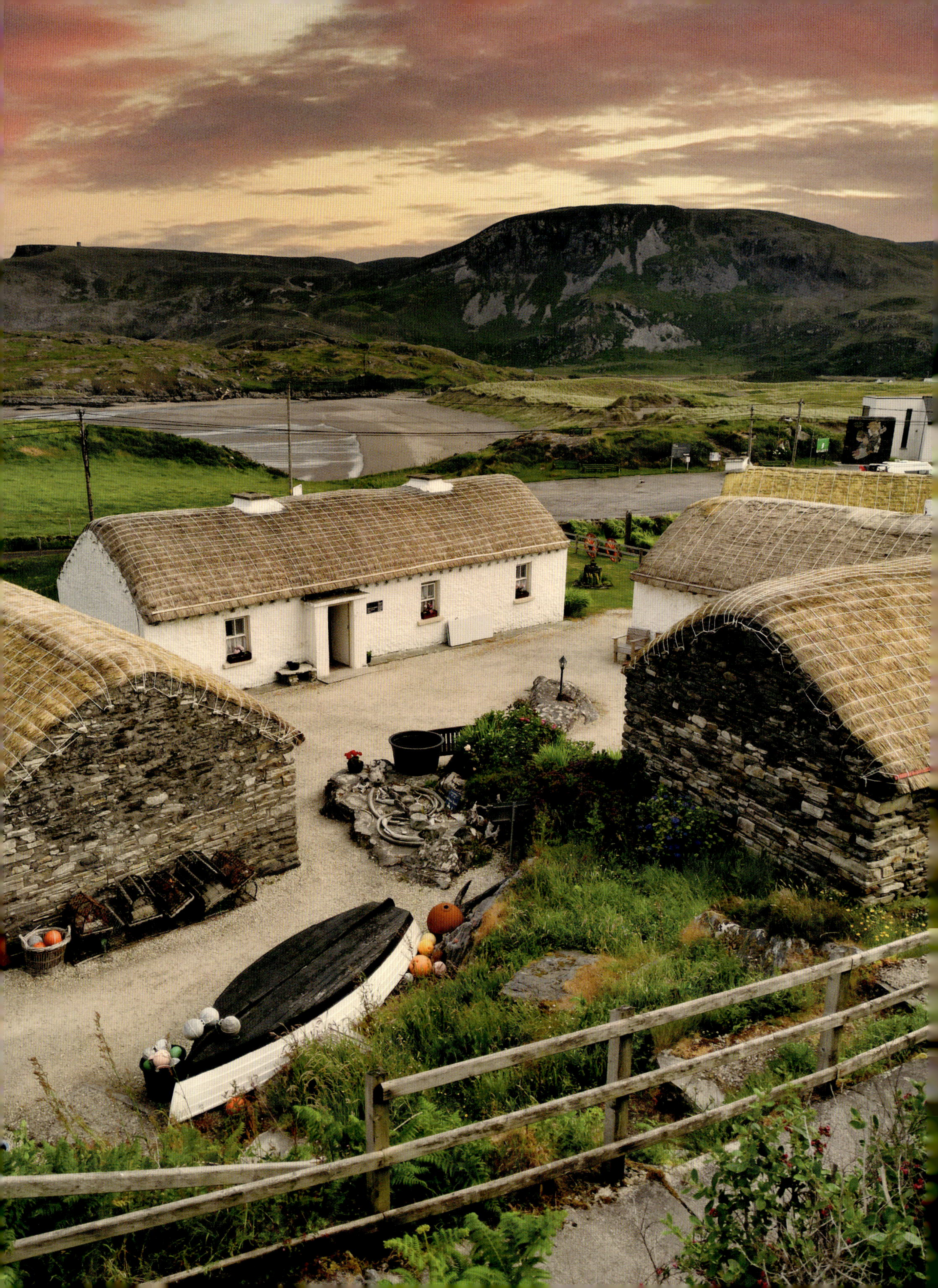

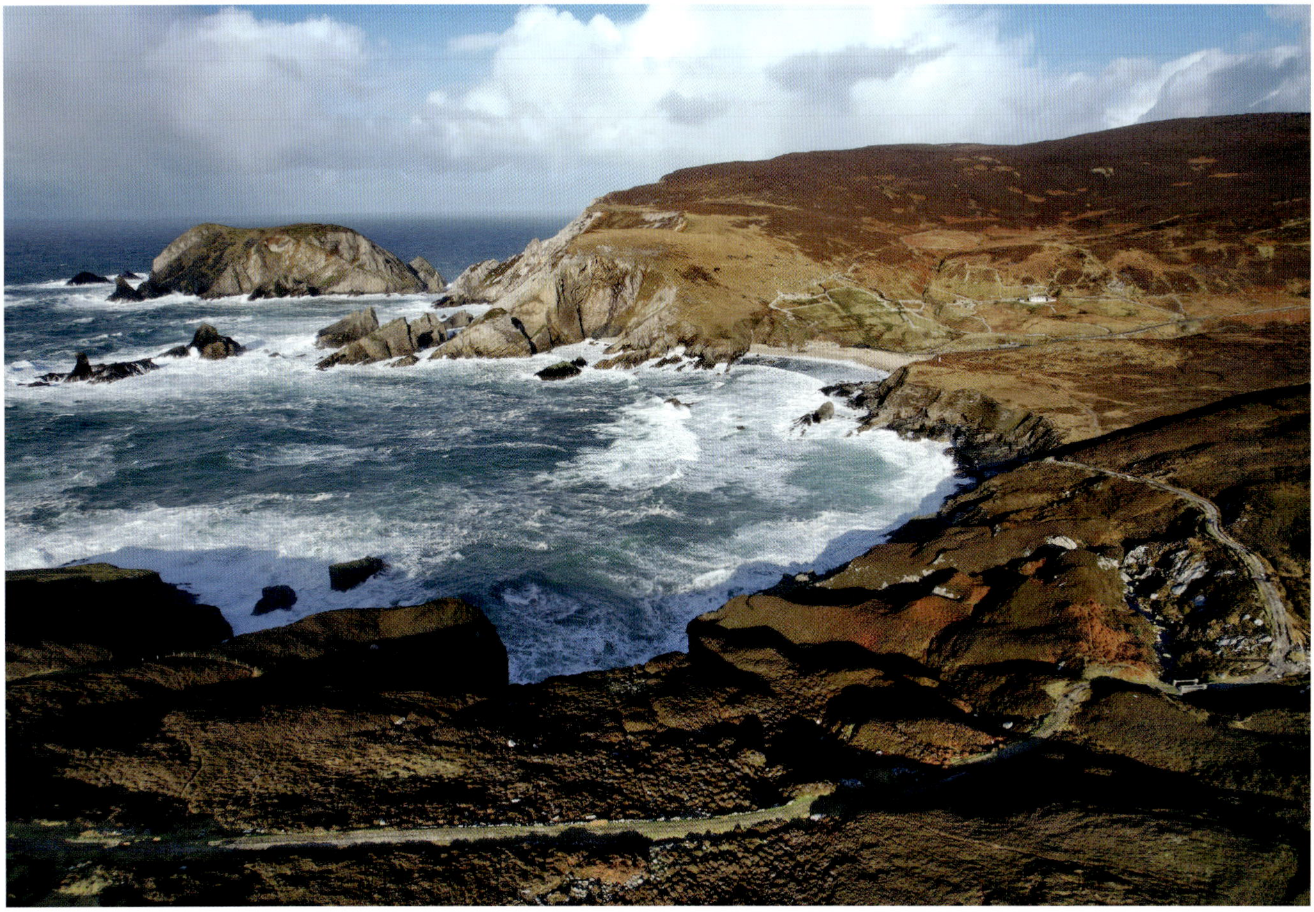

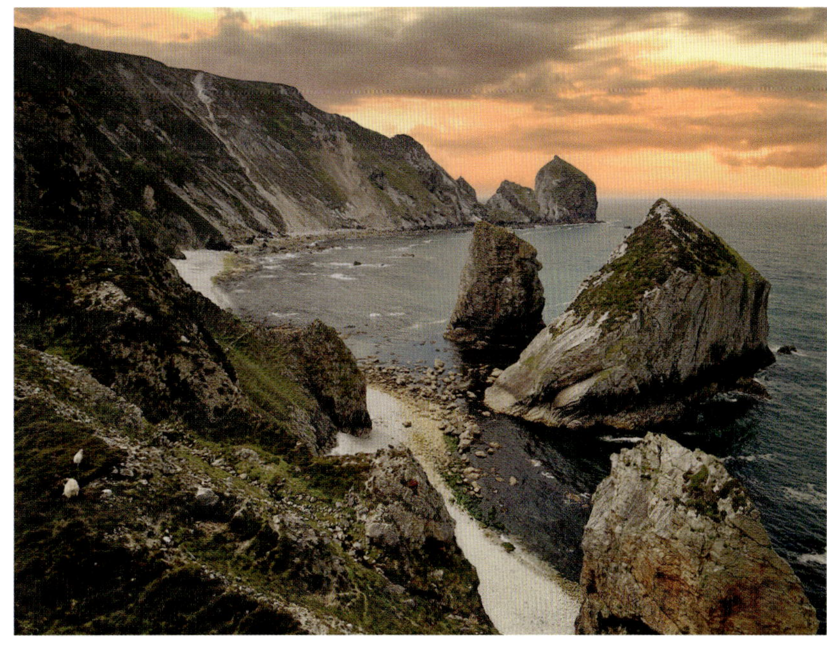

Above: The rough and rugged cliffs of An Port with its succession of sea stacks.

Right: Glenlough Bay, where the Welsh poet Dylan Thomas holidayed in the summer of 1935.

Opposite: Glencolmcille Folk Village, which was opened in 1967.

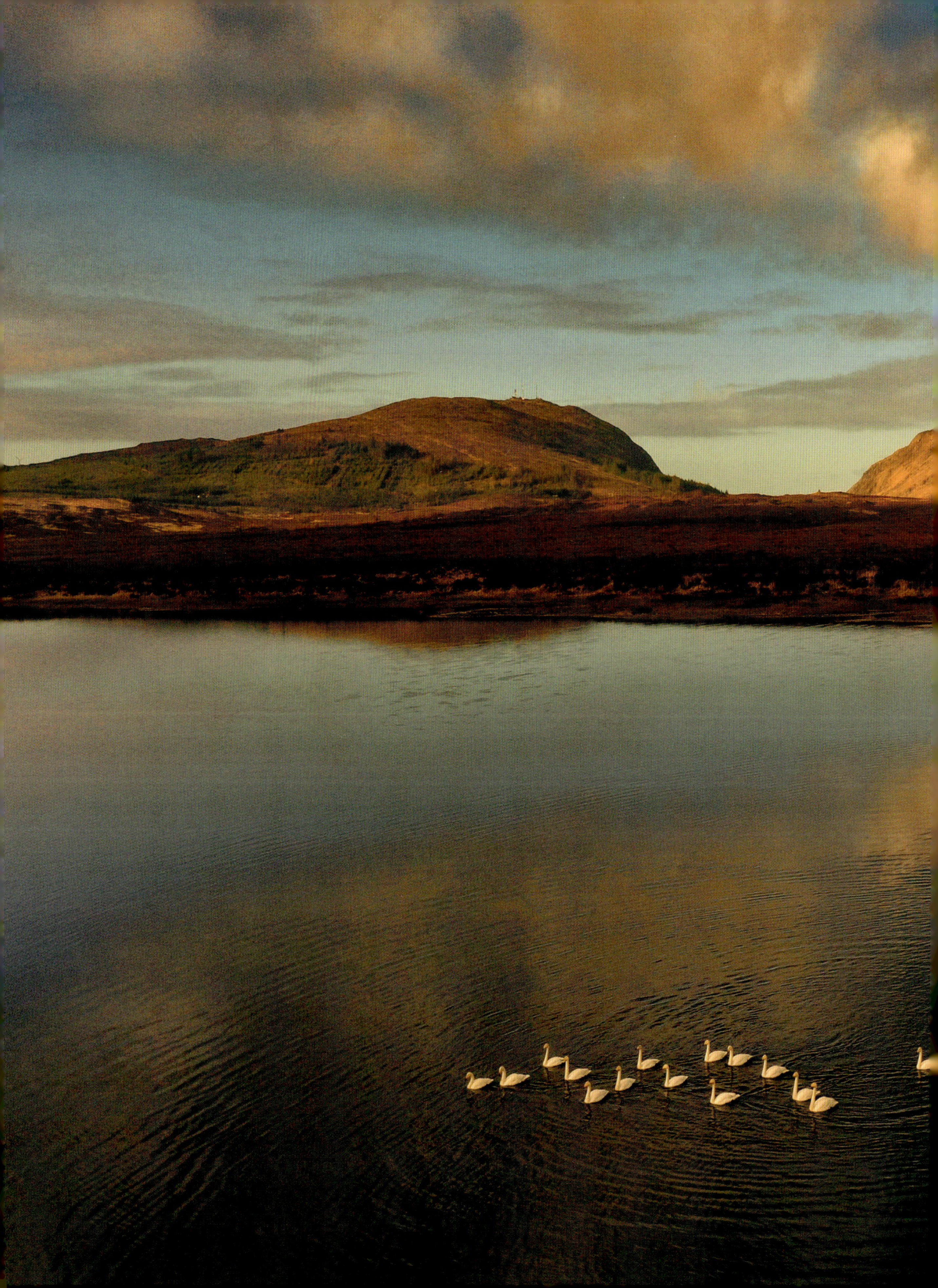

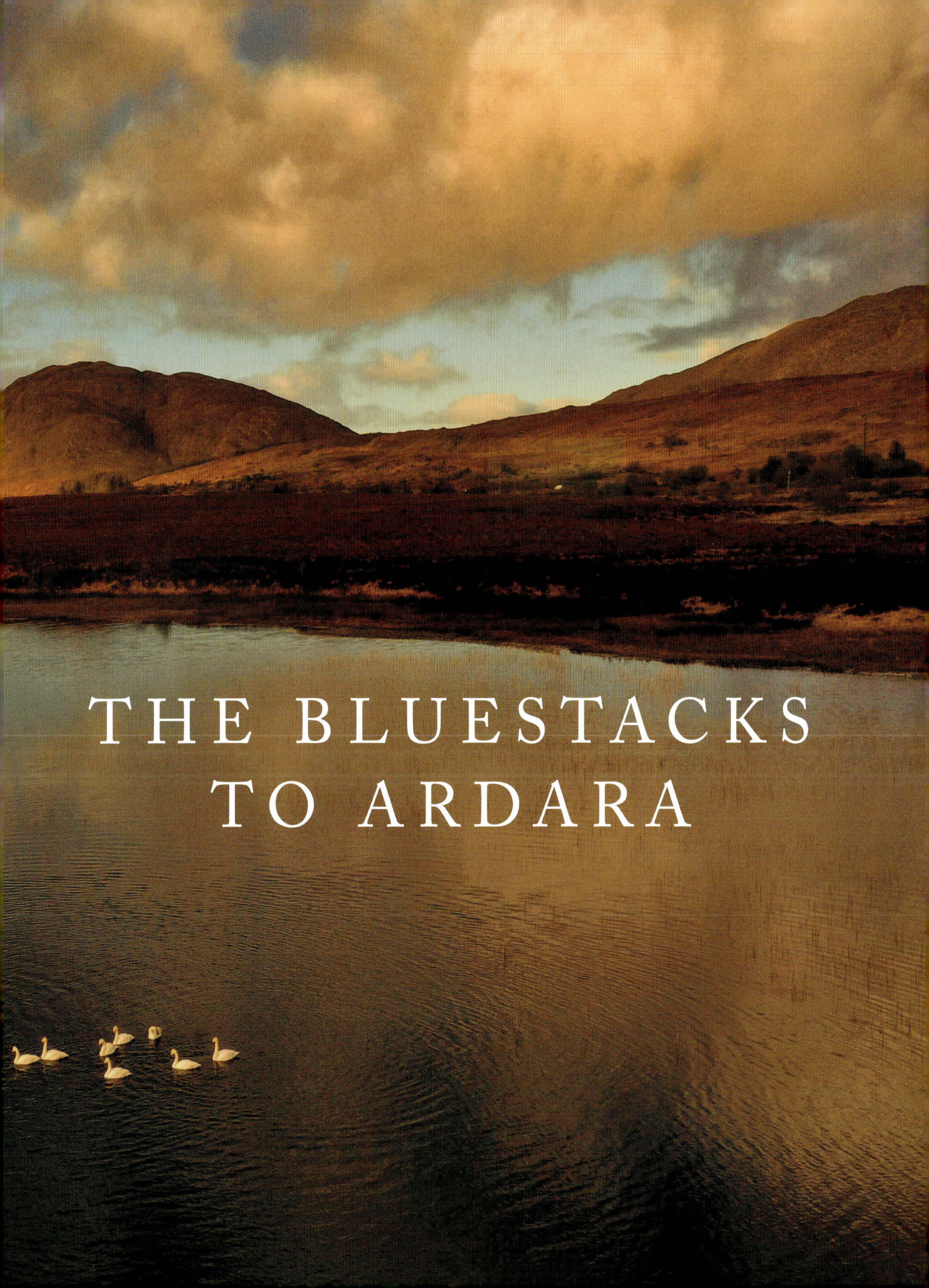

THE BLUESTACKS
TO ARDARA

County Donegal is criss-crossed with rugged mountains – the Bluestack Mountains in the south and, in the north, the Derryveagh Mountains. The road north from Donegal town to Ballybofey through Barnesmore Gap with the meandering Lowerymore River is one of the greatest scenic routes in Ireland.

Previous pages: Swans resting on Lough Mourne in March before they continue their migration journey.

White hawthorn trees and pink rhododendrons, side by side with the yellow peaflowers of gorse bushes, light up the landscape in the Bluestack Mountains.

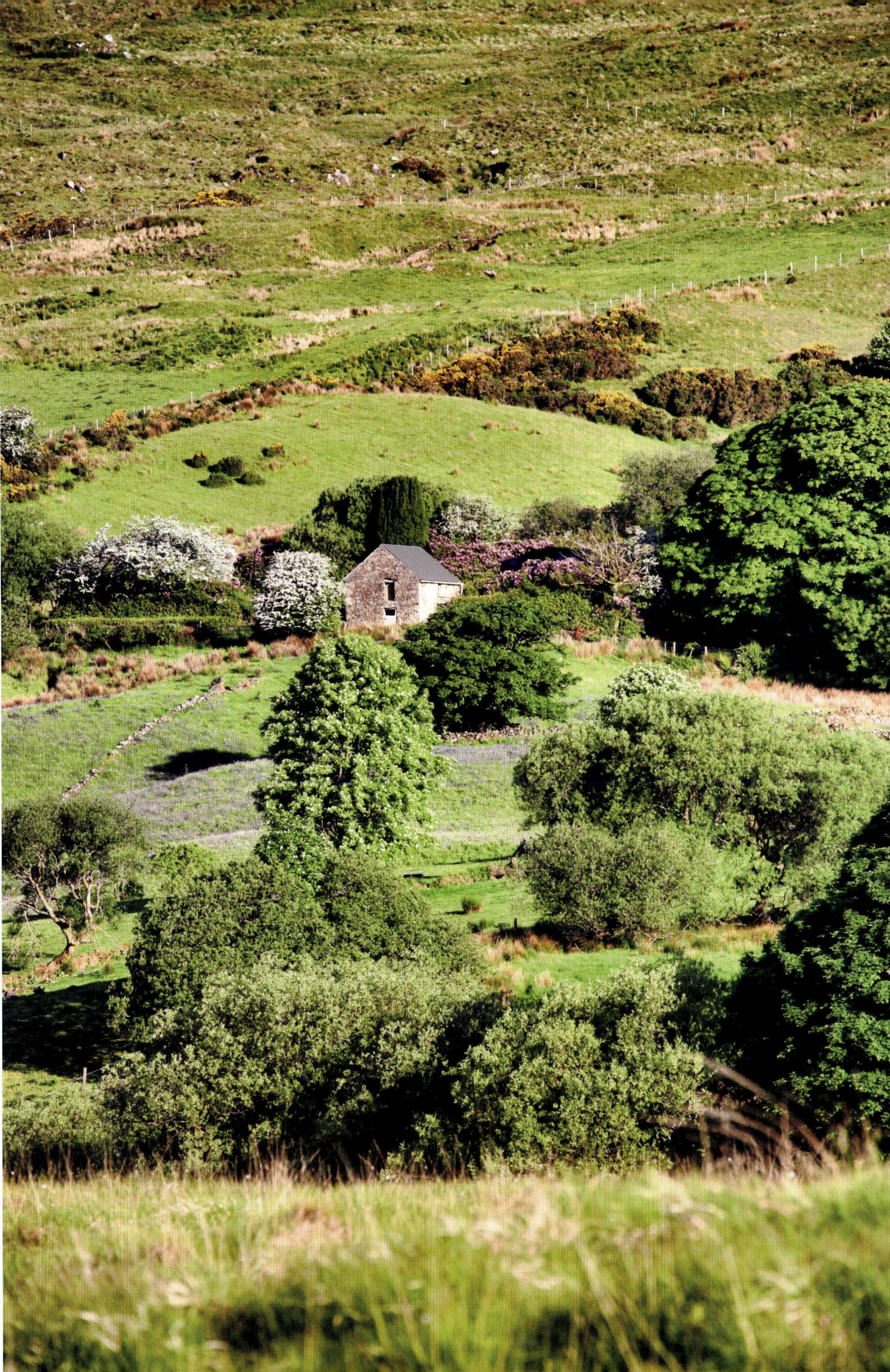

The N15 road north
from Donegal
town runs through
Barnesmore Gap in the
Bluestack Mountains.
A glacier carved this
wide, deep valley
between the impressive
towering mountains
of Croaghconnellagh
(Conell's Mountain) and
Croaghonagh (Eoghan's
Mountain). The raw,
wild landscape is a feast
for the eyes.

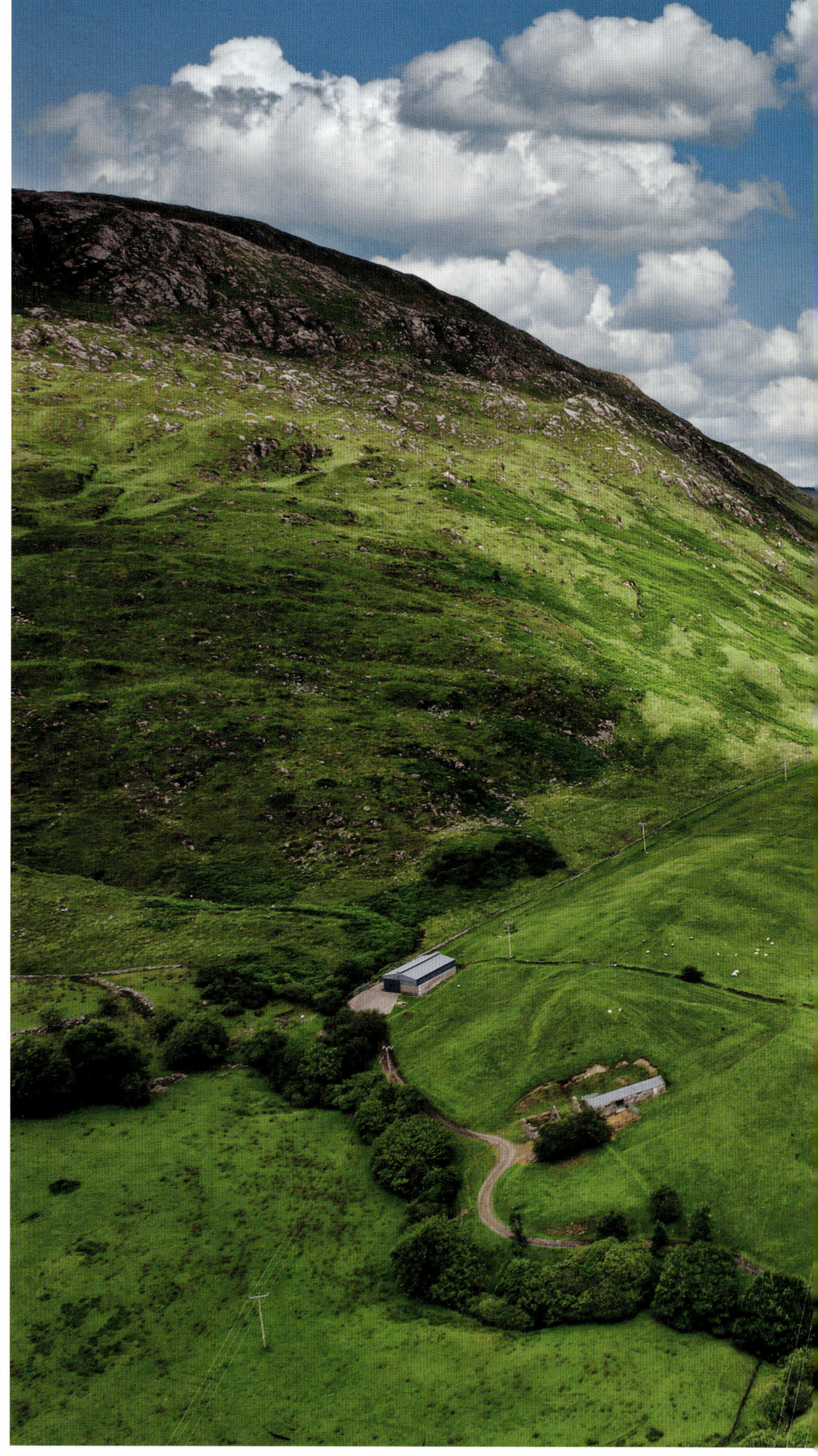

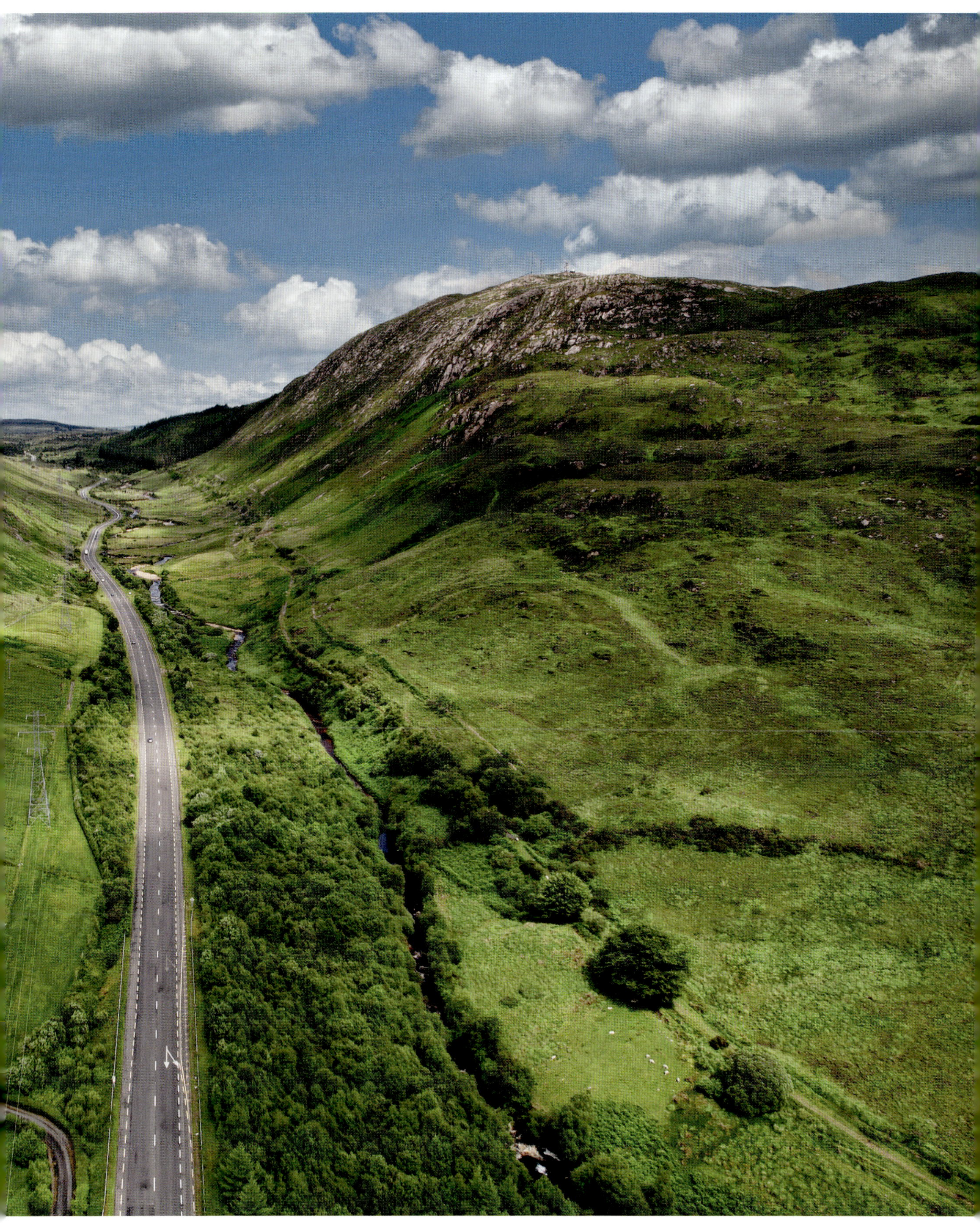

Biddys O'Barne's public house is nestled at the foothills of the Bluestack Mountains on the banks of the Lowerymore River. Originally an inn, dating back to the eighteenth century, it was a stopping point for coaches where horses were rested and travellers relaxed before the next stage of their journey through Barnesmore Gap.

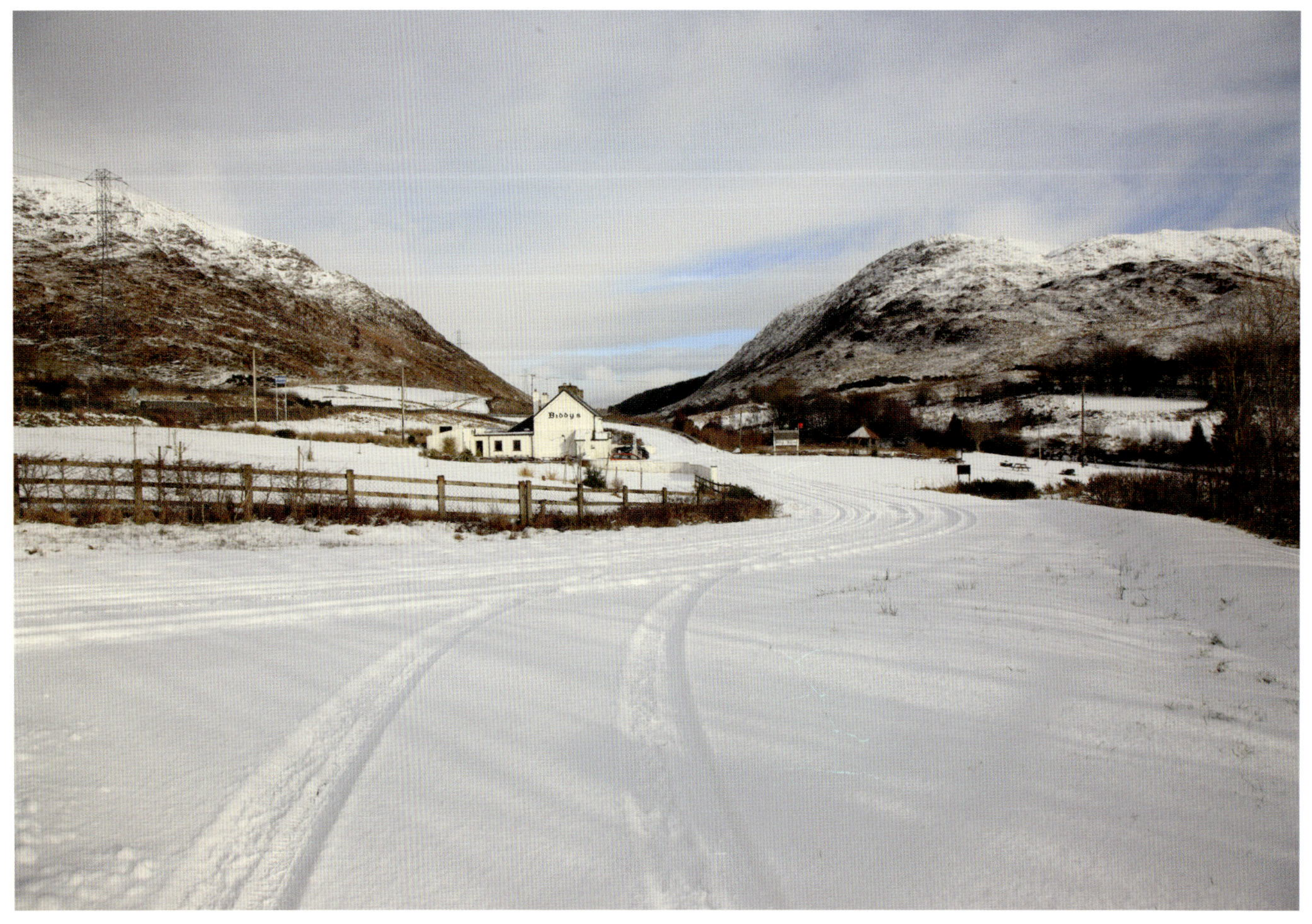

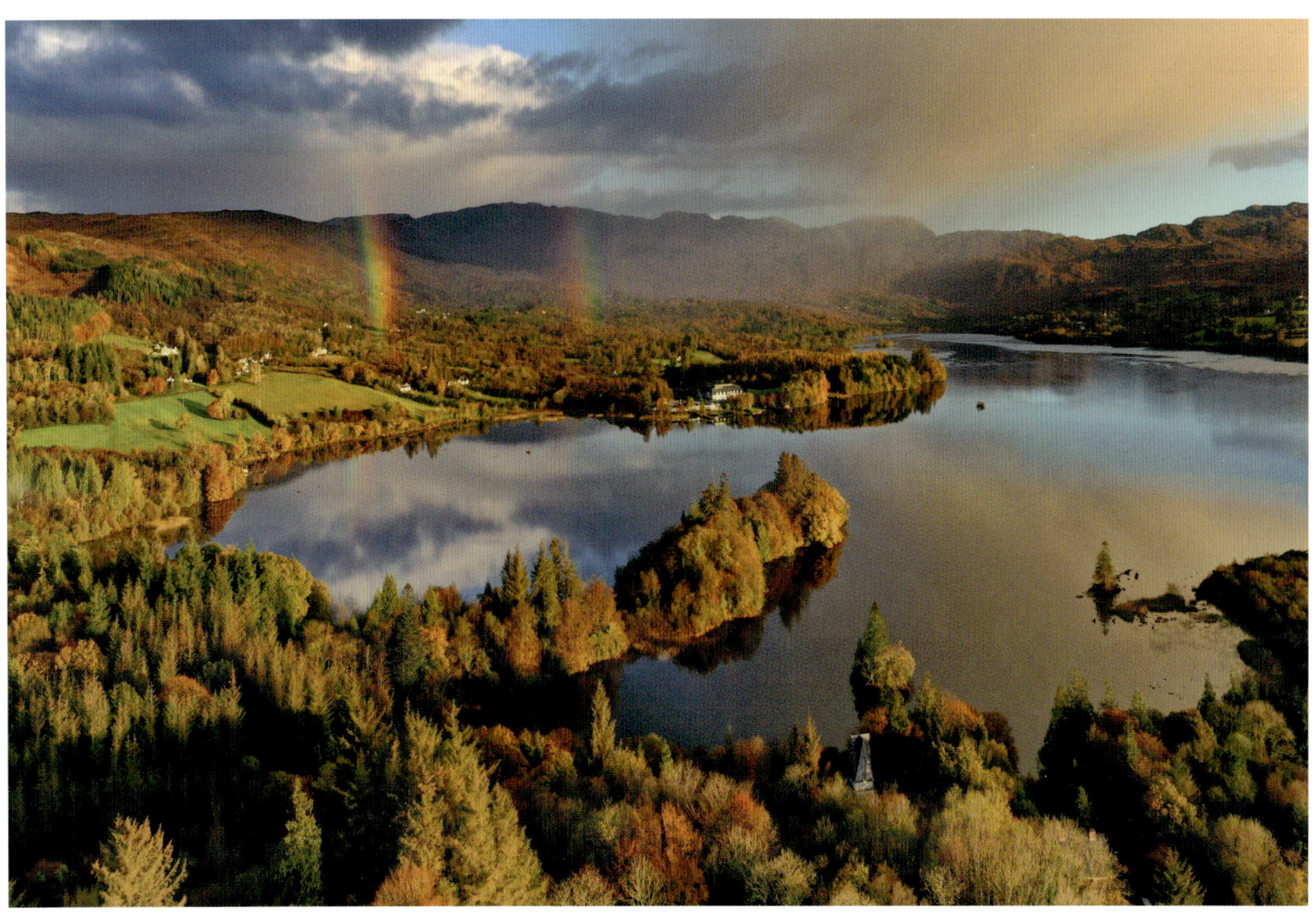

Lough Eske is one of the jewels in the Donegal crown, in an exquisite setting of tree-fringed shores and surrounded by a horseshoe of mountains. It is timeless but ever changing, with the shifting moods of the mountains and the sky at sunrise. The tower of the Church of Ireland, built in 1846, can be seen peeping up above the trees to the southwest of the lake.

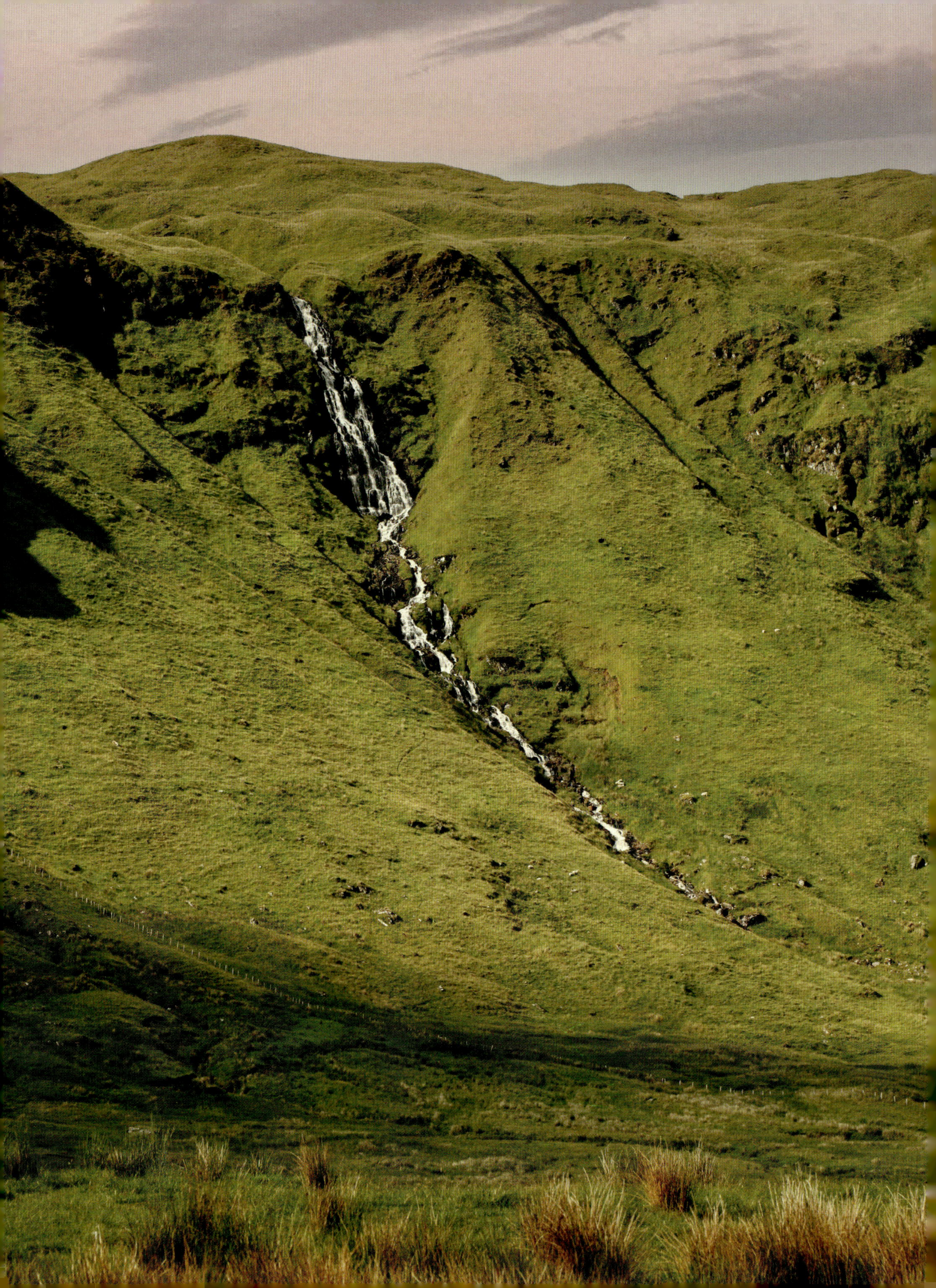

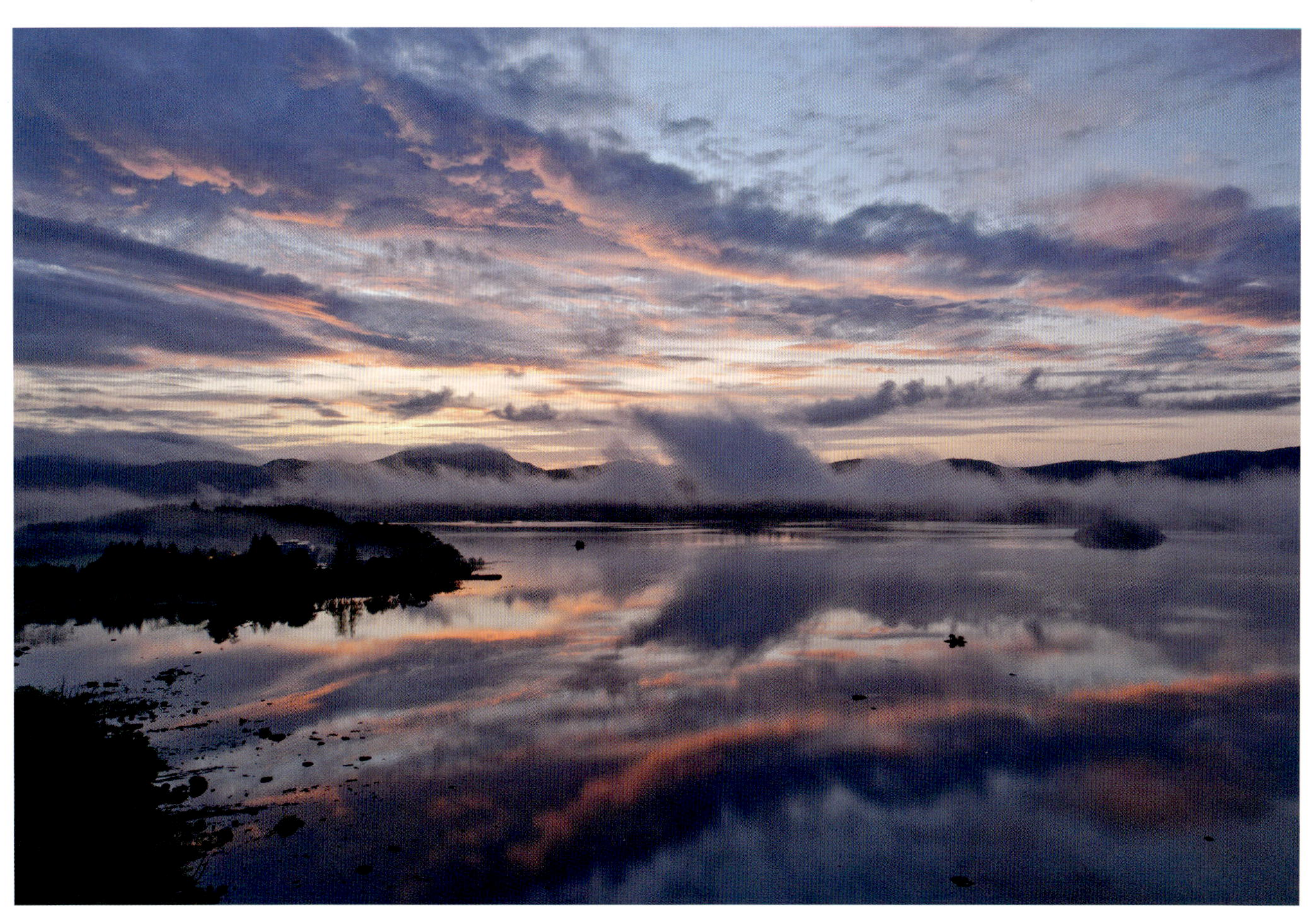

Nothing is quite as magical as the mirror reflections, shrouded partly in mist, at Lough Eske.

Opposite: The magnificent Sruell valley is a steep-sided grassy glen. On three sides, the mountains tower to over 600 metres (over 1,970 feet). The Grey Mare's Tail waterfall tumbles down Binnasruell Mountain from Lough Asgartha, twitching and turning as it descends, like a horse's twitching tail. The valley is part of the long-standing hiking route from Lough Eske to Ardara.

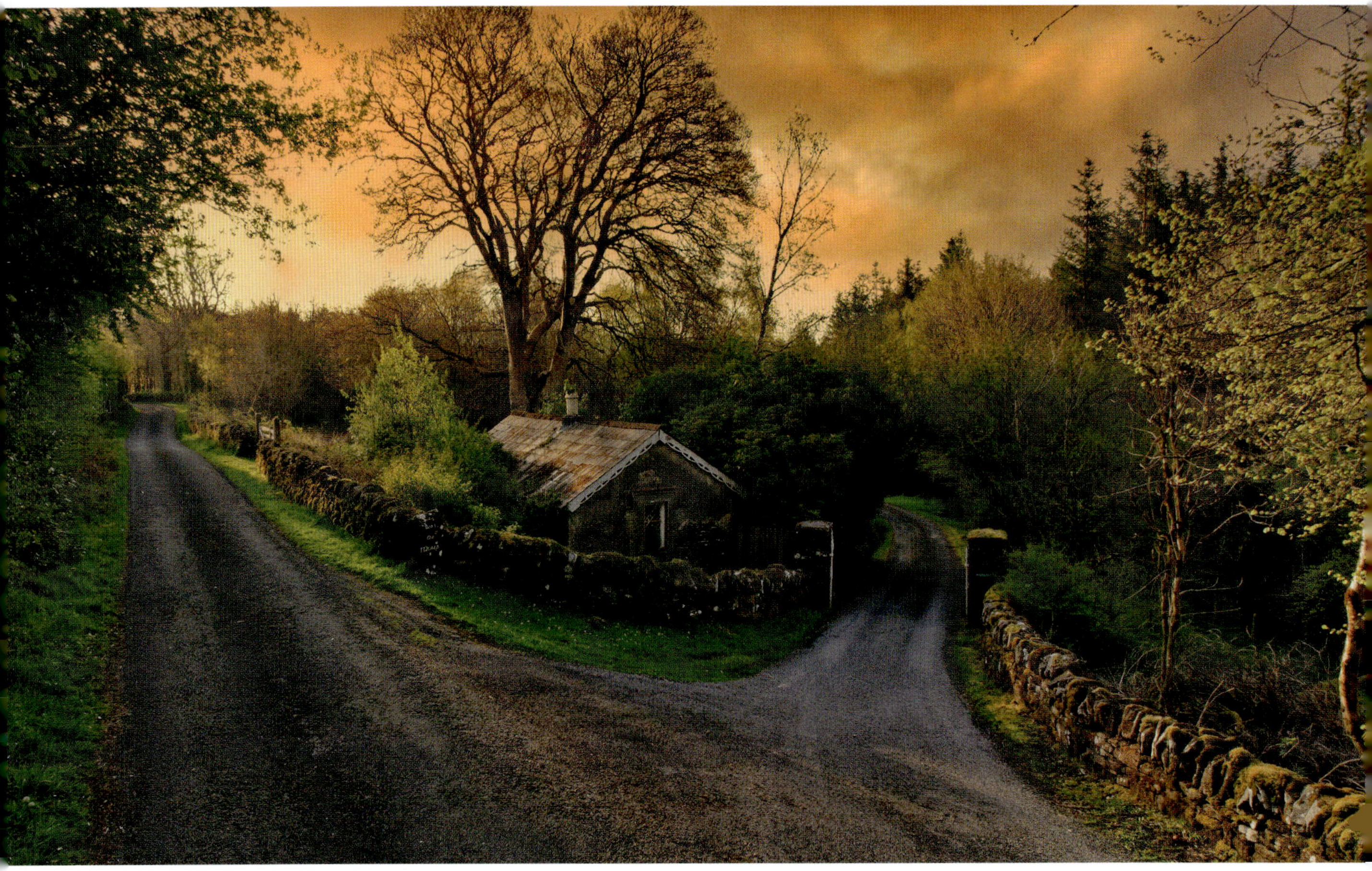

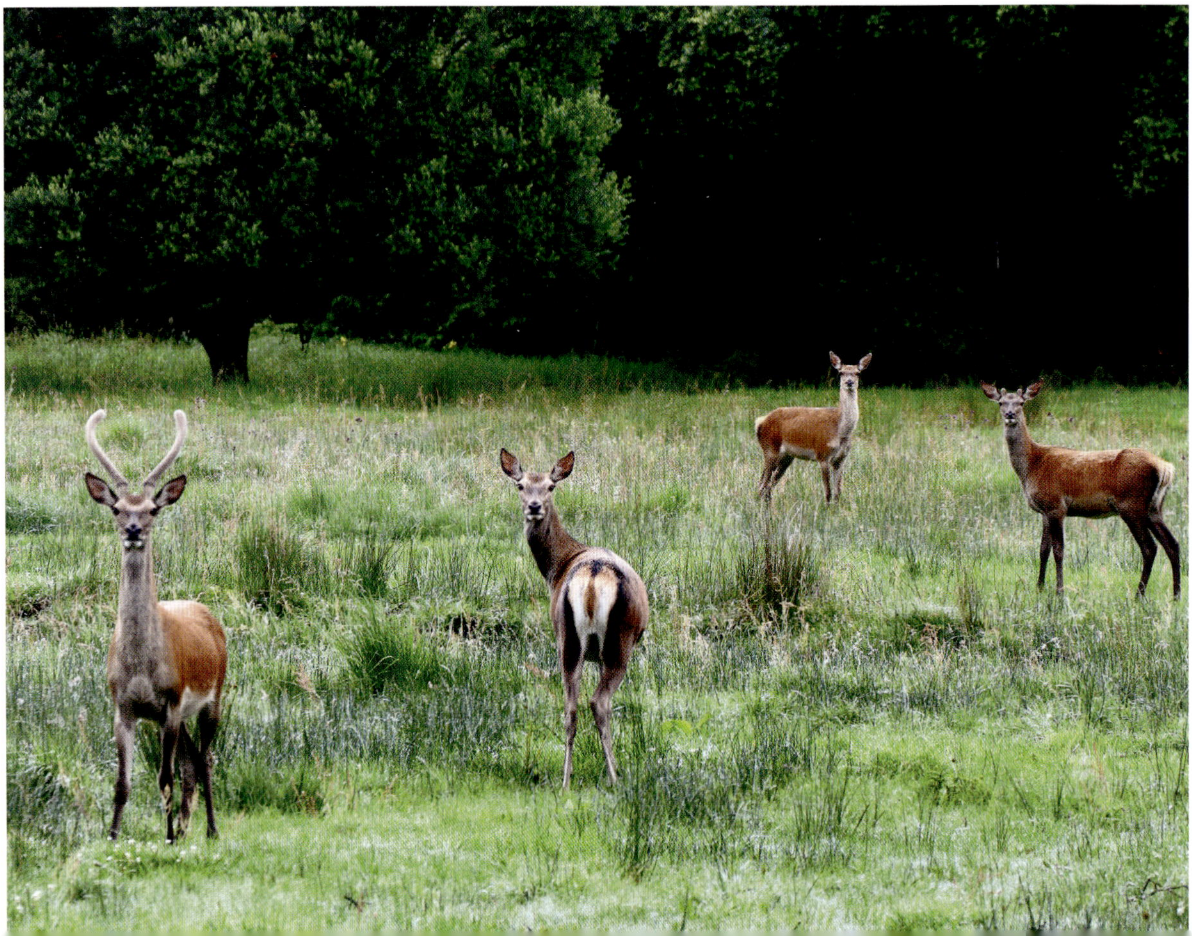

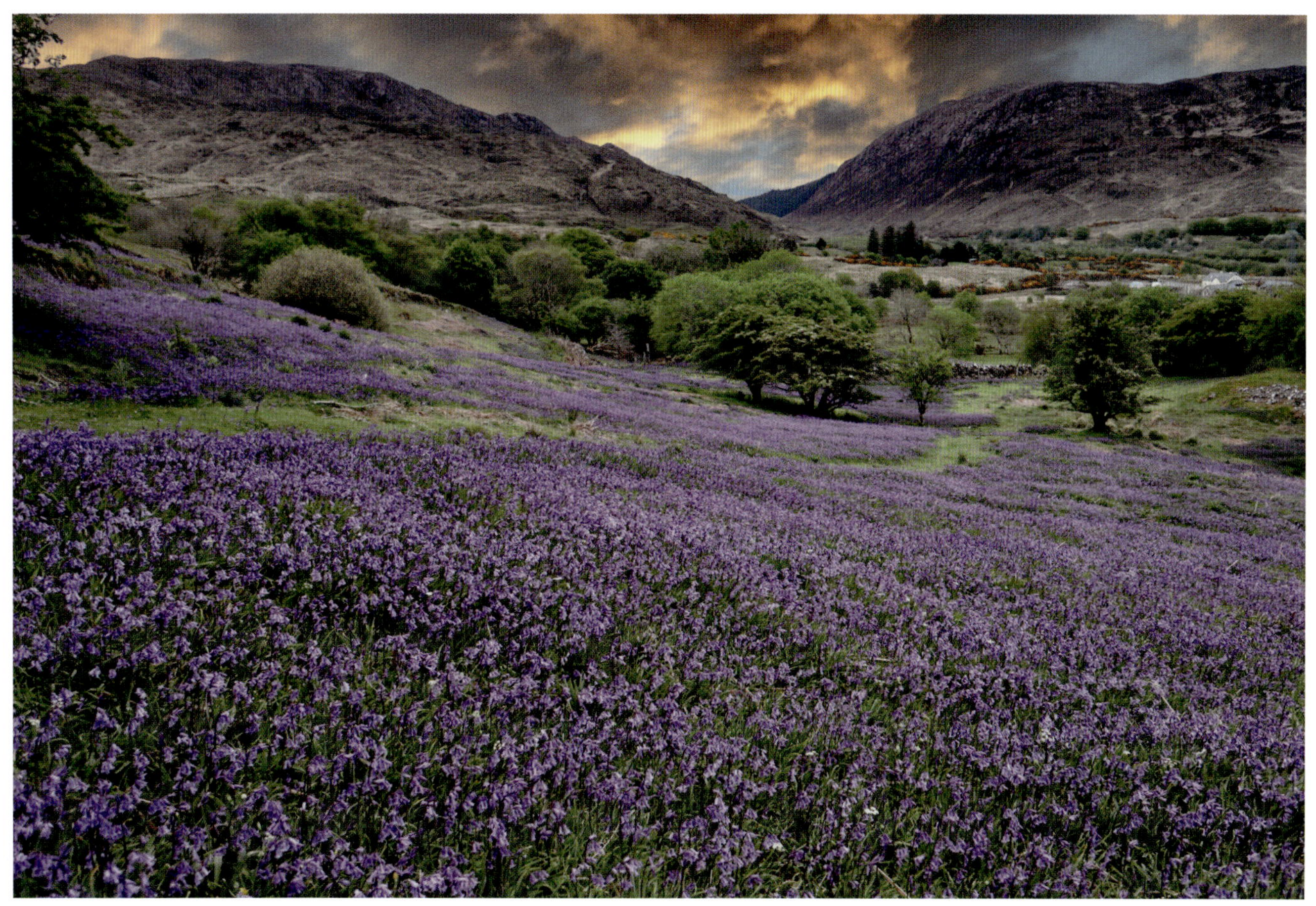

A meadow of bluebells in May with the sun rising behind Barnesmore Gap.

Opposite, top: Ardnamona Gate Lodge at Greenan. The house and gardens remain private but a woodland walkway, almost three kilometres long, has been developed by the National Parks & Wildlife Service and is open to the public.

Opposite, bottom: A family of graceful Sika deer pause from their grazing in a meadow just before dawn.

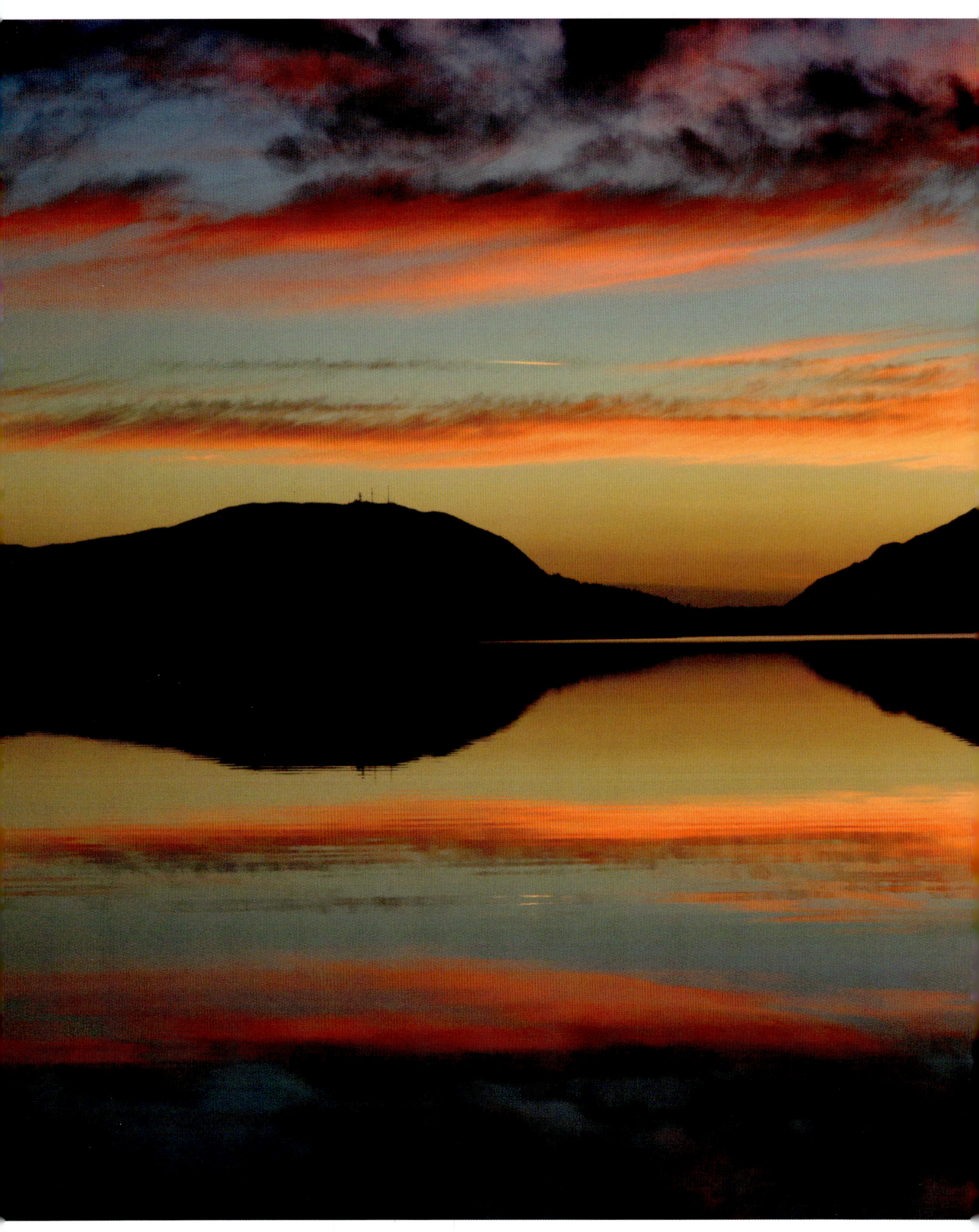

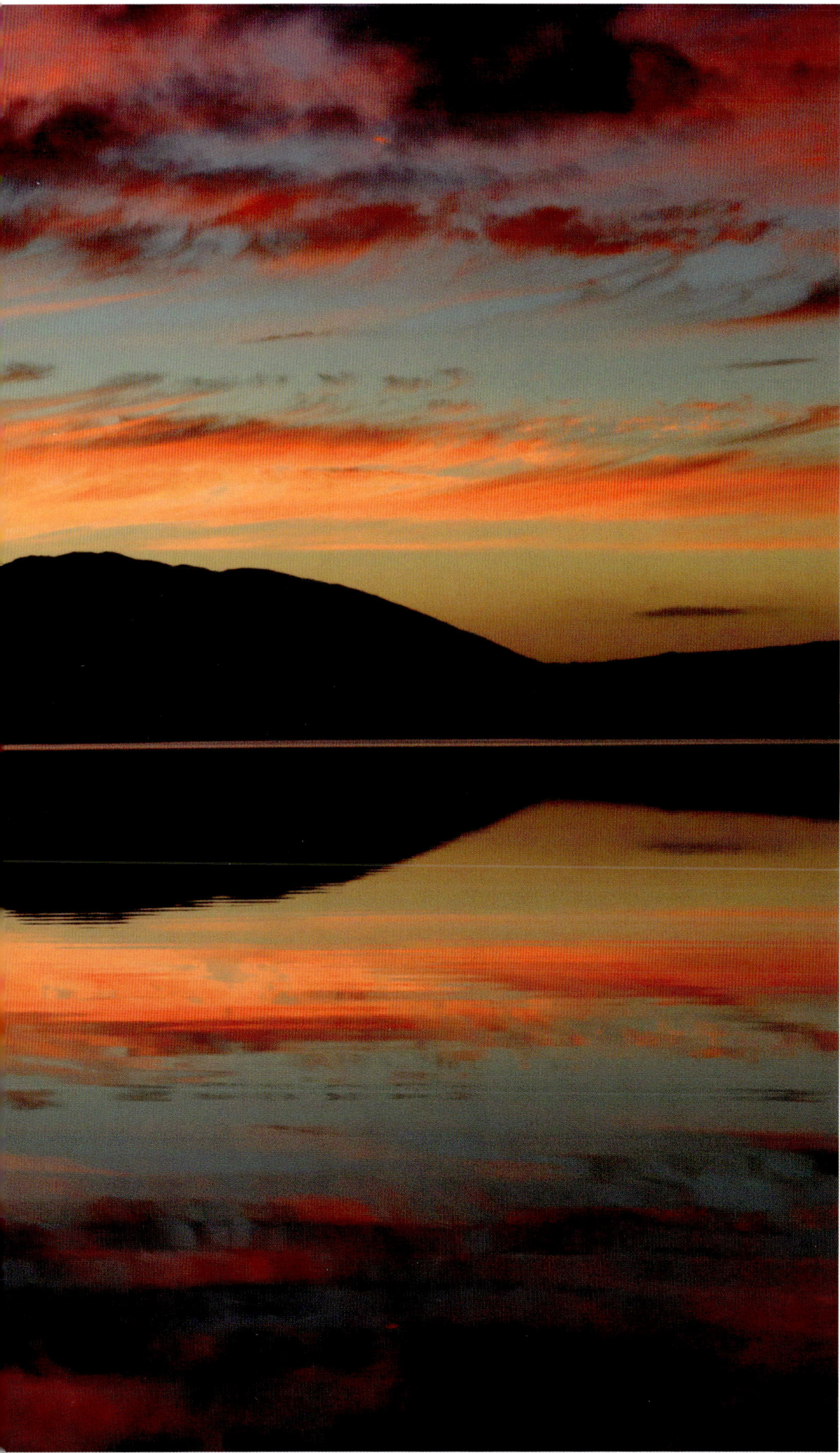

Mirror reflections at Lough Mourne. A striking view of the changing moods of the Bluestack Mountains, Croaghonagh (on the left) and Croaghconnellagh, after the sun dropped below the horizon.

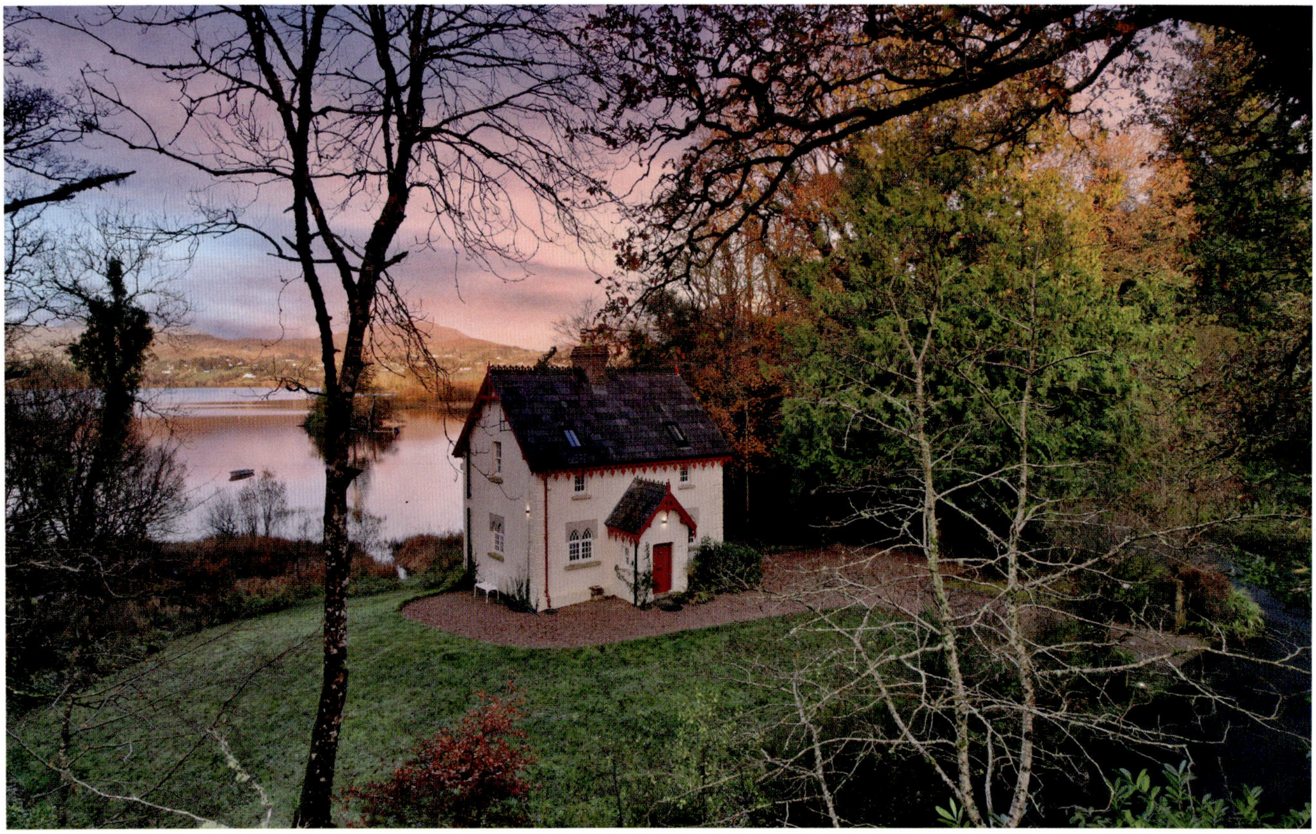

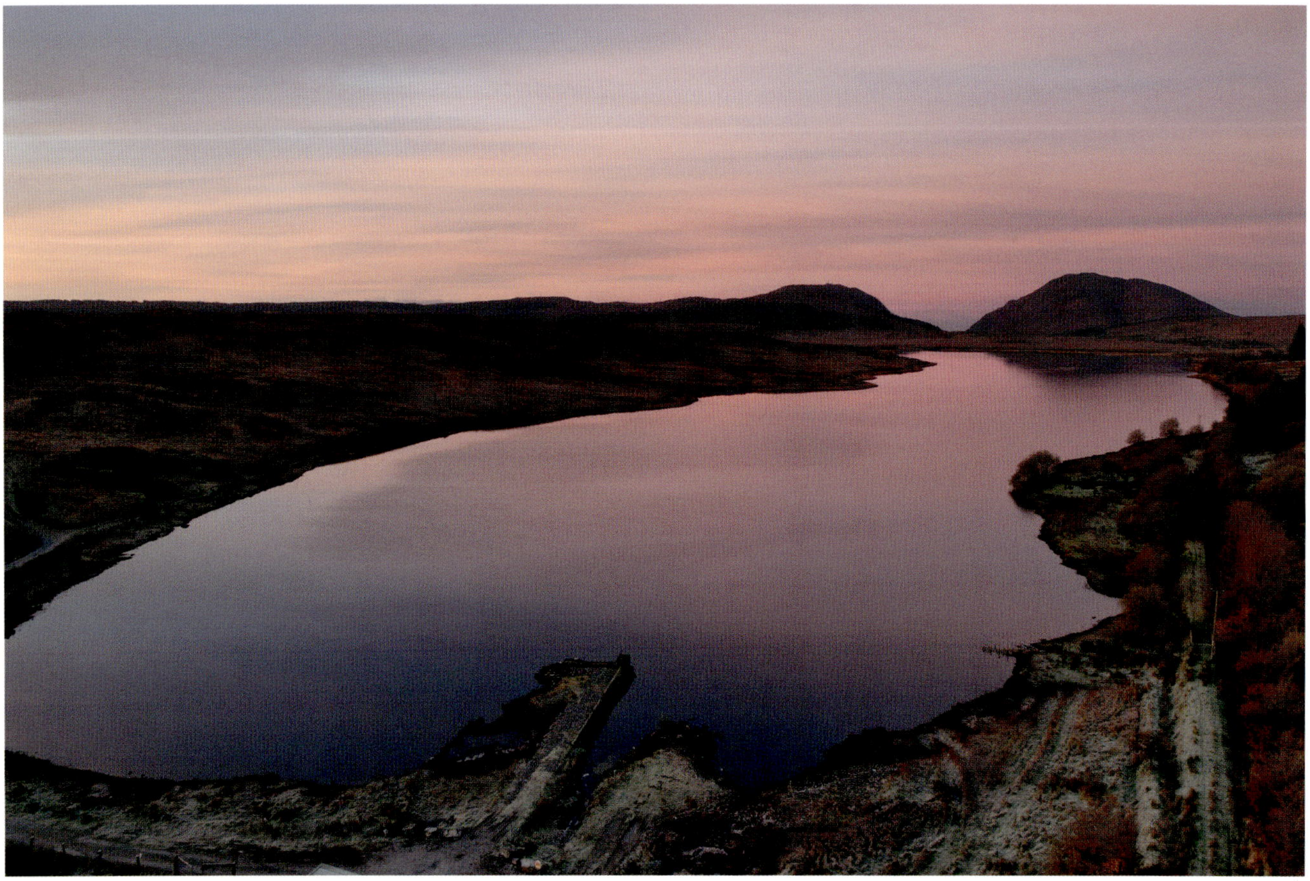

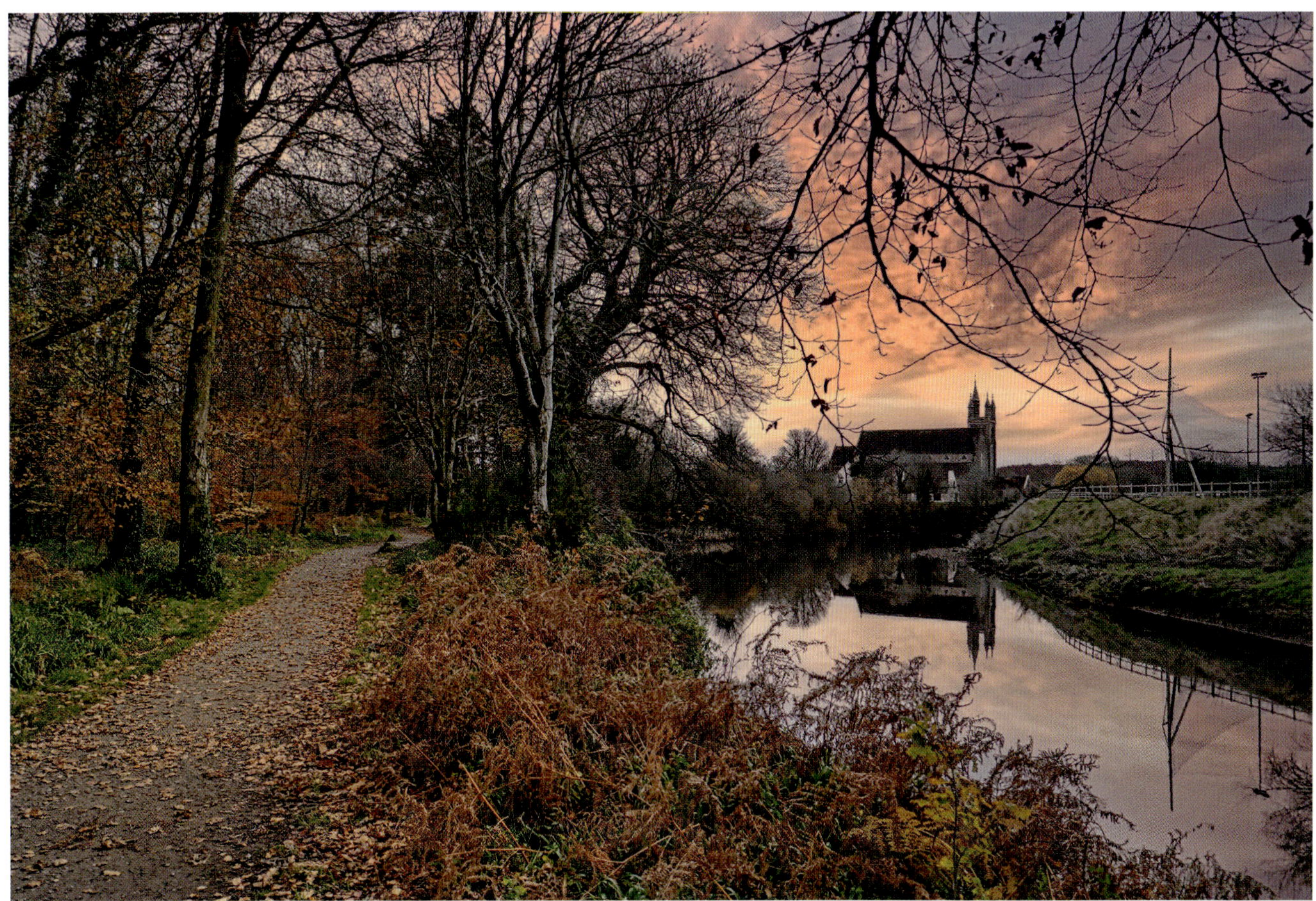

Drumboe Woods is a hidden gem along the banks of the River Finn at Stranorlar. Scenic walking paths, stunning scenery and rich history attract locals and visitors alike. The woodland path runs alongside the river, with the Church of Mary Immaculate reflected in the water.

Opposite, top: The former gate lodge to Lough Eske Castle, known as 'Wee Kate's', was built as a fishing lodge for the estate guide and his family in 1852. It has been painstakingly restored and transformed into this hideaway by the present owner, who took great care to retain all the original features. On a damp, cold morning just before sunrise, the dark clouds are lit up with wisps of pink.

Opposite, bottom: Before sunrise at Lough Mourne. The tranquil waters are home to pike, roach, brown trout and the European eel (a critically endangered species) while the lakeshore has abundant wildlife.

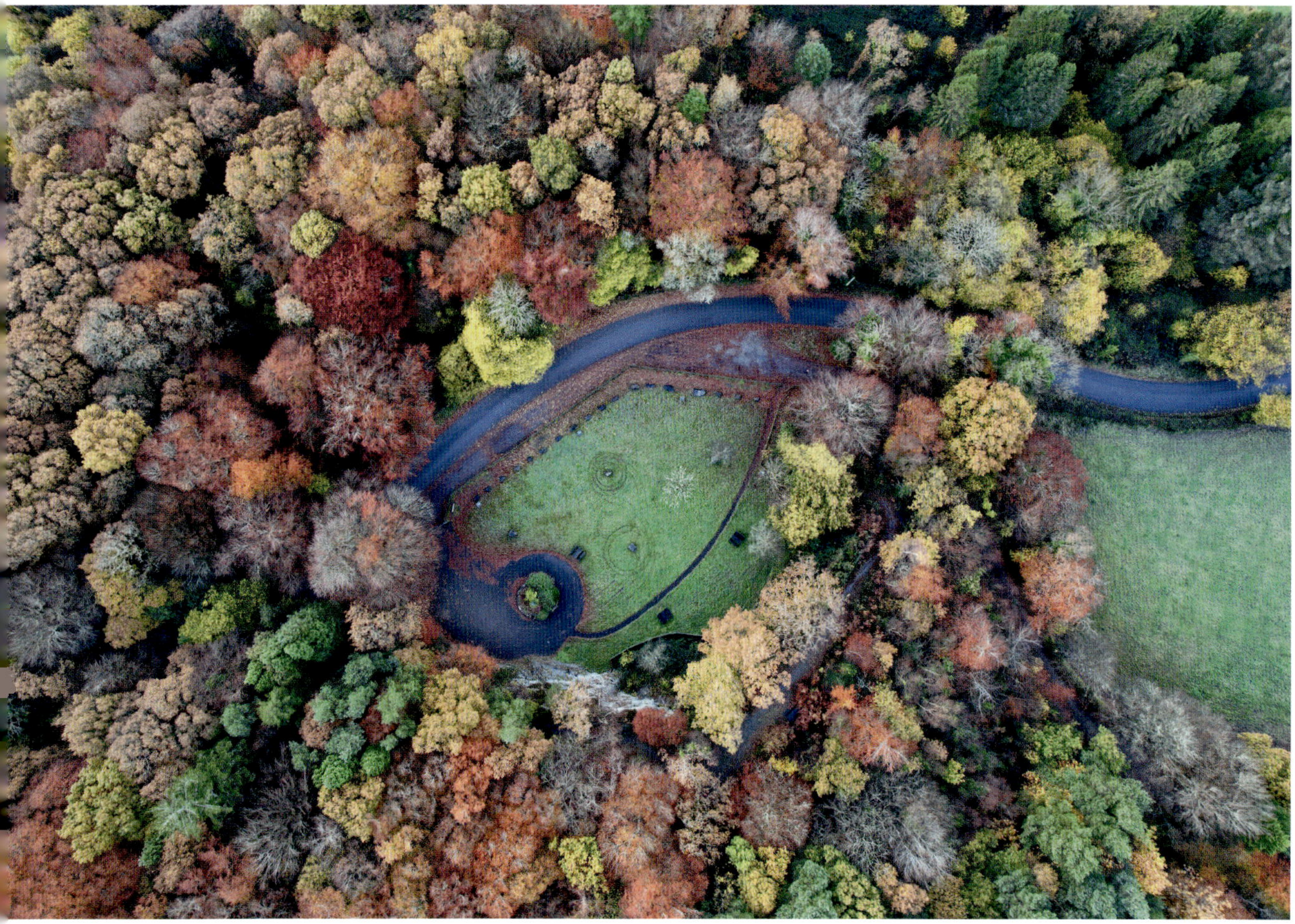

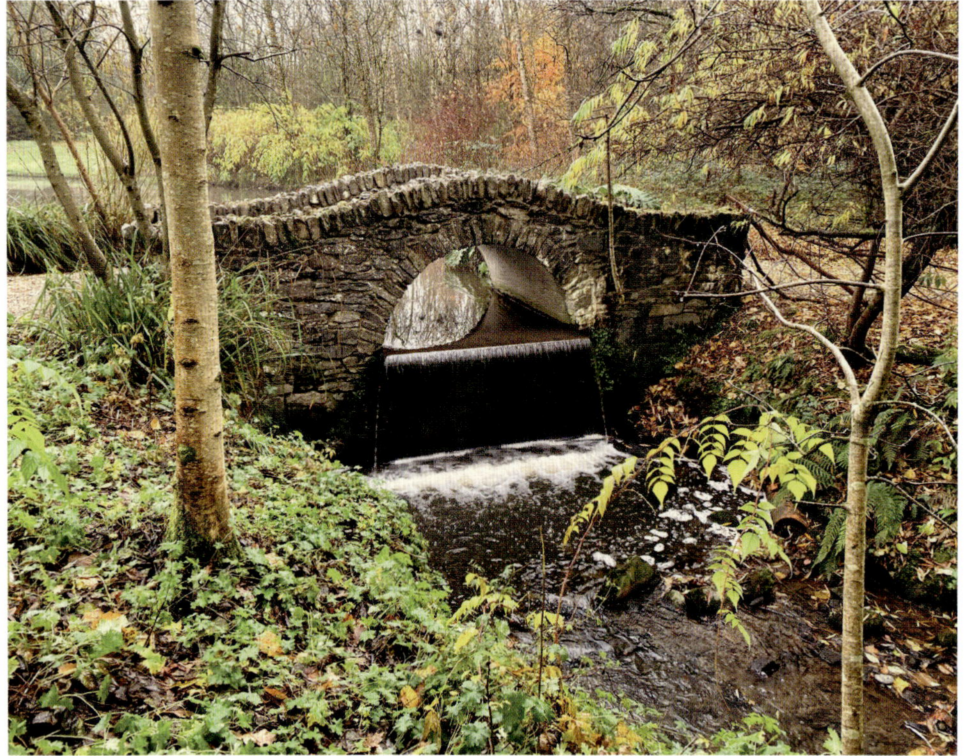

Above: A bird's-eye view of russet autumnal colours at Gort Scith picnic area, Stranorlar.

Left: Peace and tranquillity at Oakfield Park, Raphoe, with the gentle sound of water flowing under the bridge.

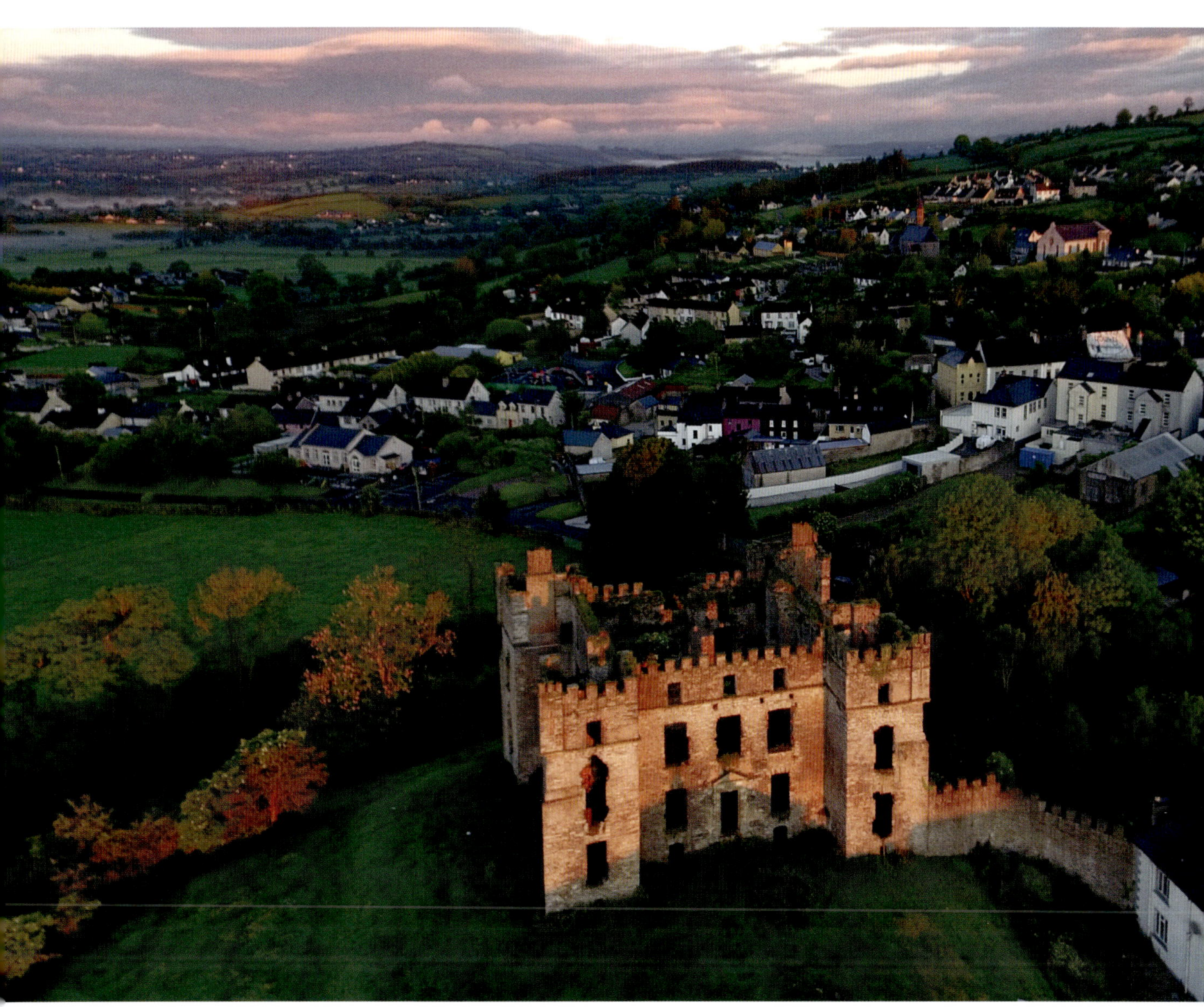

Raphoe Castle, or the Bishop's Palace as it is also known, sits atop a hill overlooking the town of Raphoe. It was built in 1636 by John Leslie, Bishop of Raphoe ('the Fighting Bishop'). Stones from a local round tower were used to construct the four-storey fortified home. It was destroyed in 1838 by an accidental fire from coals that fell out of a grate in an upper room and ignited the flooring. Since then, the Bishop's Palace has been in ruins.

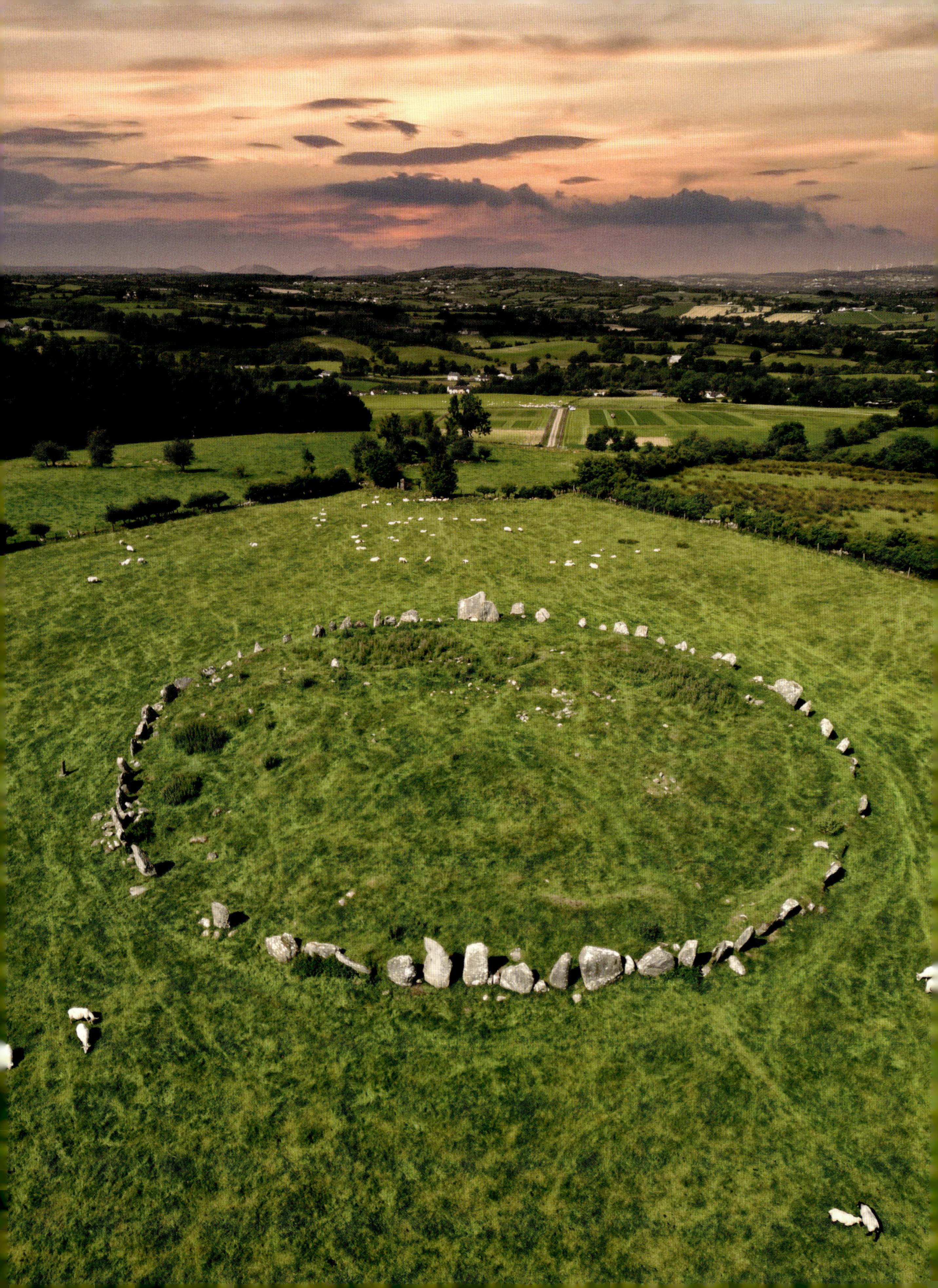

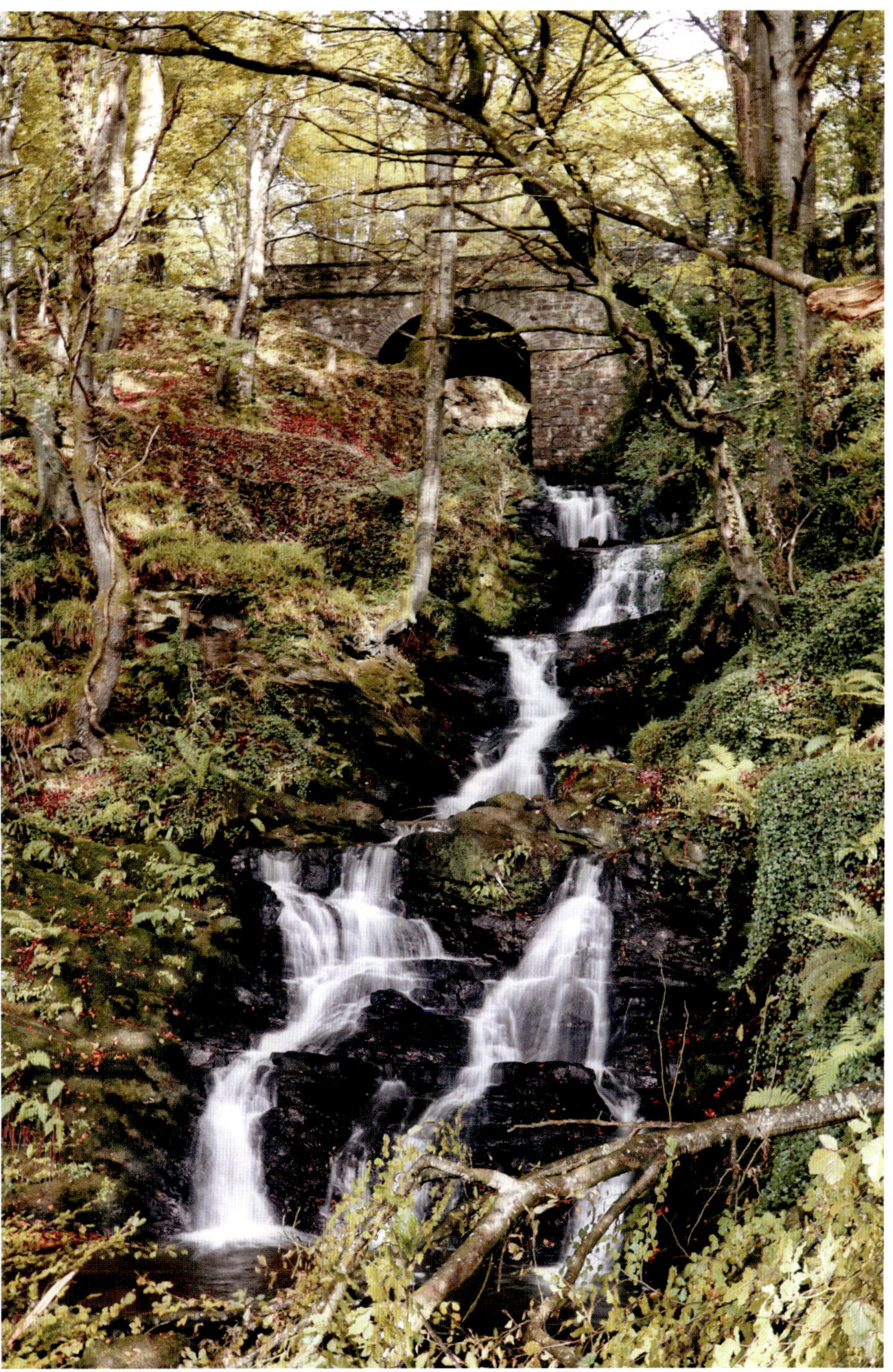

Waterfall Bridge at Burnside, Raphoe. The sound of rushing water cascading down over the rugged rocks echoes through the woods.

Opposite: The Beltany Stone Circle is one of the largest and earliest stone circles in Ireland, with a diameter of forty-four metres (145 feet). It was originally comprised of eighty upright stones, of which sixty-four still stand, and may date to *c.* 1400 BC. The name 'Beltany' derives from the spring festival of Bealtaine, or Beltane, which marks sunrise on the first day of May.

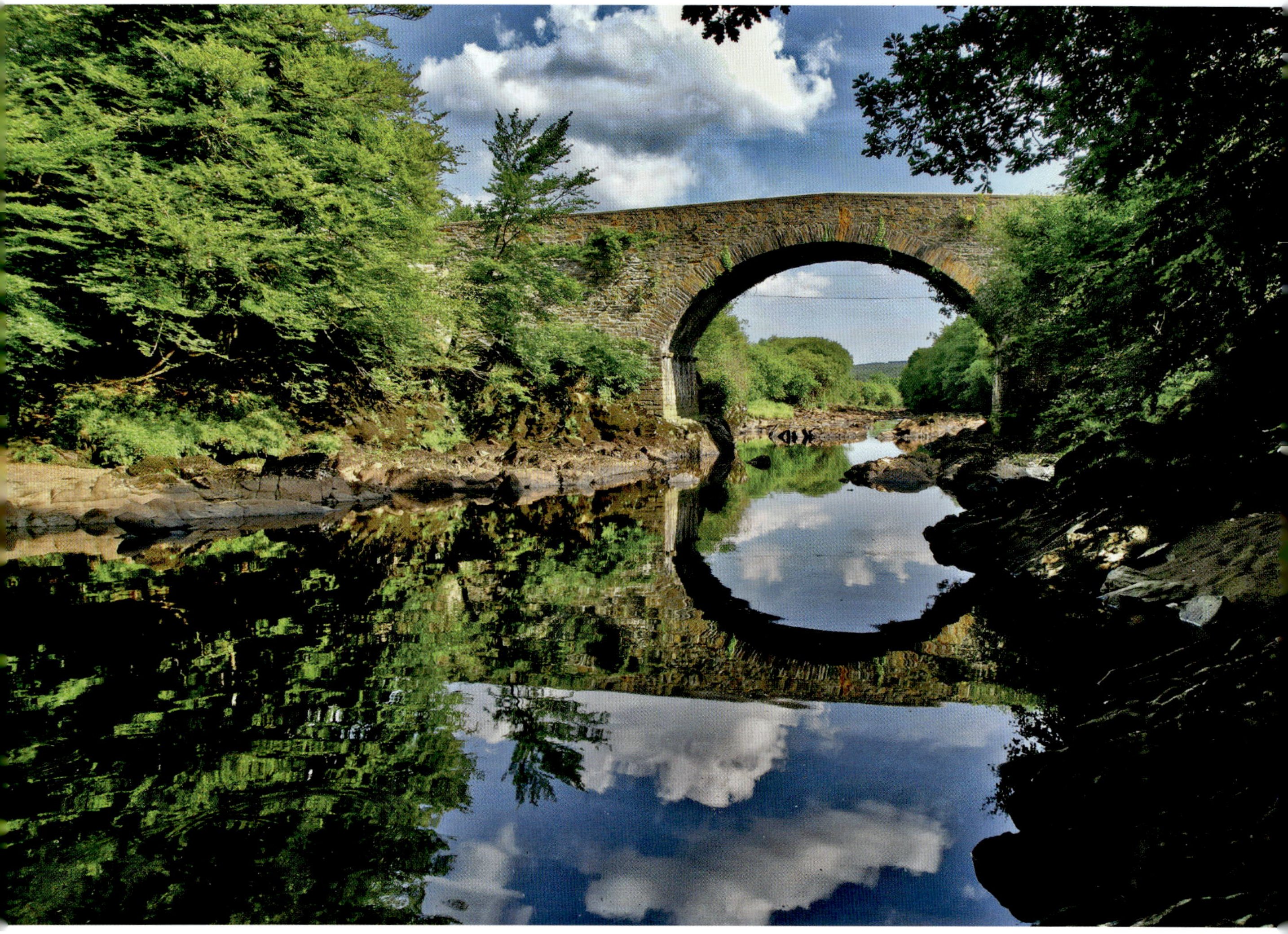

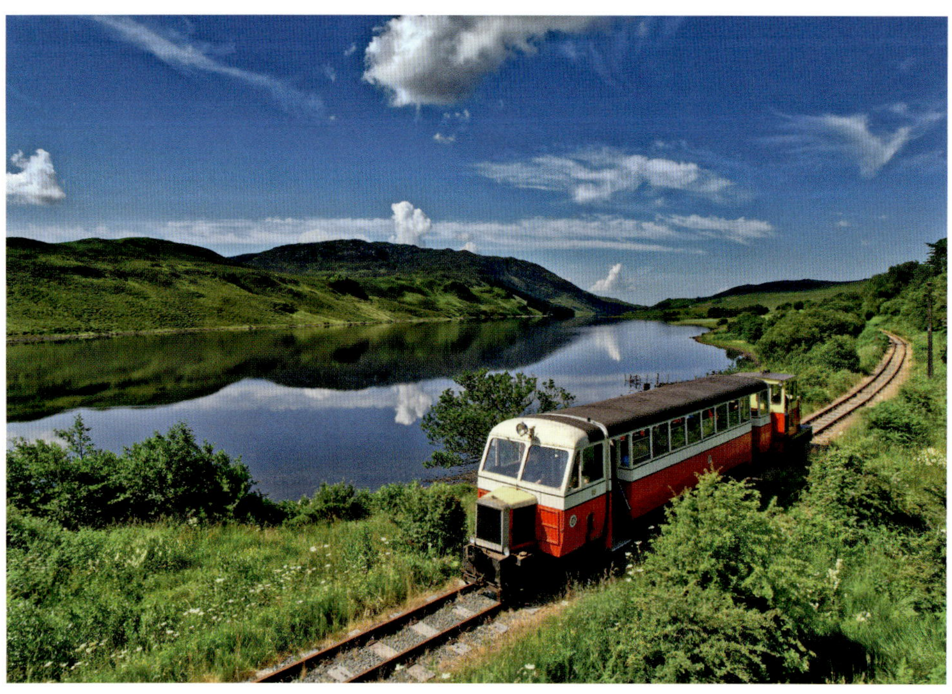

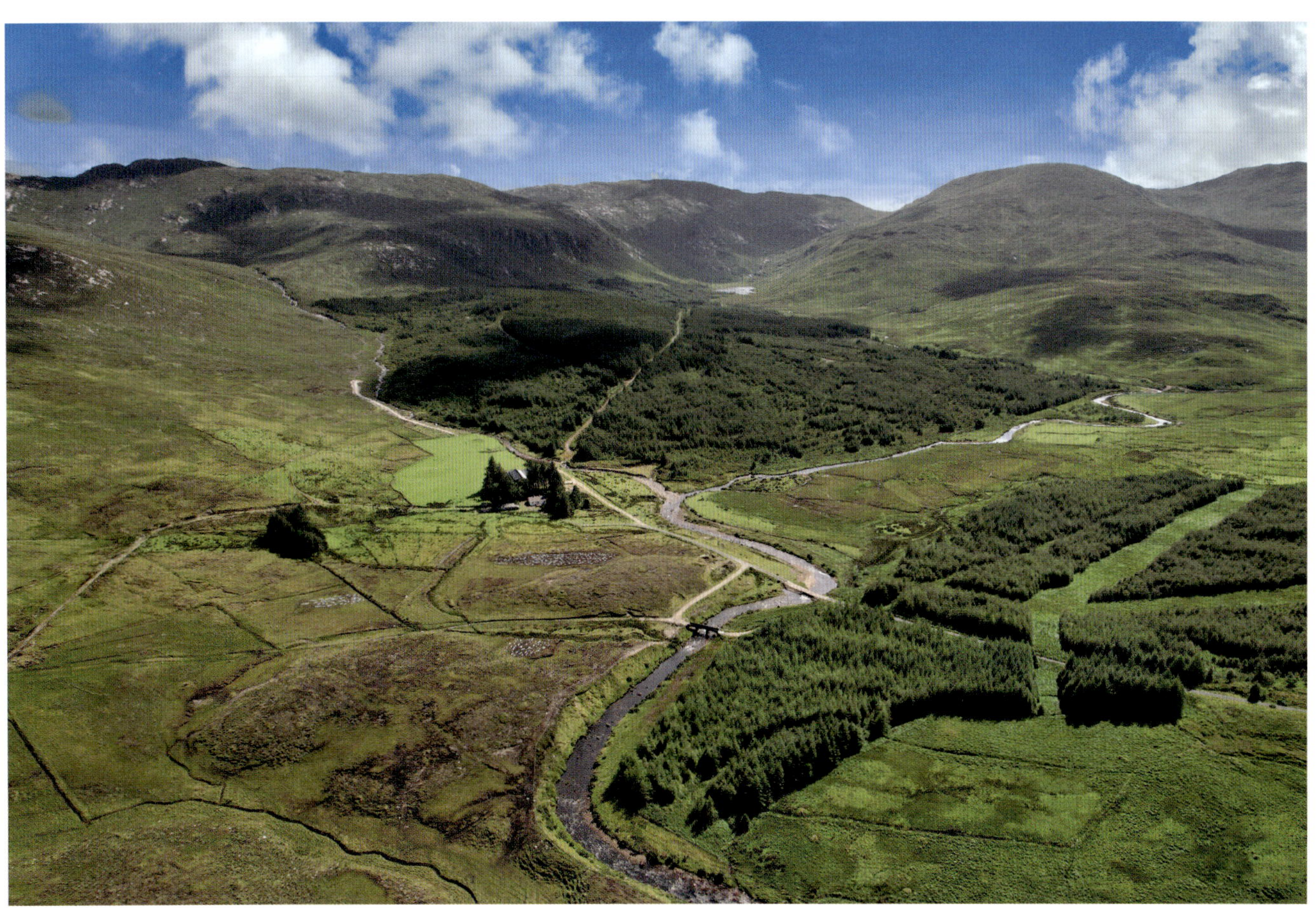

Croaghgorm Mountain, standing 674 metres (2,211 feet) tall, is the highest of the Bluestack Mountains, and the third highest in the county. On 31 January 1944, during the Second World War, a Royal Air Force Sunderland plane crashed on the mountain, killing seven RAF crewmen from 228 Squadron. Wreckage from the plane can still be seen on the mountain's slopes. A plaque was unveiled there in 1988 in their memory.

Opposite, top: Ivy Bridge at Cloghan towers above the waters of the River Finn, adding charm and character to its surroundings.

Opposite, bottom: Lough Finn, nestled below the mountains of Aghla and Screig, is approximately five kilometres long and almost a kilometre wide. The nearby village of Fintown, or Baile na Finne, is named after Finngeal, a figure from Irish mythology who, it is said, drowned in the lough trying to save her brother Feargamhain. Donegal's only operational narrow-gauge railway, an Mhuc Dhubh ('the Black Pig'), takes visitors along the northern shore of Lough Finn and back.

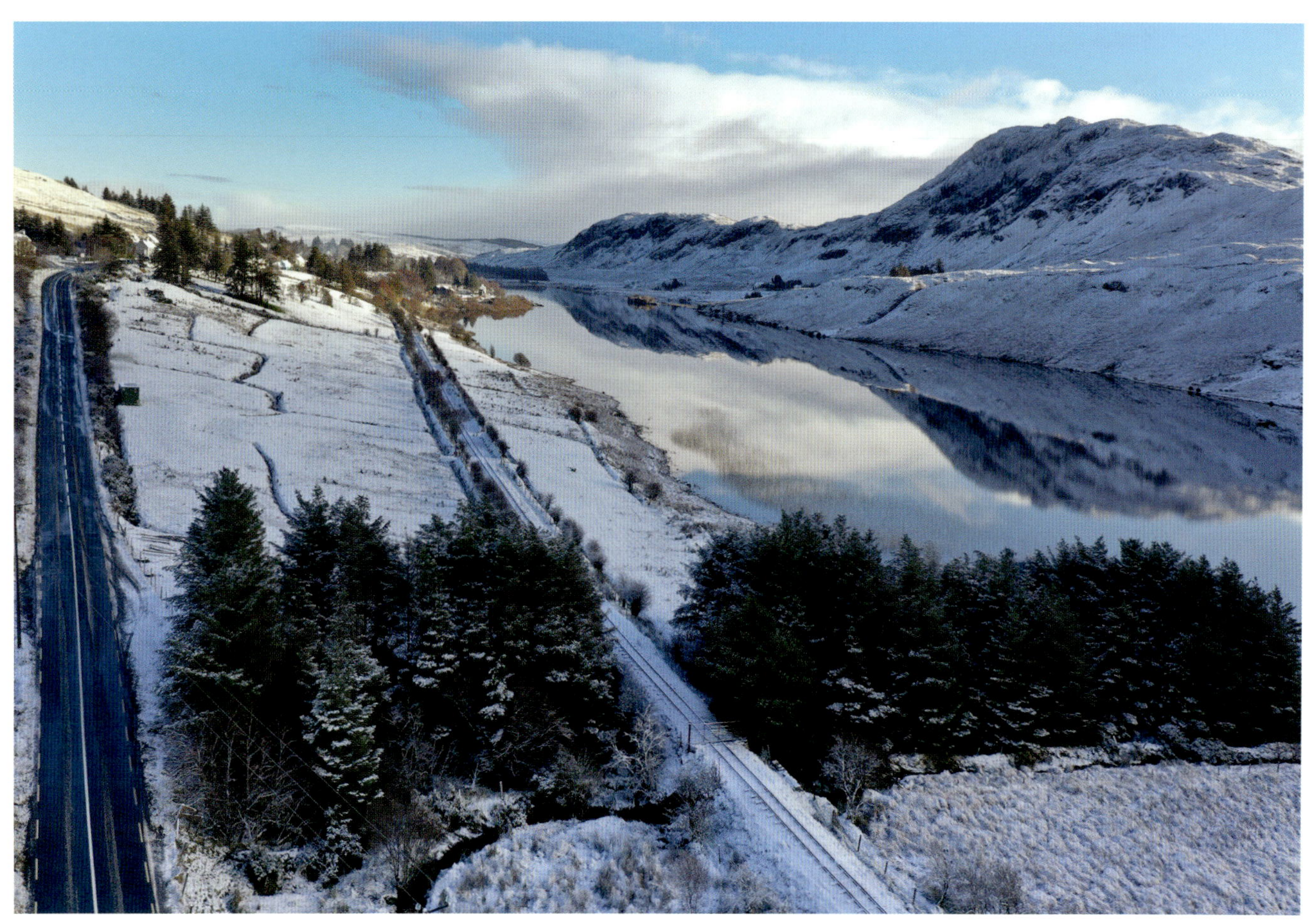

The lakeside setting of Lough Finn's narrow-gauge railway was described by the late playwright Brian Friel as being 'as scenic a stretch of railway as anything to be found in Switzerland or Minnesota'. Especially true with a blanket of snow!

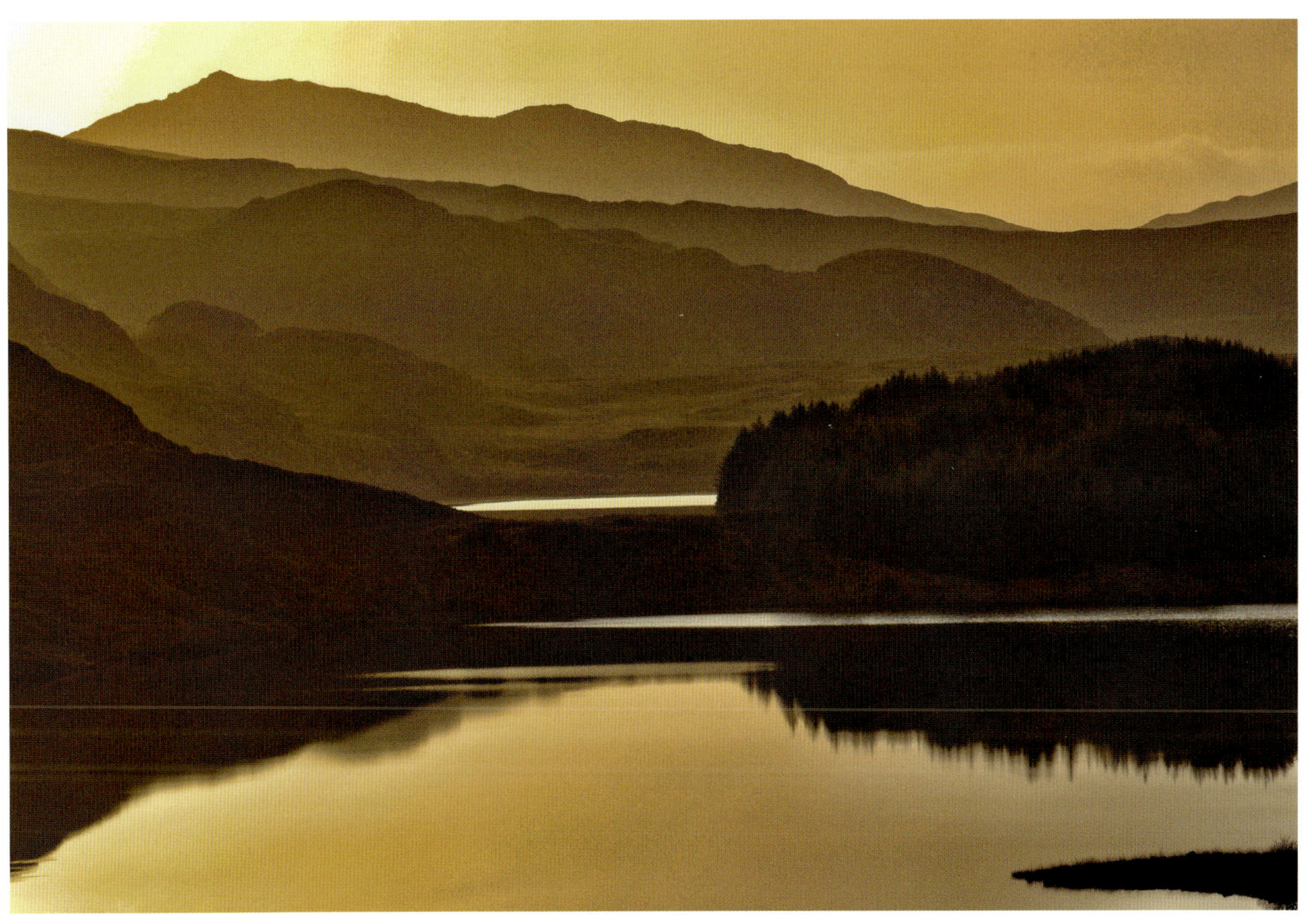

The evening sun casts a tranquil glow over Lough Ea. Located in the foothills of the Bluestack Mountains in the upper reaches of the glens of Glenties, it is the source of the Owenea River which eventually empties into the Atlantic at Ardara. Croveenananta (476 metres/1,562 feet) looms large in the background while the Sitka spruce of the lake's island are reflected in the water.

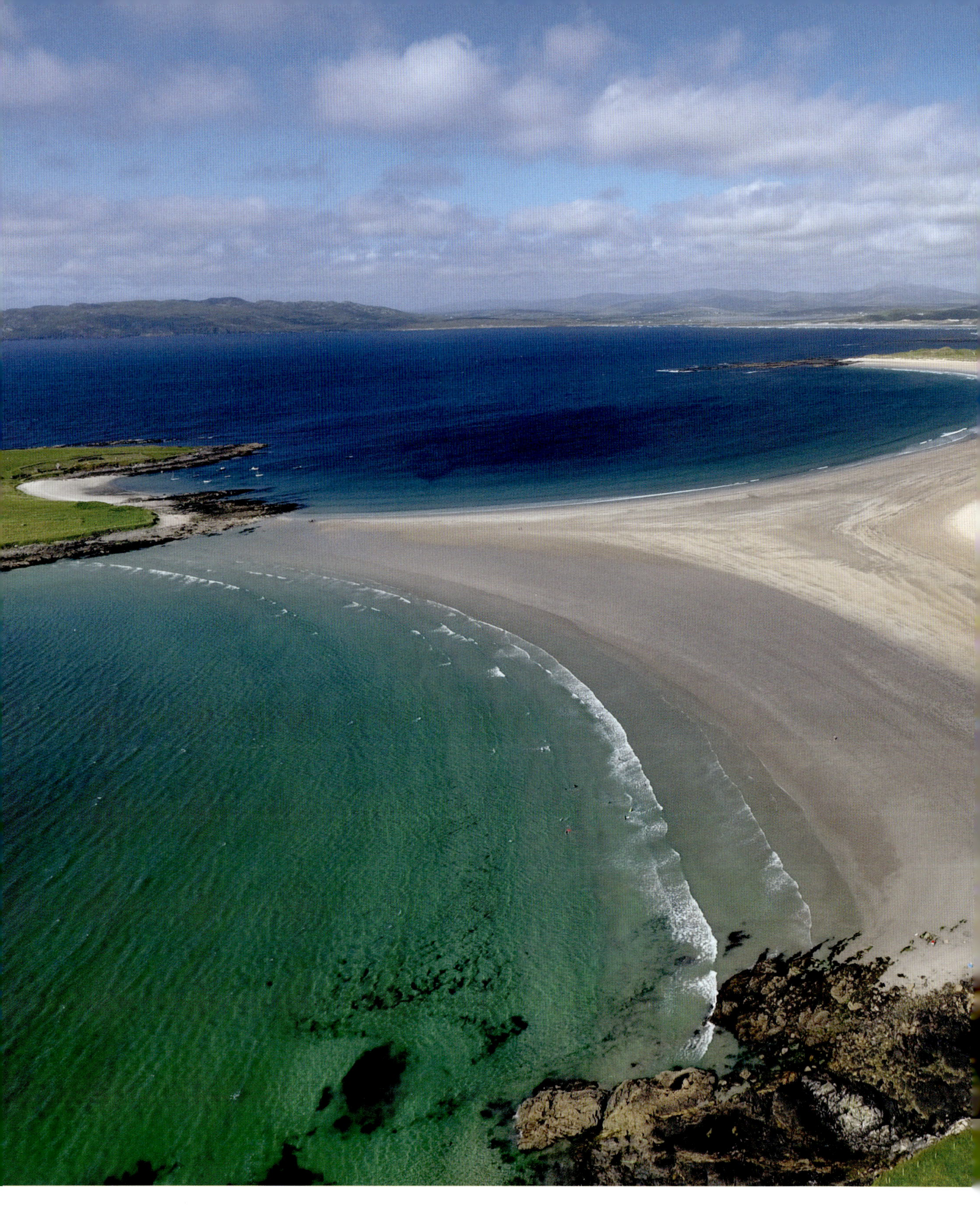

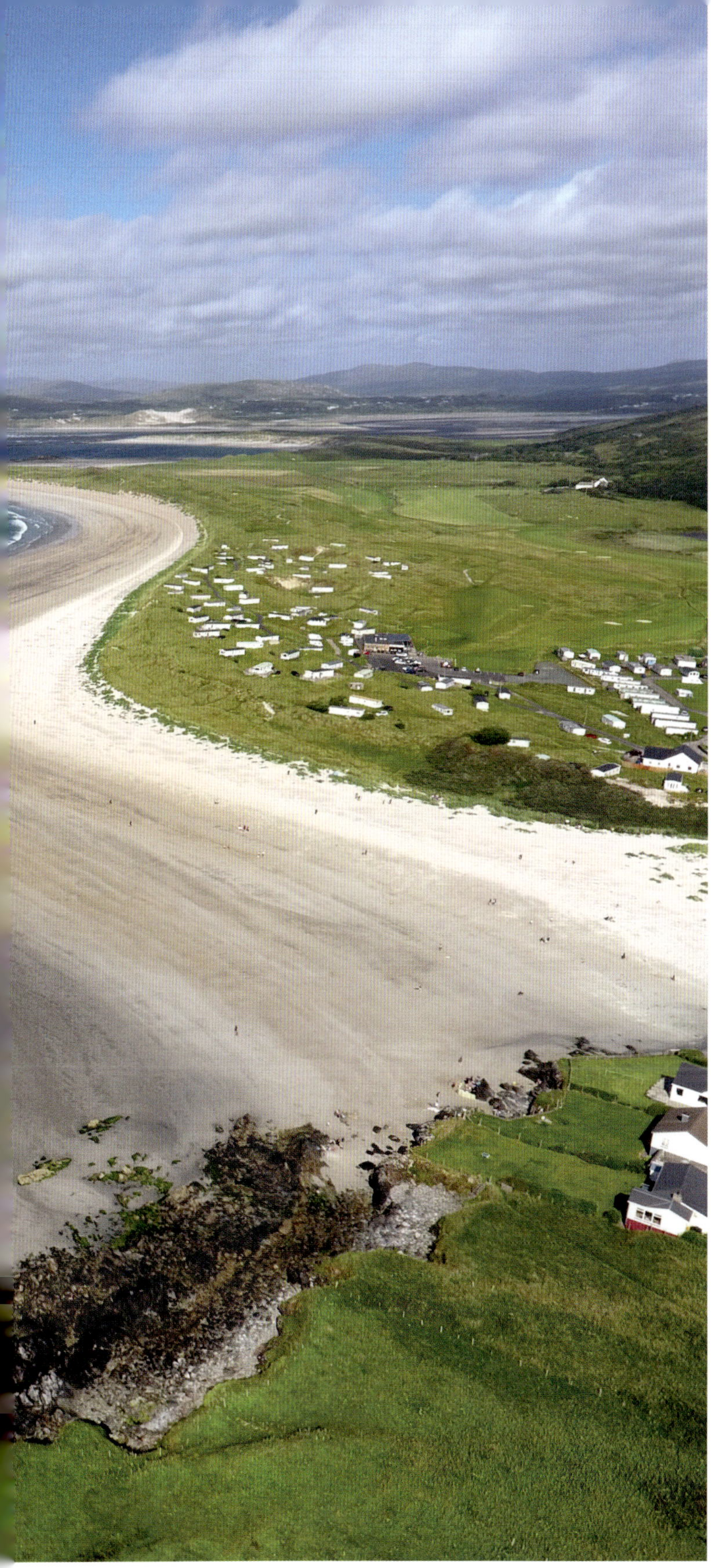

Left: Portnoo/Narin Strand is an expansive golden-white sandy beach backed by low dunes and is one of the most beautiful on the Atlantic coast. It is just a stone's throw from Ardara, Glenties and Dungloe. Inishkeel Island (middle left) can be reached by foot at low tide and is well worth a visit, with its early Christian church, holy wells and beautifully decorated stone slabs. A small community used to live on Inishkeel in the past, and in 1841 there were twenty-three inhabitants recorded, but it was later abandoned.

Below: A friendly goat and her adorable kid on a country lane.

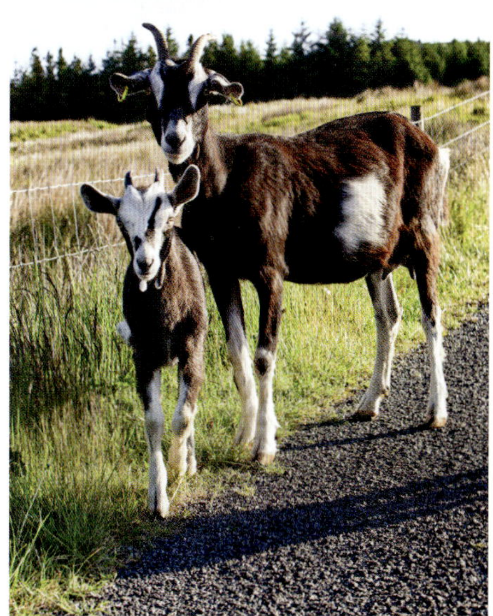

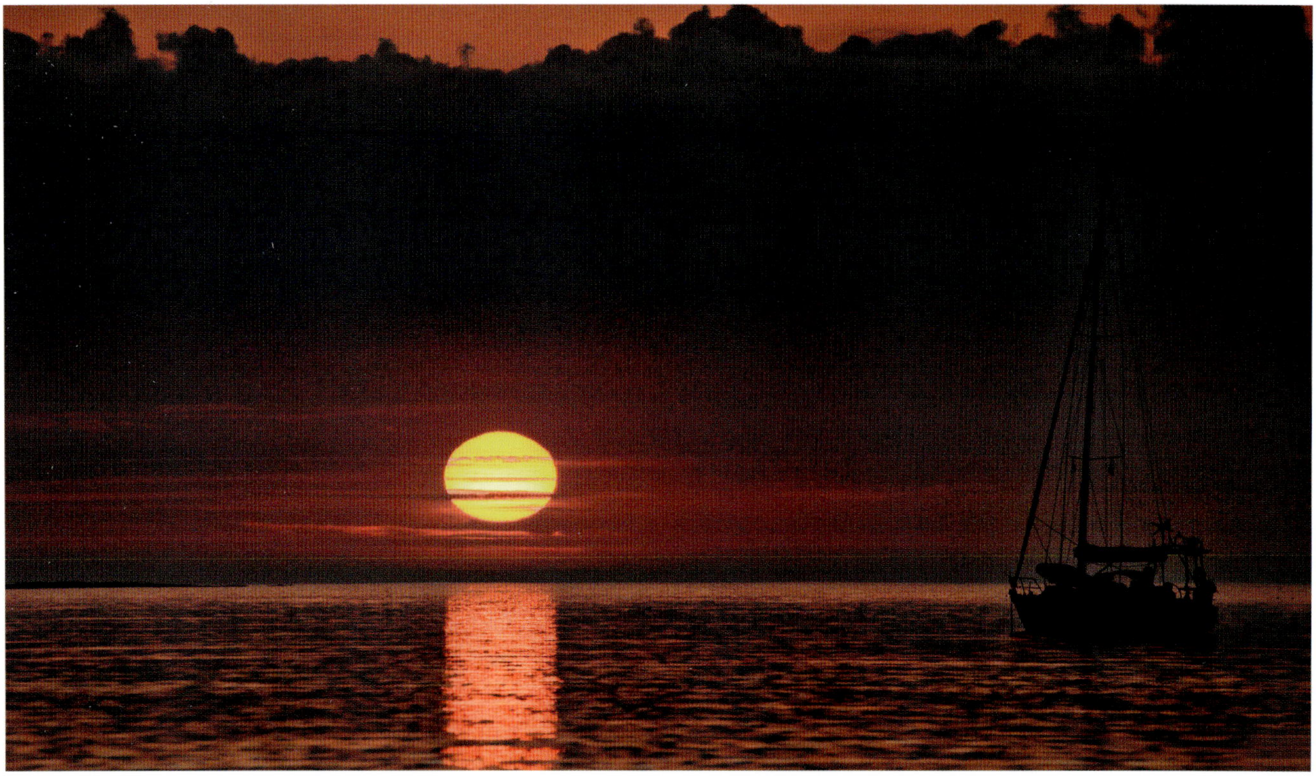

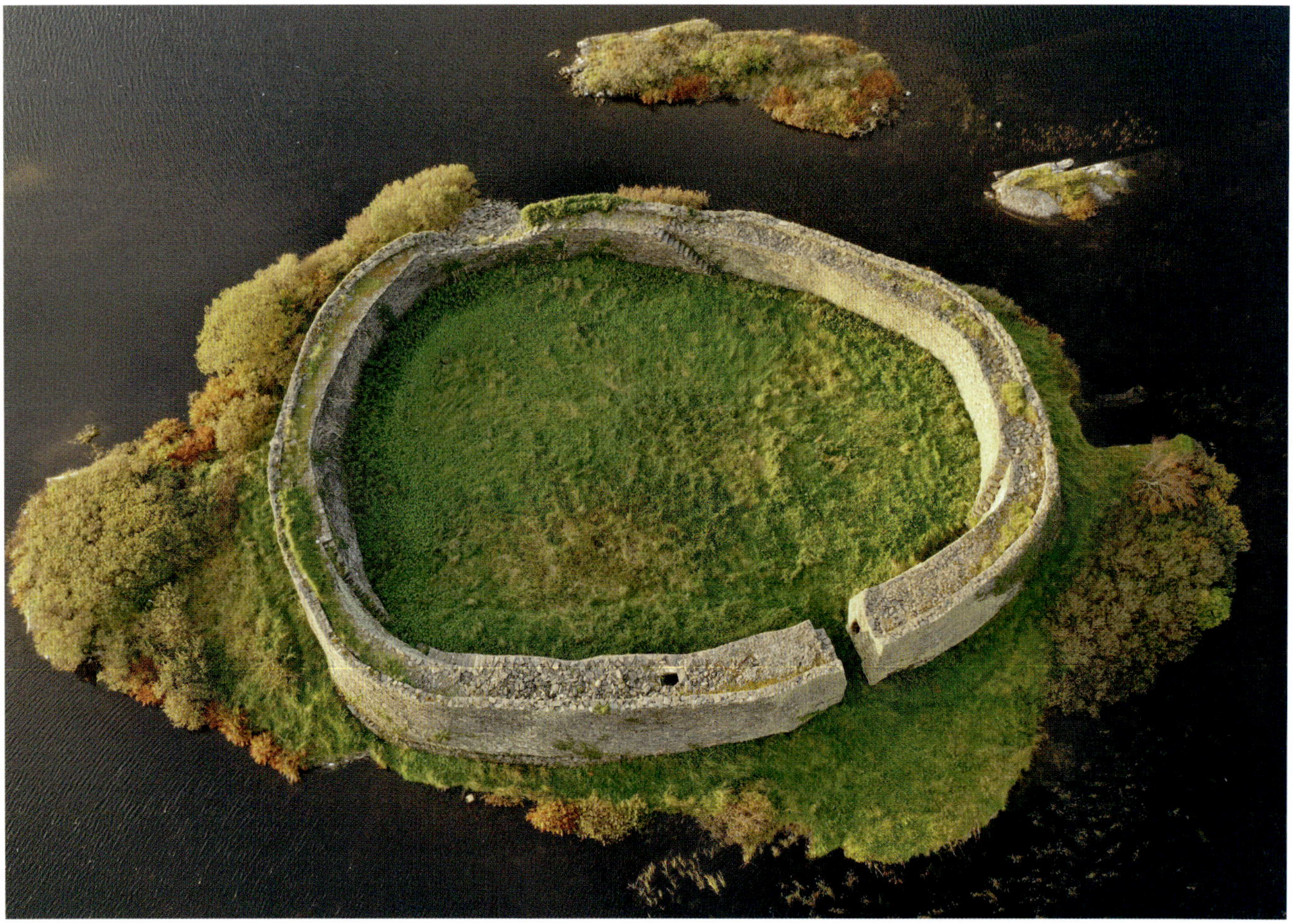

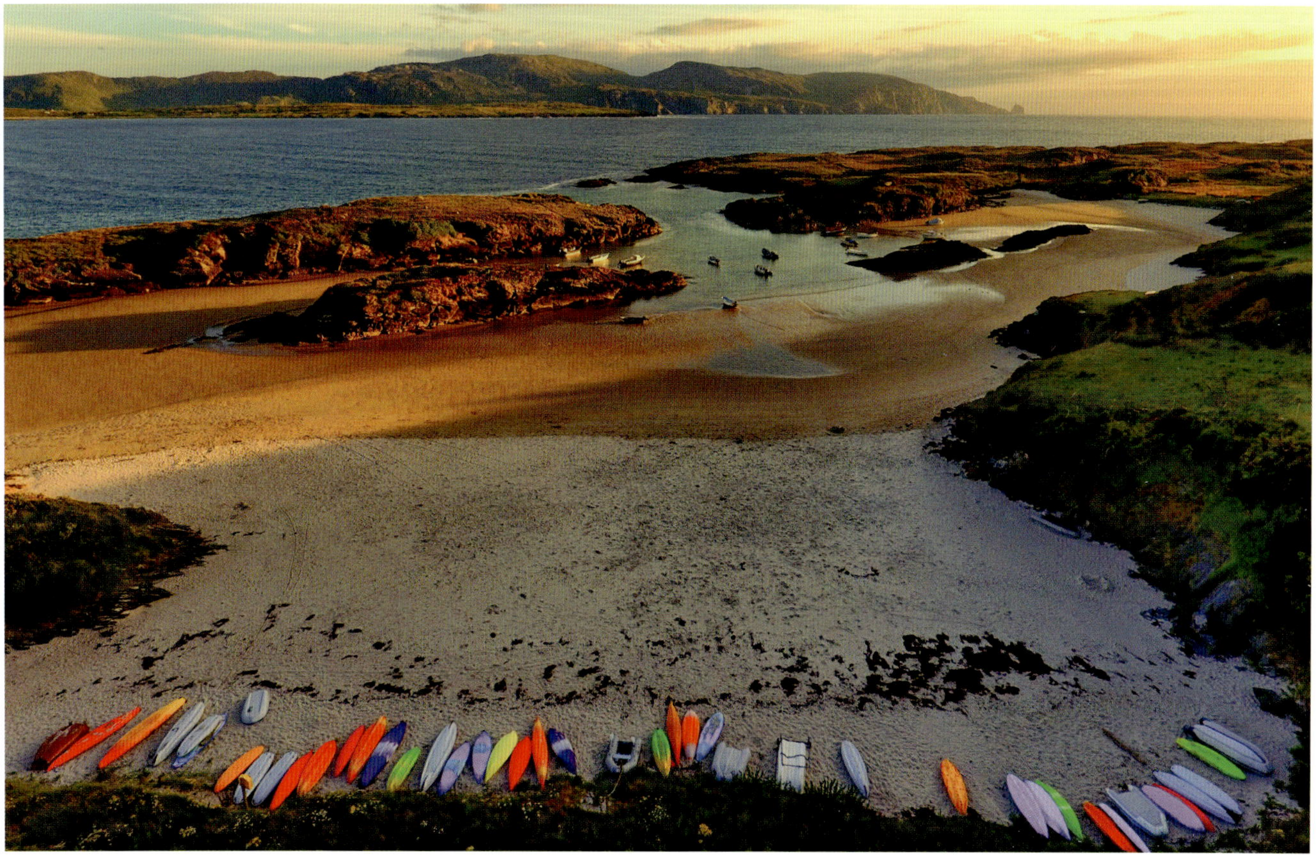

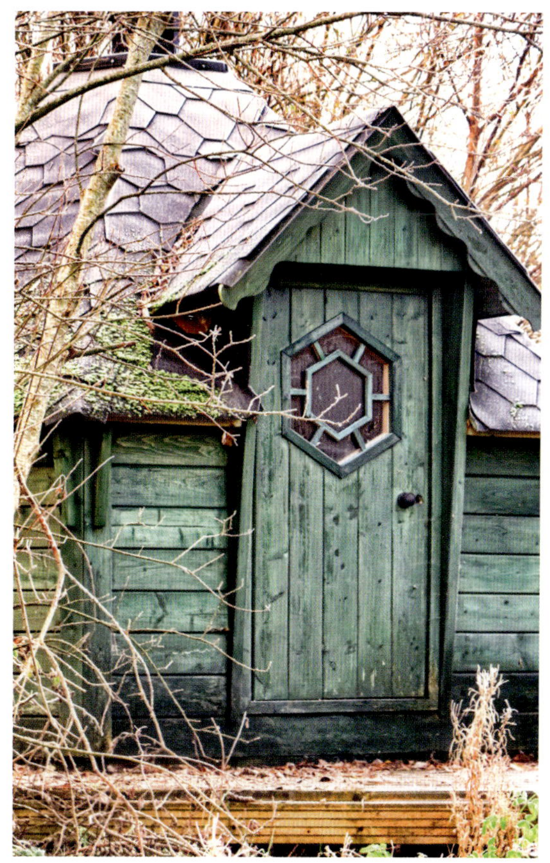

All the colours of the rainbow! A few miles west of Portnoo is the fishing and holiday hamlet of Rosbeg, situated on one of Donegal's most entrancing headlands. Life in Rosbeg is focused around the sea and the great outdoors, with swimming, surfing, sailing, kayaking and fishing all being popular.

Right: An old rustic hut sits in the heart of the woods, nestled among the trees.

Opposite, top: Sailing away, at Inishkeel island.

Opposite, bottom: Doon Fort is spectacularly sited on a small island in the middle of Loughadoon, just outside the picturesque village of Portnoo. This large drystone fort is similar to the Grianán of Aileach in Inishowen and is likely to date to the early medieval period.

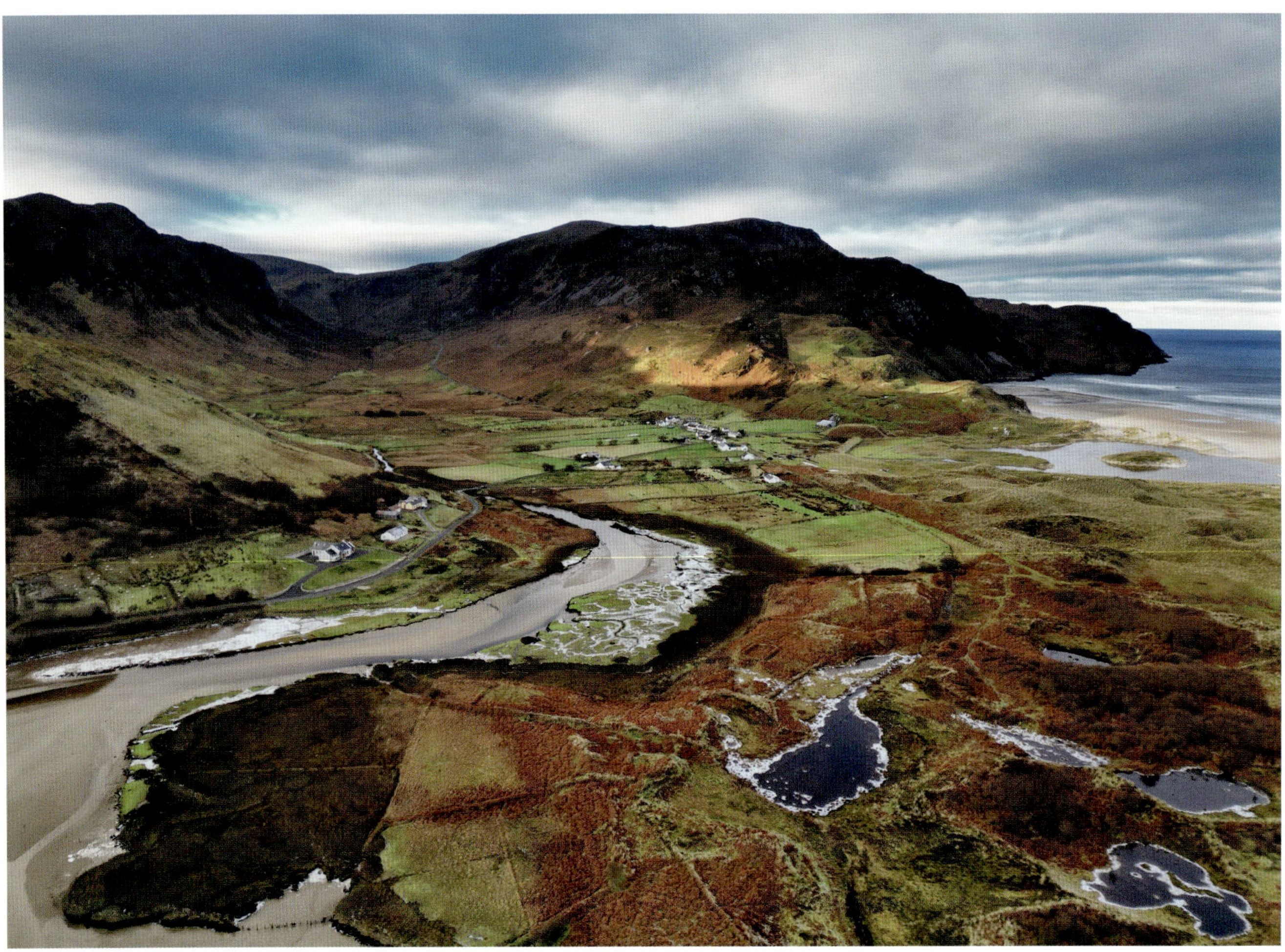

Near Ardara is Loughros Beg Bay, Maghera Beach and caves. The ice and glistening frost patterns are courtesy of Mother Nature. From the spectacular Granny Pass, a narrow, winding road etches its way through the Slievetooey Mountains, with the Glen River running alongside the road through the valley. Pockets of morning light enhance even more some of the most beautiful scenery in Donegal.

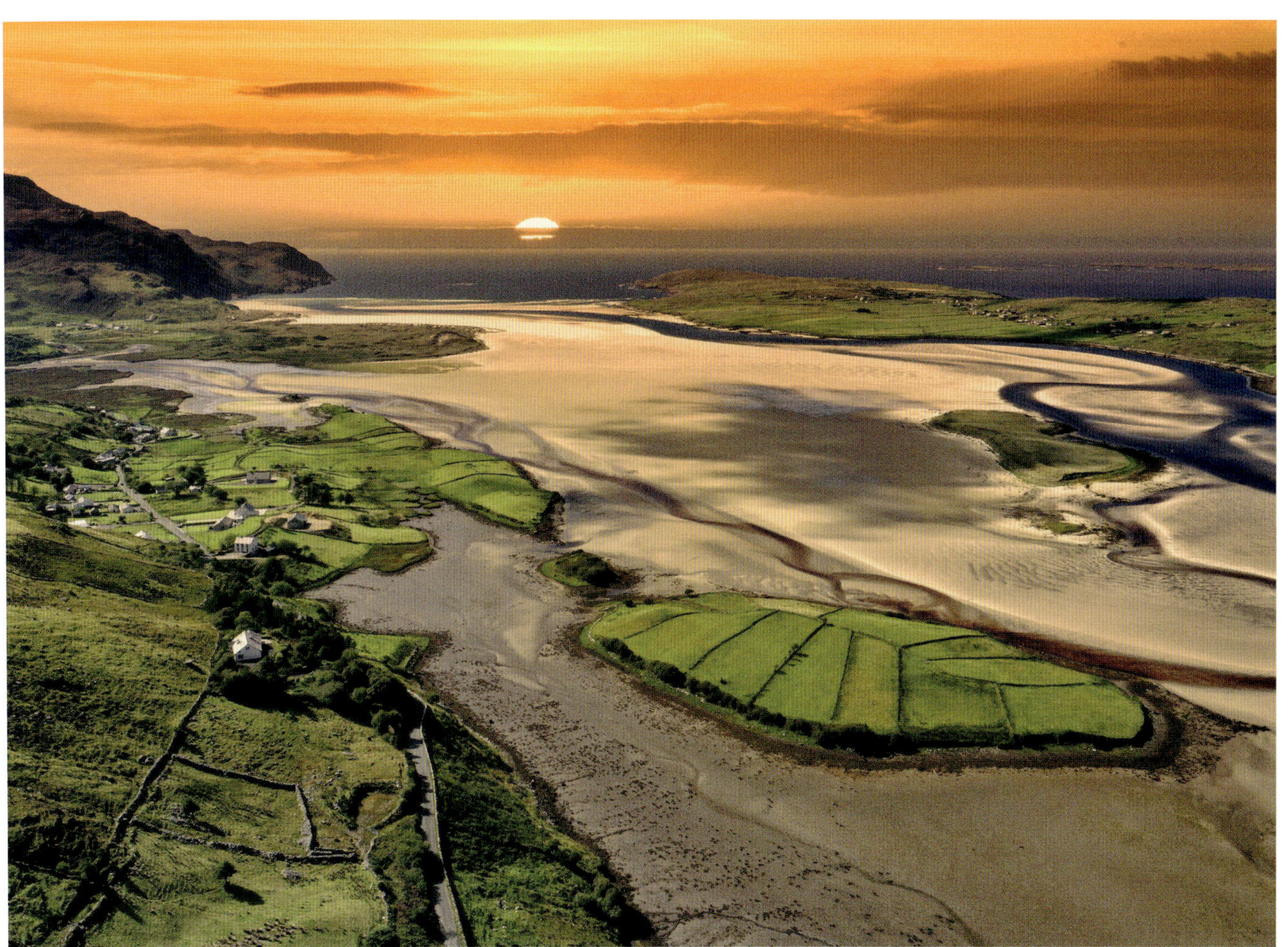

The island field of Illancreeve is situated near Assaranca Waterfall and Maghera Beach. It has an area of a little more than eight acres, comprising twelve small fields, which are usually manicured to perfection by grazing sheep for most of the year. After the sheep are moved, the fields are sown out and become a hive of activity once a year as local farmers gather to save the harvest.

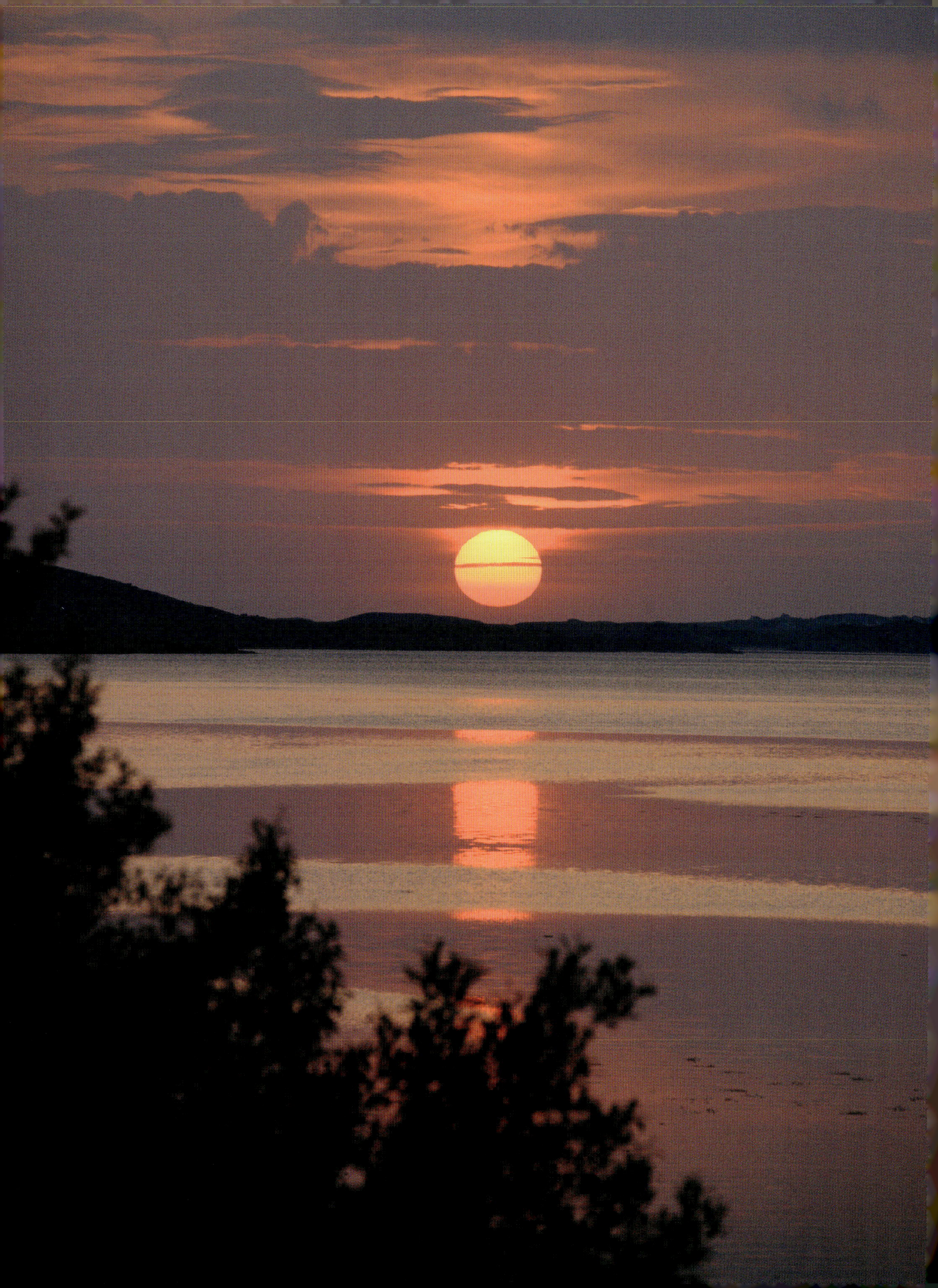

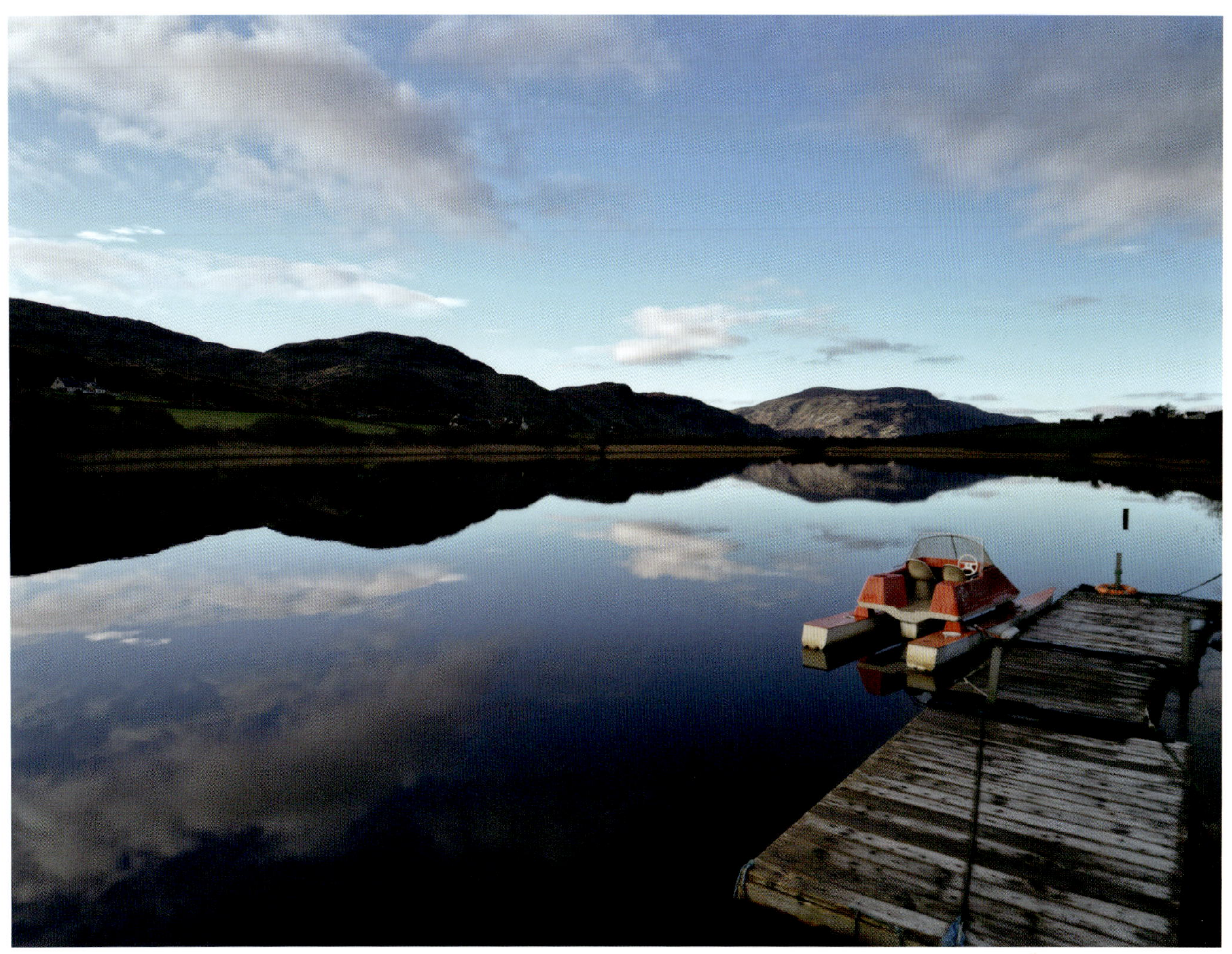

The still, uninterrupted beauty of Shanaghan Lake reflects the landscape that surrounds it. Located outside Ardara, it is home to the successful Loughros Point Rowing Club.

Opposite: At Loughros Beg Bay. The soft yet vibrant colours of sunset are particularly beautiful when reflected on water.

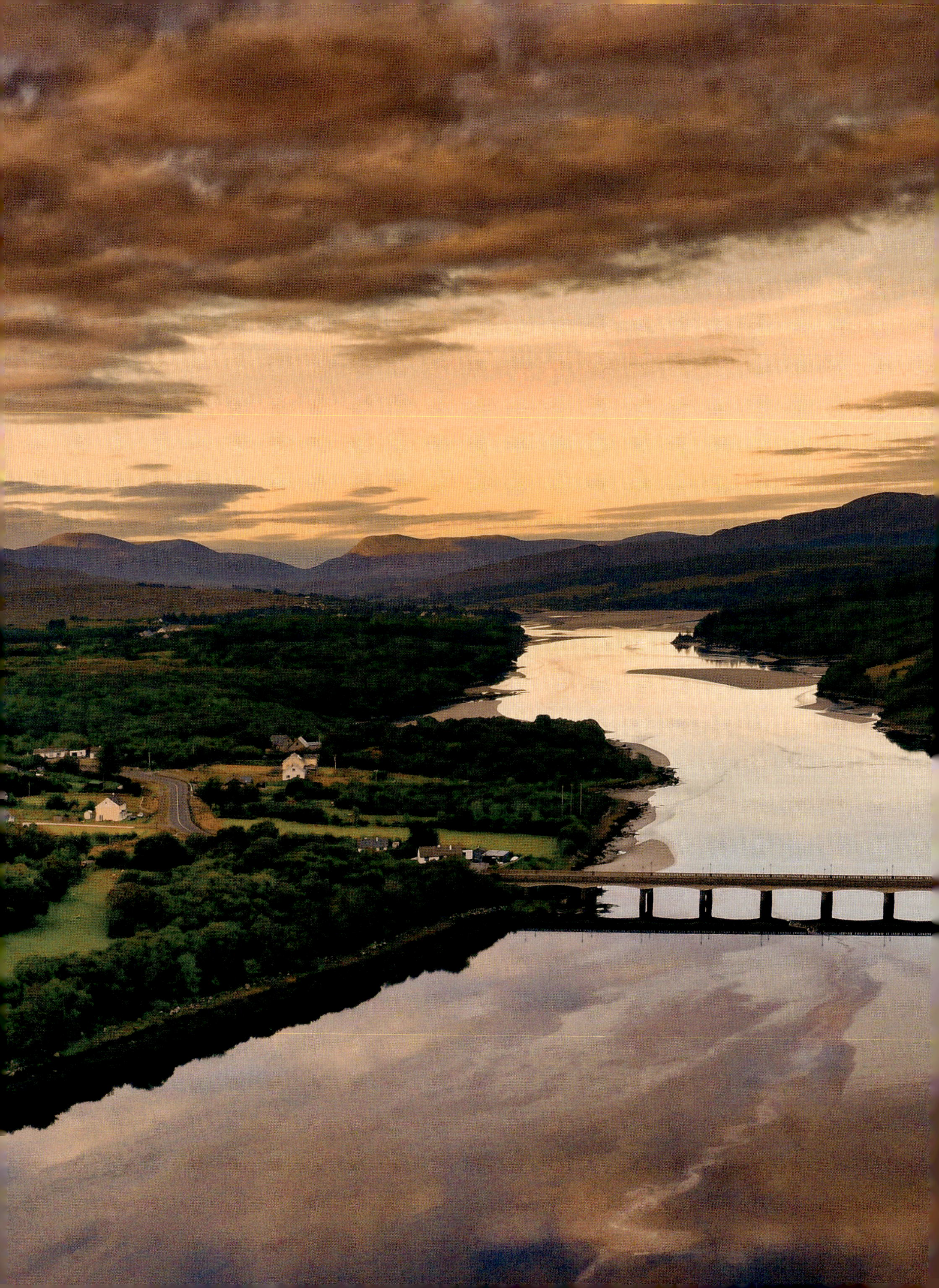

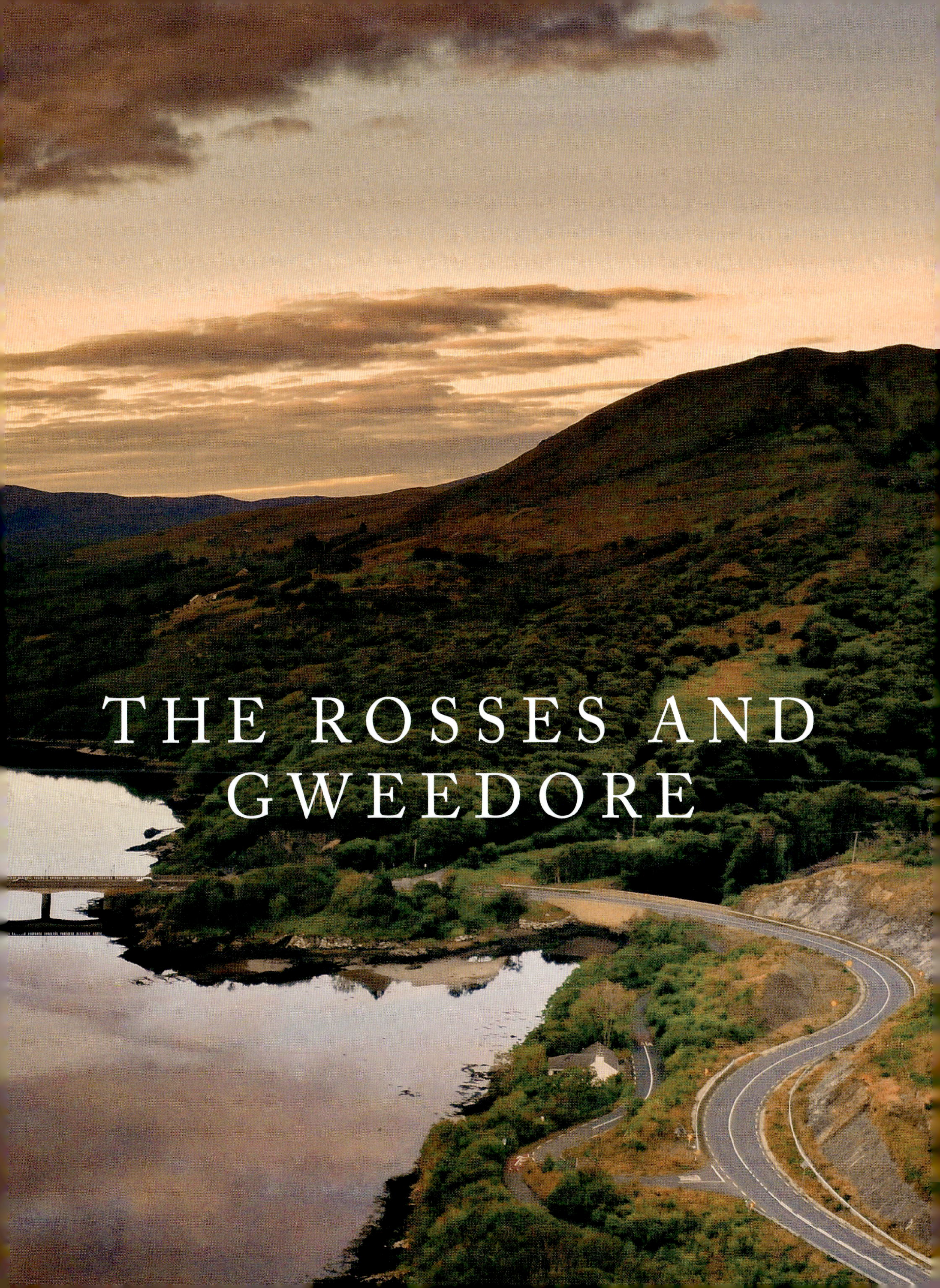
THE ROSSES AND
GWEEDORE

The Rosses and Gweedore are at the heart of Gaelic-speaking Donegal. Drive from Churchill to Doochary with the Derryveagh Mountains on one side and Glendowan Mountains on the other to experience one of the most remote and hauntingly beautiful areas in the country, with mountains, deep glens, rivers, lakes and waterfalls. Glenveagh National Park, the second-largest national park in Ireland, lies in the heart of the wild and rugged landscape of the Derryveagh Mountains, of which Errigal is the highest peak.

Previous pages: The Gweebarra Bridge, built in 1953, carries the N56 road over the Gweebarra River, near Lettermacaward.

Opposite, top: 'Leave nothing your but footprints.' Dooey's Green Coast award-winning beach is sandwiched between Gweebarra Bay and Trawenagh Bay, close to Lettermacaward. Drive with caution and respect on the narrow, winding roads leading to this beach.

Opposite, bottom: Tír na Draíochta ('the Land of Magic') in Dungloe is a children's art and story trail, opened in 2022. The story walk features a series of original artworks that were created to enchant children, based around the tale of a Norwegian troll who got lost in bad weather and wound up in Dungloe where he has been befriended by the local fairies.

Right: One of the fairy houses at Tír na Draíochta.

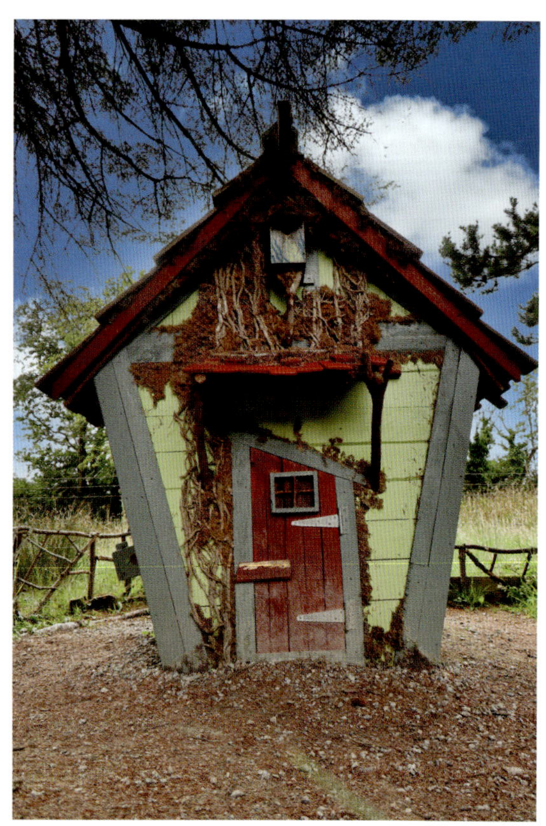

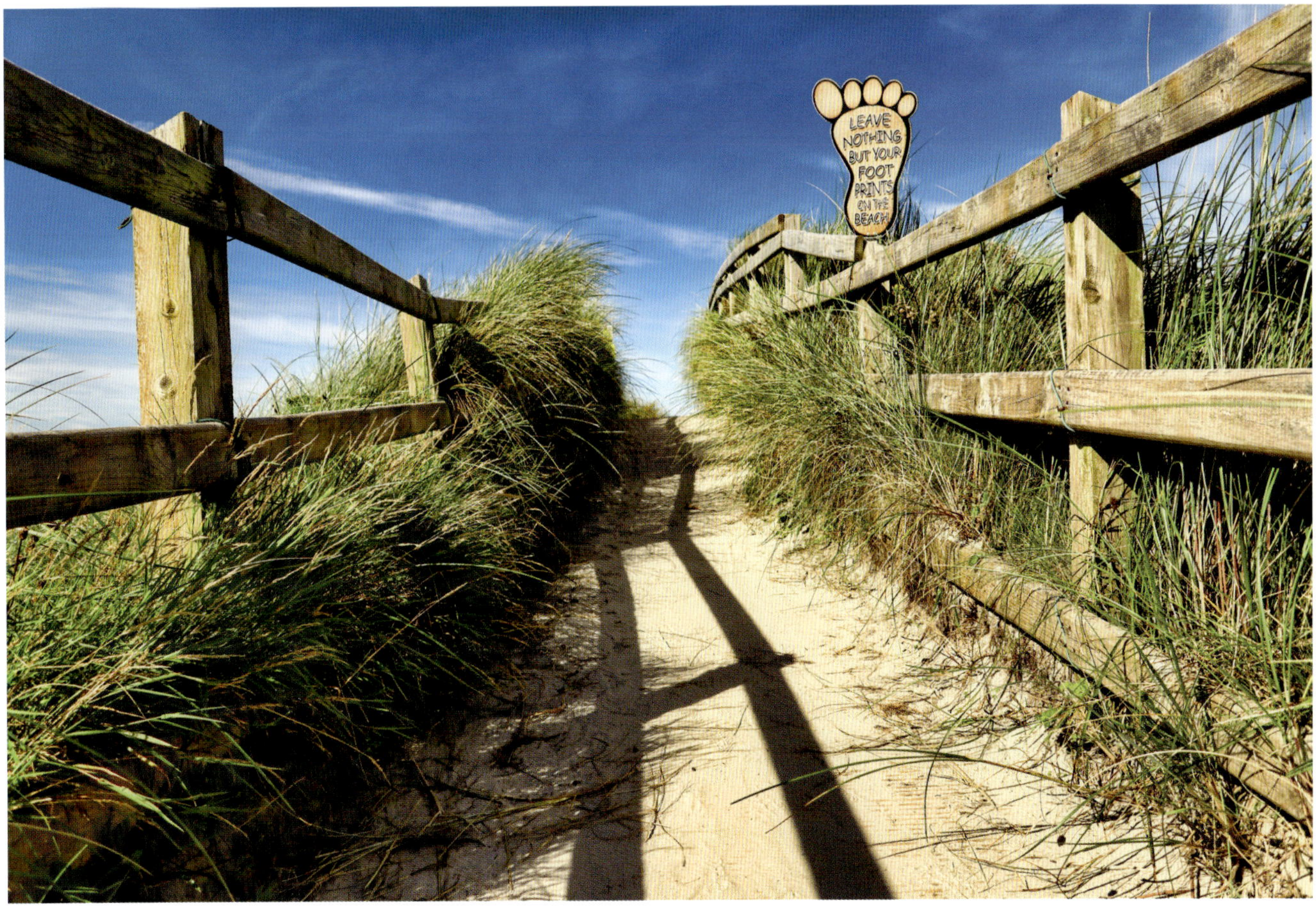

LEAVE
NOTHING
BUT YOUR
FOOT
PRINTS
ON THE
BEACH

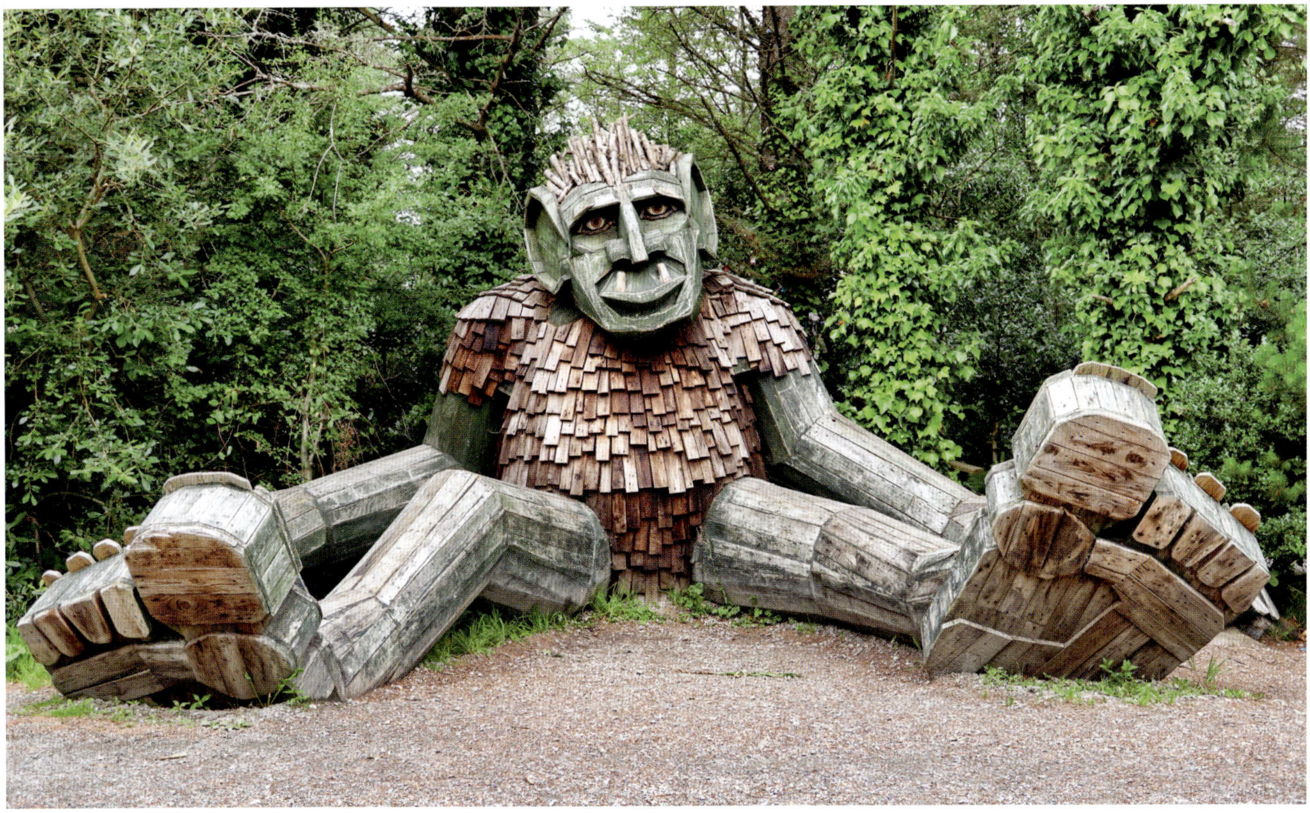

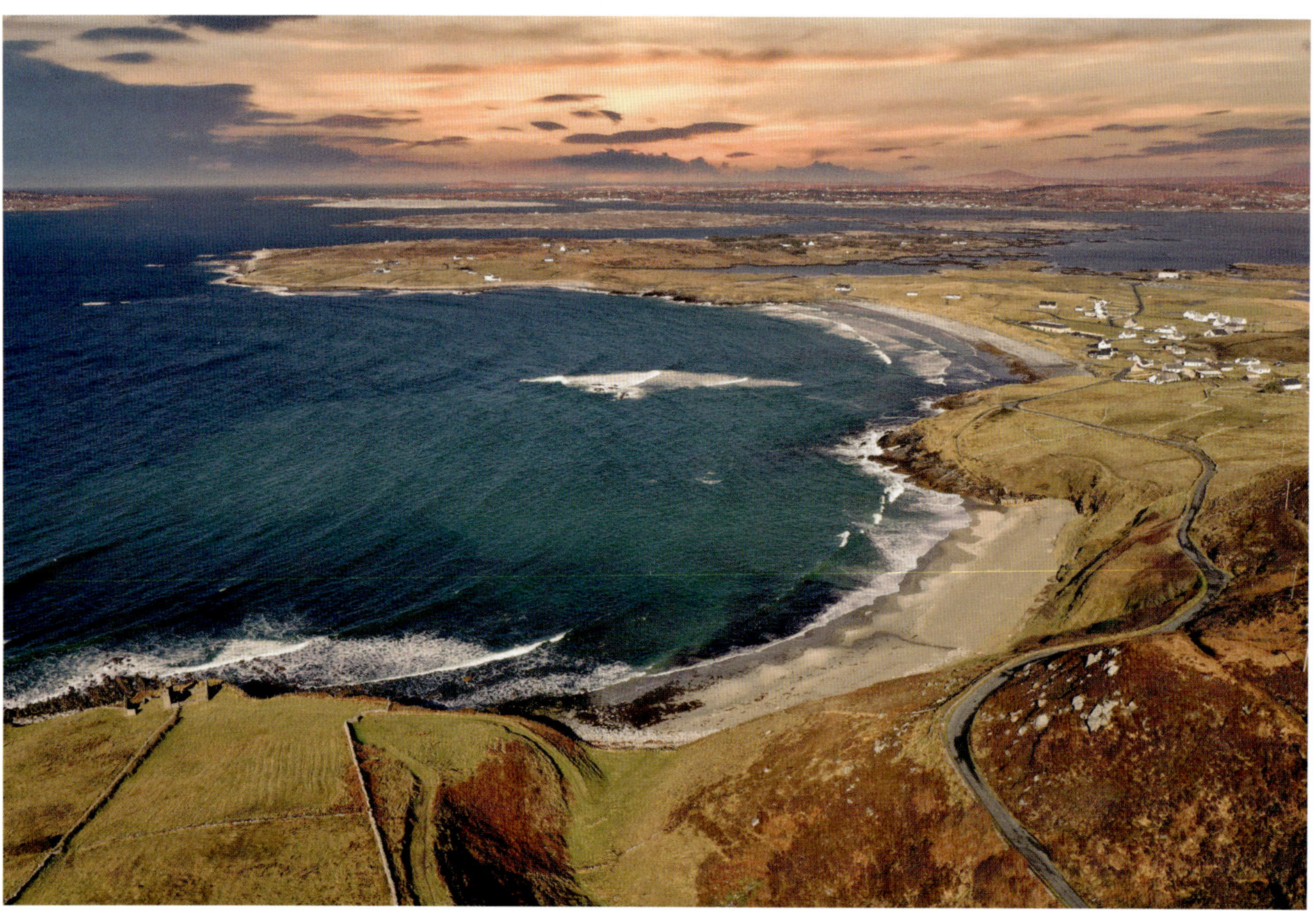

The village of Maghery is perched on the west coast of the Rosses, surrounded by beaches, islands, lakes, hills, caves and sea arches. It is rich in historical heritage, with monuments dating back five millennia, and its variety of habitats supports abundant wildlife. It is also the starting point of a spectacular drive which winds out to the headland, making it a little-known jewel on the Donegal coast.

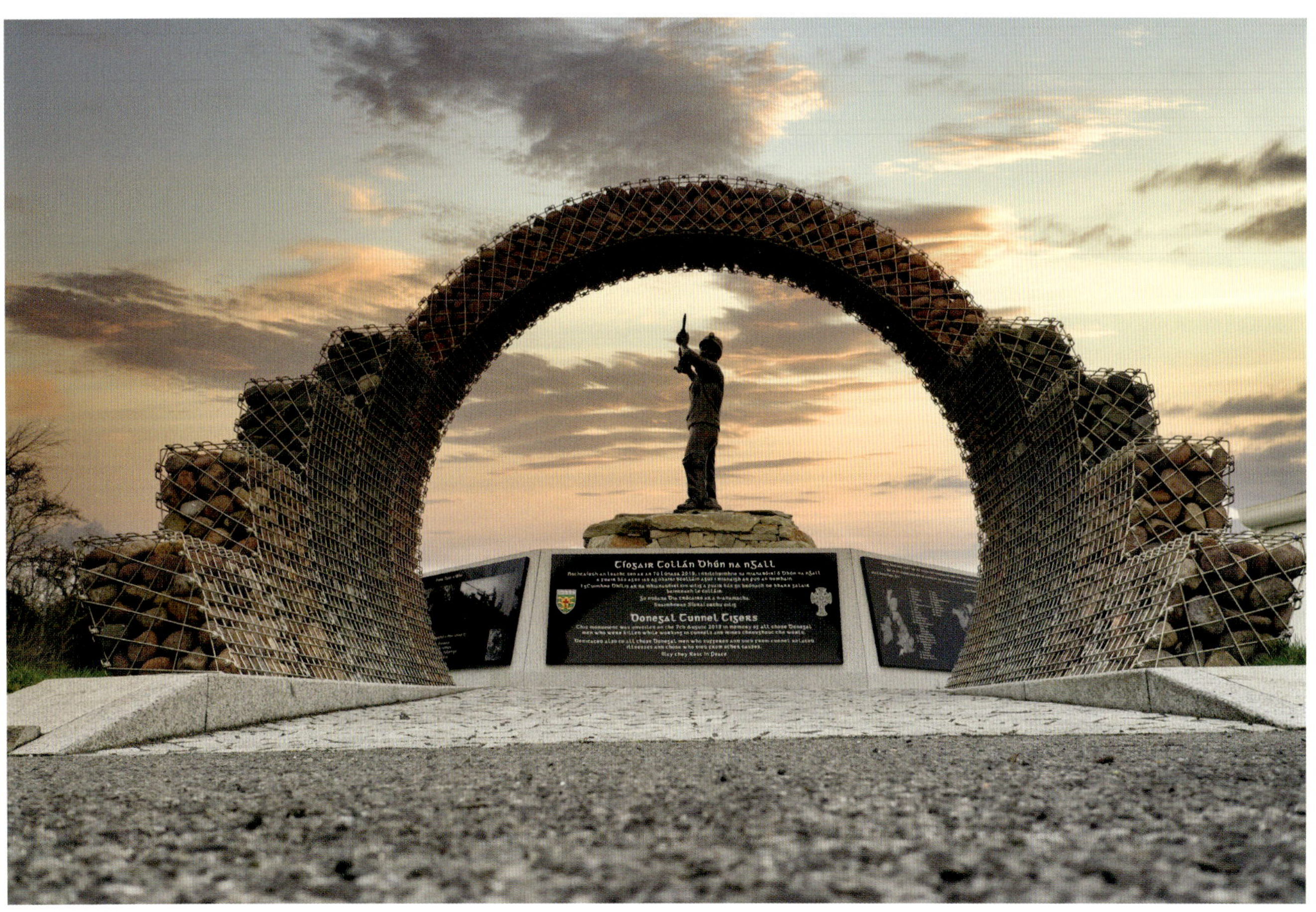

This impressive memorial, situated in the grounds of St Crona's Church, Dungloe, is in honour of the legendary Donegal Tunnel Tigers who died overseas. The Tunnel Tigers were workers on projects such as the Channel Tunnel, the London Underground and the Clyde Tunnel. The monument includes the names of seventy-seven people from the area who died while working on these projects and is also dedicated to the many who suffered life-changing illnesses or injuries because of unsafe working conditions. An archway entrance leads to a hand-carved granite statue of a Tunnel Tiger.

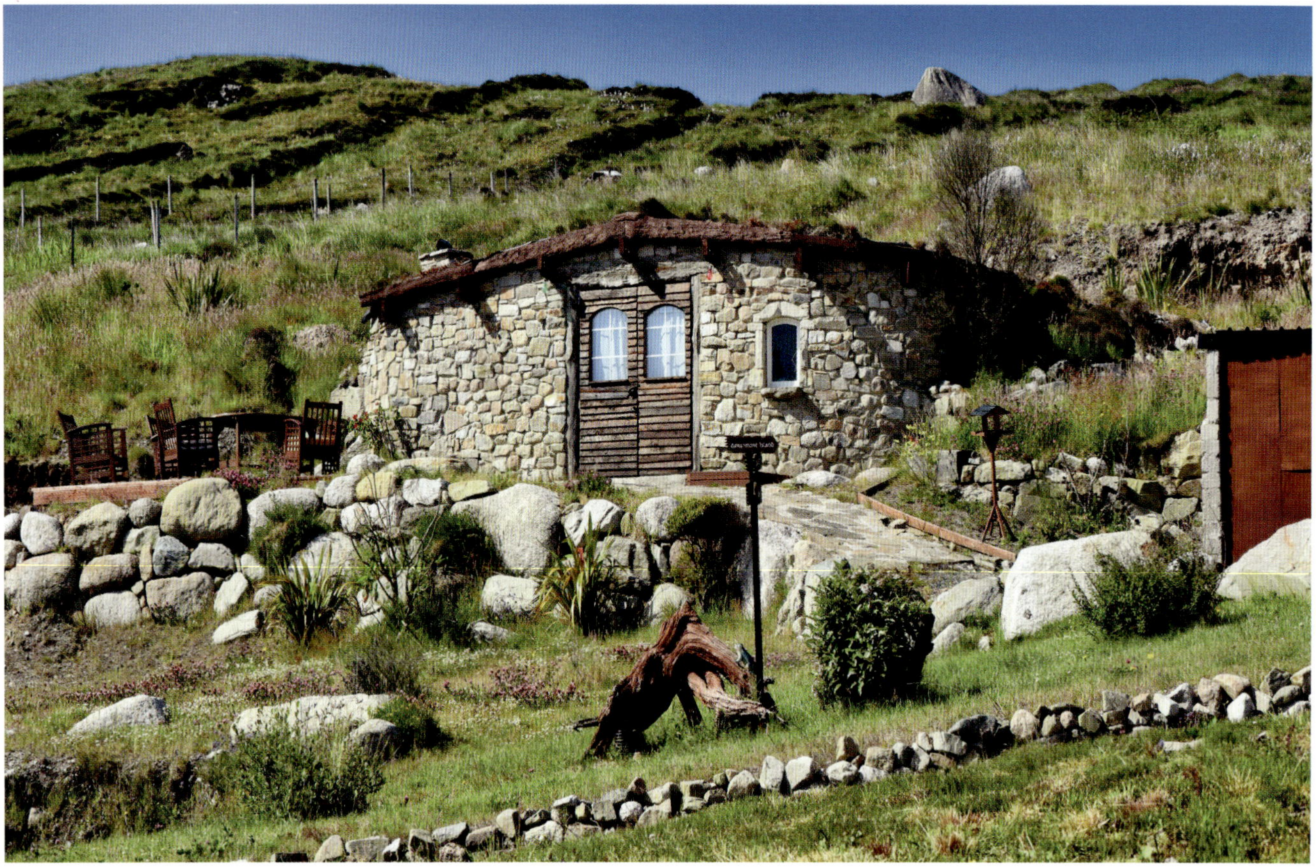

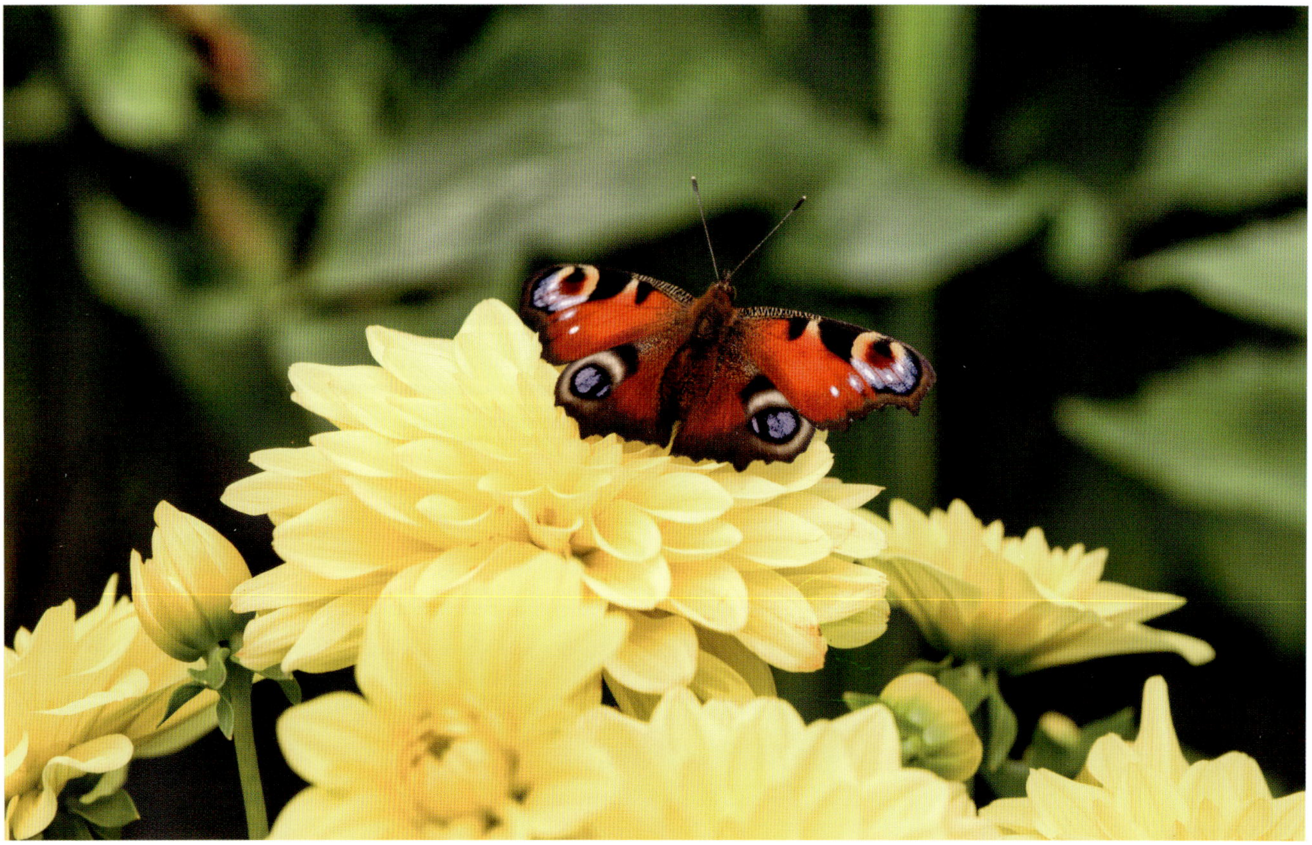

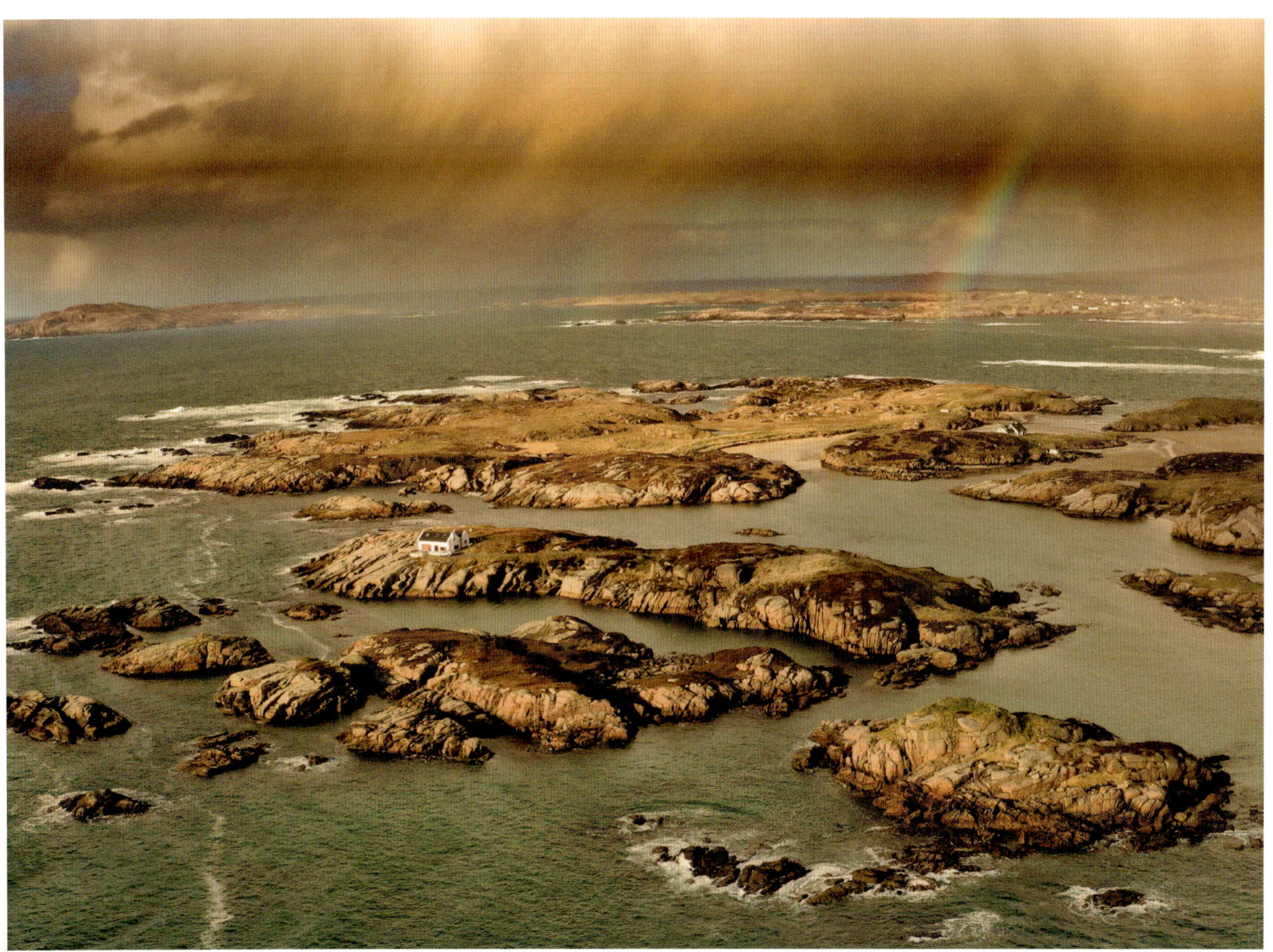

Fall Island (Oileán an Easa), northwest of Burtonport, is a mere 200 metres (656 feet) long, with one solitary house built on the granite bedrock. Access is possible at low tide when the ocean floor reappears between the island and the mainland. Timing is everything in order to stay safe!

Opposite, top: A unique little house on Arranmore, complete with a bog oak sculpture in the garden.

Opposite, bottom: A peacock butterfly sipping nectar from the blossoms.

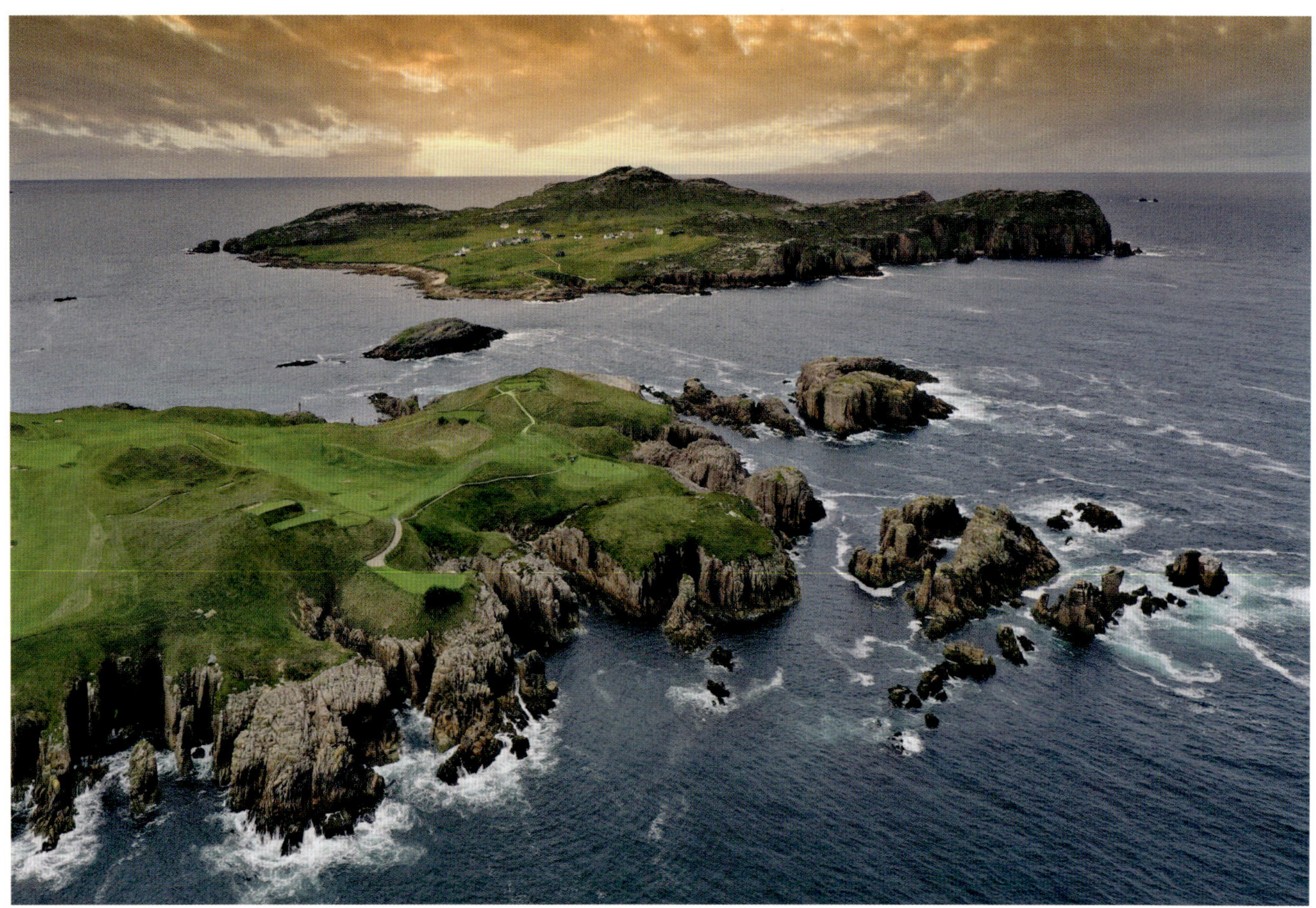

There's a magical nine-hole golf course on the northern clifftop of Cruit Island. The signature sixth hole (pictured) is one of the best, most beautiful and most terrifying par threes in the world. Owey Island (top of picture) lies just a short distance off Cruit. The name Owey – 'uaigh' in Irish – means grave, but a more popular interpretation is 'cave'. It is the spectacular setting of Owey that gives it its character. The power of the Atlantic is unrelenting in this isolated far northwest corner of Donegal. There is a remarkable collection of intact traditional thatched houses that seem frozen in time, and are mostly still owned by the original families. The walls are made from pink granite, quarried locally.

The gentle curve of Mullaghderg Beach near Kincasslagh is popular with walkers. Enticing as it looks, however, swimming is not allowed, owing to dangerous currents.

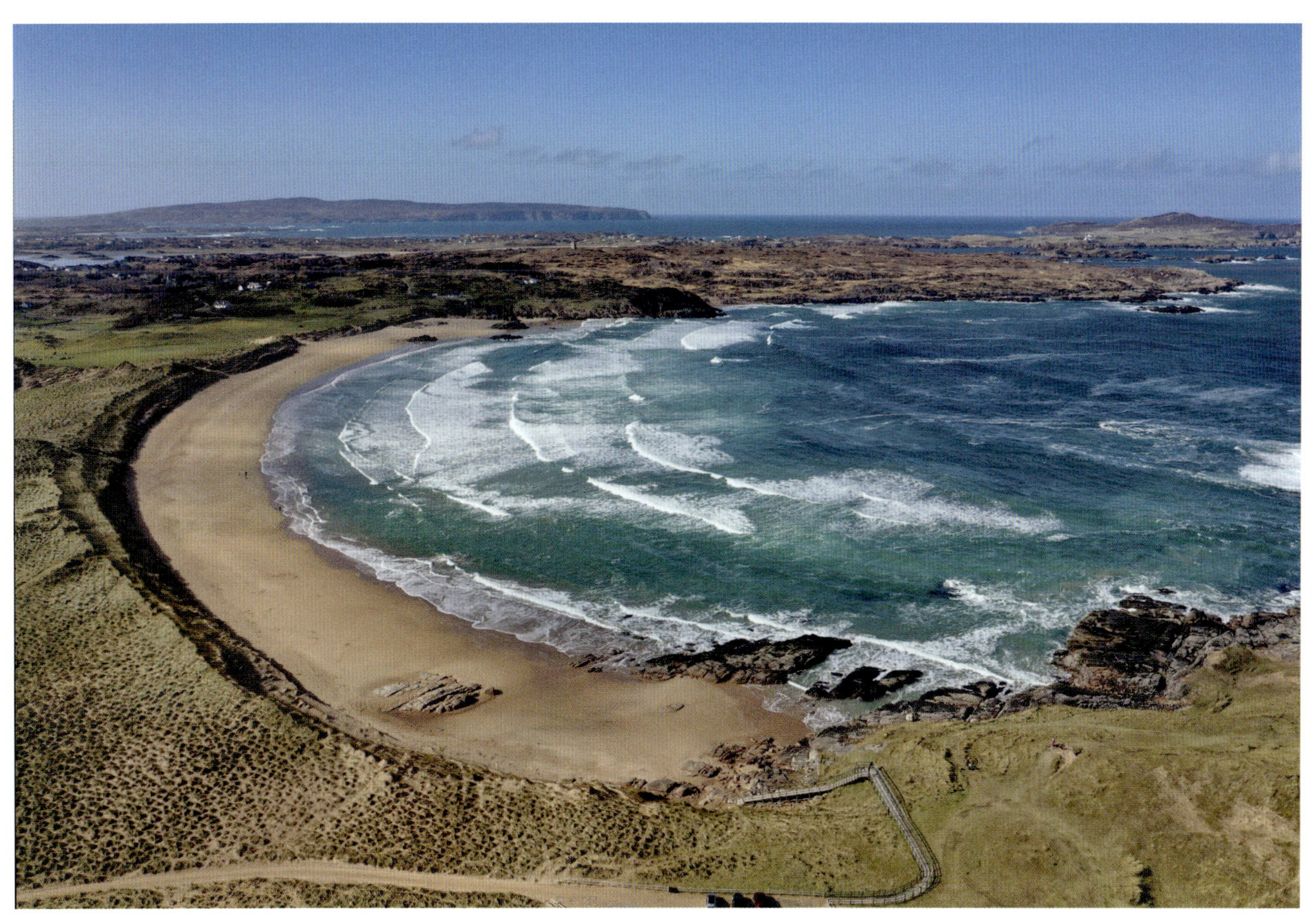

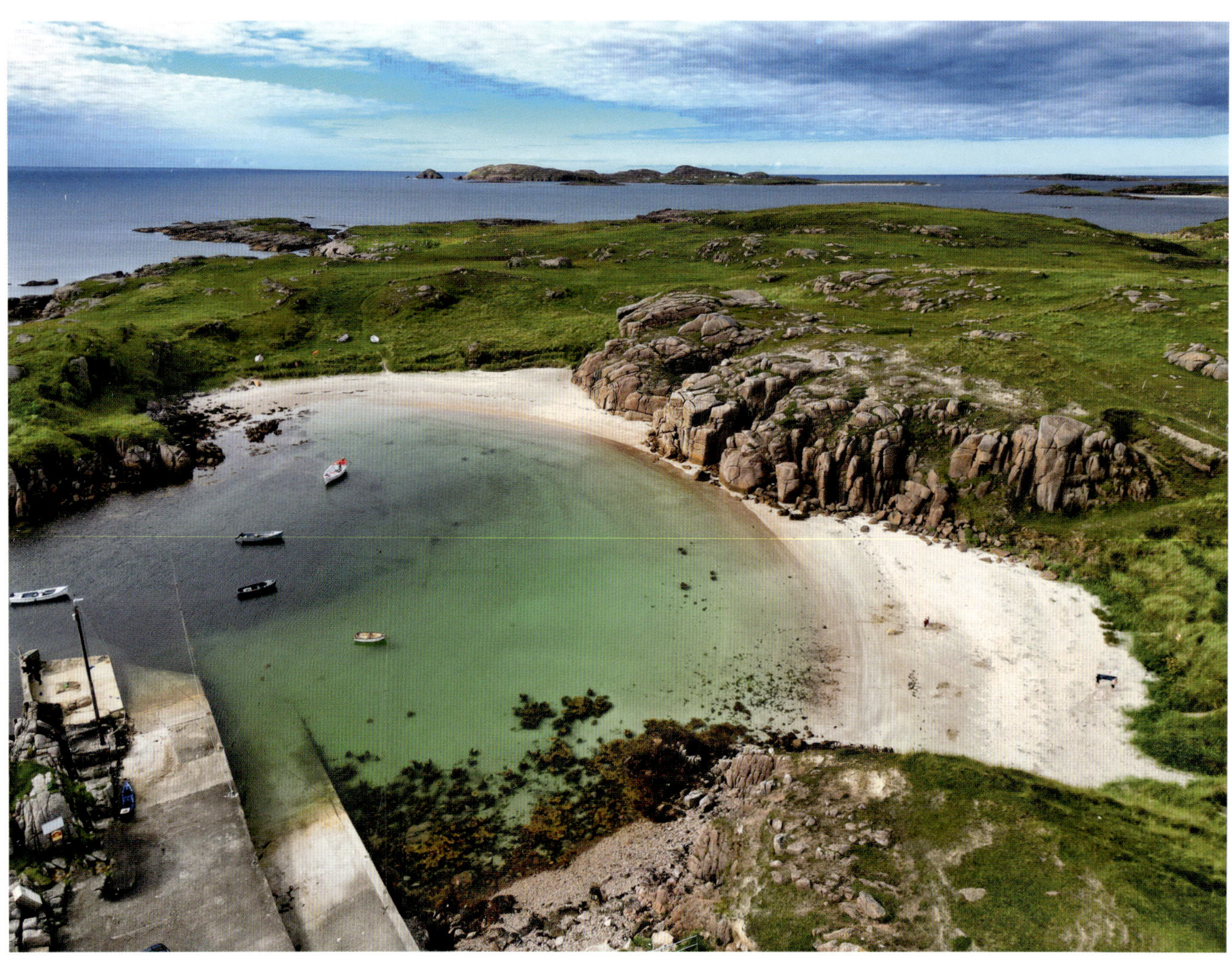

The secluded semicircular bay of the Boat Strand, Carnboy, Carrickfinn.

Opposite: Bunbeg is a fishing village in the heart of the Gaeltacht, the Irish-speaking district, of Gweedore, and is Europe's smallest active harbour. The port was built in the late 1830s by local landowner Lord George Hill to encourage fishing. He had a grain store constructed on the quay, and opened a shop and a bakery. By the 1890s, this was a busy port, with herring and mackerel being the main catches. Lobster and crab from the islands were brought first by currach, then by cart, rail, steamer and rail again to reach London restaurants.

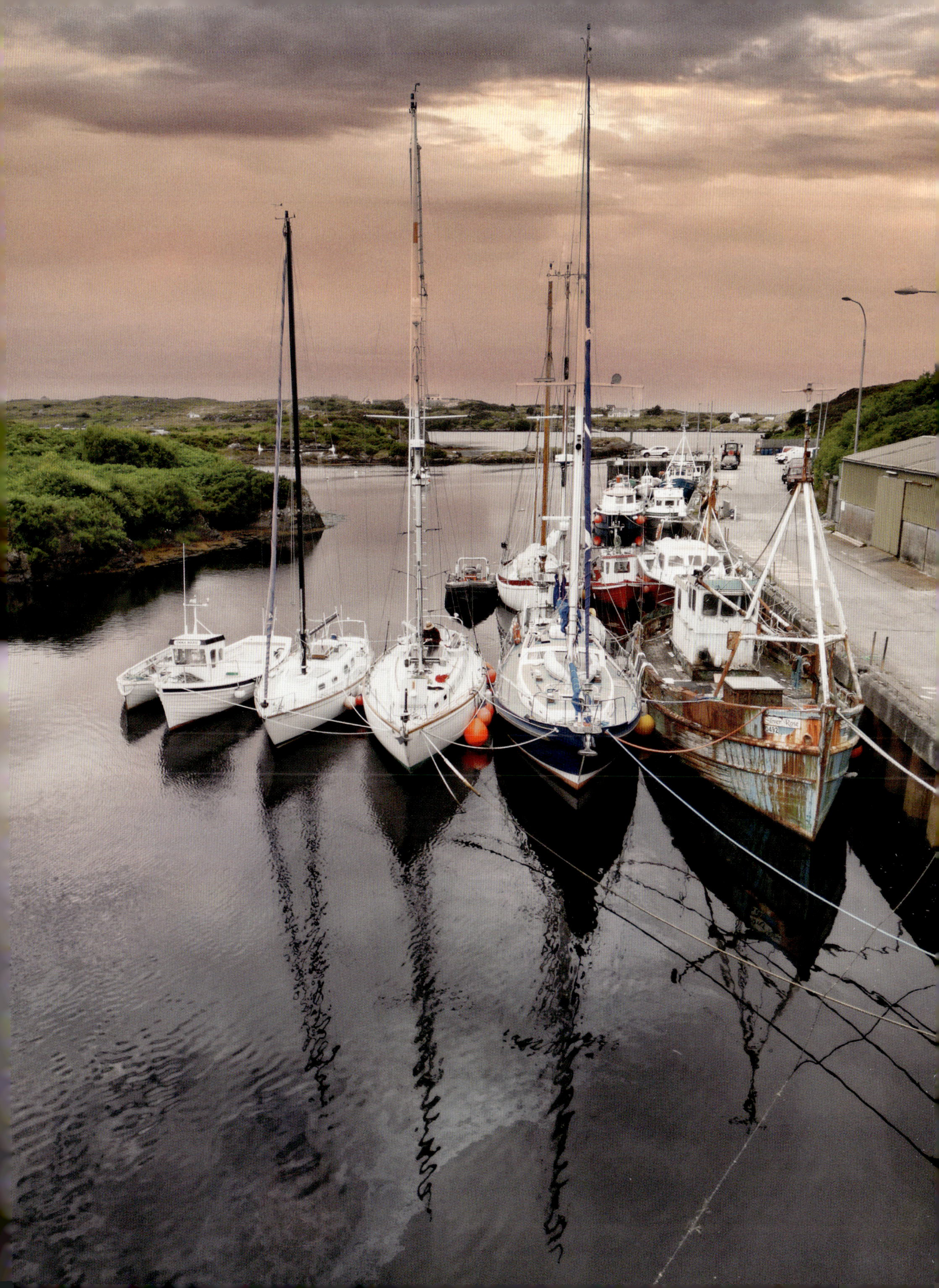

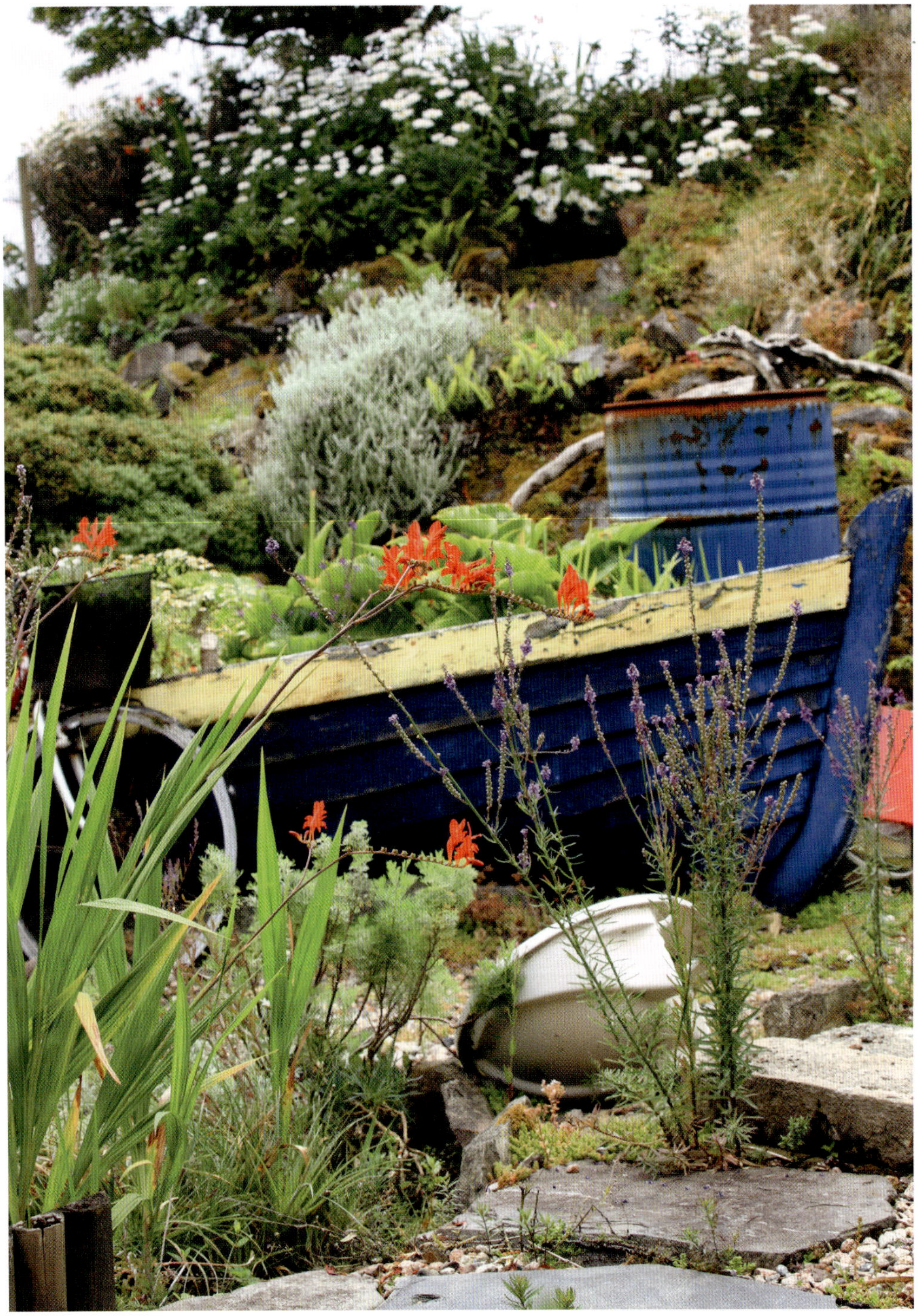

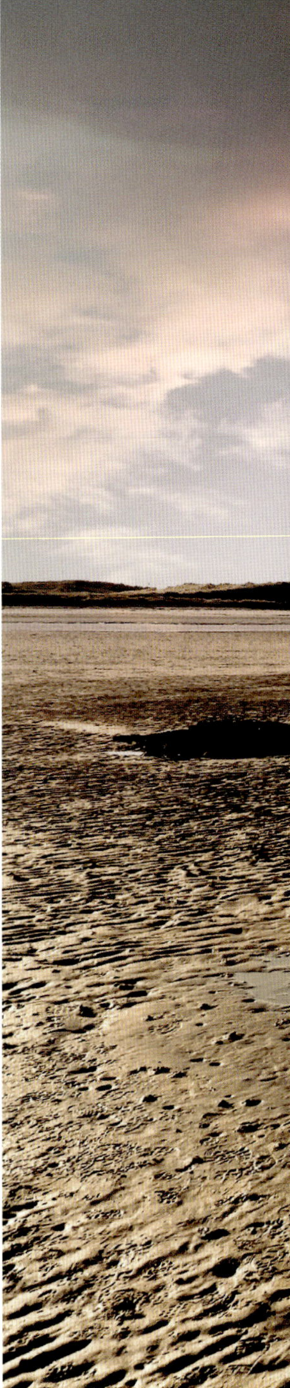

'Jack's Garden'. Nestled among wildflowers lies a weathered old boat inviting thoughts of the stories it could tell.

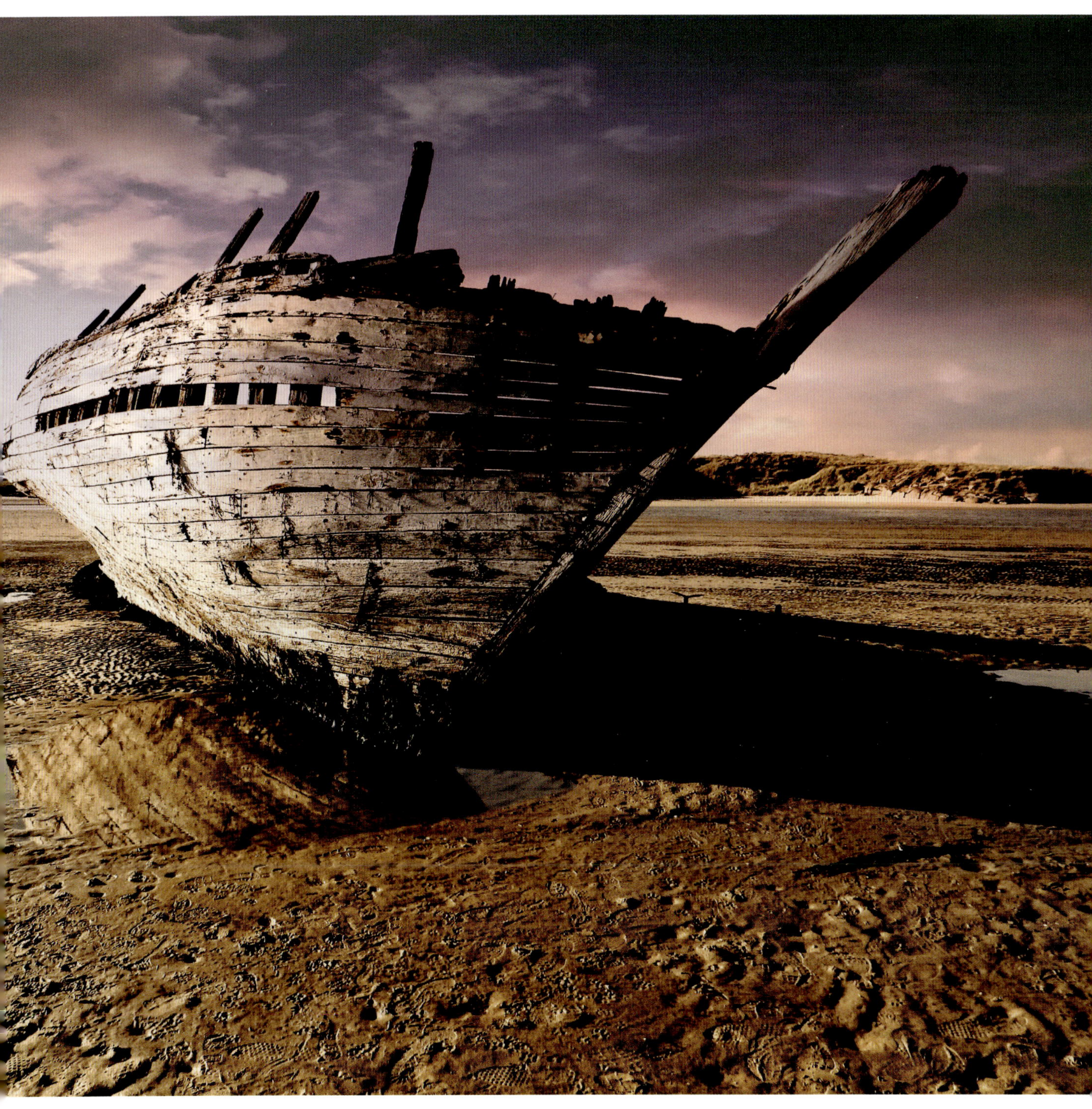

Bád Eddie on Magheraclogher Beach was built in Brittany in France. Originally named *Ami Des Flots* ('Friend of the Waves'), it was renamed *Cara na Mara* ('Friend of the Sea'), and later became known as *Bád Eddie* ('Eddie's Boat'), after its owner. It came ashore to Magheraclogher Beach for minor repairs in 1977 but has been stranded here ever since. Today, it is a beloved icon for the local community and an inspiration for painters, poets, writers and musicians alike, and is one of Ireland's most photographed landmarks.

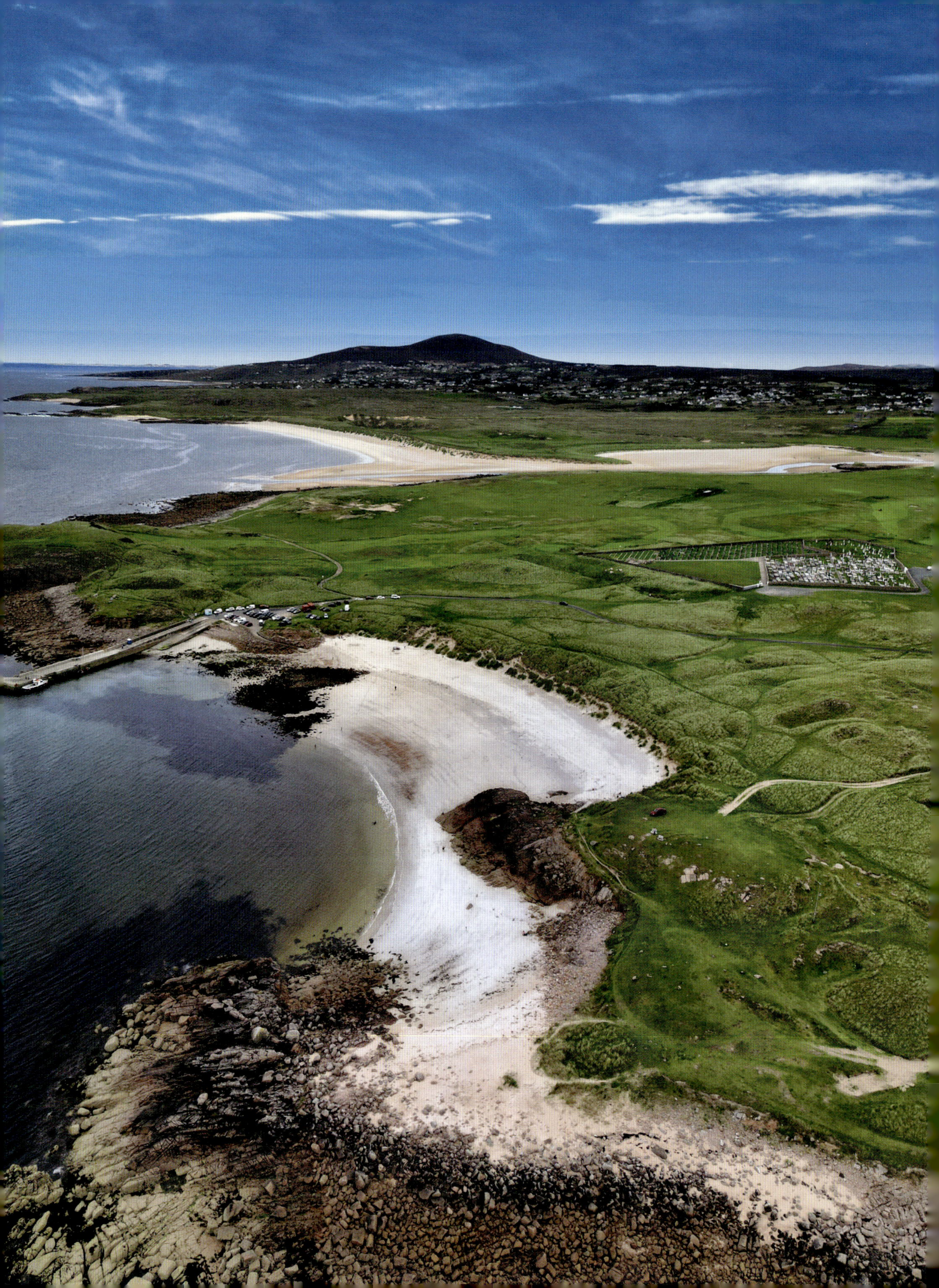

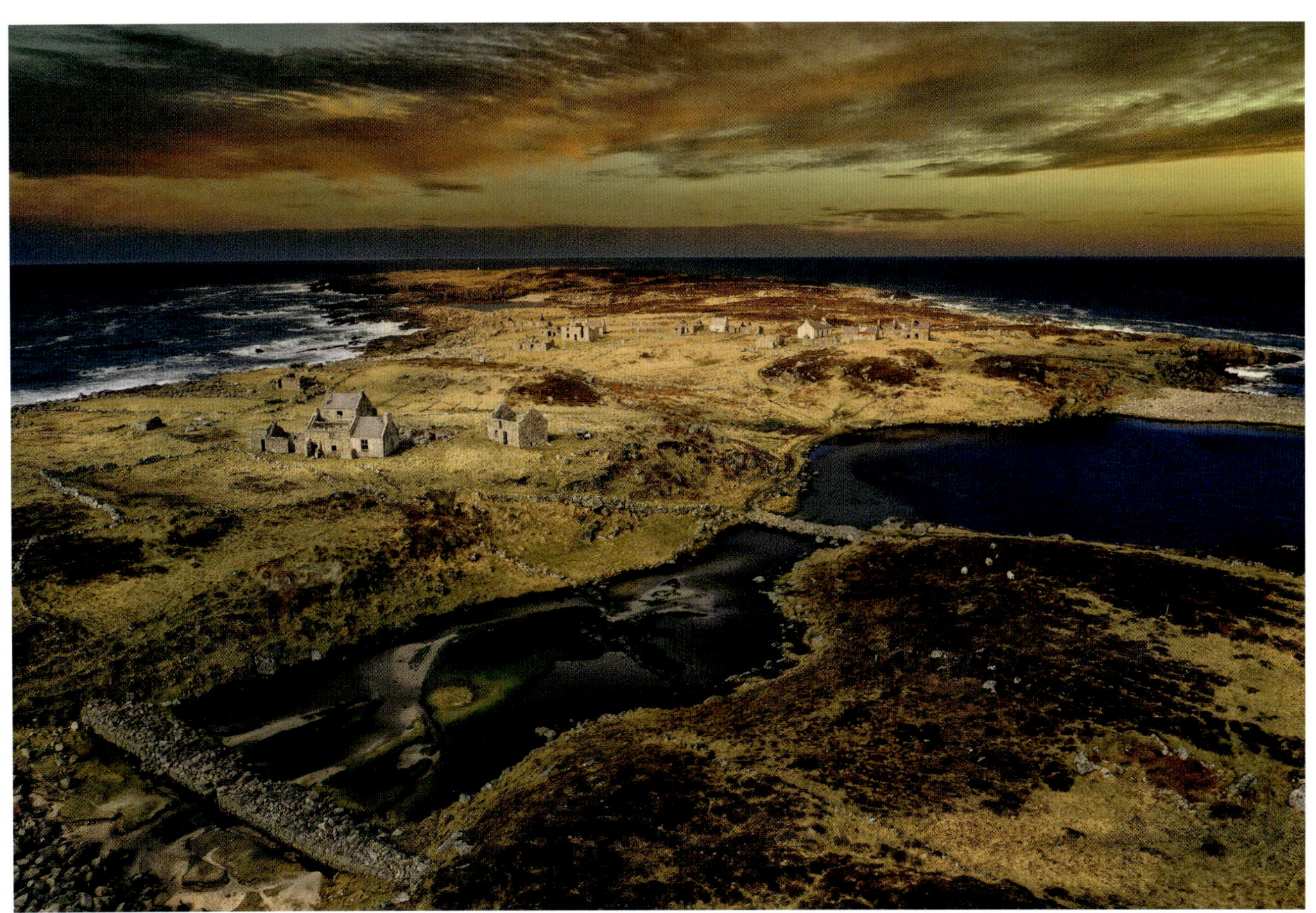

Inishsirrer, off the coast at Gweedore, is the farthest north of a line of islands stretching from Arranmore to Bloody Foreland. A close-knit community of twelve families lived here in the first half of the twentieth century, and were renowned for their expertise in sailing, rowing and fishing. By 1943, only seven families remained. The young left and got married, while others went to Scotland for work. The school was about to close because of the lack of children and, if someone got ill, there were rarely enough able-bodied men available to row them to the mainland. The last residents had no choice but to leave. The scene aches with both beauty and sadness. One cannot have anything but the deepest respect for the people who reared families on the island, where life was hard and precarious.

Opposite: Trá Dhearg ('the Red Beach') and St Mary's Graveyard at Magheragallan, Derrybeg.

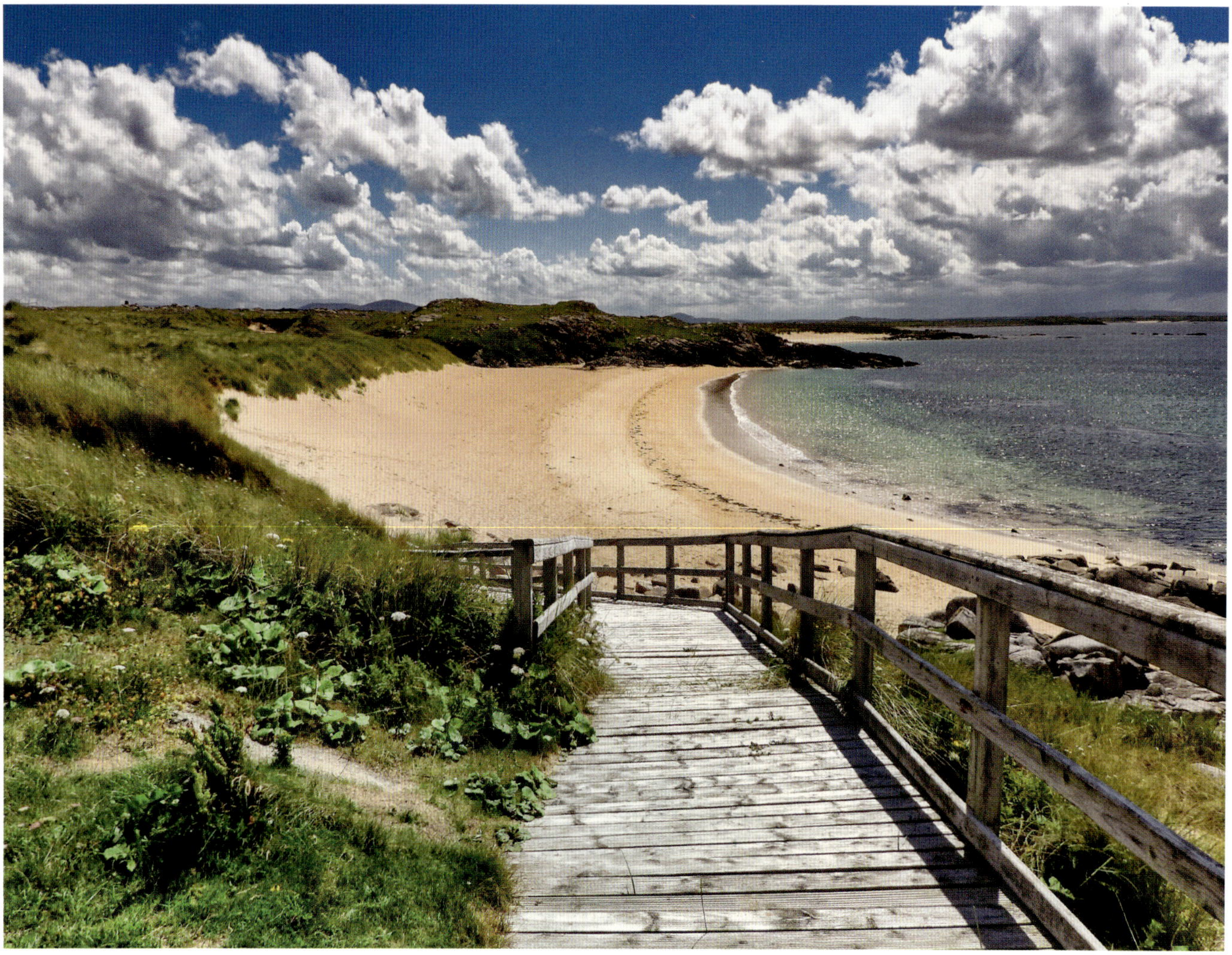

The boardwalk to Glassagh Beach in Gweedore.

Opposite: Bloody Foreland, or Cnoc Fola, gets its name from the many red hues of the setting sun as it sinks in the west. Across the hills are numerous stone walls, made of granite boulders, dating back to the 1890s. Livestock still graze in the tiny fields.

Right: Lambs and ewe.

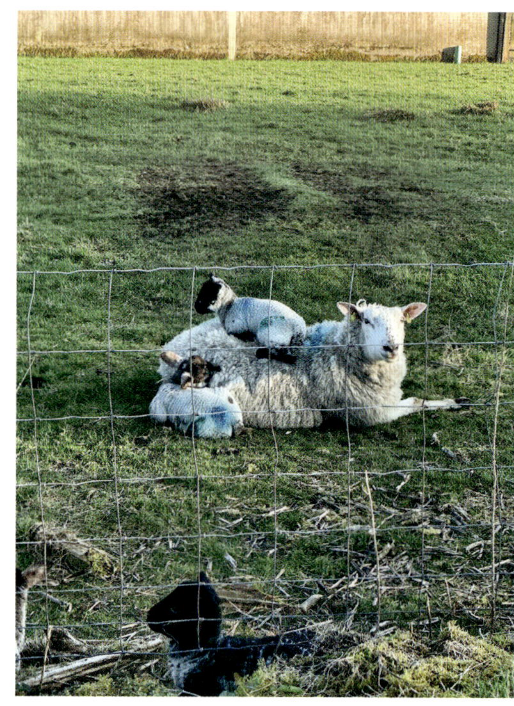

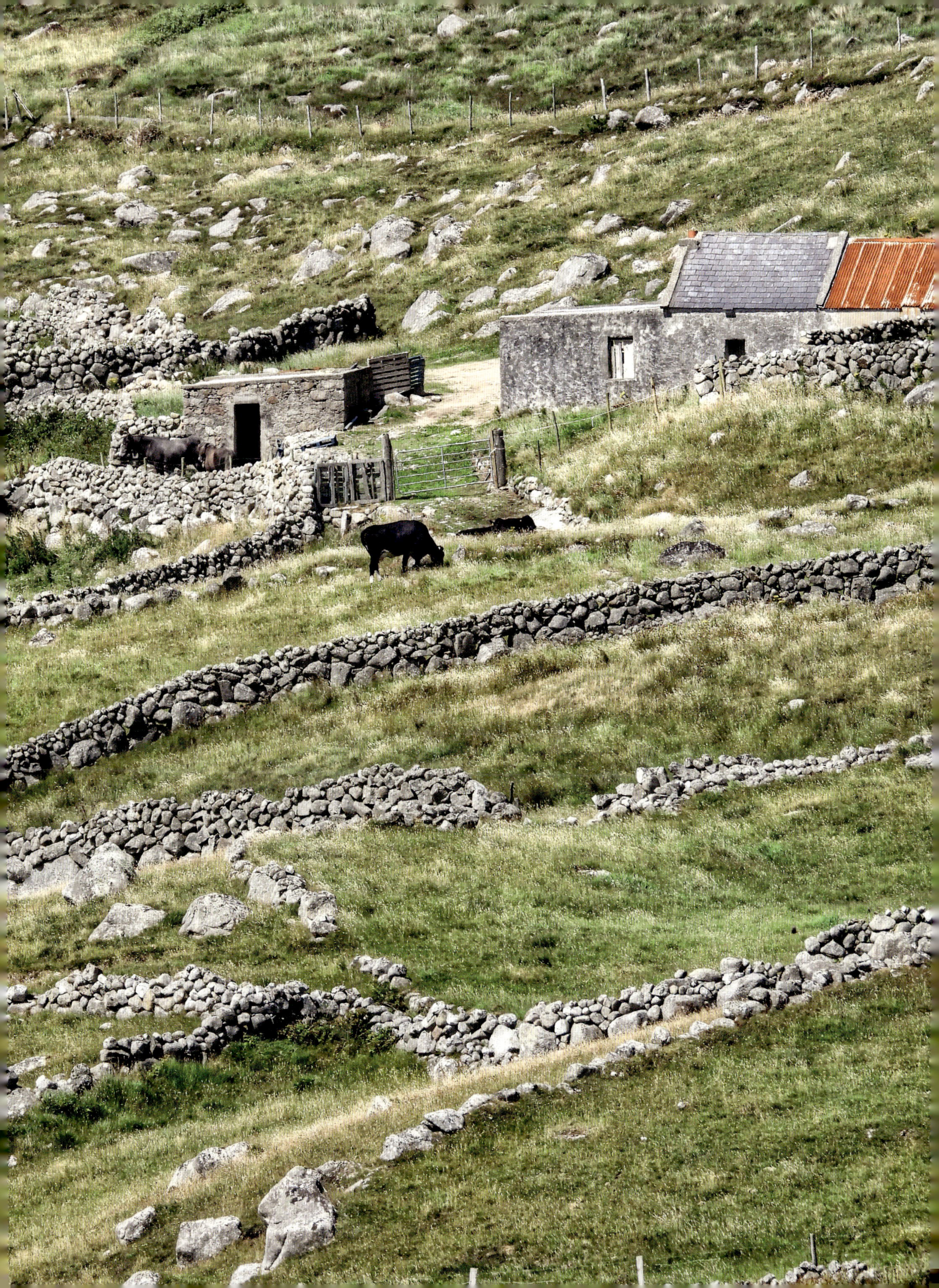

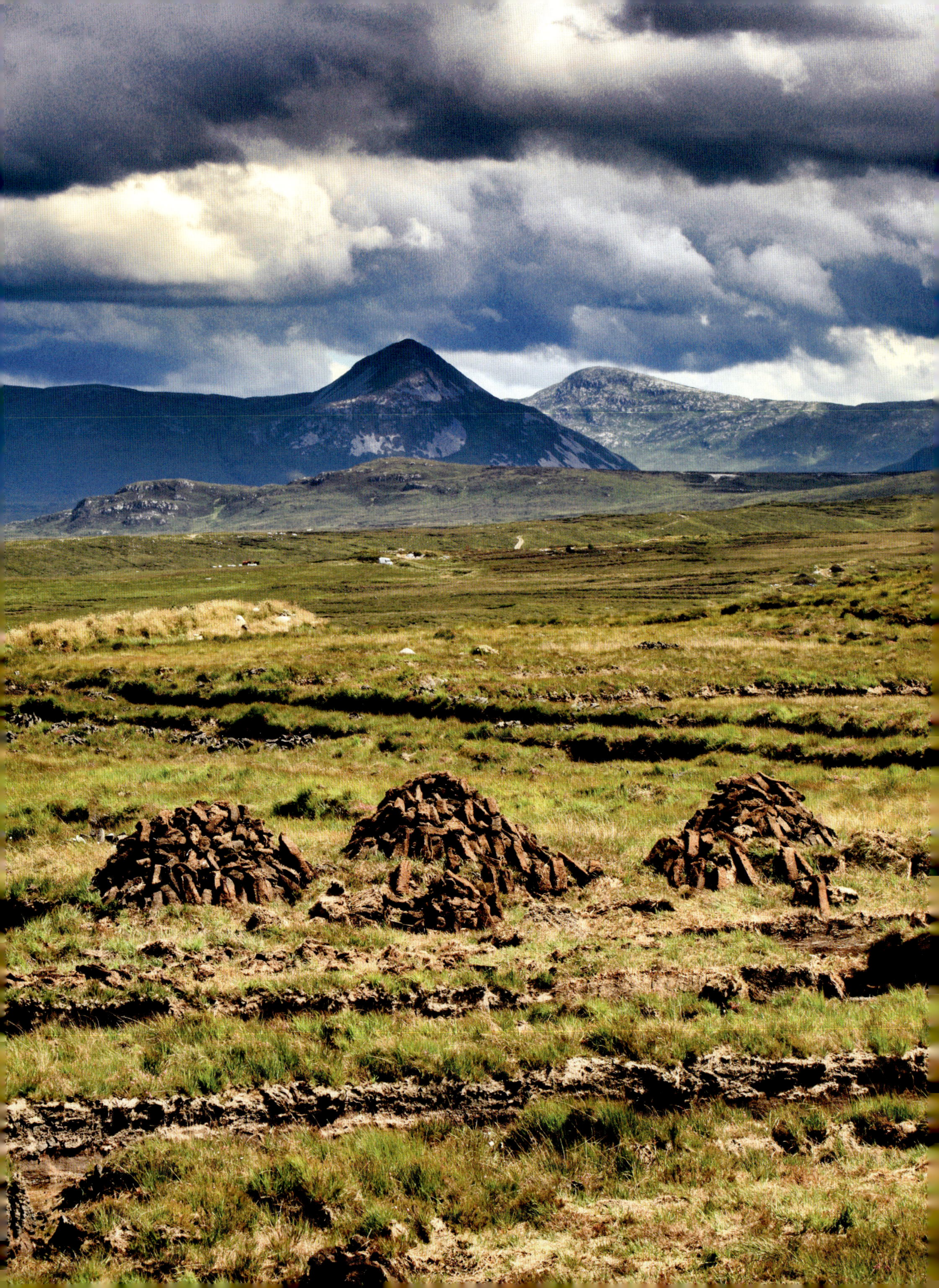

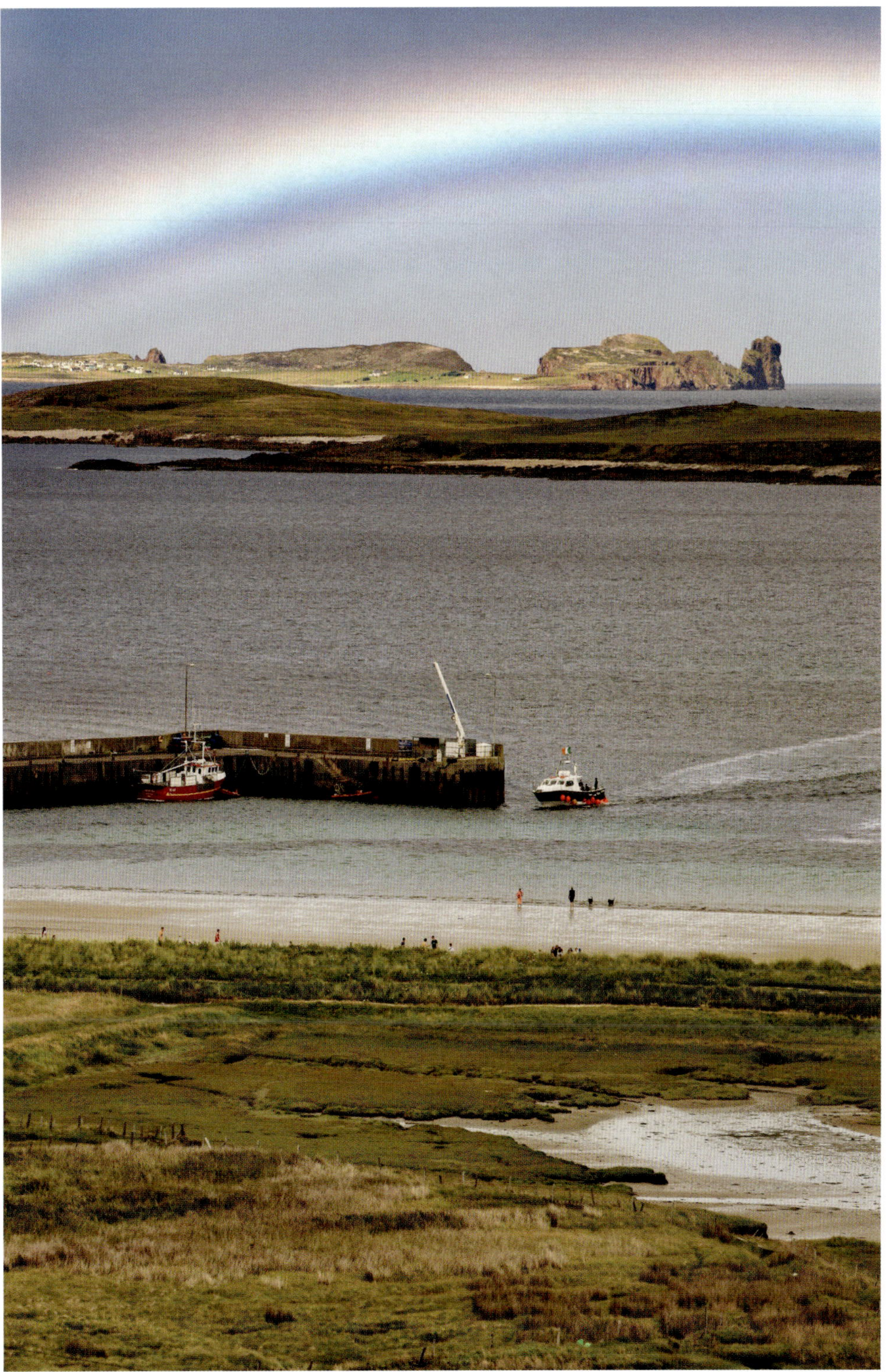

Magheraroarty Pier with Tory Island 14.5 kilometres in the distance. Tory is the most remote inhabited island of Ireland.

Opposite: 'Winning' the turf is a labour-intensive process of cutting, drying and removing sods from the bog during the summer months.

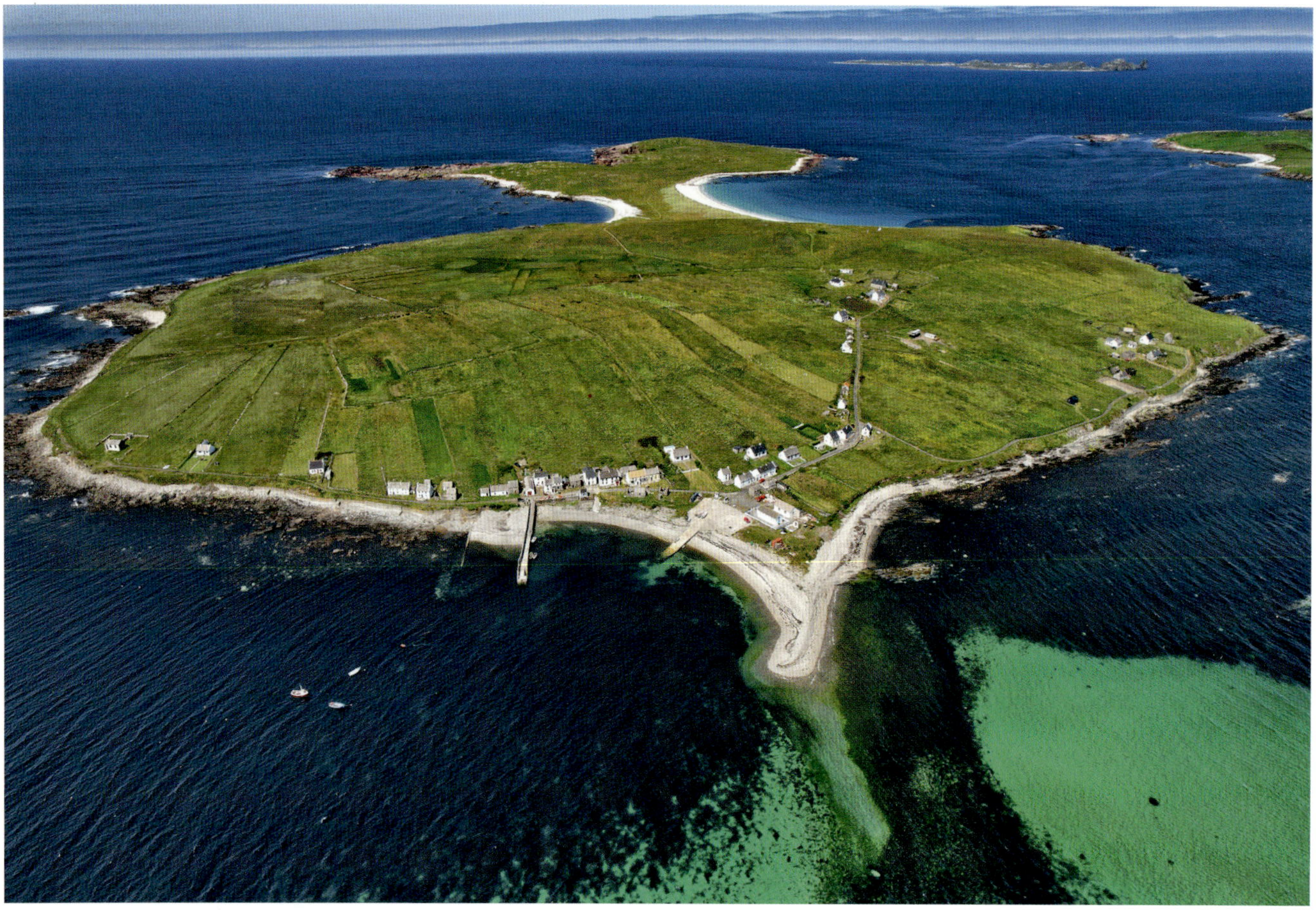

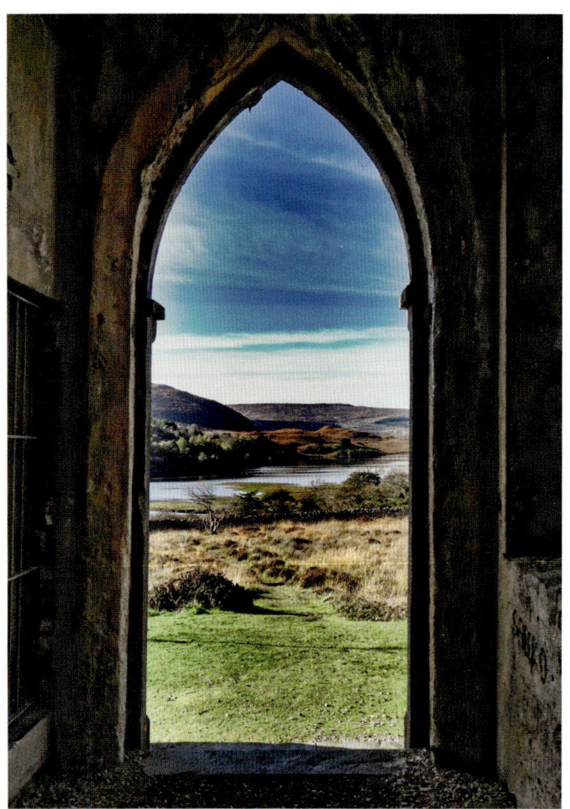

Above: Inishbofin (from the Irish 'Inis Bó Finne', meaning 'Island of the White Cow') lies minutes by boat from the pier at Magheraroarty, Gortahork. In 1929, Arthur Kingsley Porter, a professor at Harvard University, bought Glenveagh Castle in the heart of the Derryveagh Mountains. He also built a house on Inishbofin, which he used for weekend breaks with his wife, Lucy. On 8 July 1933, while out walking on the island, he disappeared. There is much speculation to this day as to what fate befell him.

Left: A view of Dunlewey Lough from the doorway of the old Church of Ireland, Dunlewey.

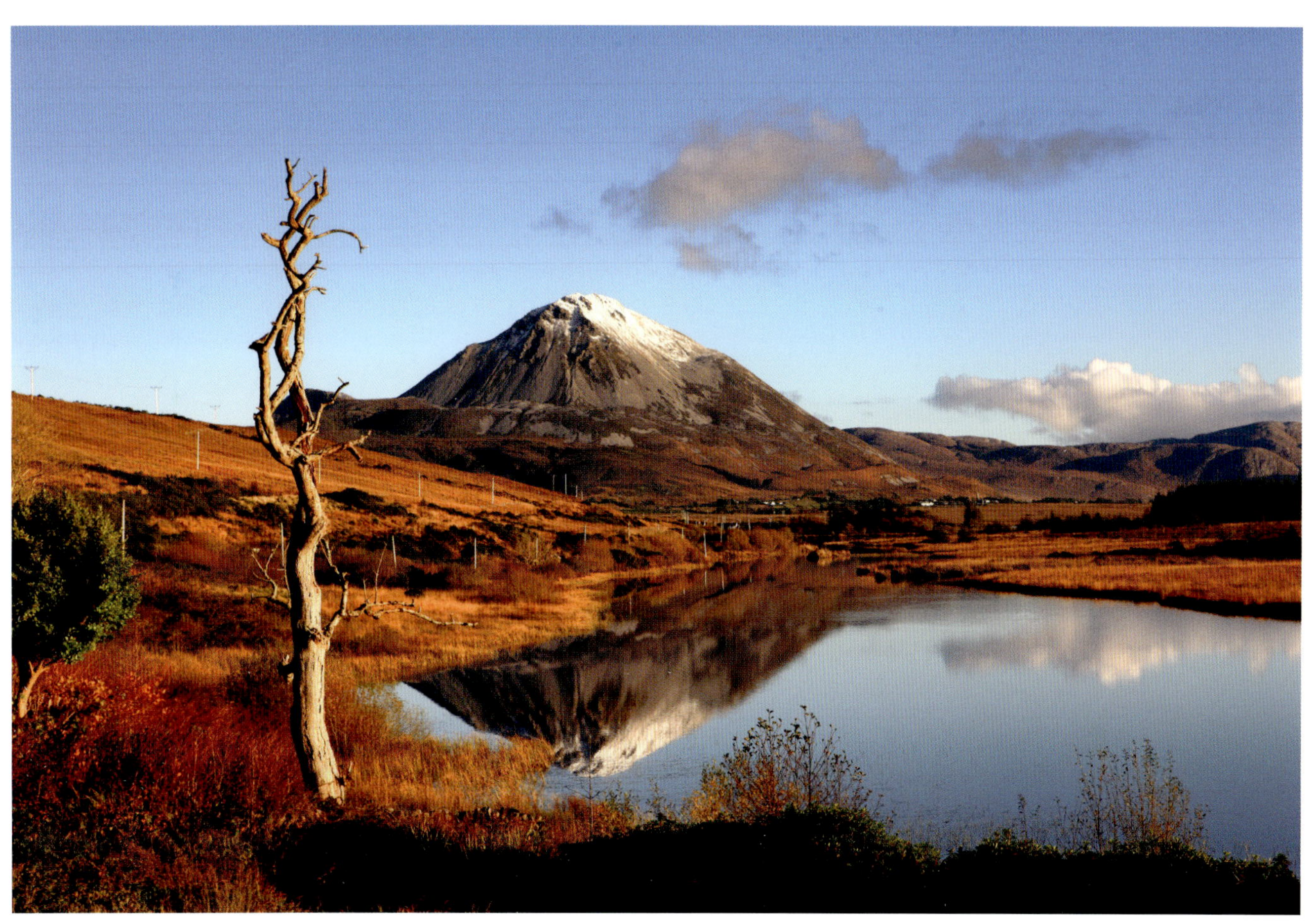

Errigal (An Earagail), rising to 751 metres (2,464 feet), is the tallest peak in the Derryveagh Mountains and in the county. It is the southernmost of the Seven Sisters mountain chain, the other sister peaks being Muckish, Crocknalaragagh, Aghla Beg, Ardloughnabrackbaddy, Aghla More and Mackoght. Errigal's quartzite peak makes it one of Ireland's most iconic landmarks.

According to legend, this huge glaciated glen acquired its name – the Poisoned Glen – when Balor, the one-eyed giant king of Tory, was killed here by his exiled grandson, Lú Lámhfhada, who struck him with a stone. Balor fell to the ground and the poison from his eye split the rock and poisoned the glen. The less-interesting truth is that it resulted from a spelling error. The local name, An Gleann Neamhe ('the Heavenly Glen'), was misspelt by an English cartographer as An Gleann Neimhe ('the Poisoned Glen').

The Church of Ireland church was built from locally sourced white marble and blue quartzite in the mid-1800s, overlooking nearby Dunlewey Lough.

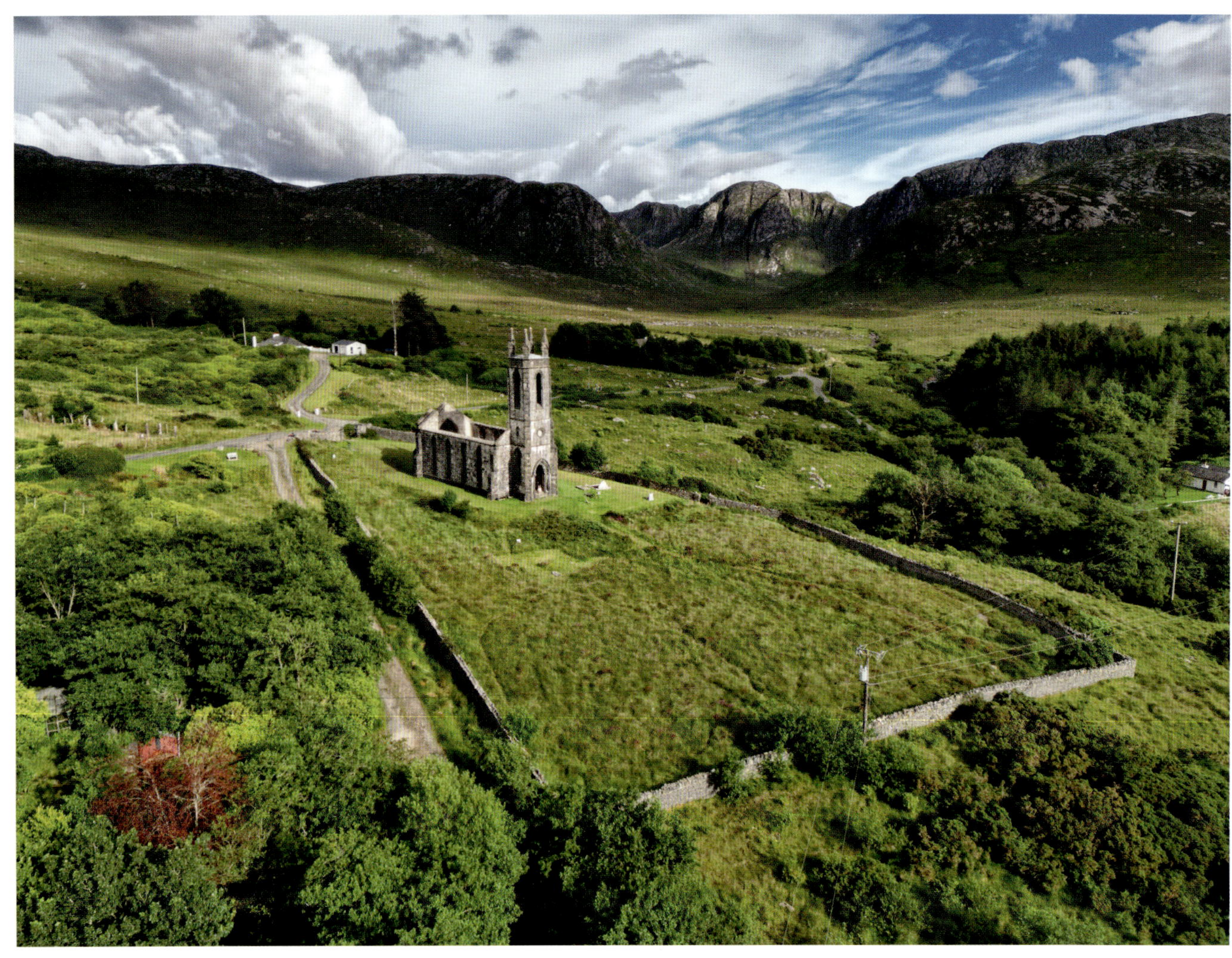

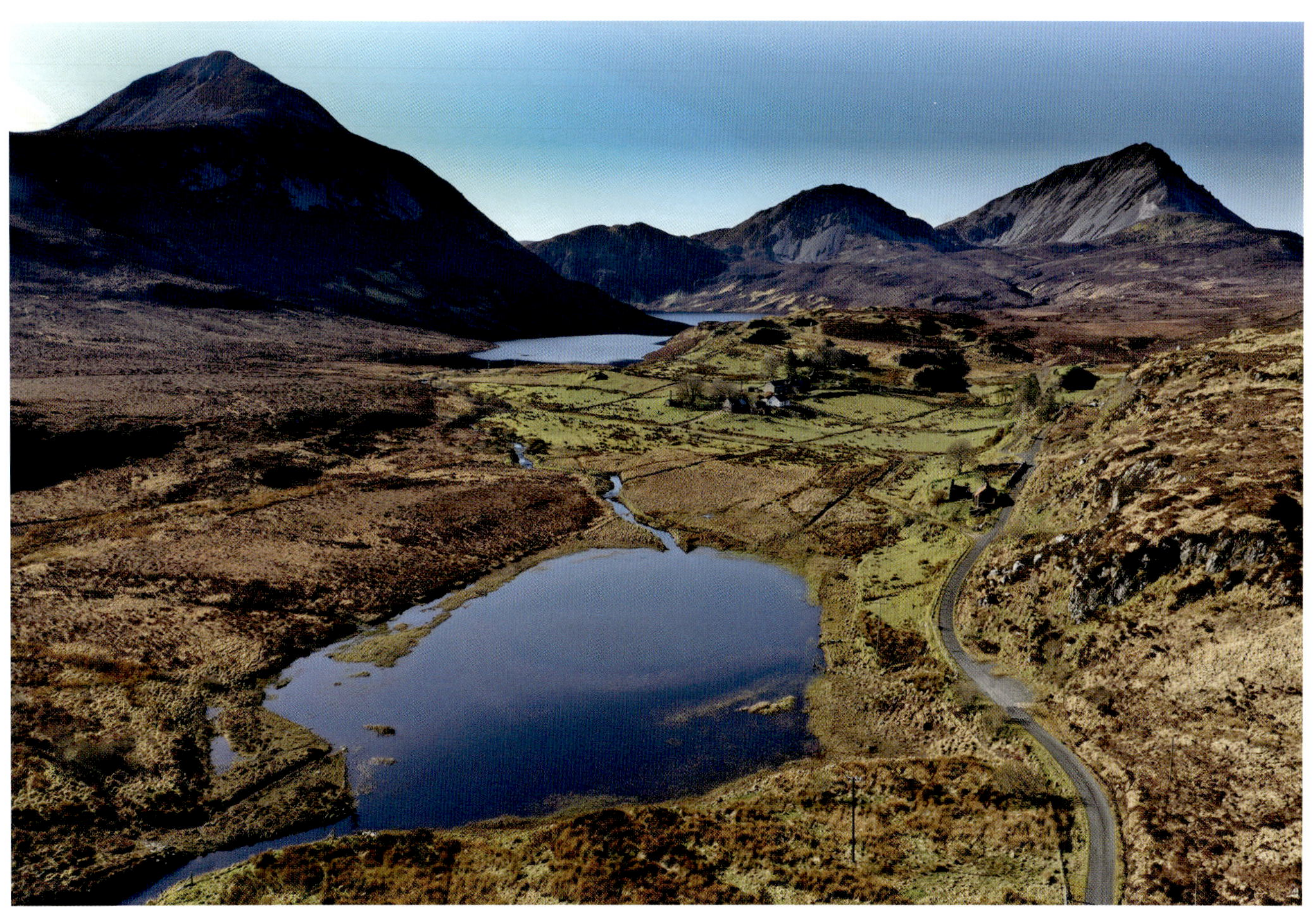

The Derryveagh Mountains of (left to right) Errigal, Mackoght and Aghla More. In the foreground is Procklis Lake with the Tullaghbeg River linking it to Lough Altan in the distance.

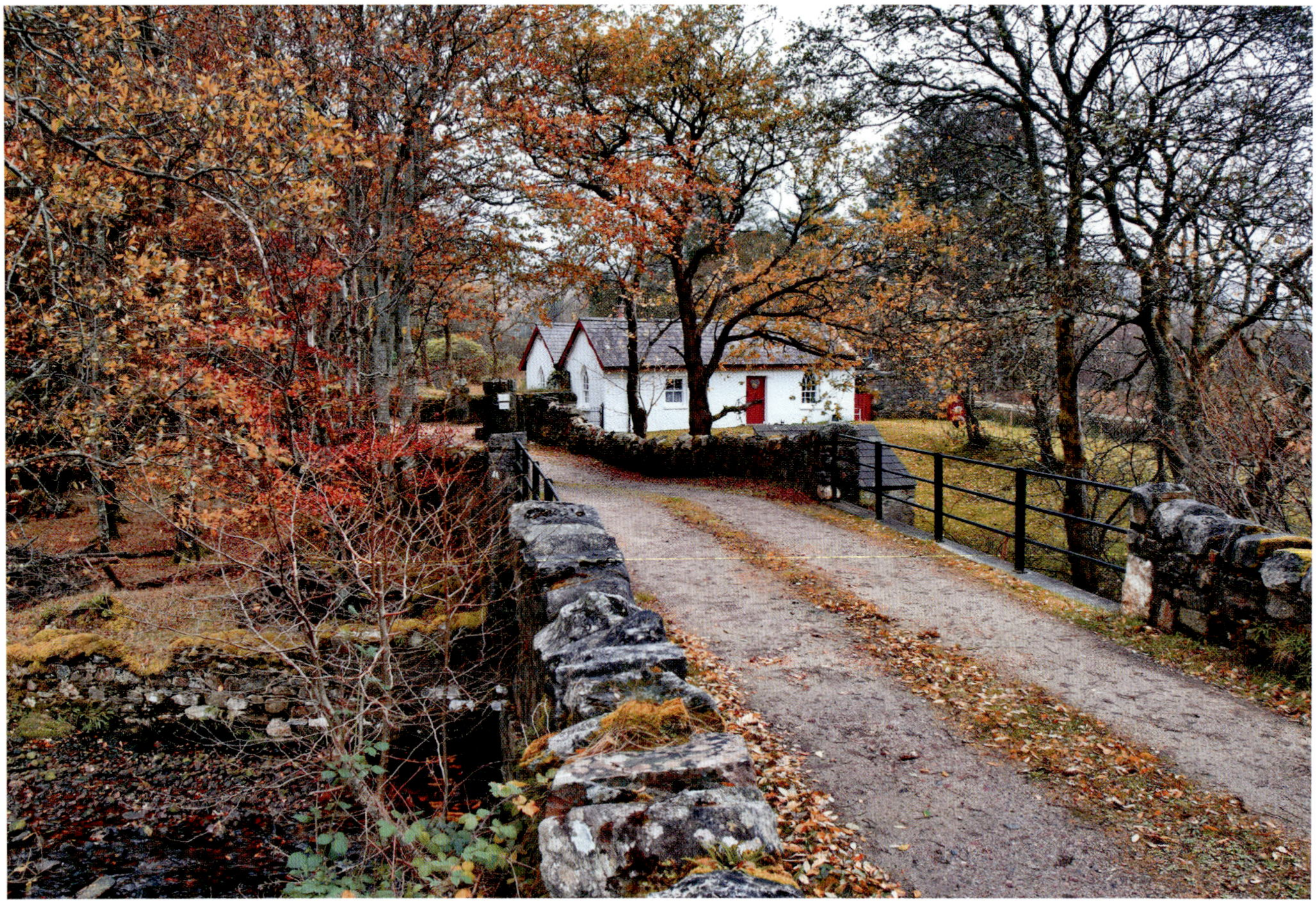

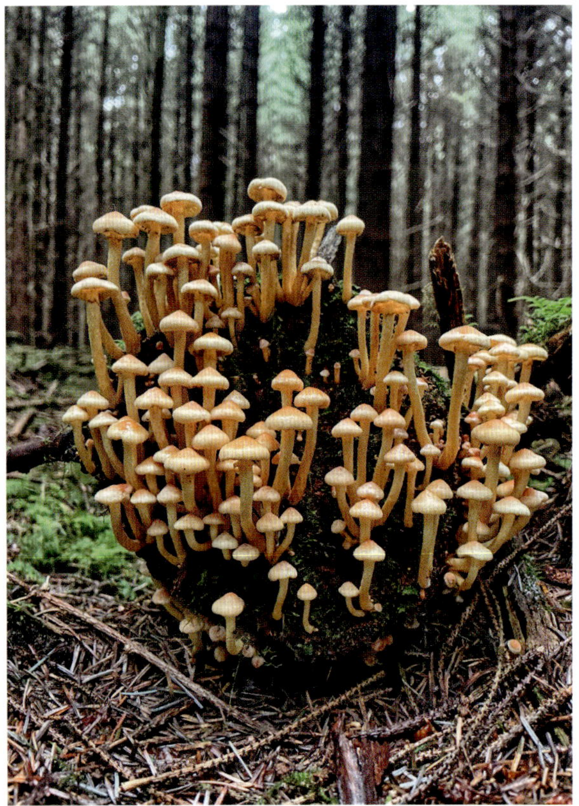

Above: The Gate Lodge at Dunlewey.

Left: An exuberance of *Hypholoma capnoides* mushrooms growing from a fallen tree trunk.

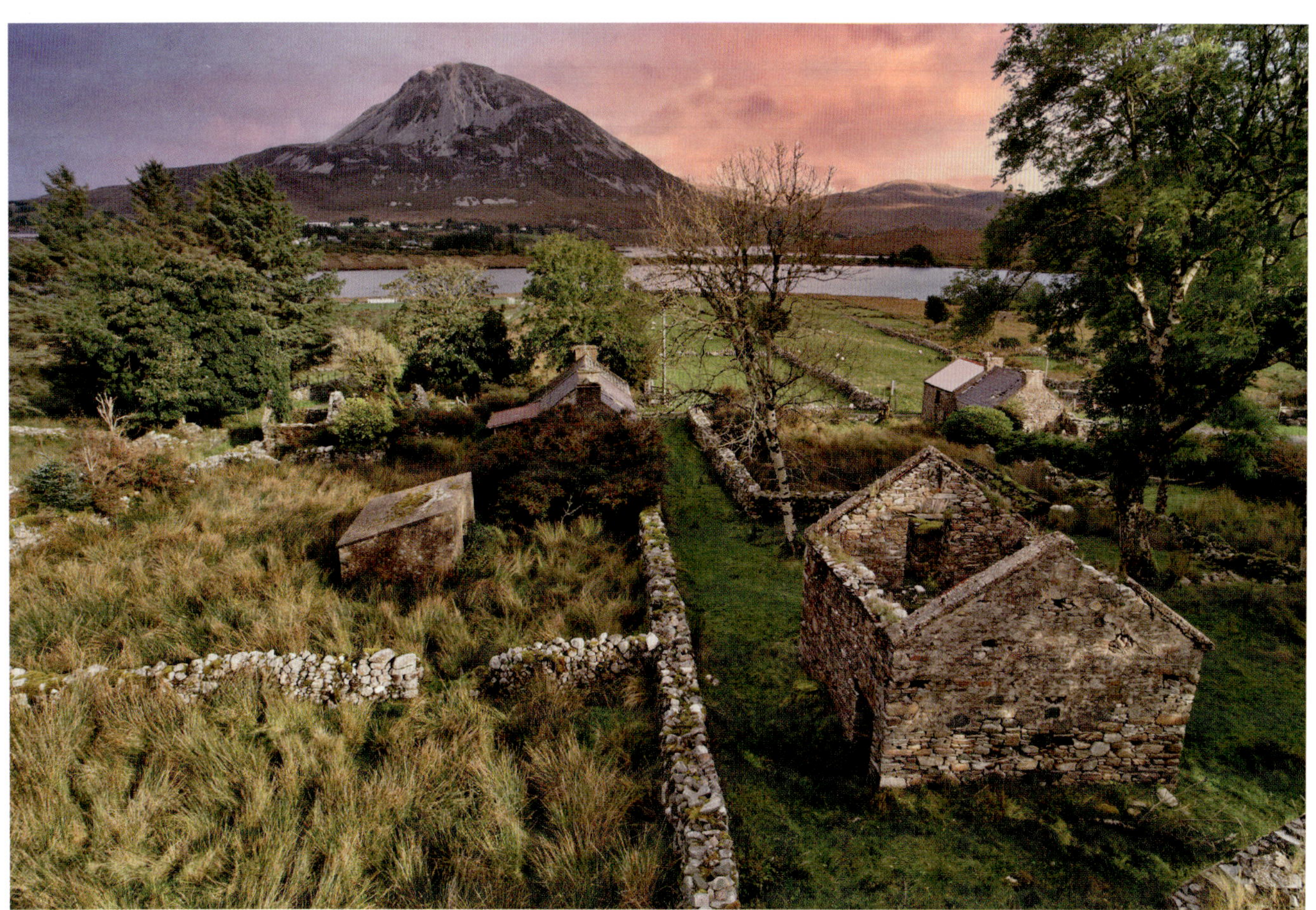

The deserted village of Glentornan is nestled on the shore of Dunlewey Lough, overlooked by majestic Errigal. According to census records, forty to fifty people lived here until 1911. It was gradually abandoned, mainly through emigration.

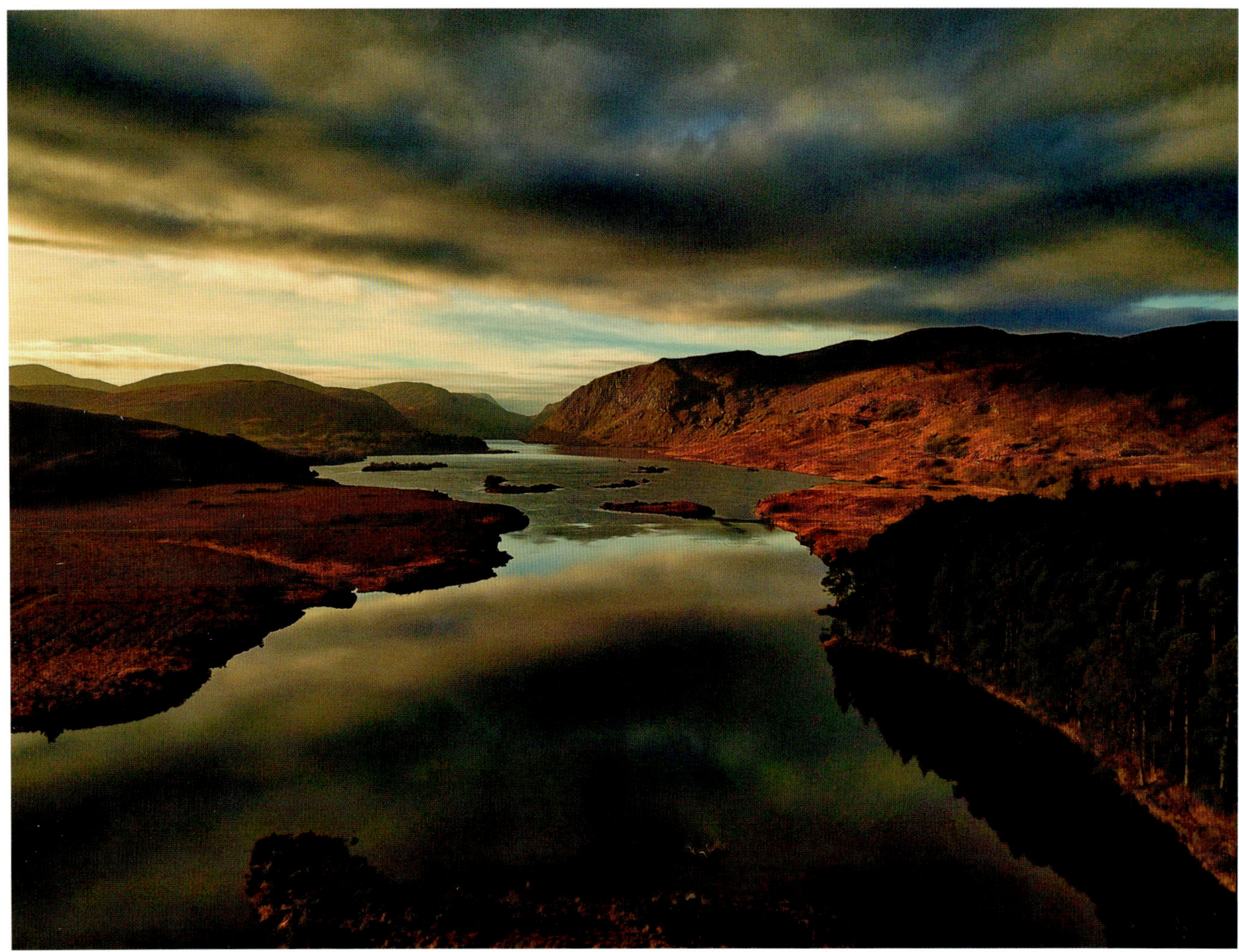

Lough Beagh, surrounded by the 16,000 hectares of Glenveagh National Park, lies in the narrow Glenveagh Valley between the Derryveagh and Glendowan Mountains. Steep granite cliffs rise on both sides of the lake to heights of about 300 metres (1,000 feet). The lake has numerous small islands at its northern end. The national park includes most of the Derryveagh Mountains, the Poisoned Glen and part of Errigal, and saw the successful reintroduction of the golden eagle in 2001.

Opposite: Glenveagh Castle sits close to the southeastern shore of Lough Beagh. Made from rough-hewn granite, the crenellated mansion was built in the 1870s and designed by John Townsend Trench, a cousin of John Adair, the original owner of the Glenveagh estate. It consists of a four-storey rectangular keep with walls one and a half metres (five feet) thick, with battlemented ramparts, turrets and a round tower.

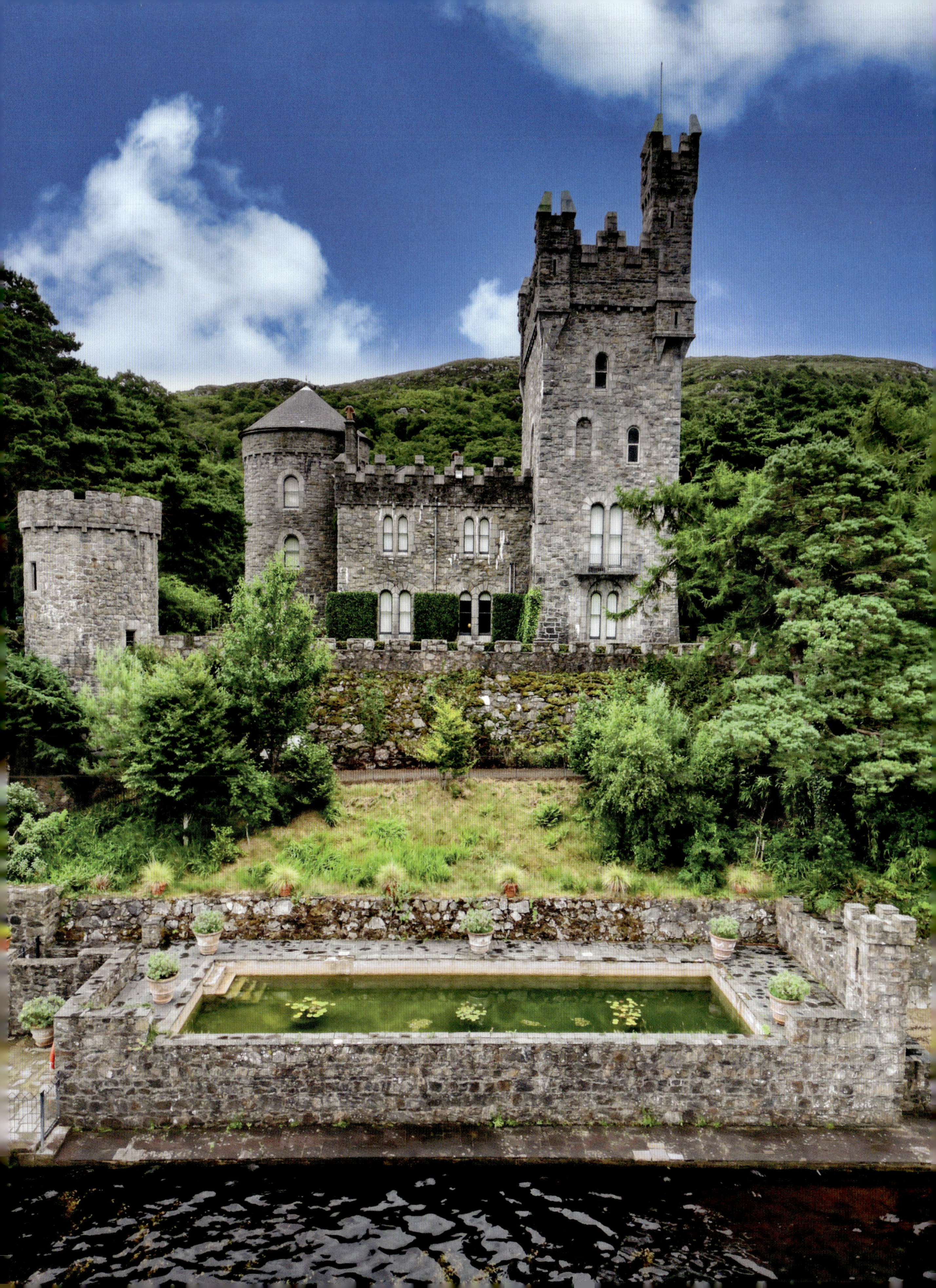

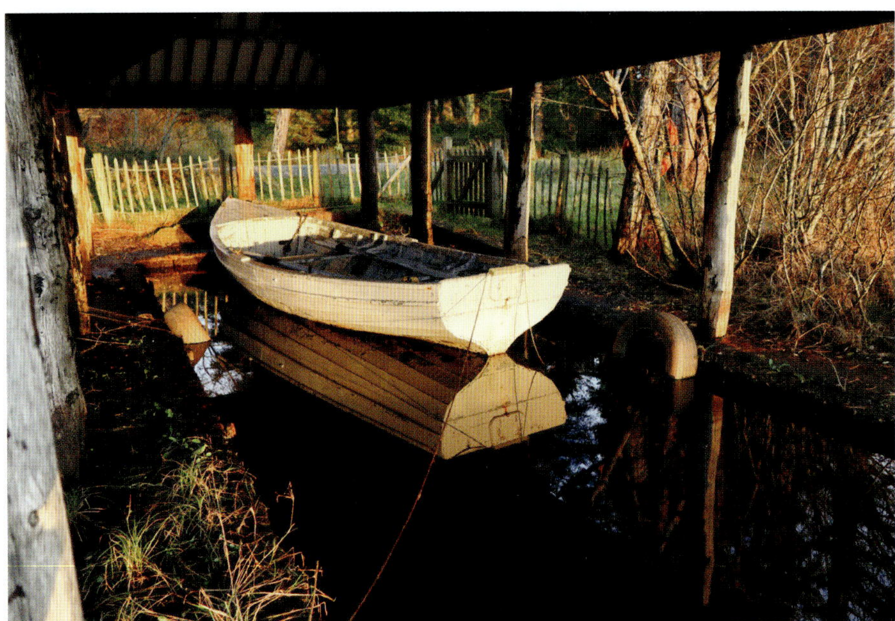

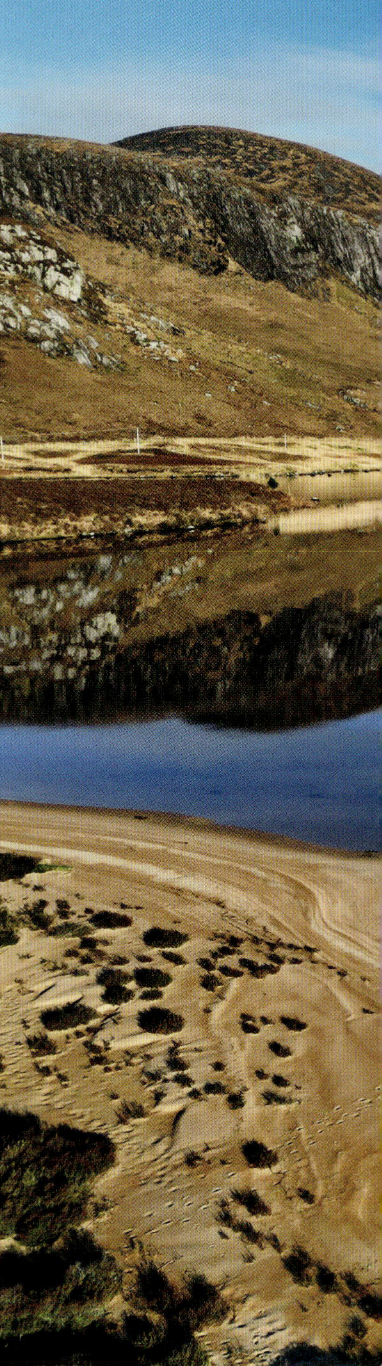

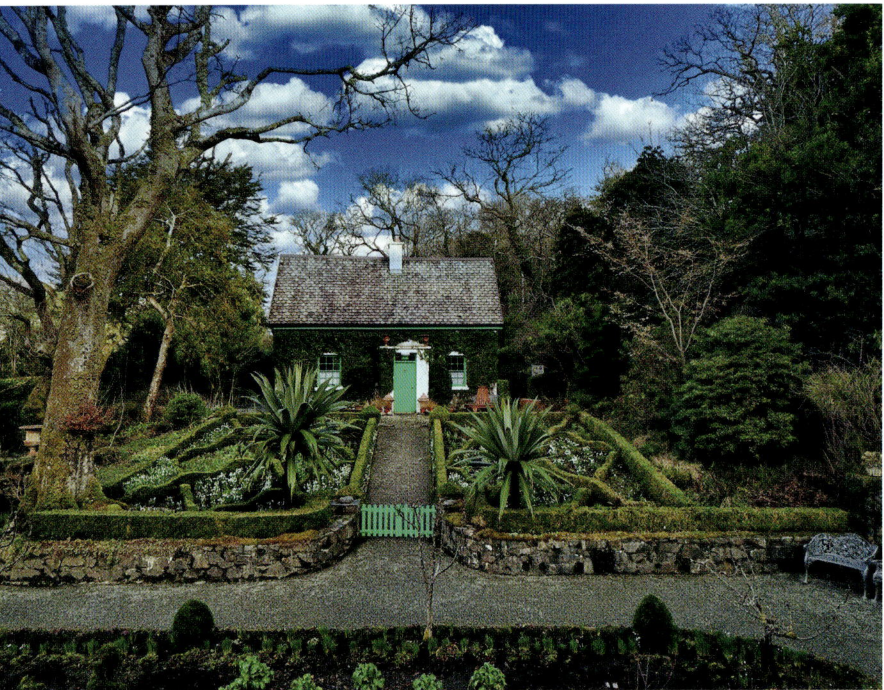

Top: Last light on the boathouse at Glenveagh.

Bottom: The Gardener's Cottage is in the walled garden in the grounds of Glenveagh Castle. It occupies an area where stone was quarried to build the castle and is now a beautiful combination of the practical and the ornamental. Lived in until recently, it has since been adapted to house archives associated with the history of the gardens. The neat little garden in front of the cottage, with its carpet of snowdrops, is a beautiful place, almost spiritual, a great spot to reflect!

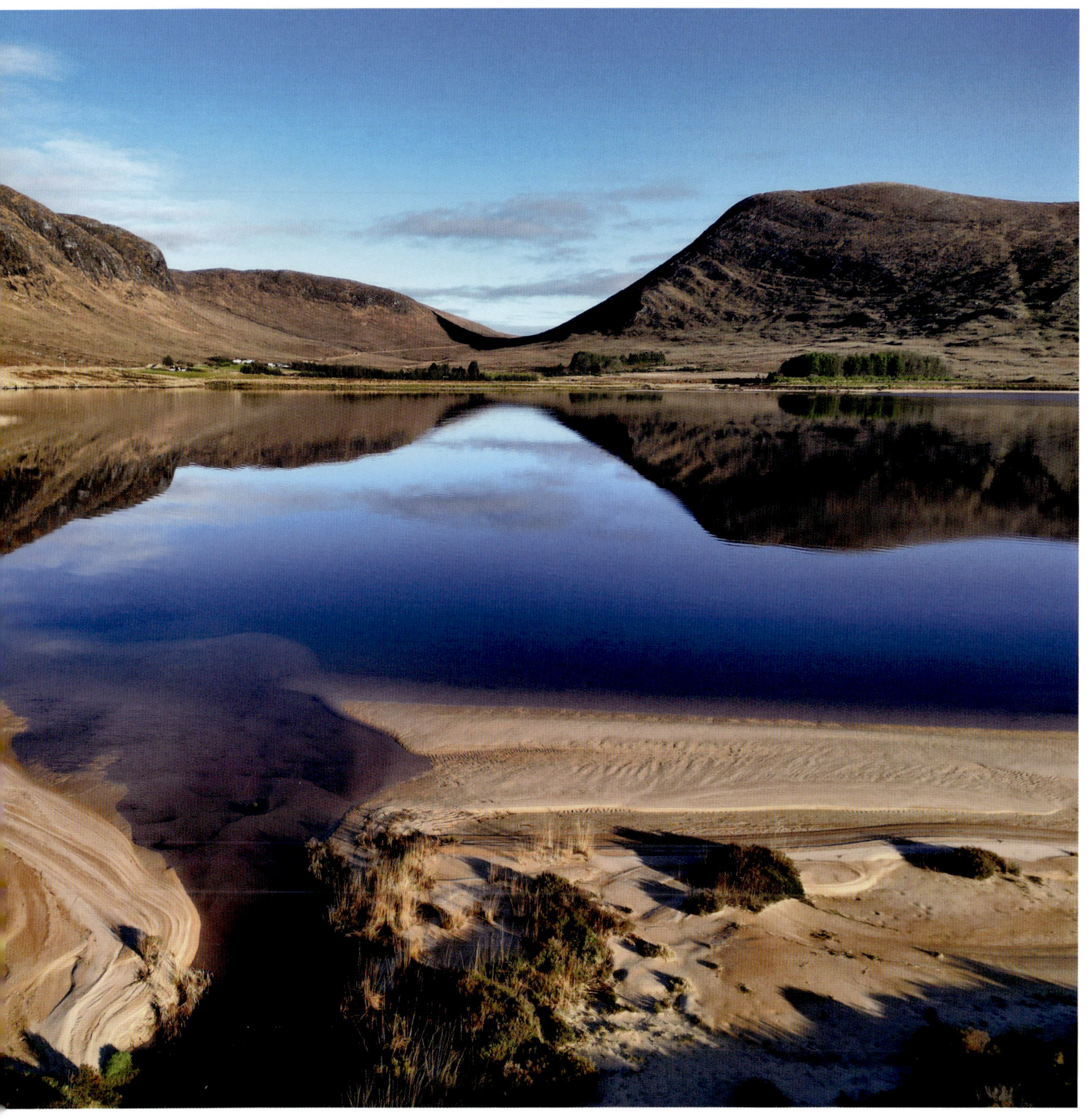

Lough Barra lies just to the east of the R254 road, approximately nine kilometres northeast of the village of Doochary and boasts its very own beach! The sand creates a stunning contrast to the vibrant blue water. Lough Barra Bog Nature Reserve, to the right of the lake, is part of the most extensive lowland blanket bog in Ireland's northwest.

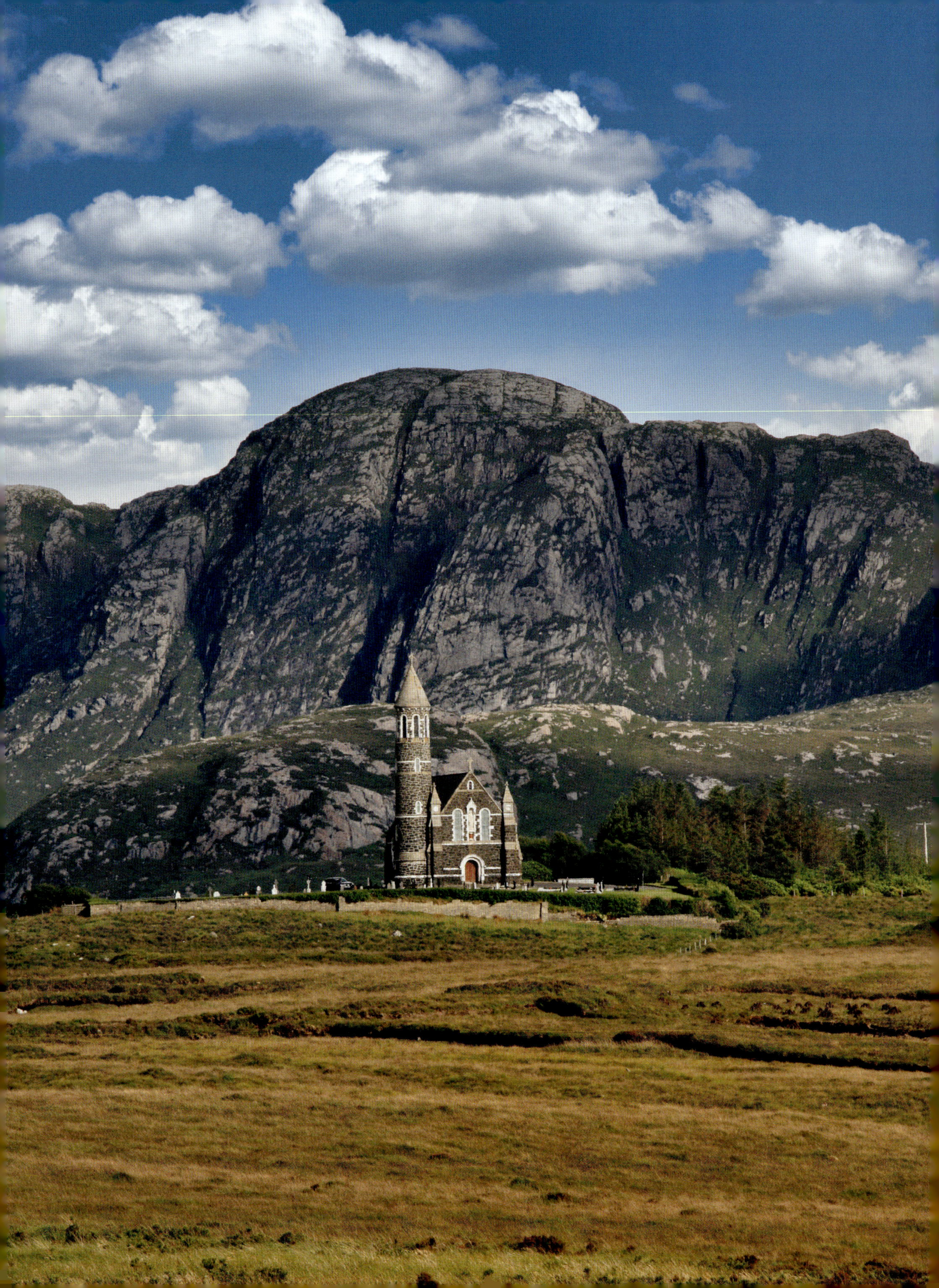

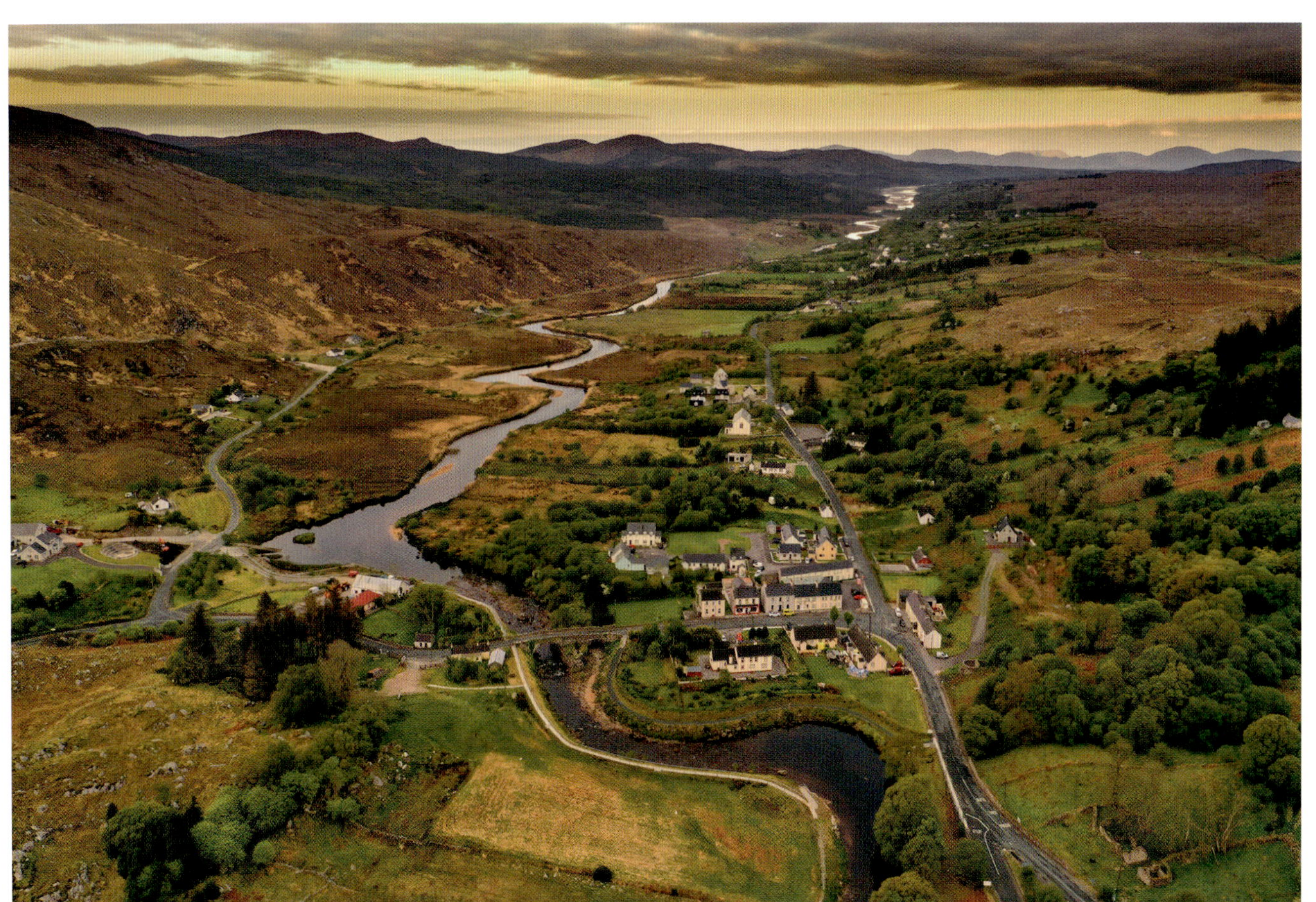

The small Gaeltacht village of Doochary (meaning the 'Black Weir') is an oasis of tranquillity in the Rosses where a bridge crosses the Gweebarra River, which meanders through the village as it makes its way to the sea. Every turn on the road unfolds a new and stunning landscape of rugged mountains, deep glens and many lakes. Doochary's neighbours are Dungloe to the west, Fintown to the east, Maas to the south and Glendowan to the north. At the edge of the village is a holy well, Tobar Shorcha (Sarah's Well), the waters of which are reputed to cure skin problems. There is also a granite icehouse, built around 1850, which was used by a landlord of the time to preserve fish caught in the river. With extensive walking and cycling routes, Doochary is a haven for anyone with a love of the great outdoors.

Opposite: The Hiberno-Romanesque Church of the Sacred Heart in Dunlewey was built in 1877.

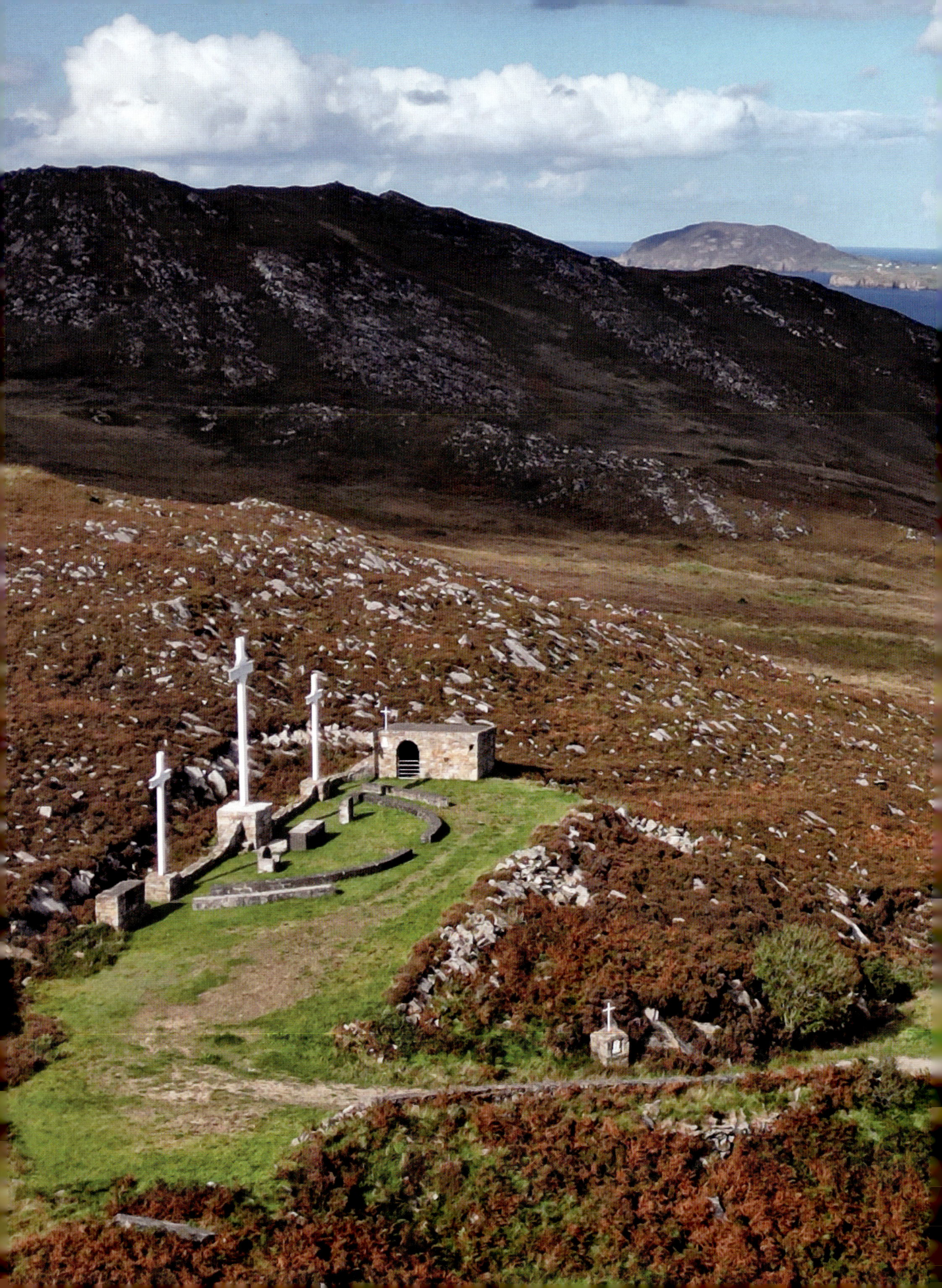

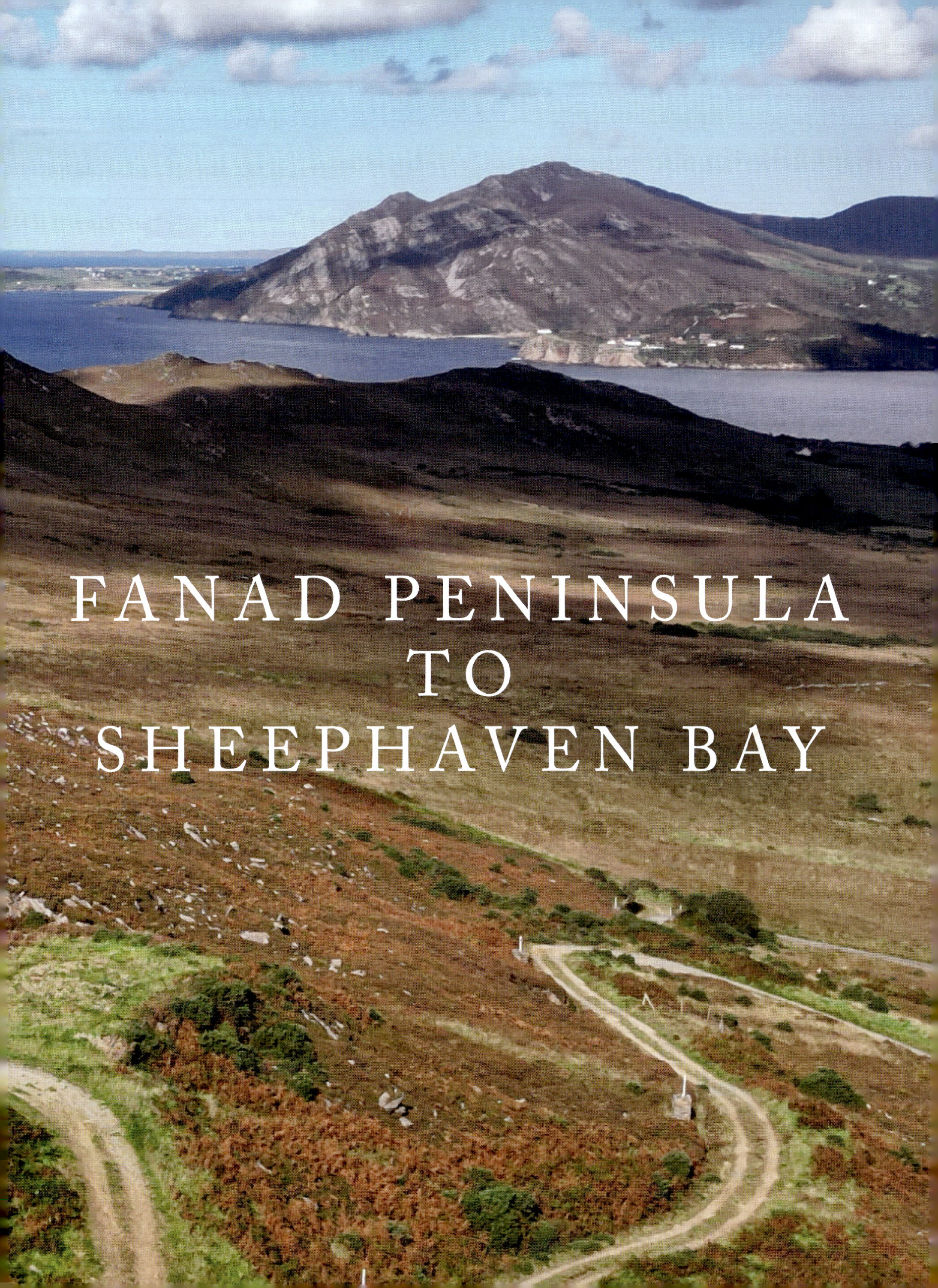

FANAD PENINSULA
TO
SHEEPHAVEN BAY

Fanad Peninsula to Sheephaven Bay in the north possesses dramatic cliffs, expanses of golden sand and dunes. Ards Forest Park offers walking trails and beaches. Doe Castle is a sixteenth-century medieval fortress, with Muckish Mountain enhancing the scenery of the area.

Previous pages: The Way of the Cross is an unusual pilgrimage walk on the edge of Knockalla Mountain, with the Stations of the Cross for silent contemplation along the way. Whatever your beliefs, this is an awe-inspiring and peaceful place. The views of Dunree Head and the Urris Hills in Inishowen are stunning.

Opposite: The towering spire of St Eunan's Cathedral in Letterkenny is visible from all over the town. It was built between 1890 and 1900 in the French Gothic Revival style and, according to the National Inventory of Architectural Heritage, is one of the finest cathedrals in Ireland.

Highland cows are known for their distinctive long horns and shaggy coats. Their hardiness and ability to graze on rougher pastures make them a preferred option for Donegal farmers.

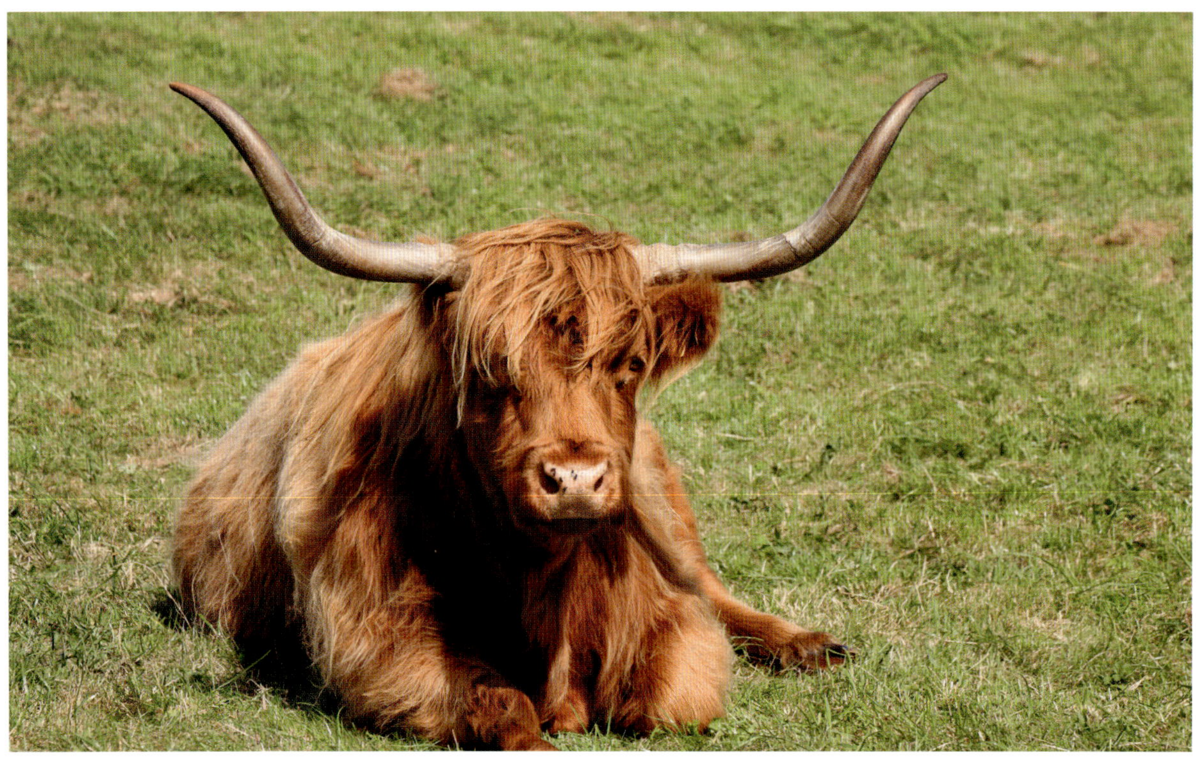

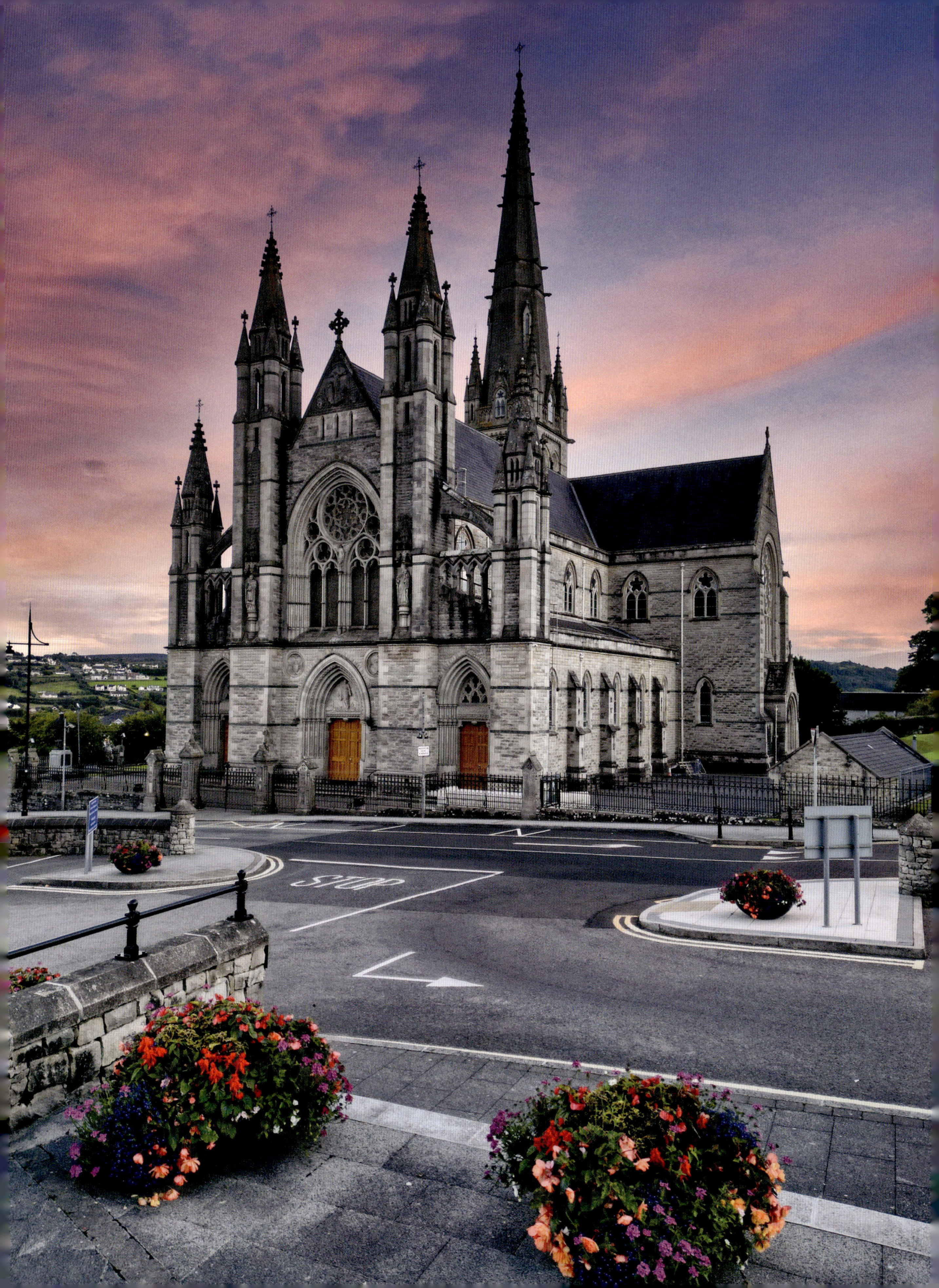

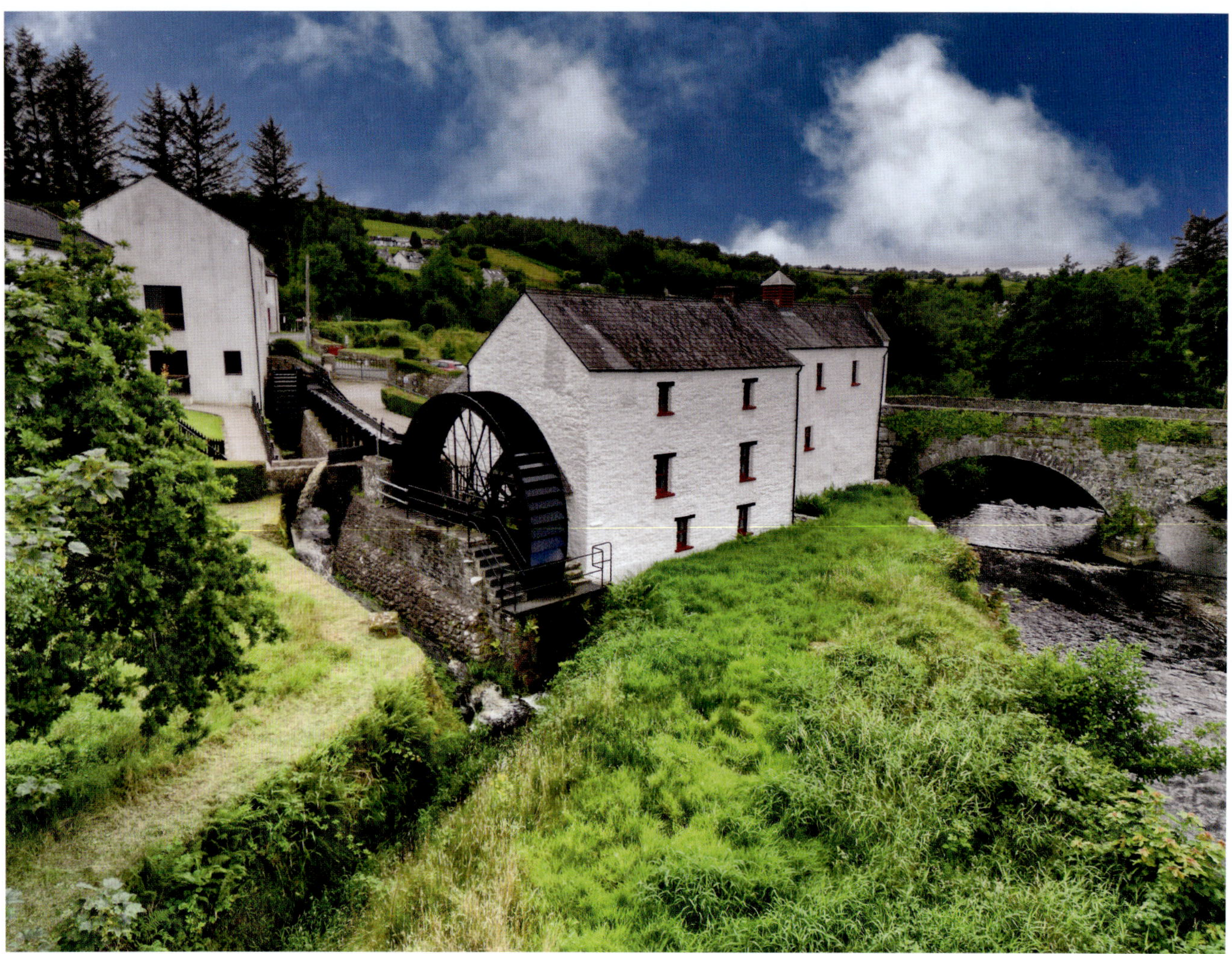

Newmills Corn and Flax Mills has one of the largest operating waterwheels in the country. The millrace is a kilometre long and powers two separate mill wheels, one for grinding oats and barley and the other for flax, which visitors can see in action on a guided tour.

Opposite, top: The ruins of Killydonnell Friary are to be found on the shores of Lough Swilly near Ramelton. It was a Franciscan friary, founded in 1471 by the ruling O'Donnell family. Old legend says that the bell of Killydonnell was stolen by raiders from Tyrone who then set out to sea with it in a small boat. When a sudden storm hit, both the crew and the bell were drowned. The bell is said to be heard tolling at midnight every seven years. If anyone hears it, they are doomed to die before the next time it rings, or so the legend goes.

Opposite, bottom: Autumn at Drummonaghan Woods, Ramelton.

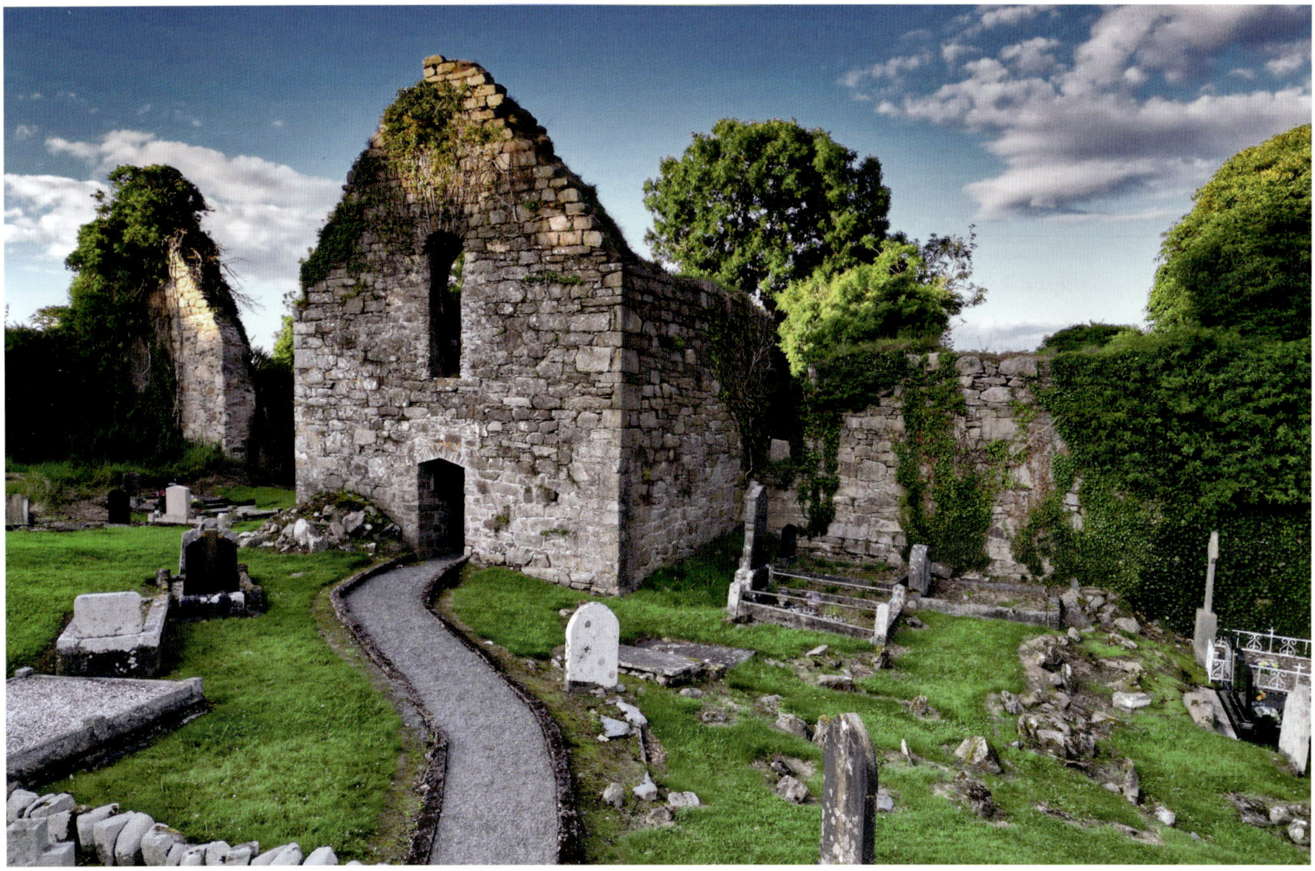

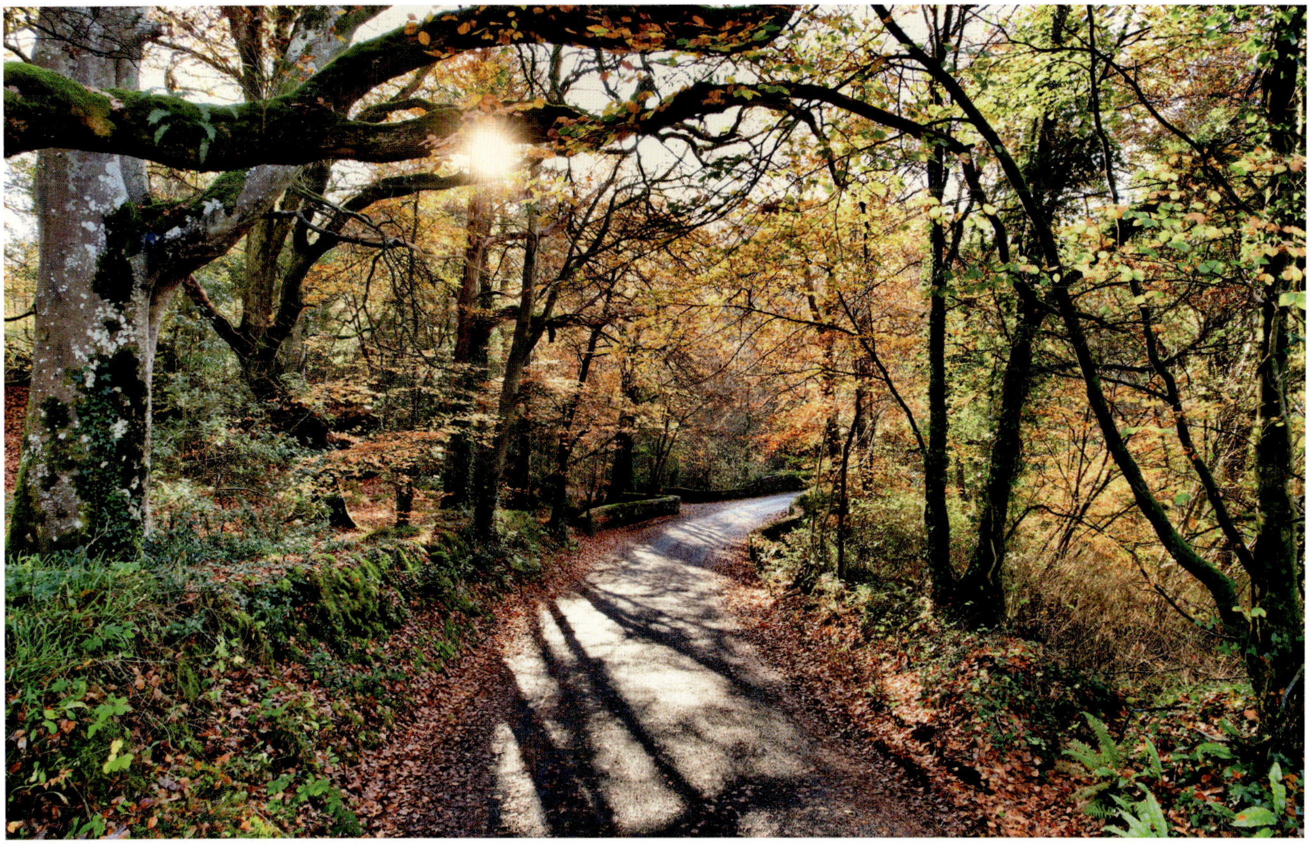

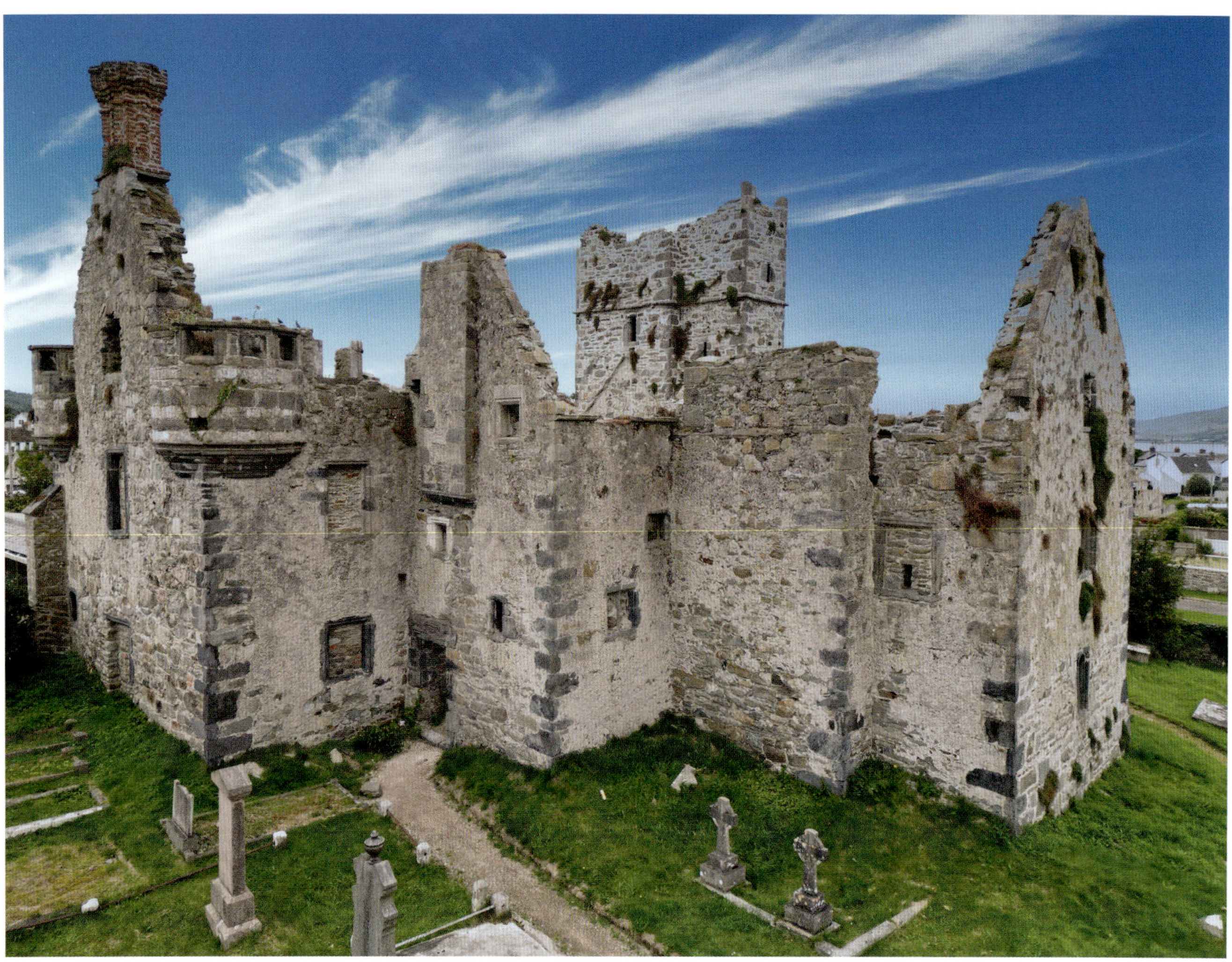

Rathmullan Abbey was a Carmelite foundation, built between 1508 and 1516. In 1601, it was used as a barracks and in 1617 it became the castle residence of the Protestant Bishop of Raphoe, Andrew Knox. The chancel was later used as the parish church until 1814, when it was abandoned.

Opposite: The seaside resort of Rathmullan, on the western shores of Lough Swilly, boasts a stretch of sandy beach measuring nearly three kilometres. It hosts a wide range of outdoor activities, with some of the finest sailing, fishing and sightseeing opportunities in the vicinity.

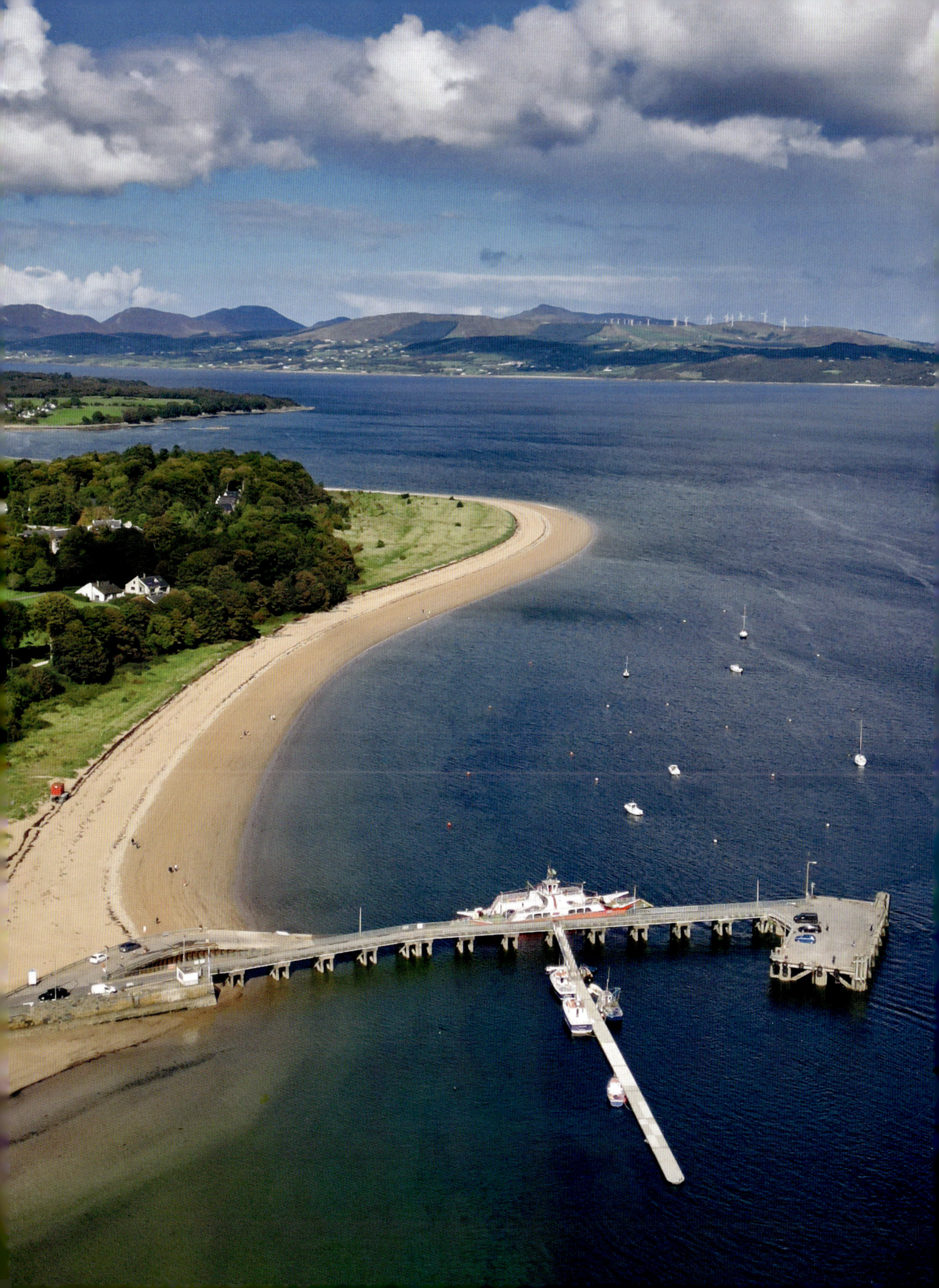

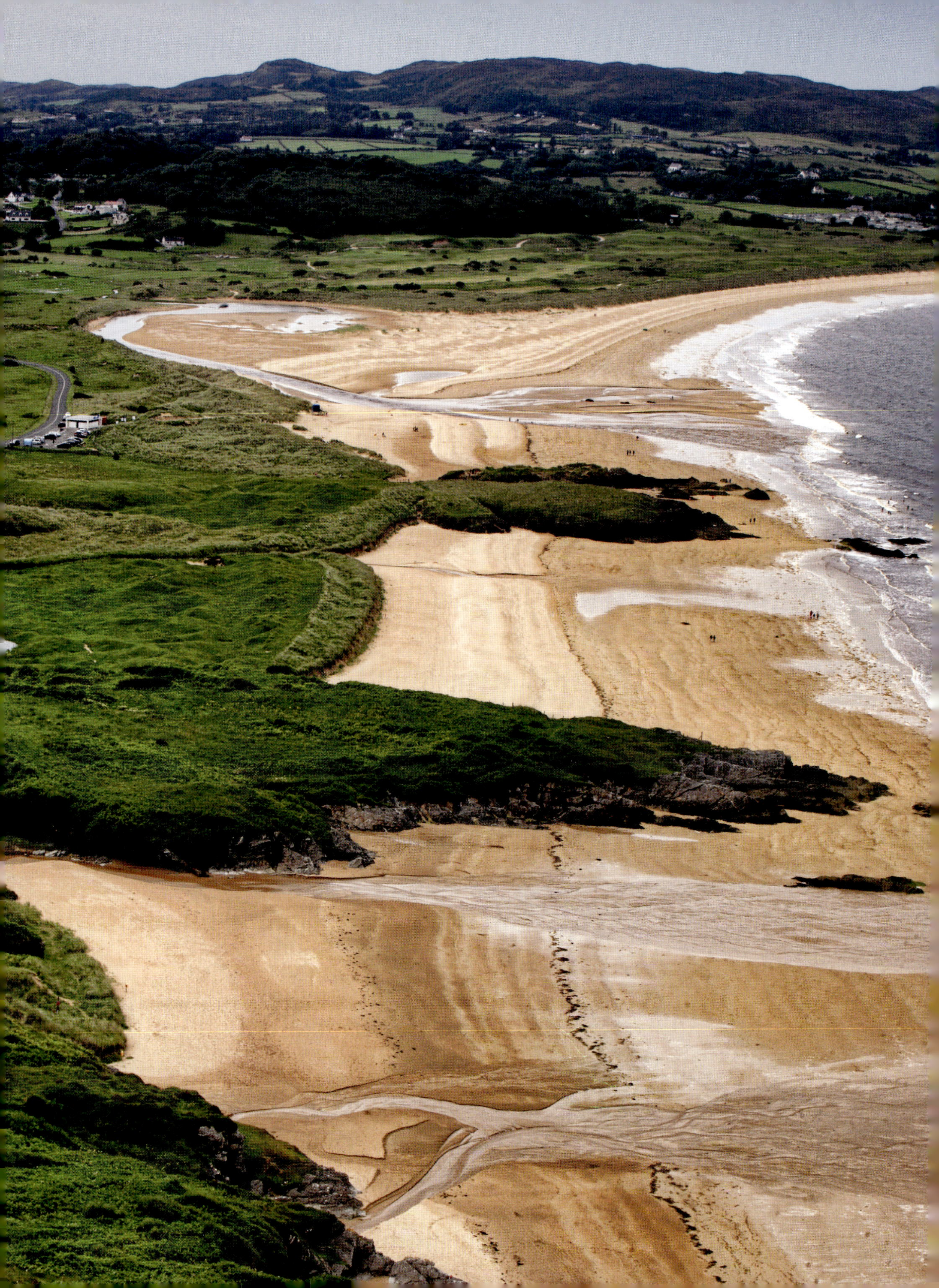

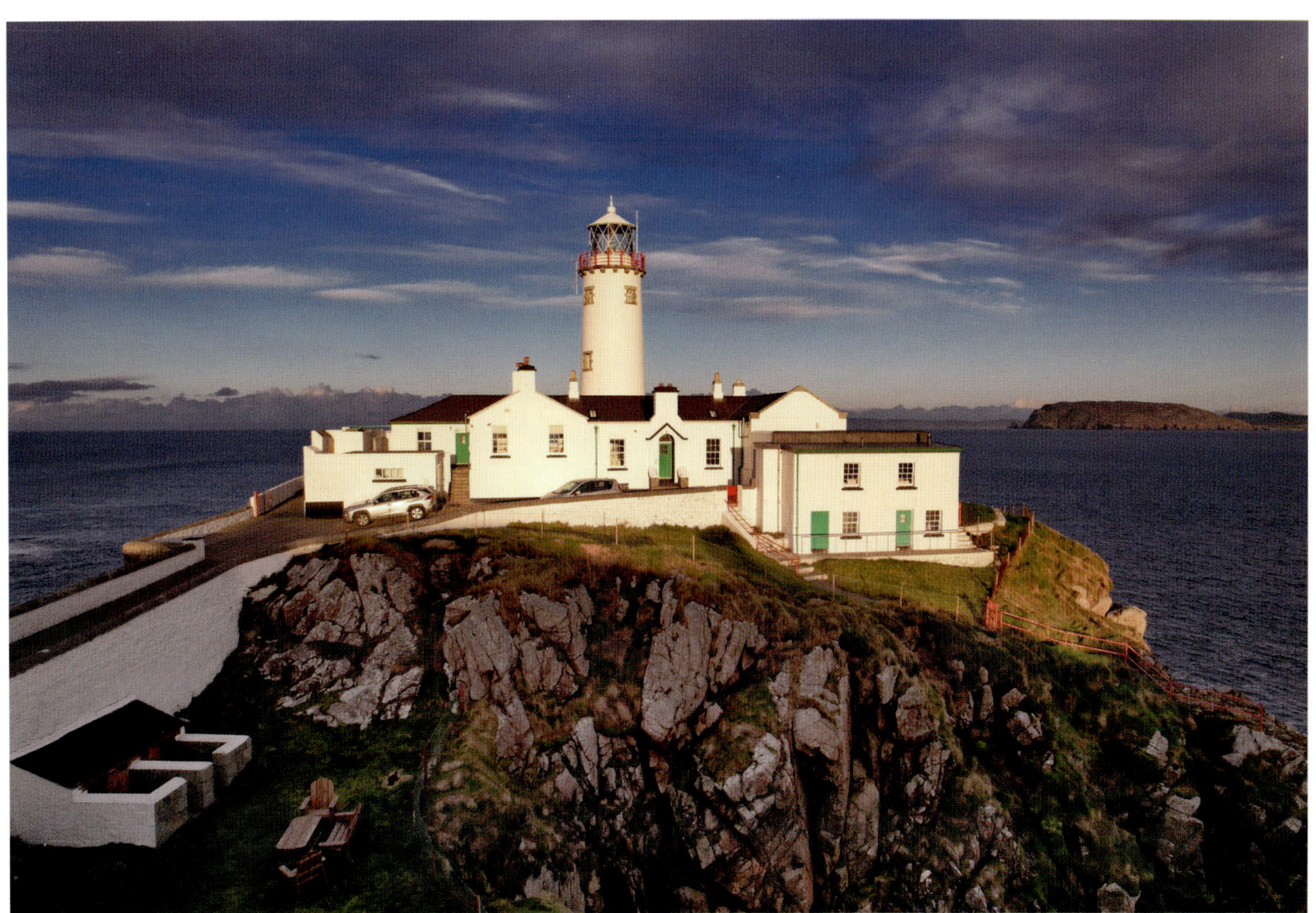

The iconic Fanad lighthouse was designed by civil engineer George Halpin and first lit on 17 March 1817. The construction of a light was called for following a tragedy in December 1811, when the frigate HMS *Saldanha* struck rocks near Fanad Head during a violent storm, with the loss of 250 crew.

Opposite: Ballymastocker Bay, also known as Portsalon Beach, is a spectacular crescent of long, sandy beach on the western shore of Lough Swilly. It stretches from Portsalon to the Knockalla Hills.

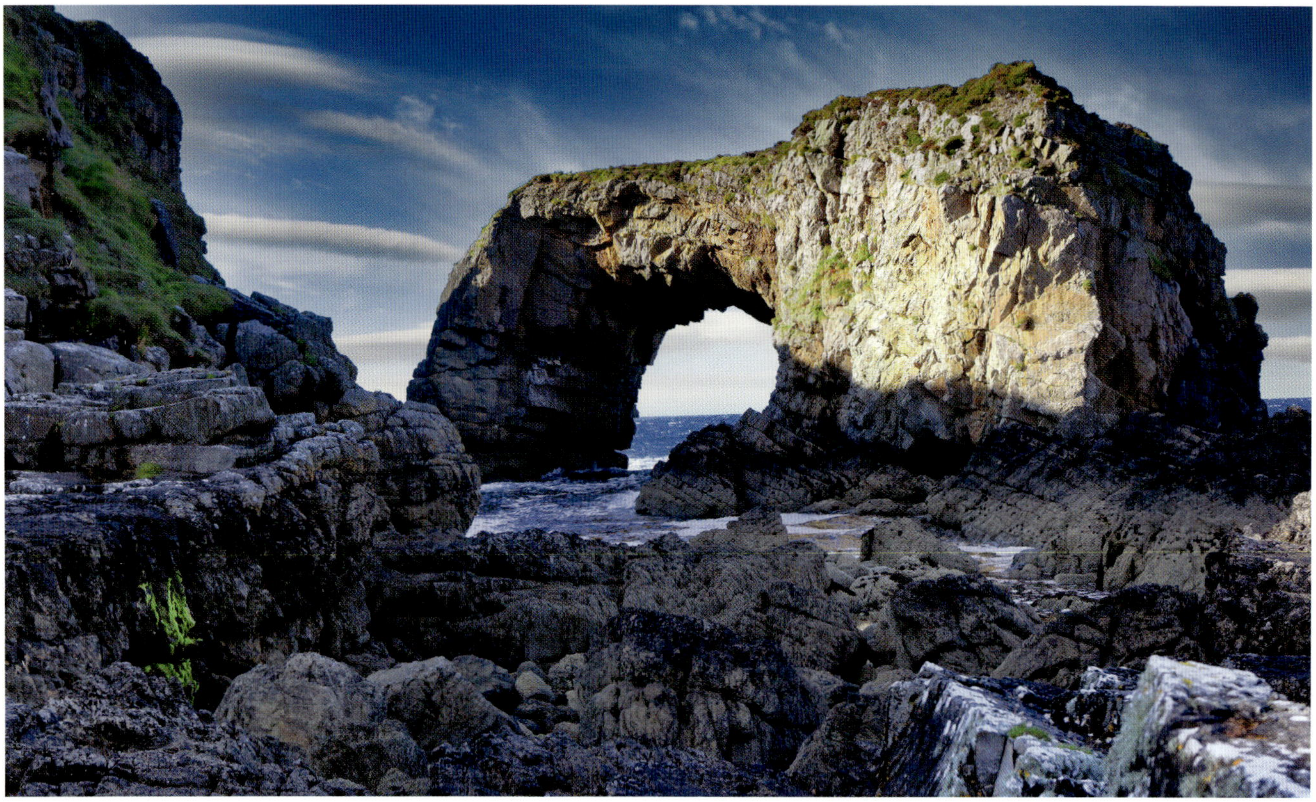

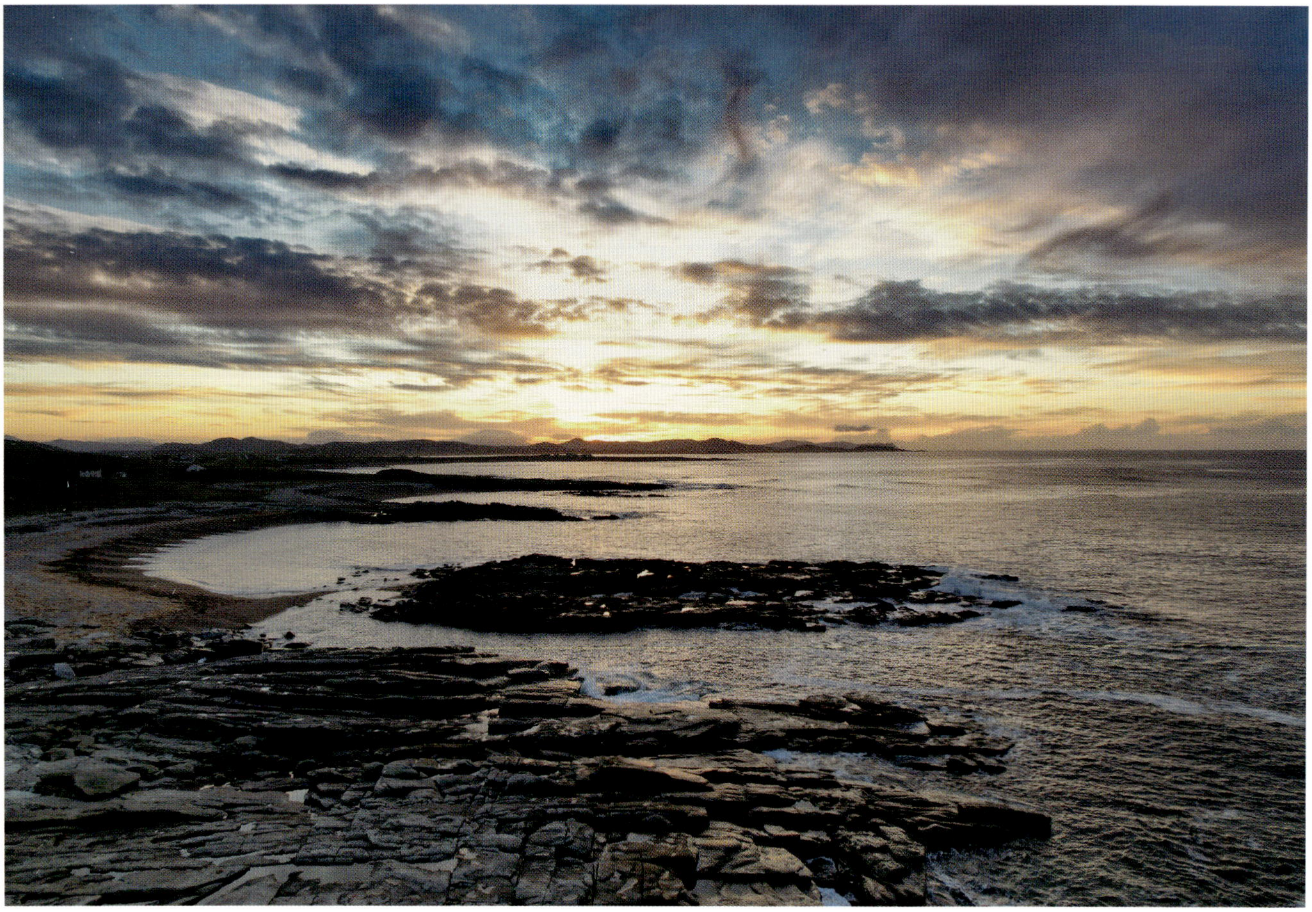

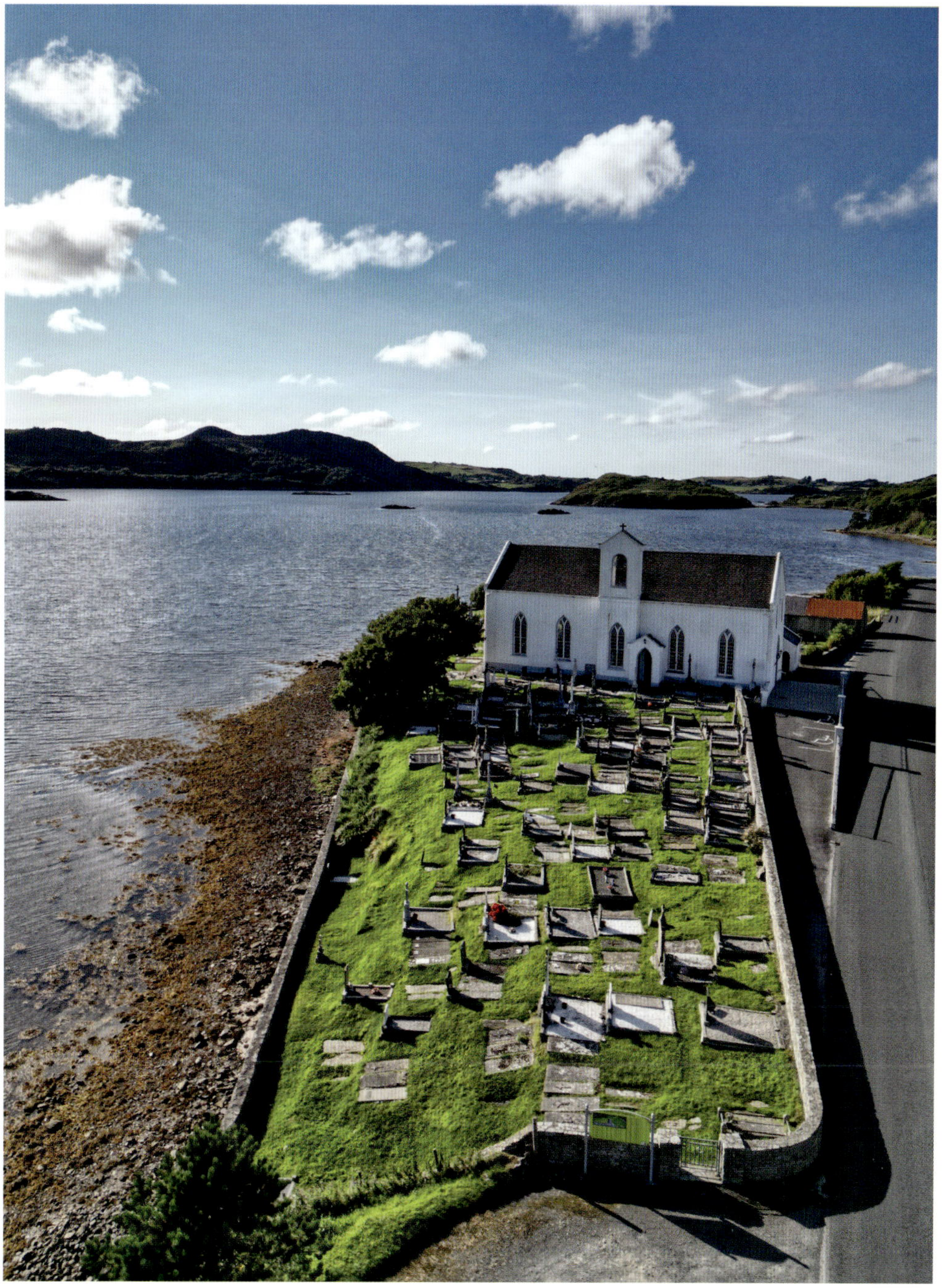

St Columba's Church at Massmount, Mulroy Bay, was built in the early 1780s. Around sixty years later, the original church was extended, reroofed and a bell tower erected. Wood for the roof was brought by raft from Araheera across Mulroy Bay and those same beams are still part of the roof, over 180 years on. It's the perfect example of peace and tranquillity. Croaghan Island is visible directly behind it.

Opposite, top: Great Pollet Arch on Fanad Head is Ireland's largest sea arch.

Opposite, bottom: Ballyhiernan Beach stretches for over two kilometres, sandwiched between sand dunes and the Atlantic. It's a popular spot for surfers.

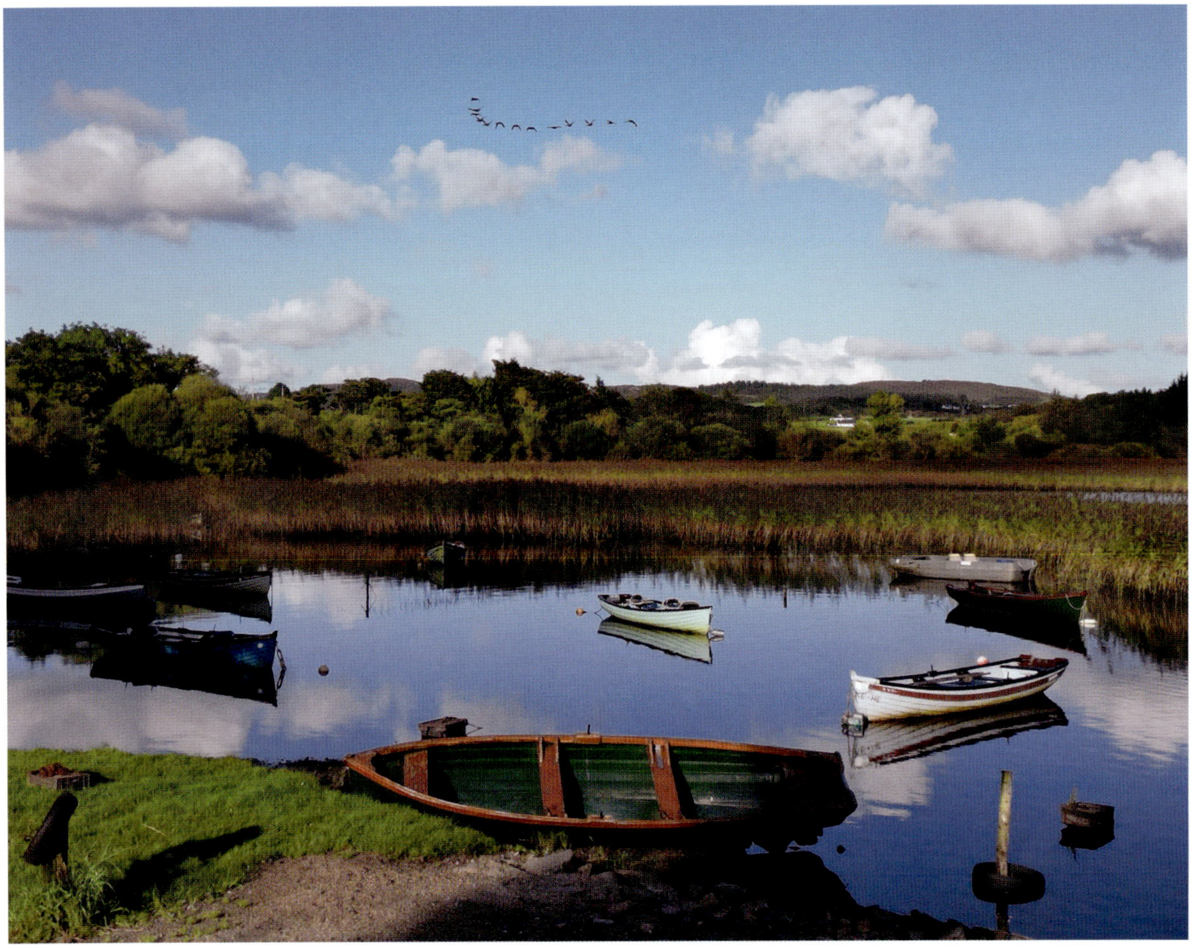

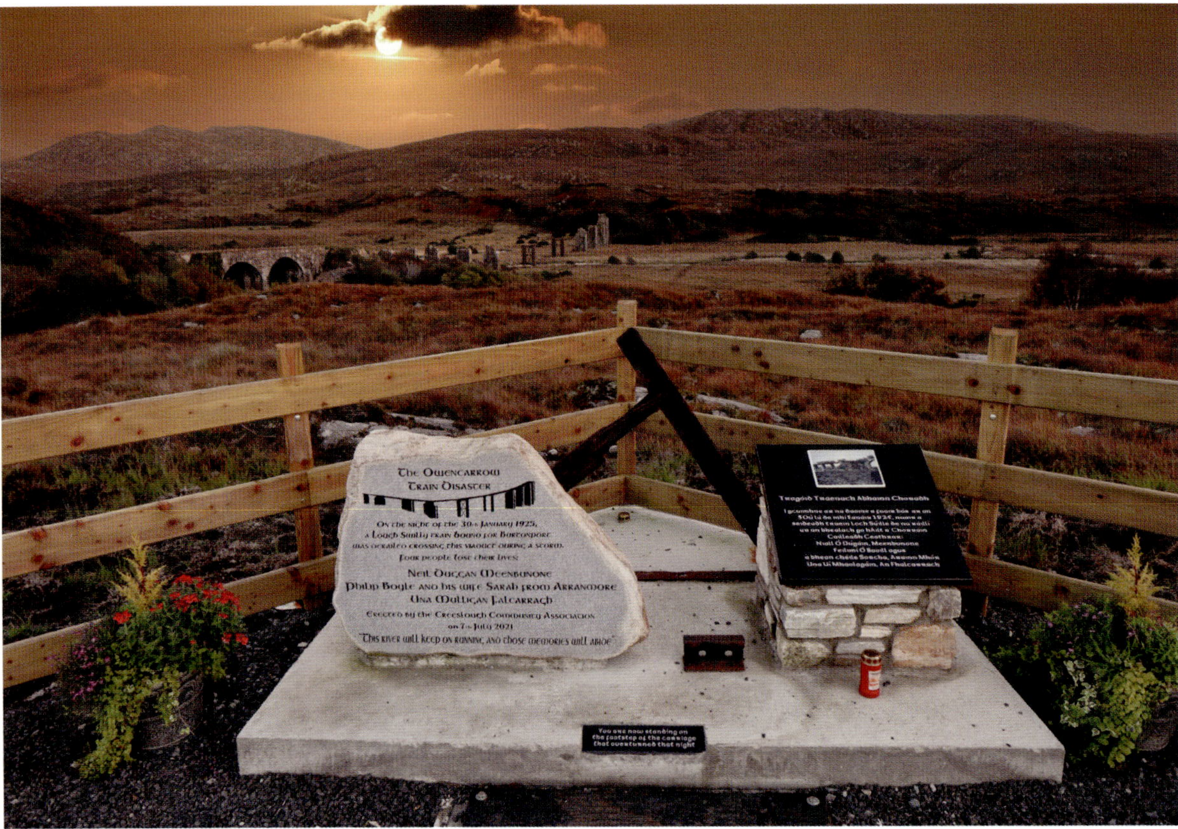

The Owencarrow
Train Disaster

On the night of the 30th January 1925,
a Lough Swilly train bound for Burtonport
was derailed crossing this viaduct during a storm.
Four people lost their lives:

Neil Duggan Meenbunone
Philip Boyle and his wife Sarah from Arranmore
Una Mulligan Falcarragh

Erected by the Creeslough Community Association
on 7th July 2021

"This river will keep on running, and those memories will abide"

Tragóid Traenach Abhainn Chraoibh

I gcuimhne ar na daoine a fuair bás ar an
30ú lá de mhí Eanáir 1926, nuair a
raibeadh traein Loch Súilí ar na railí
ar an bhealach go hAit a' Chorráin
Ceithre Cheathrar:
Niall Ó Dúgáin, Meenbunone
Feilimí Ó Baoill agus
a bhean chéile Sorcha, Árainn Mhór
Úna Uí Mhaolagáin, An Fhalcarrach

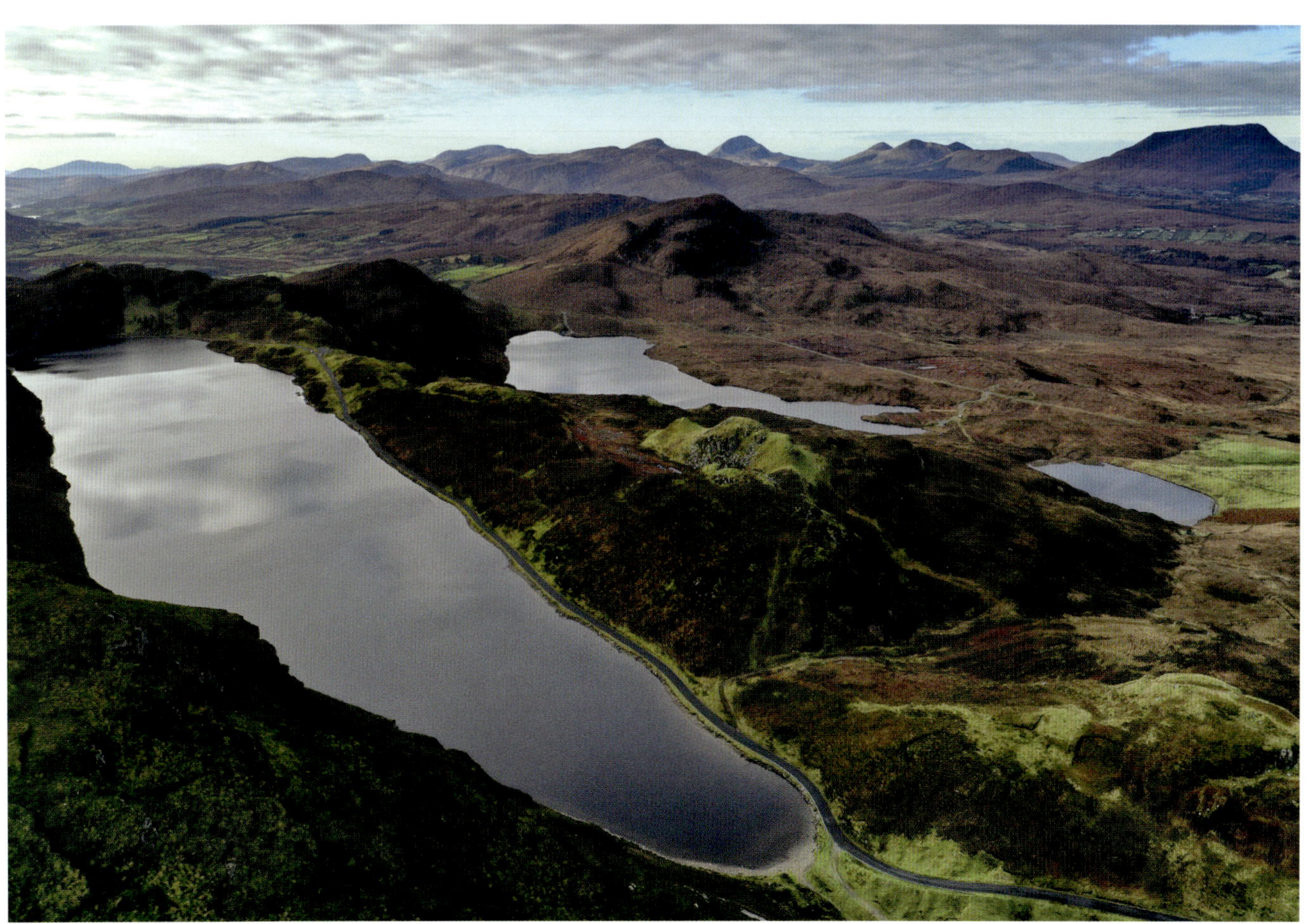

Lough Salt is a long, narrow mountain lake, set in a stunning landscape of valleys and hills, with the Derryveagh Mountains in the distance.

Opposite, top: Lough Fern, south of Milford, is a popular fishing spot, containing brown trout, salmon, three-spined stickleback, perch and the critically endangered European eel. Part of the Leannan River Special Area of Conservation, it is home to Milford & District Angling Club. At its northern end are two islands, one of which is a crannóg.

Opposite, bottom: The monument to the Owencarrow Disaster, the worst accident in the history of the Lough Swilly Railway. In a terrifying incident in January 1925, high winds blew two carriages of a Burtonport-bound train off the Owencarrow Viaduct. Several passengers were tossed out of the damaged carriages in the accident and four perished.

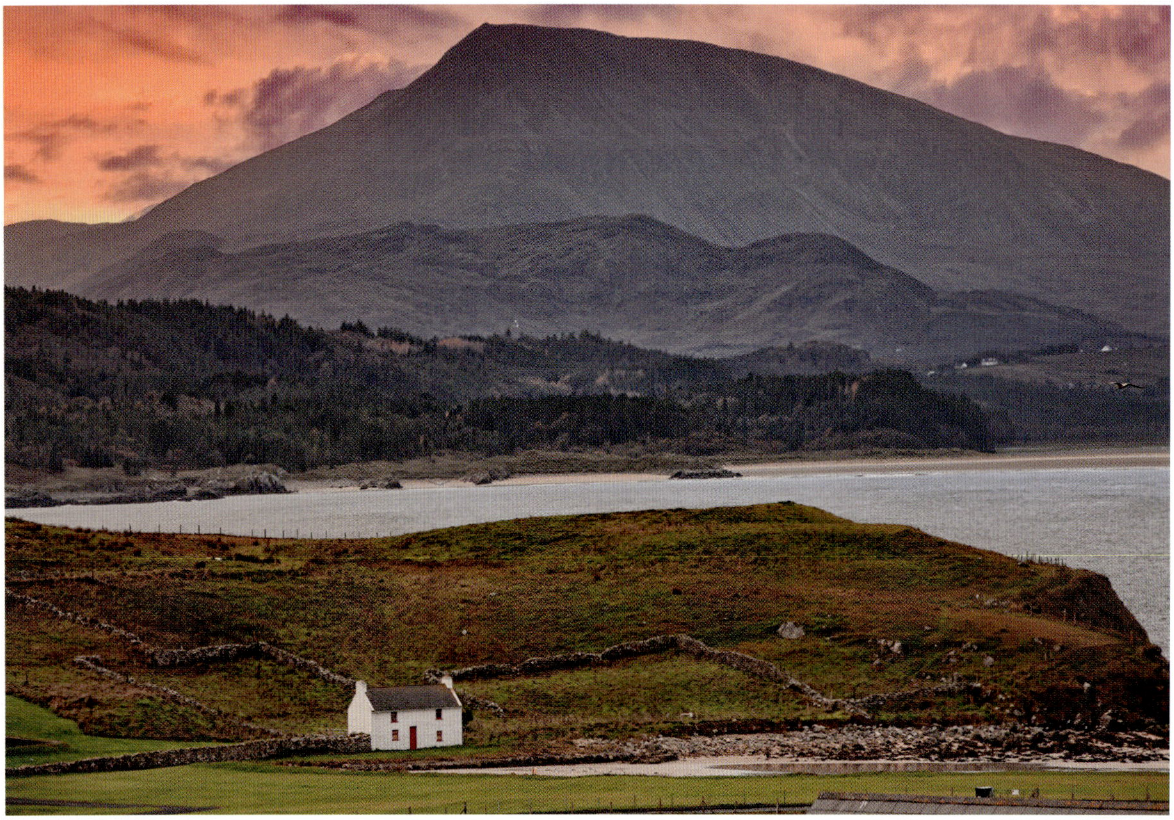

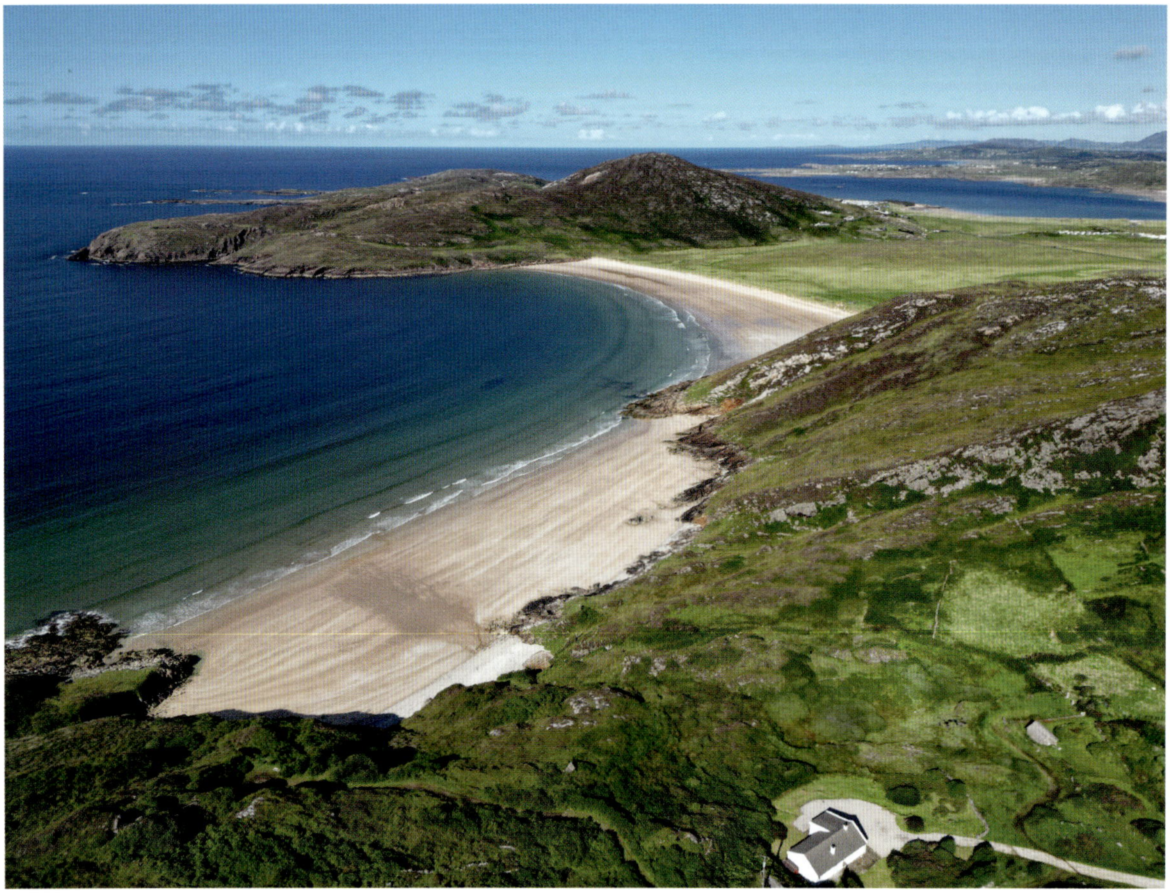

Opposite, top: A picture-perfect whitewashed cottage at the southern end of Tra Beg Beach, in Downings, with the unmistakable outline of Muckish Mountain in the background.

Opposite, bottom: Trá na Rossan Bay, Rosguill, Downings.

Dooey is one of the most secluded and picturesque little coves on the Rosguill Peninsula near Downings. In the distance is the towering Horn Head.

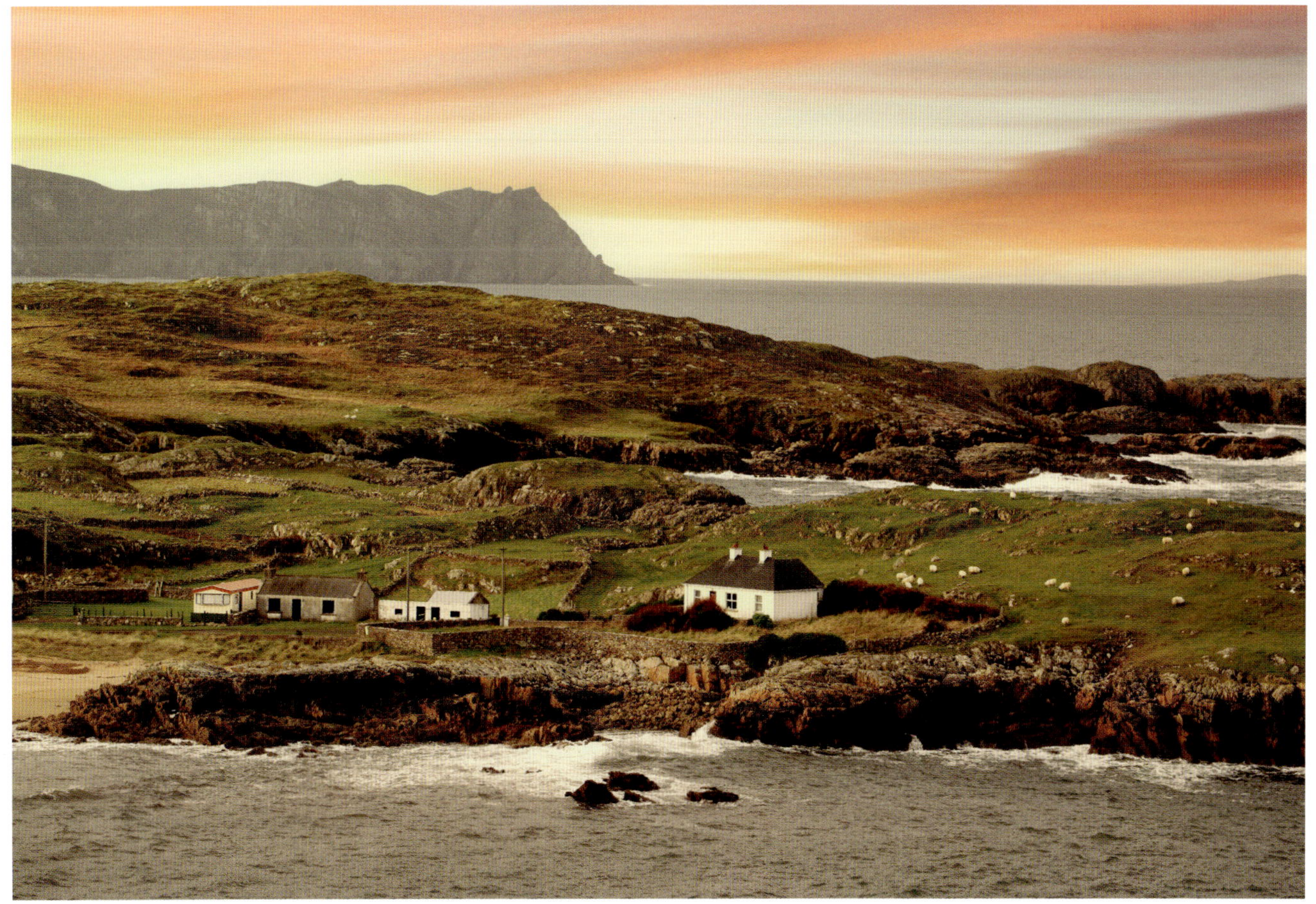

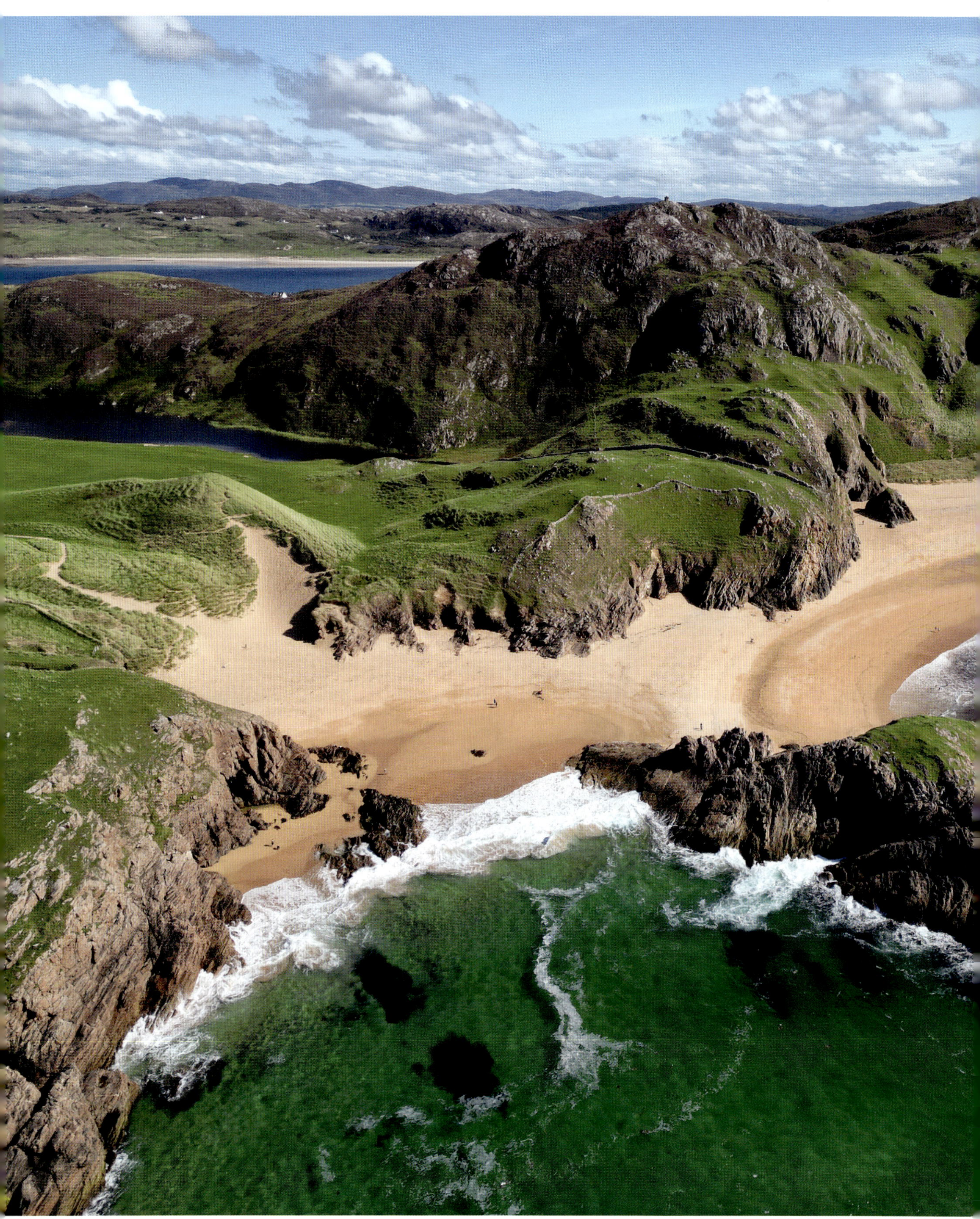

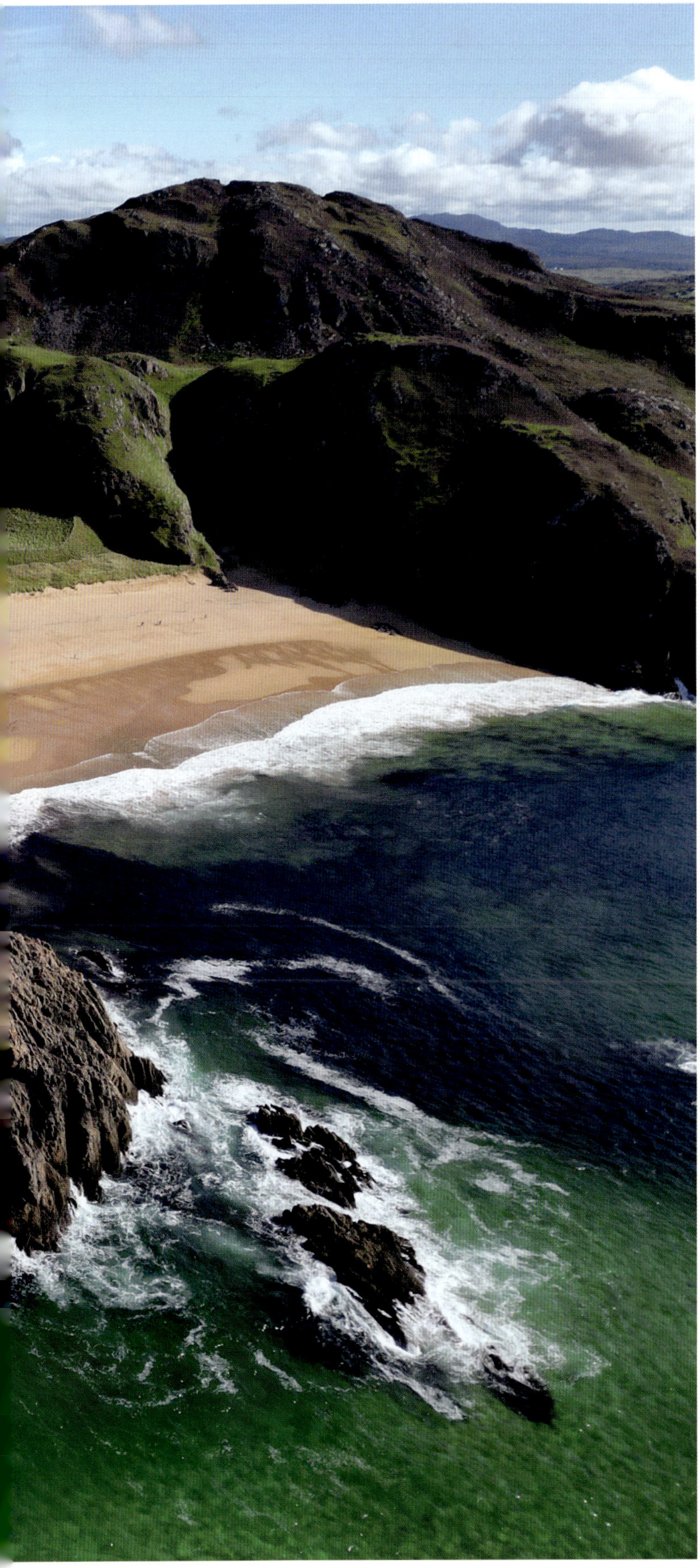

Left: Boyeeghter Bay, also known as Murder Hole Beach, is on the western side of Melmore Head on the Rosguill Peninsula. Nestled between towering cliffs, with a breathtaking expanse of golden sands, crystal-clear waters, caves, coves and dunes, the allure of this coastal gem lies in its unspoiled nature. When the tide is in there are two beaches. Rough Island is the small island fifteen metres (fifty feet) offshore. Swimming is not advised here.

Below: Looking out from a cave onto Murder Hole Beach.

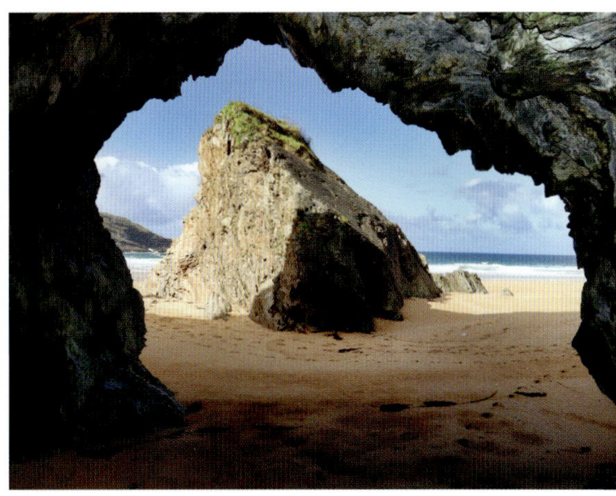

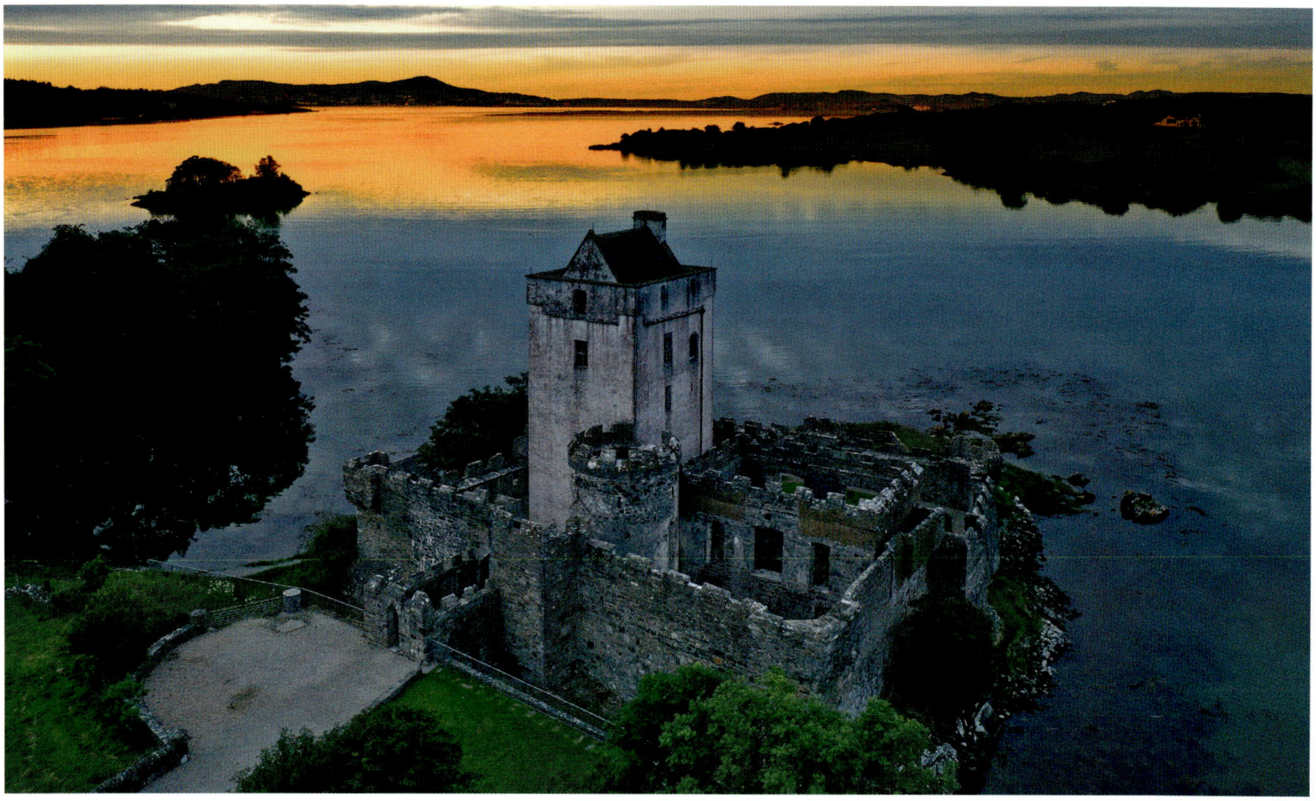

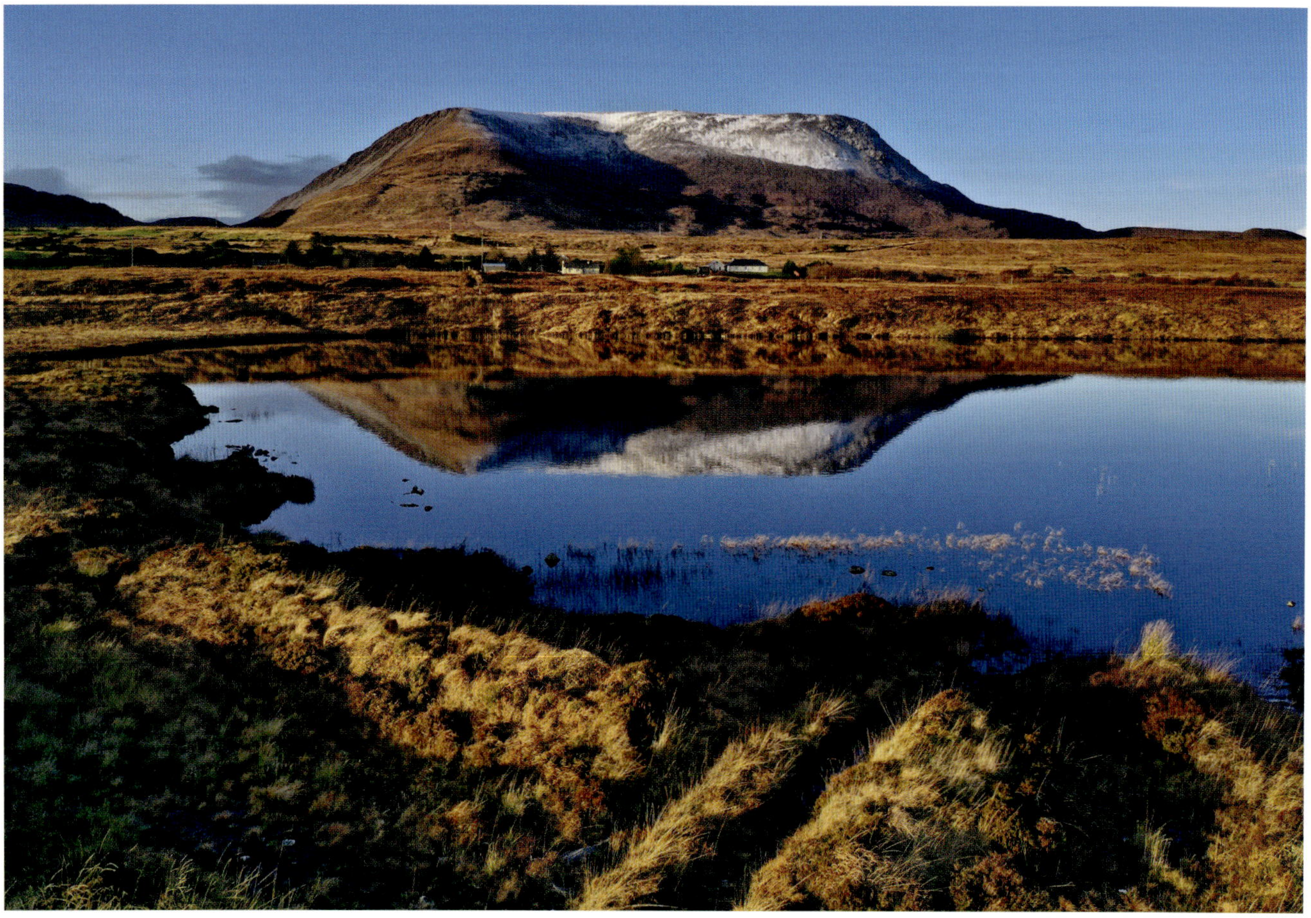

Opposite, top: The spectacularly sited fifteenth-century Doe Castle at Sheephaven Bay, near Creeslough village. For almost two centuries it was a stronghold of the MacSweeney clan, who were originally from Scotland. Now in the care of the Office of Public Works, it is open to visitors.

Opposite, bottom: Muckish Mountain, one of the Seven Sisters chain in the Derryveagh Mountains, is 667.1 metres (2,188 feet) high. The mountain gets its name from the Irish 'mhucais', meaning 'pig's back'. In any other area, this distinctive mountain would be an iconic landmark but with Errigal just a few miles away, Muckish tends to be overlooked.

This tiny stone bridge in the Gaeltacht district of Cloghaneely near Muckish Mountain is known locally as Droichead na nDeor ('the Bridge of Tears'). During the nineteenth century, Donegal people emigrating to Britain, America and Australia crossed this bridge on their way to the port of Derry. Their friends and families would accompany them to this spot, from where they carried on alone, hence the name.

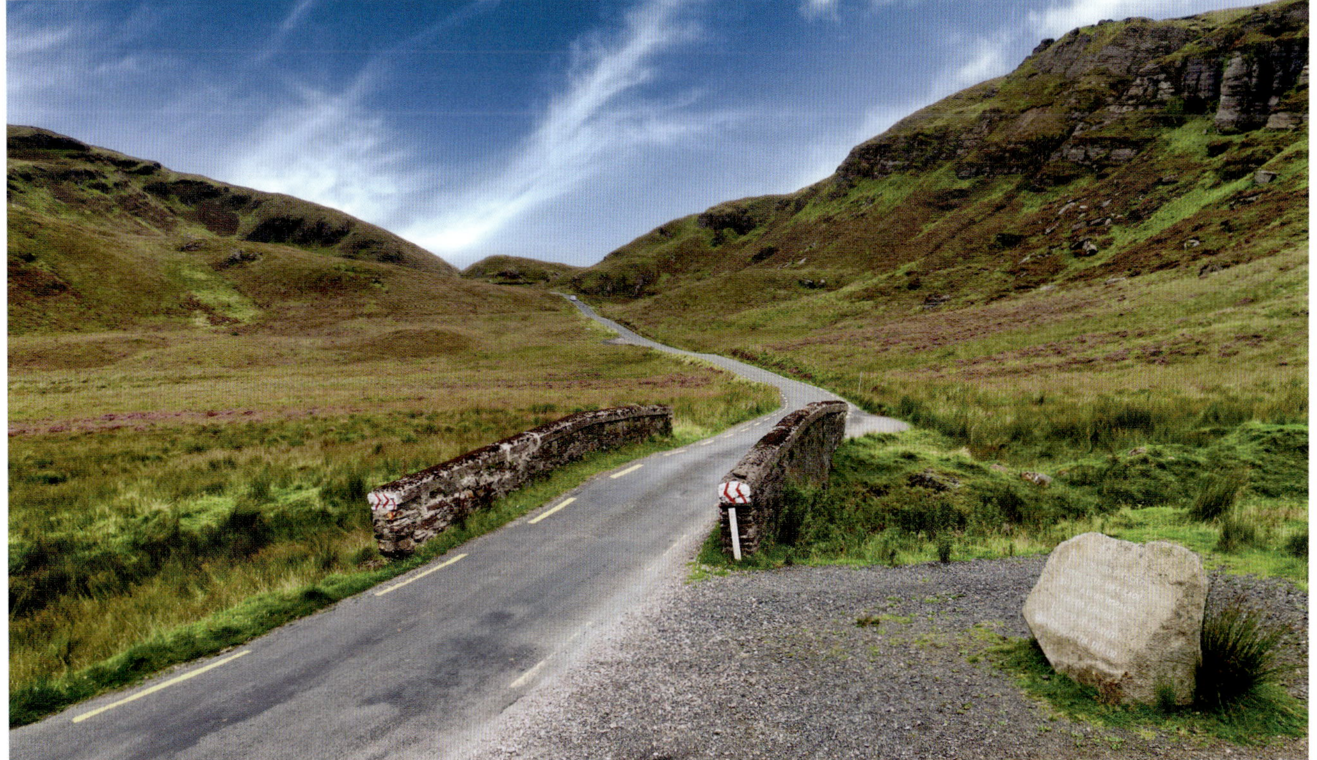

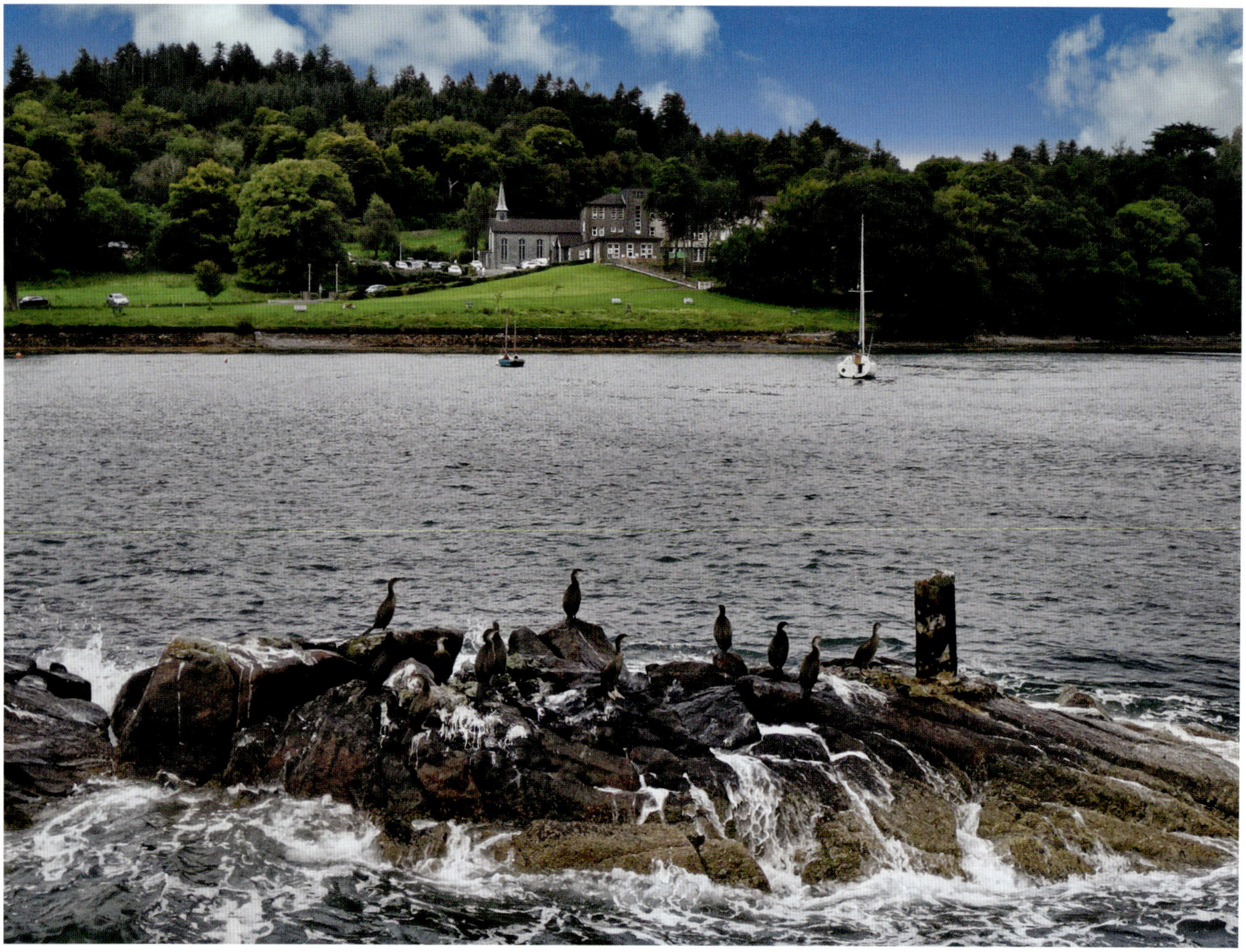

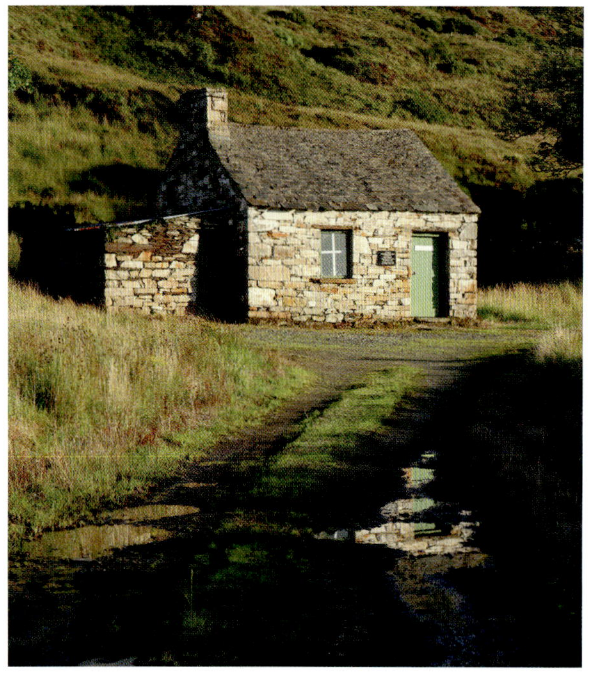

Above: Ards Friary on Sheephaven Bay backs onto Ards Forest Park, which offers several marked trails, graded from short to strenuous. The wetland trail around Master John's Marsh is a beautiful short walk, while the coastal walks include sandy shores, grassy dunes, cliffs, salt marshes and secret coves.

Left: Noreen Bawn's Cottage, the childhood home in Creeslough of Bridget Gallagher, who died in 1927, aged twenty-three, after returning home from America. The song 'Noreen Bawn' was inspired by her life and death, and the house has been restored with the help of local people.

Opposite: Lady Isabella's Beach, north of Ards Friary, has an almost tropical feel. Perfect for paddling, but swimming is not advised.

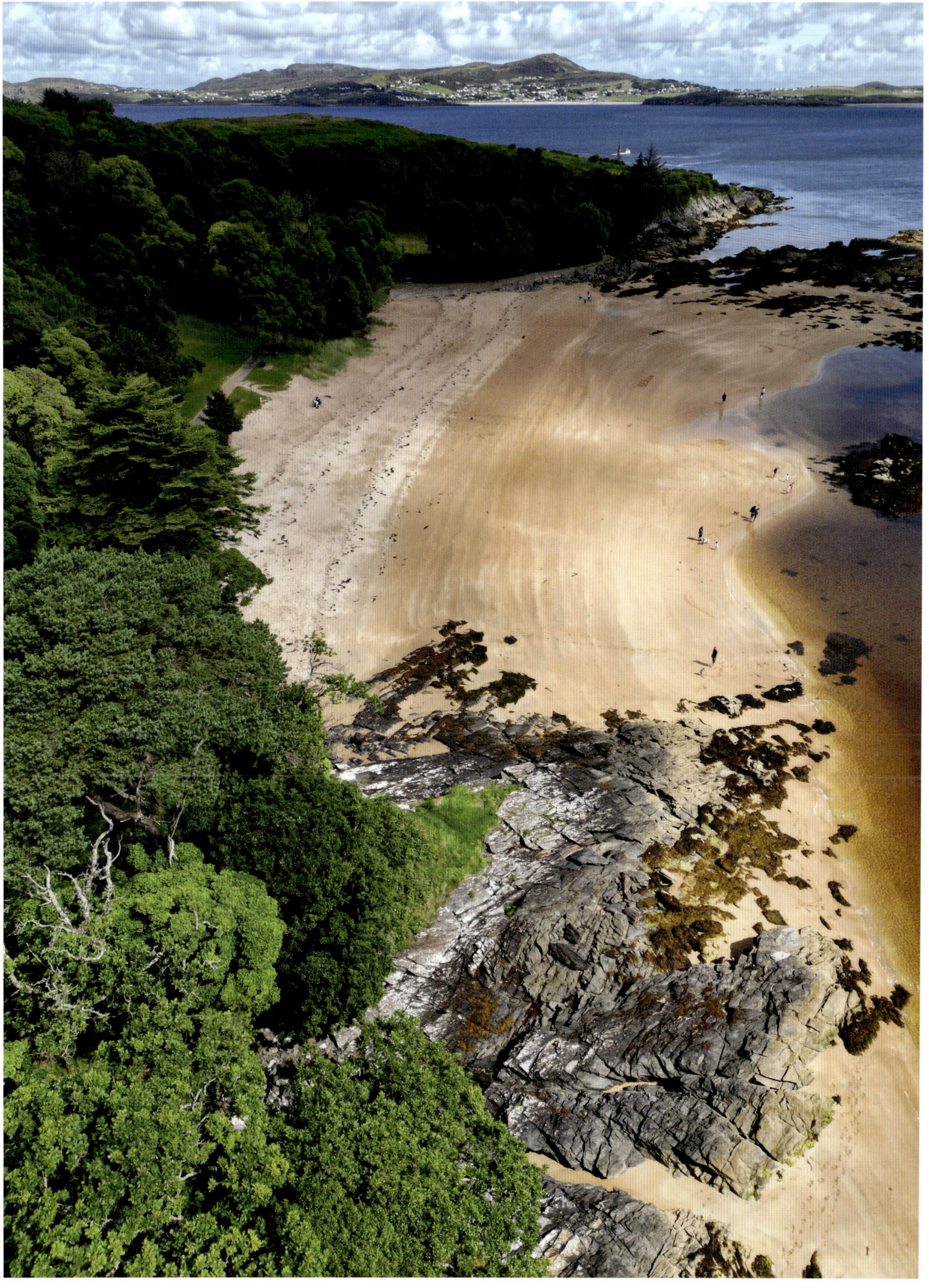

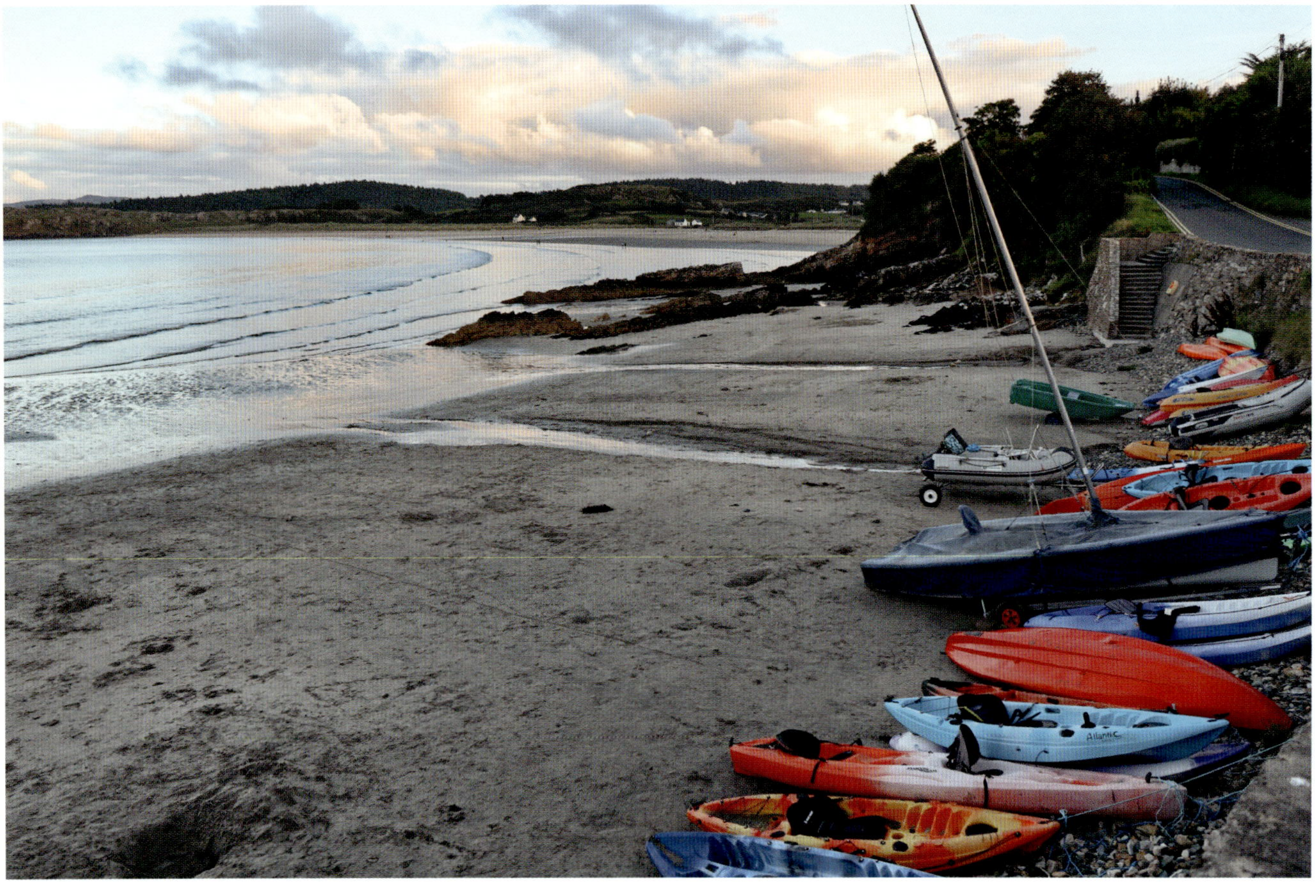

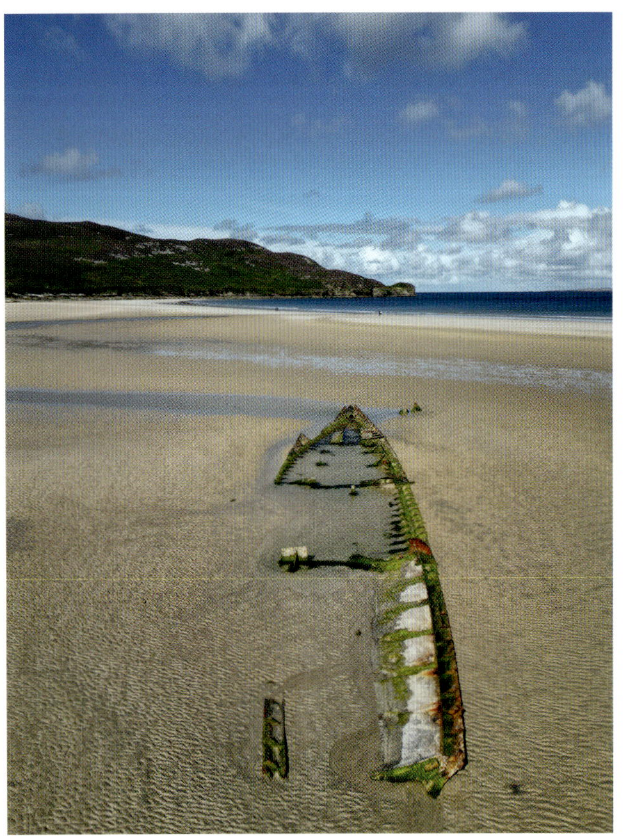

Top: The sand dunes surrounding Marble Hill Beach are rich in wildlife. Even the corncrake can be heard here occasionally.

Left: At low tide on Killahoey Beach at Dunfanaghy, the wreck of a steam trawler, the *Dinas FD63*, can be seen. The ship was stranded here on 4 December 1936.

Opposite: The steep cliffs on the Horn Head peninsula tower 180 metres (600 feet) above the Atlantic. Designated a Special Protection Area and a Special Area of Conservation, the cliffs are home to colonies of breeding seabirds, including puffin, shag, guillemot and razorbill. (Note that the weather here can change extremely quickly, and it is a dangerous place to be when mist rolls in, especially if you have no navigational experience.)

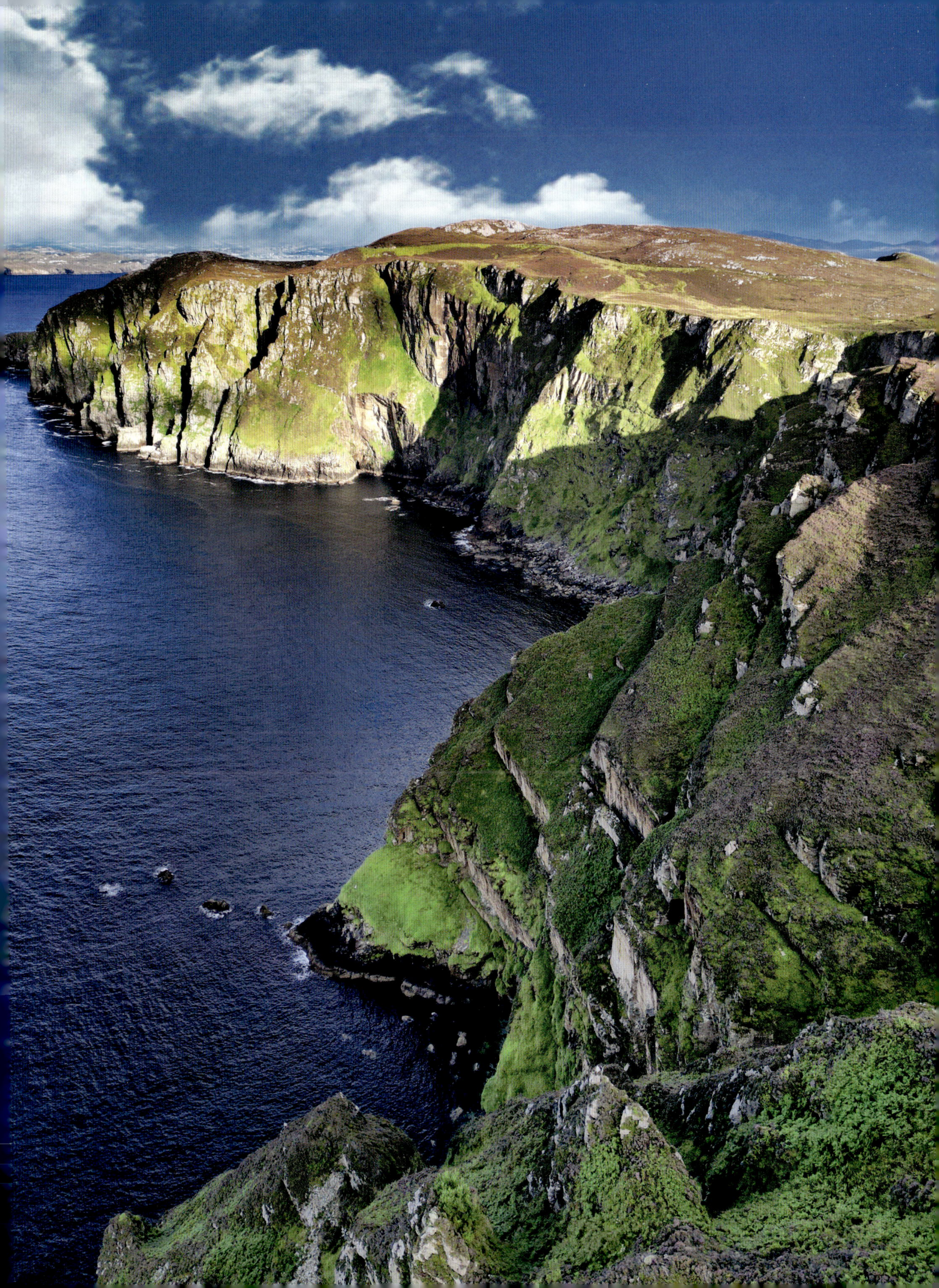

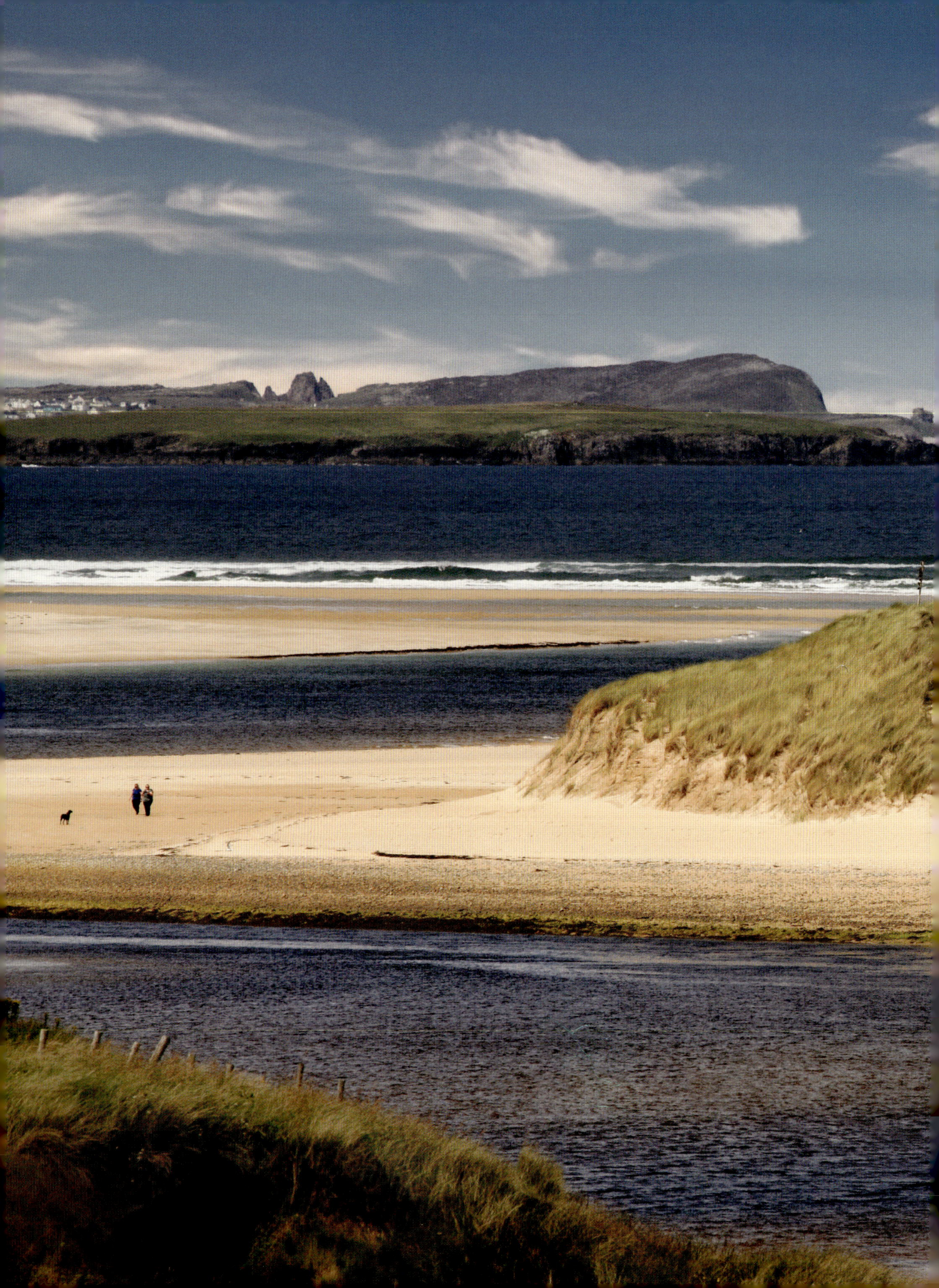

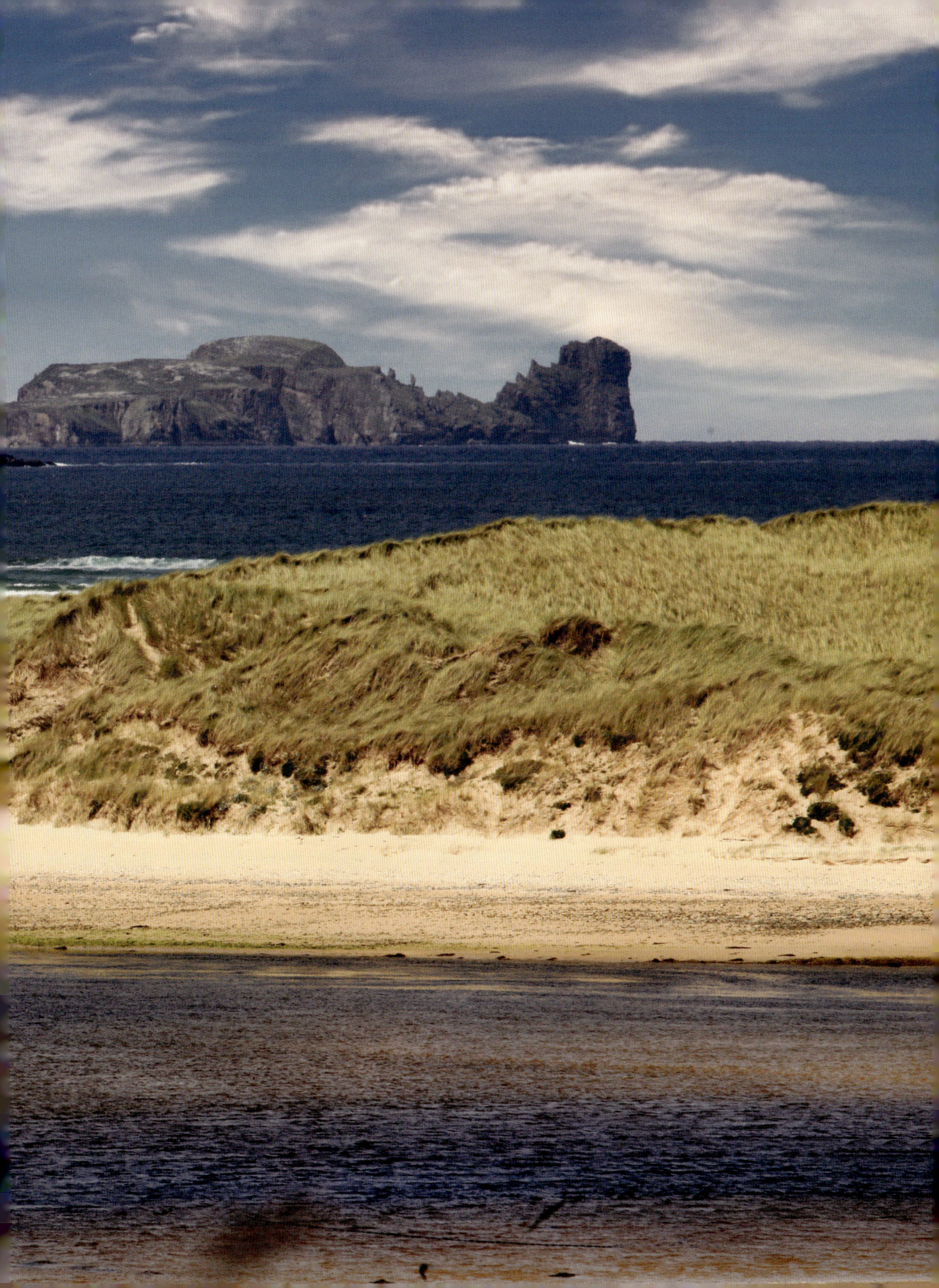

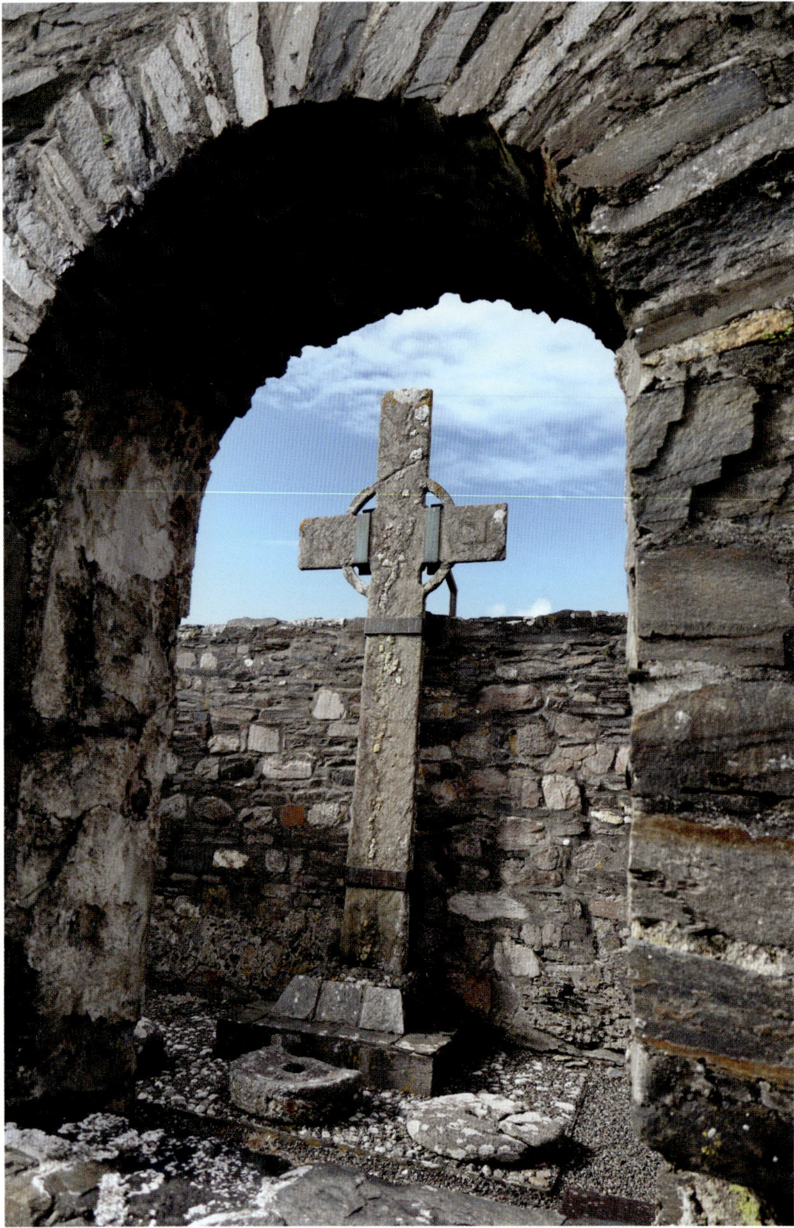

Inside the ruins of Ray Church stands an early medieval high cross, possibly dating to the eighth century. Locally known as St Colmcille's Cross, legend says it was cut from a single solid rock on the side of Muckish Mountain. The cross was damaged during a storm in 1750. It was repaired in the 1970s and strapped to the interior wall of the church.

Opposite: Tramore Strand at Dunfanaghy is a two-kilometre stretch of golden sand backed by rolling hills, with Muckish Mountain further beyond inland. It is a secluded spot and is accessible only on foot across sand dunes from the bridge on the west side of Dunfanaghy, a thirty-minute walk. As with many of Donegal's beaches, swimming is not advised here.

Previous pages: Drumnatinny Beach at Falcarragh offers miles of sandy beach and uninterrupted views across the sea to the offshore islands of Inishbofin, Inishdooey and Inishbeg, and the vertical cliffs on Tory Island in the distance.

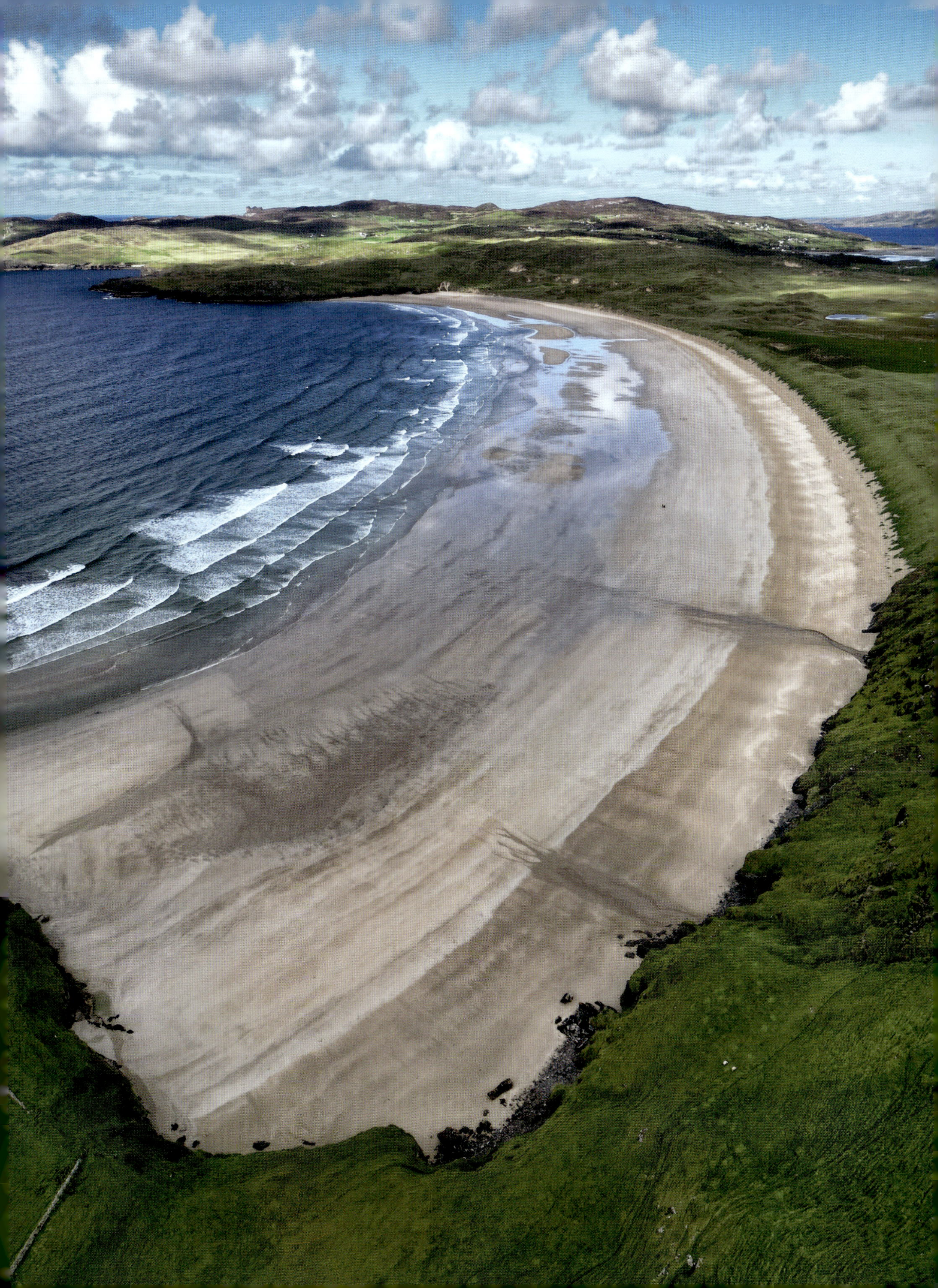

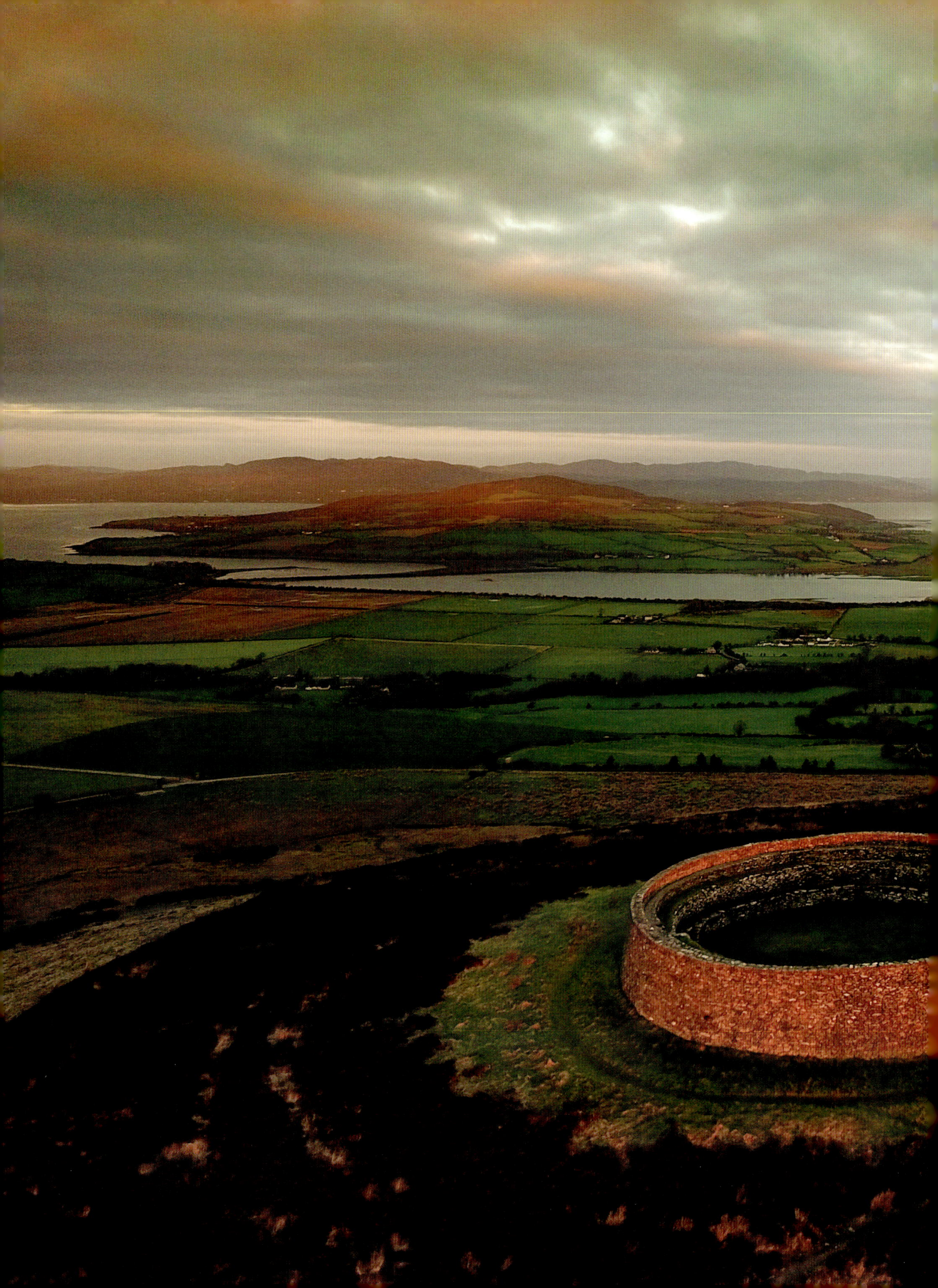

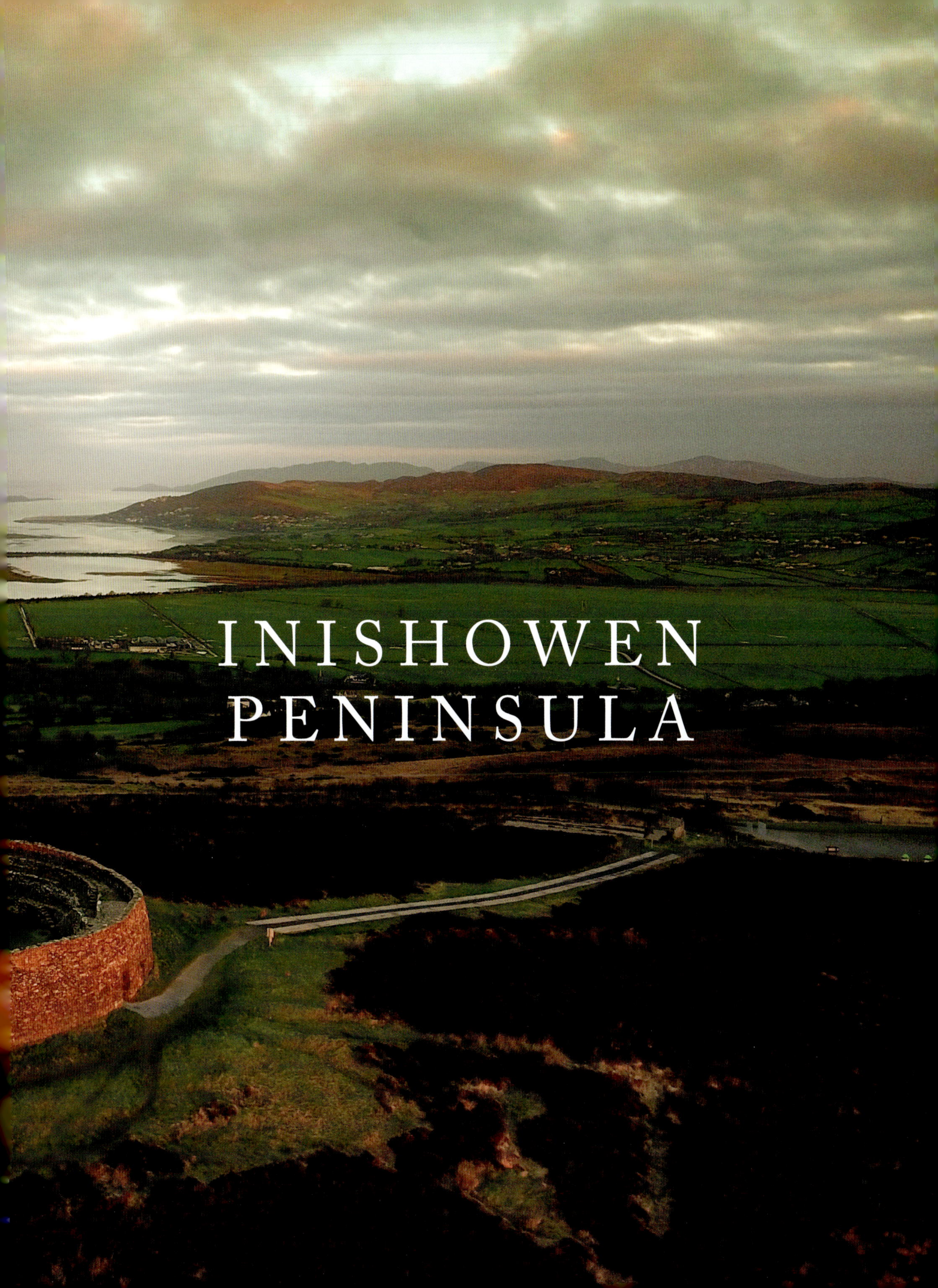
INISHOWEN
PENINSULA

The Inishowen Peninsula holds the northernmost point on the island of Ireland, Malin Head. The peninsula comprises a landscape of superb beaches, especially Kinnego Bay, Culdaff, Tullagh and Pollan, as well as the central mountain range, with towering Slieve Snaght at the middle.

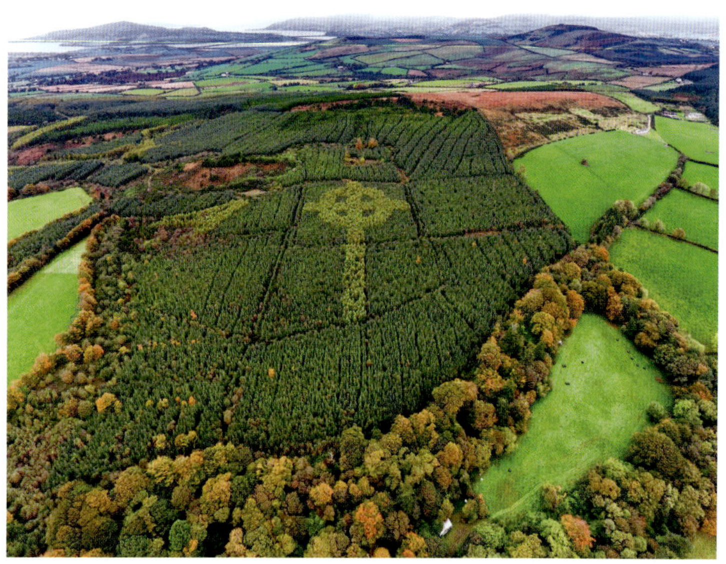

Previous pages: The Grianán of Aileach is a restored stone fort or cashel on the summit of Greenan Hill and commands wonderful views along Lough Swilly, Lough Foyle and Inch Island to the north. The name translates as 'Stony Palace of the Sun'. The fort was probably constructed in the late eighth or early ninth century AD as the capital of the Cenél nEógain, kings of this part of Ulster. In 904 and 939, Aileach was plundered by the Vikings. The final destruction of Aileach took place in 1101 at the hands of the army of Muirchertach Ua Briain, King of Munster. The lintel-covered entrance in the cashel leads into an interior enclosed by a wall that rises in three terraces and is accessible by inset stairways.

Above: Emery Celtic Cross at Bogay Hill, Killea near Newtowncunningham. This cross was spotted in 2016 by air passengers flying over Donegal. Local forester Liam Emery planted Japanese larch trees amongst surrounding evergreens before his death in 2010. The larches are similar in colour to the evergreens for much of the year, but their leaves turn a beautiful shade of gold in autumn, and the cross appears.

Opposite: The unique award-winning St Aengus' Catholic Church in Burt was built in 1967, designed by local architect Liam McCormick, who took inspiration from the circular shape of the Grianán of Aileach.

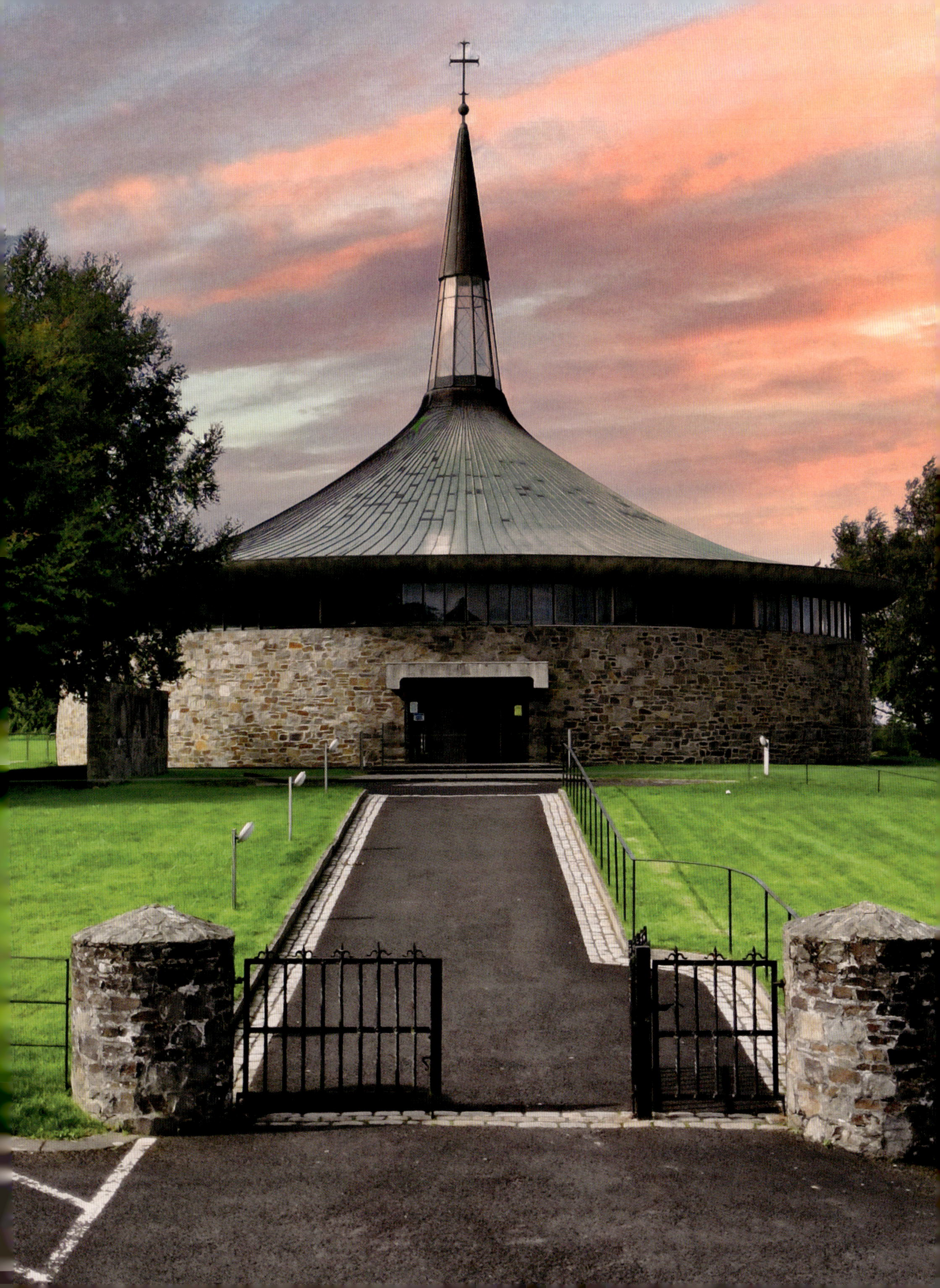

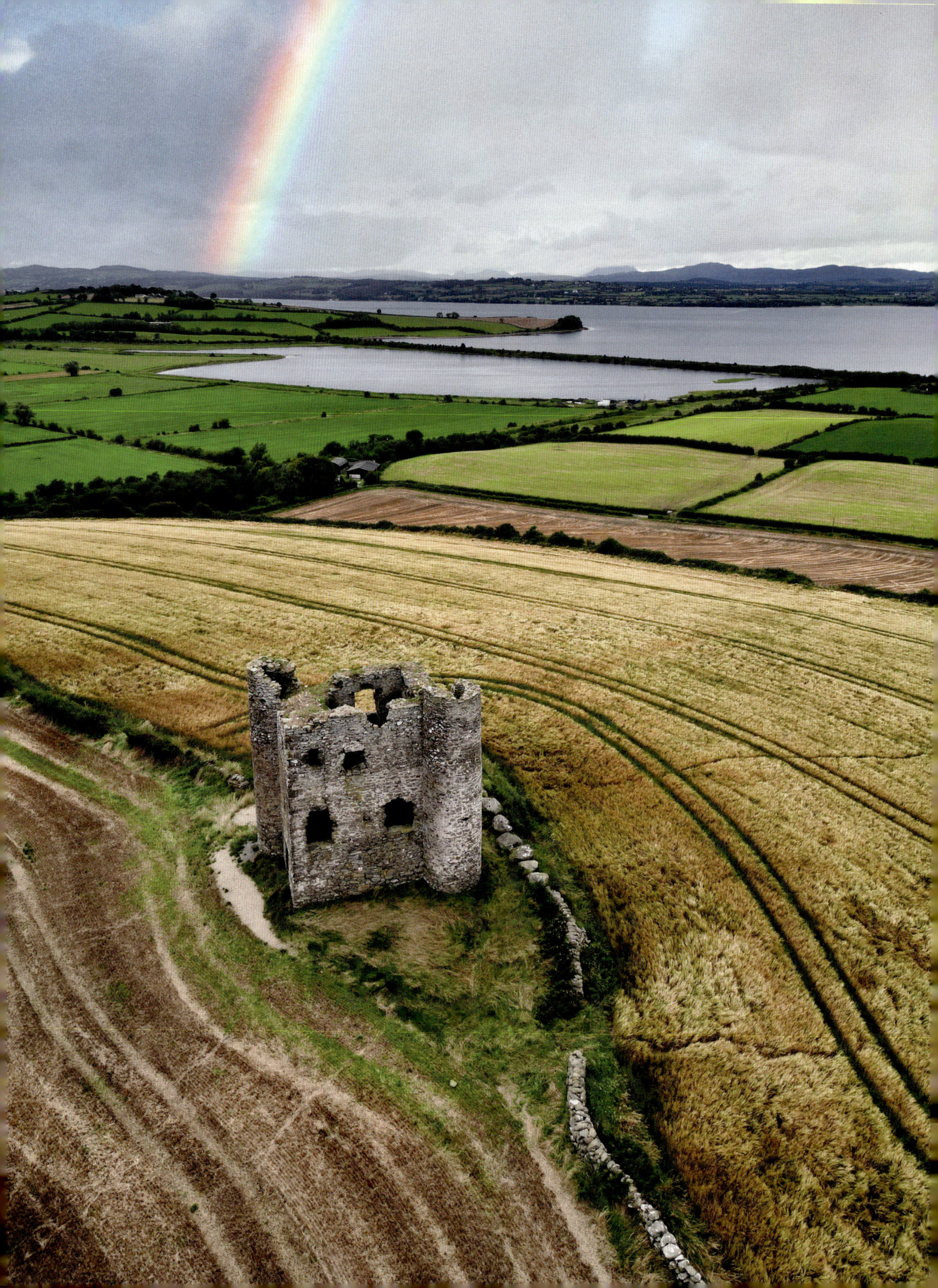

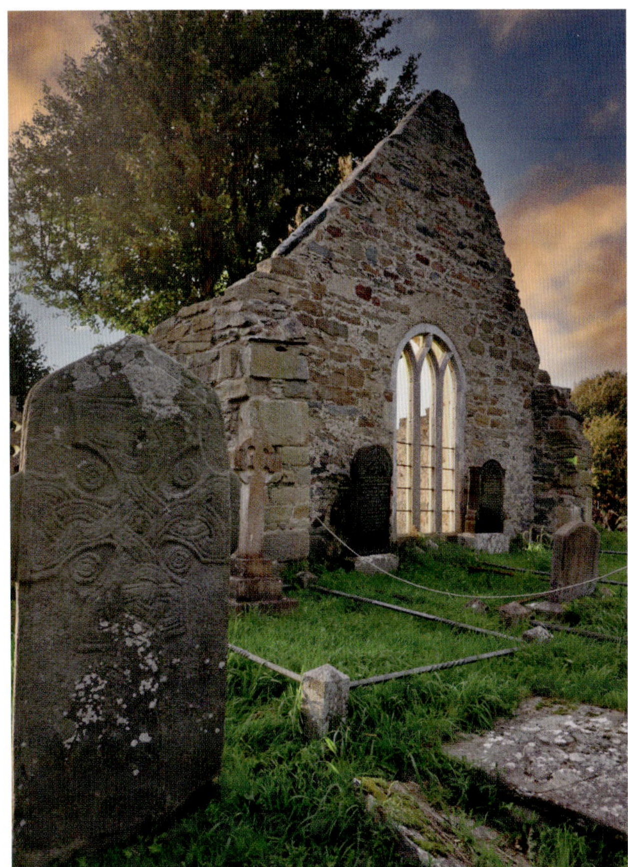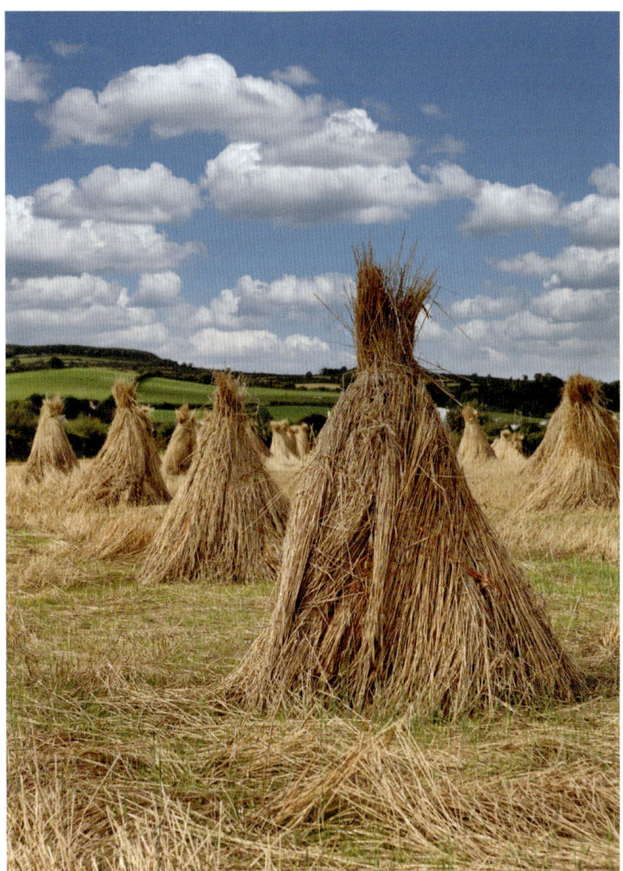

Above, left: St Mura's Cross at Fahan is a cross-inscribed slab at the site of a monastery founded in the sixth century by St Colmcille. One of his disciples, St Mura, became its first abbot. He died in AD 645 and local tradition holds that this slab, in the shape of an ordinary gravestone, marks his burial place. Its design predates the high crosses of Ireland.

Above, right: Stooks of rye straw near Manorcunningham. This straw is grown for the thatch industry in Donegal, which has the highest concentrations of thatched structures in Ireland.

Opposite: Burt Castle was built in the sixteenth century and was one of Clan Ó Dochartaigh's strongholds. The battered but imposing ruins of this ancient fortress are easily visible from the nearby road (but please note that they are on private land).

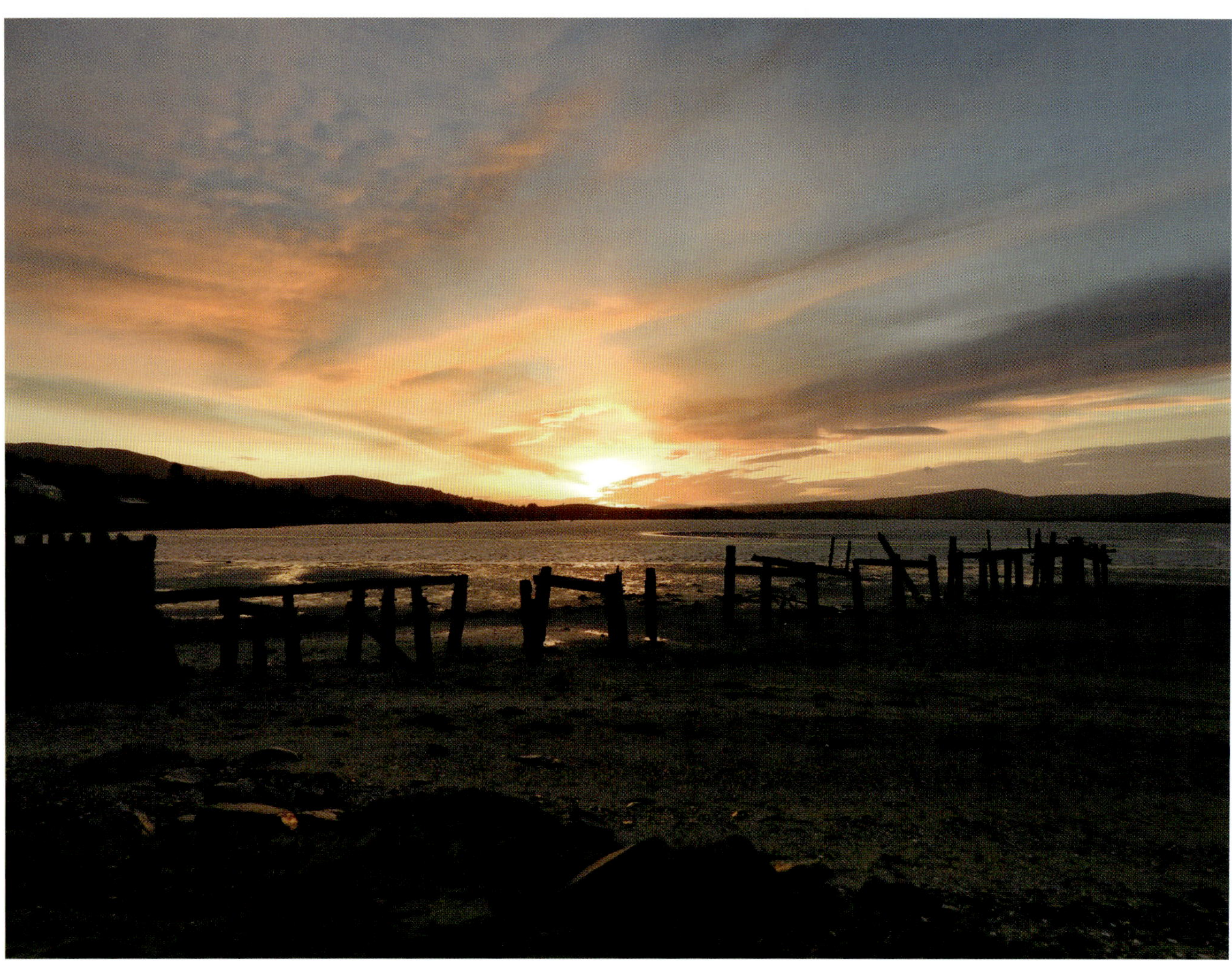

Dawn light at an old wooden pier near Fahan. Located on the western shores of Lough Swilly and built in 1922, this ruined pier has become a much-loved landmark in the area.

Opposite: When Colonel George Vaughan built Buncrana Castle in 1718, he moved the village of Buncrana to its current location to allow space around his country house for gardens. One of the first large manor houses on Inishowen, it is a rare example of the early Georgian period in Ireland.

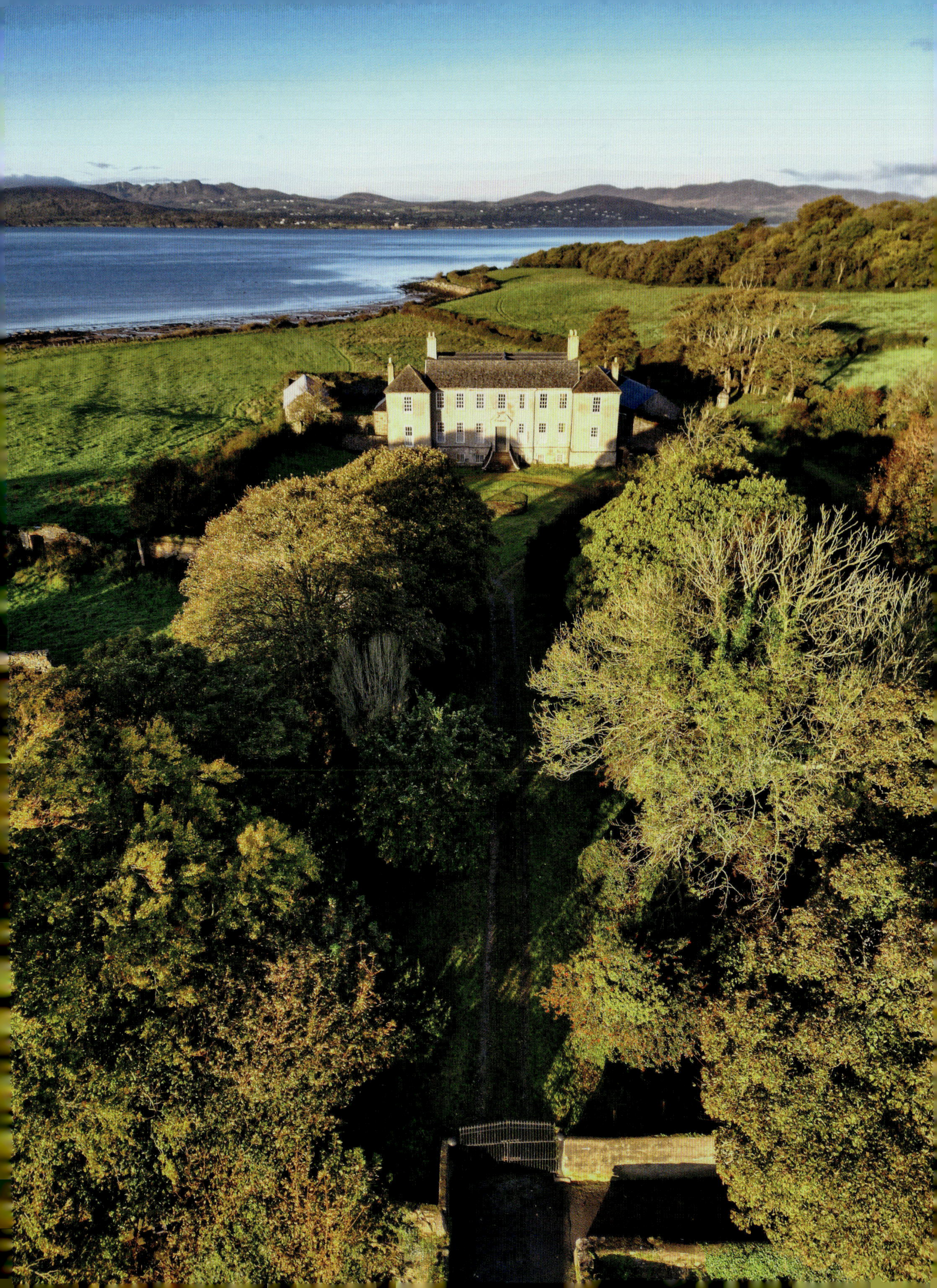

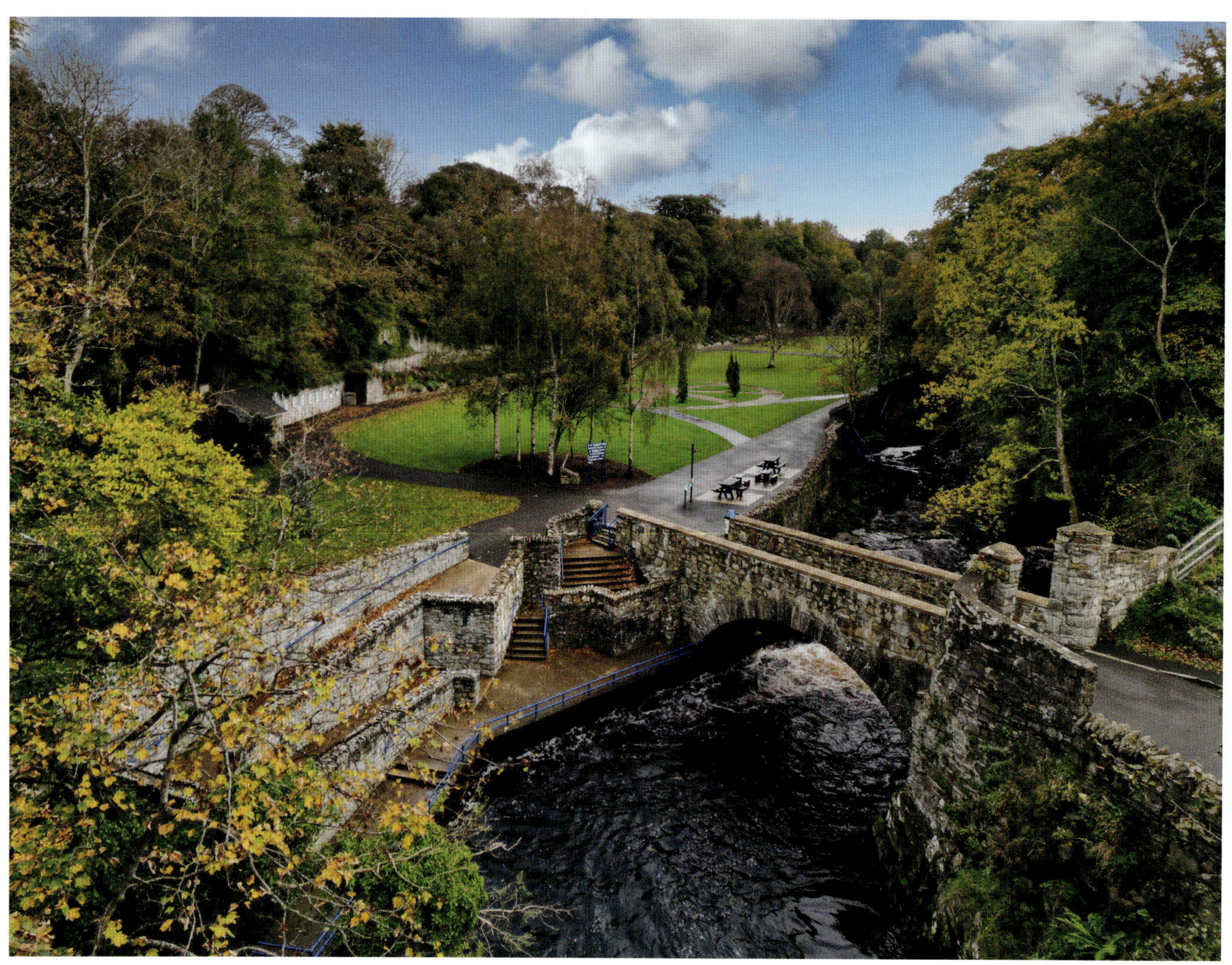

Buncrana's Swan Park is named after Harry Percival Swan, who was born in the town in 1879 and whose family operated a successful milling business here from 1868 until the early 1980s. He bequeathed the park to the people of Buncrana in 1965. Harry was a businessman, historian, author, antiquarian and founding member of the County Donegal Historical Society. Today the park provides a rich habitat for flora and fauna and is an invaluable leisure resource for both locals and visitors.

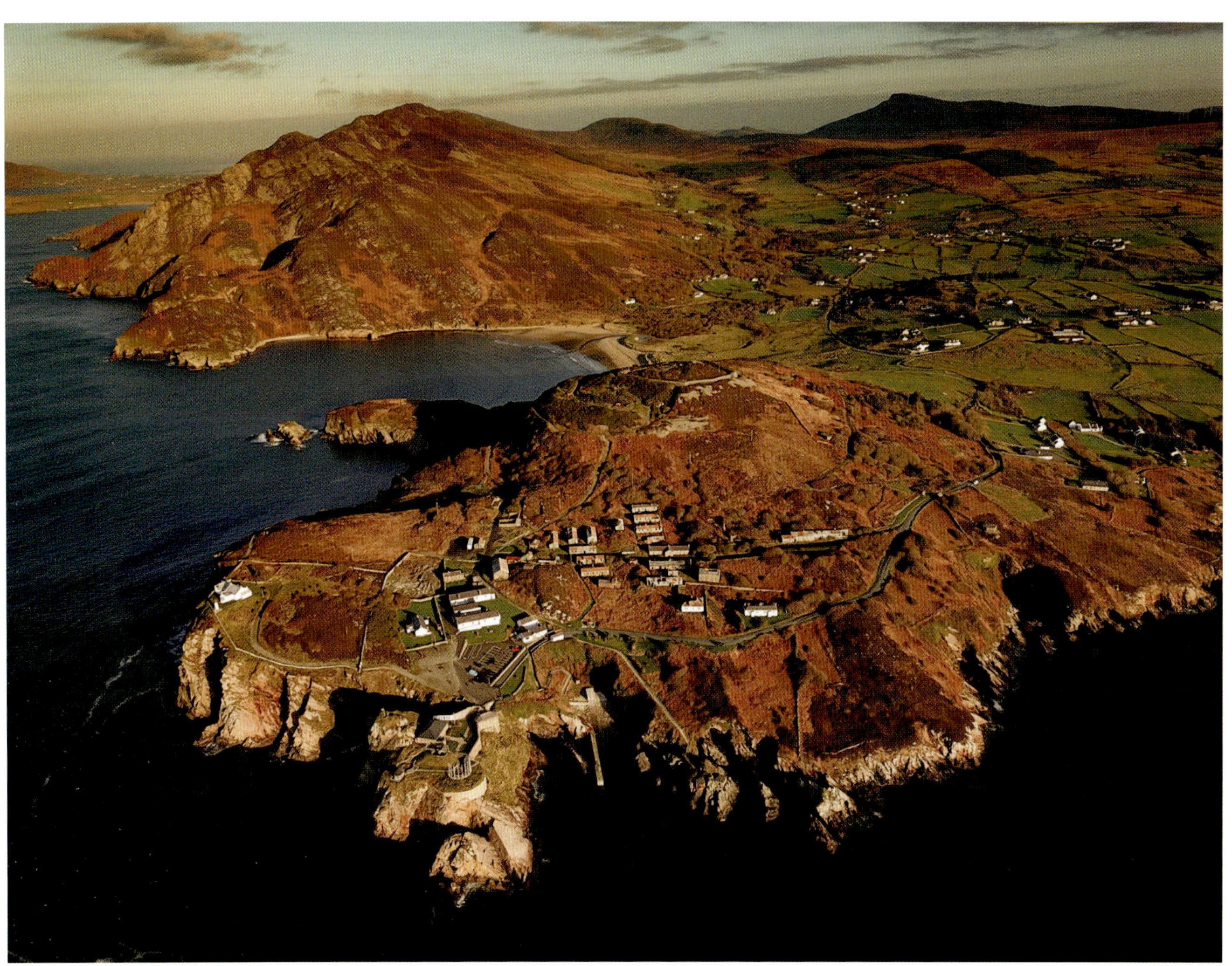

Fort Dunree (in Irish 'Dún Fhraoigh', meaning 'Fort of the Heather') is perched on a rocky outcrop overlooking Lough Swilly, demonstrating its vital role in coastal defence. Near to the spot where Wolfe Tone was brought ashore in 1798, a small fort was erected to guard against the possible return of a French invasion fleet. In the late nineteenth century, the fort was modernised and enlarged with the building of the 'top fort' on Dunree Hill. During the First World War, it stood guard whilst Admiral Lord Jellicoe's Fleet was anchored in Lough Swilly prior to engaging the German navy at the Battle of Jutland. Control of the fort was transferred to the Irish Free State just before the Second World War. Today it houses a display of military memorabilia and artefacts, along with an array of large guns from the twentieth century.

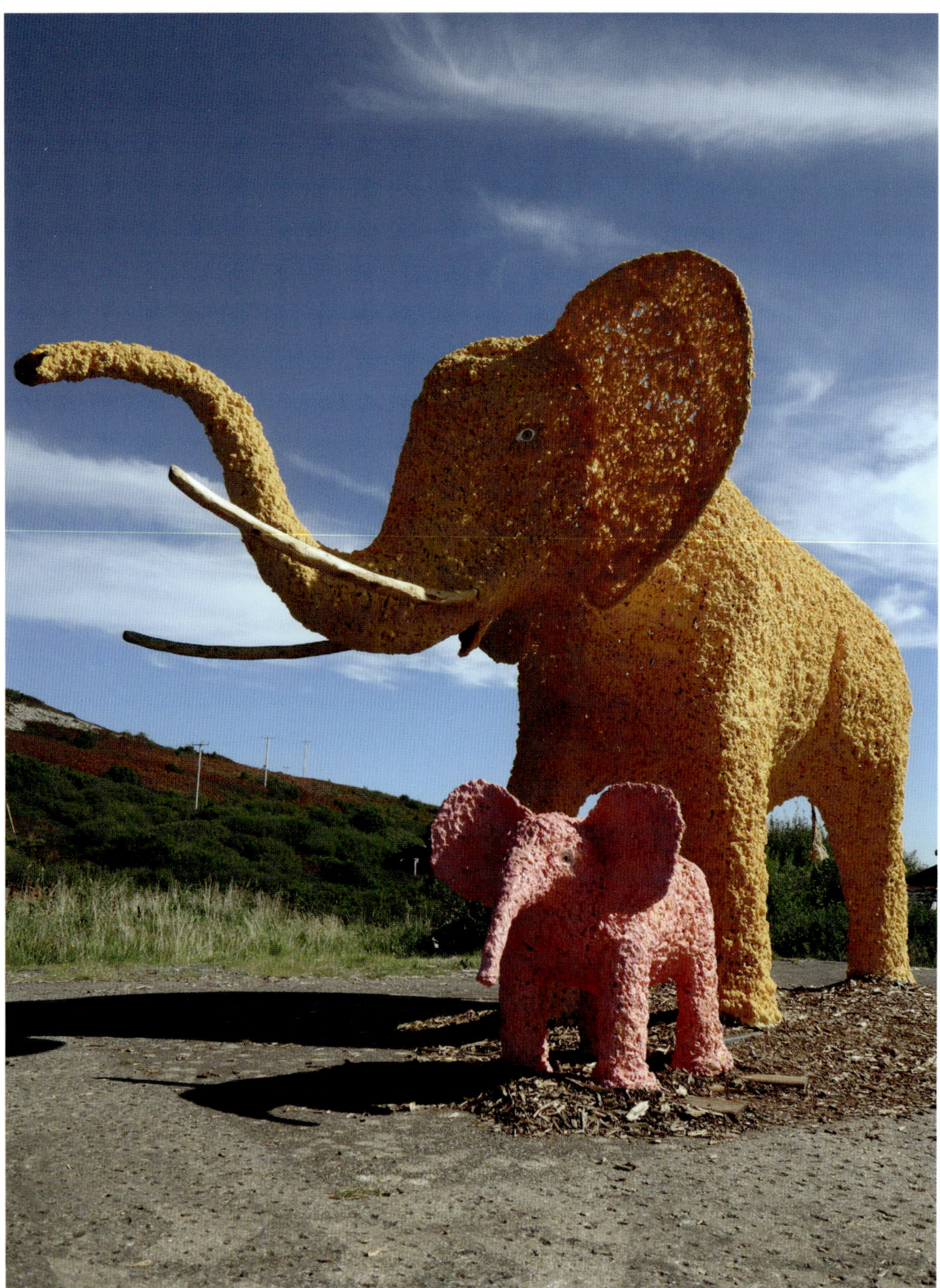

A structure in the shape of an African elephant, three metres (ten feet) high, and an accompanying pink calf, built by sculptor Kevin Harkin, was part of a temporary exhibition at Artlink Fort Dunree in 2023. Constructed from a steel frame and chicken wire, it took more than a year to complete.

Opposite: A steep and meandering road passes through the Mamore Gap between the hill of Mamore (right) and Croaghcarragh (left).

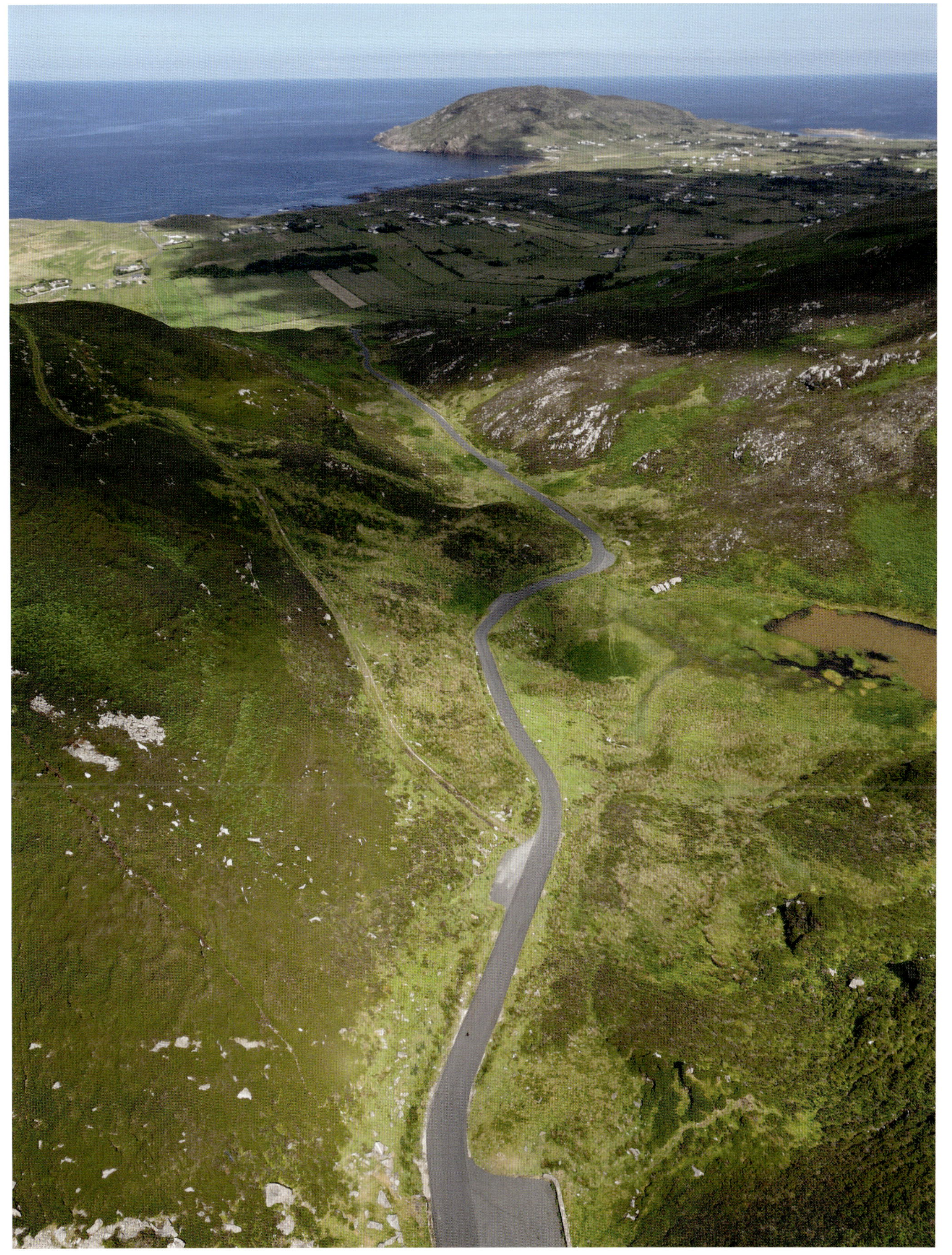

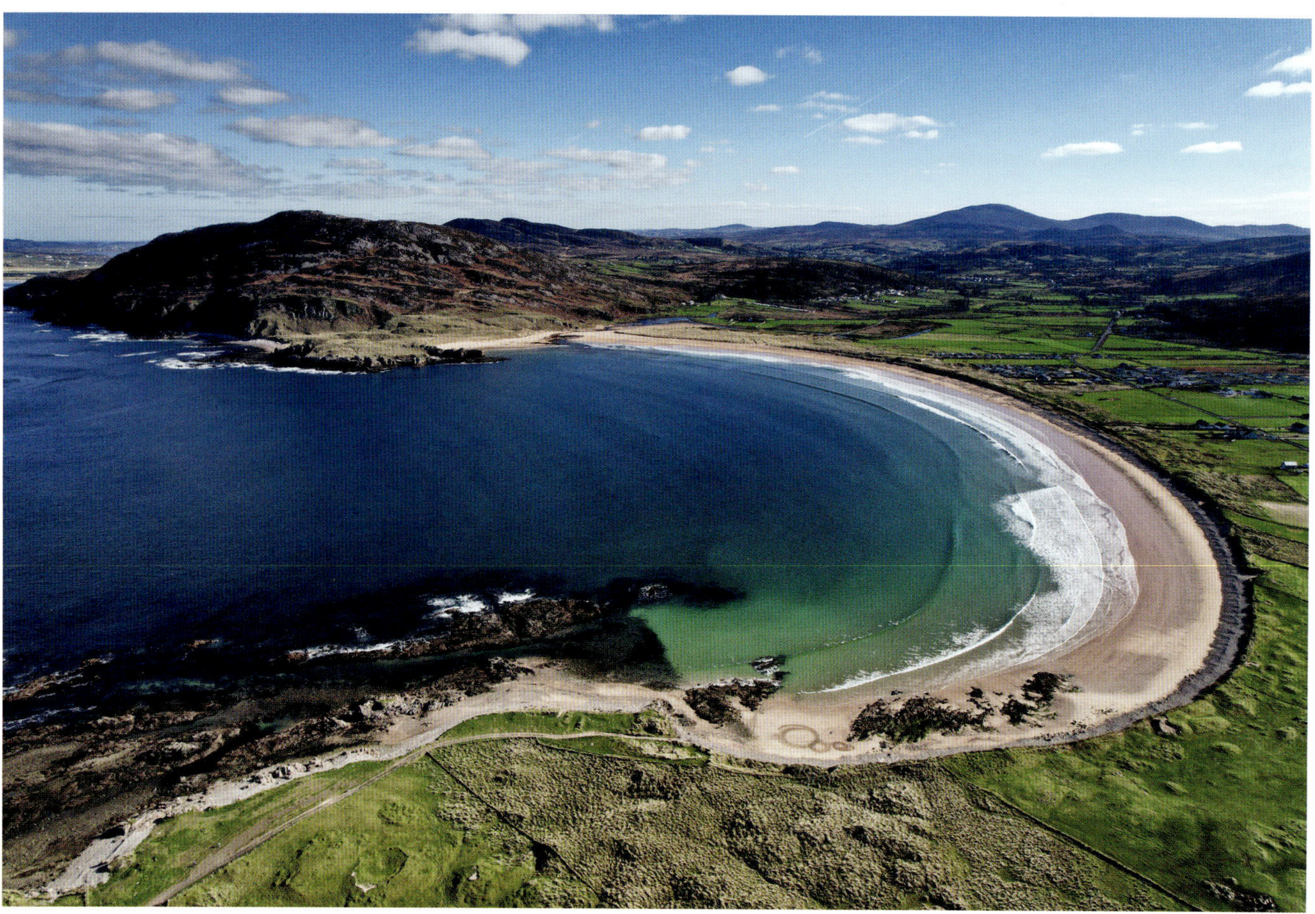

Near Clonmany is Tullagh Bay, an almost perfect horseshoe shape, with golden sands and crystal-clear waters, and bordered to the east by Binnion Hill.

Opposite: Glenevin Waterfall. When Doris Russo retired to Inishowen from the US in the early 1990s, she bought the Glen House, a B&B near Clonmany. After she moved in, to her delight she discovered a waterfall on the property. Determined to make this natural feature accessible to the community, she developed the route to the waterfall with gravel paths, footbridges criss-crossing the stream, and picnic areas. Mature deciduous woodland overhangs the path while the rugged high ground of Raghtin More Mountain provides the backdrop. Although Doris died in 2017, the project continues to develop year on year and has expanded to include walks through the Urris Hills, including an eight-kilometre trail named after her.

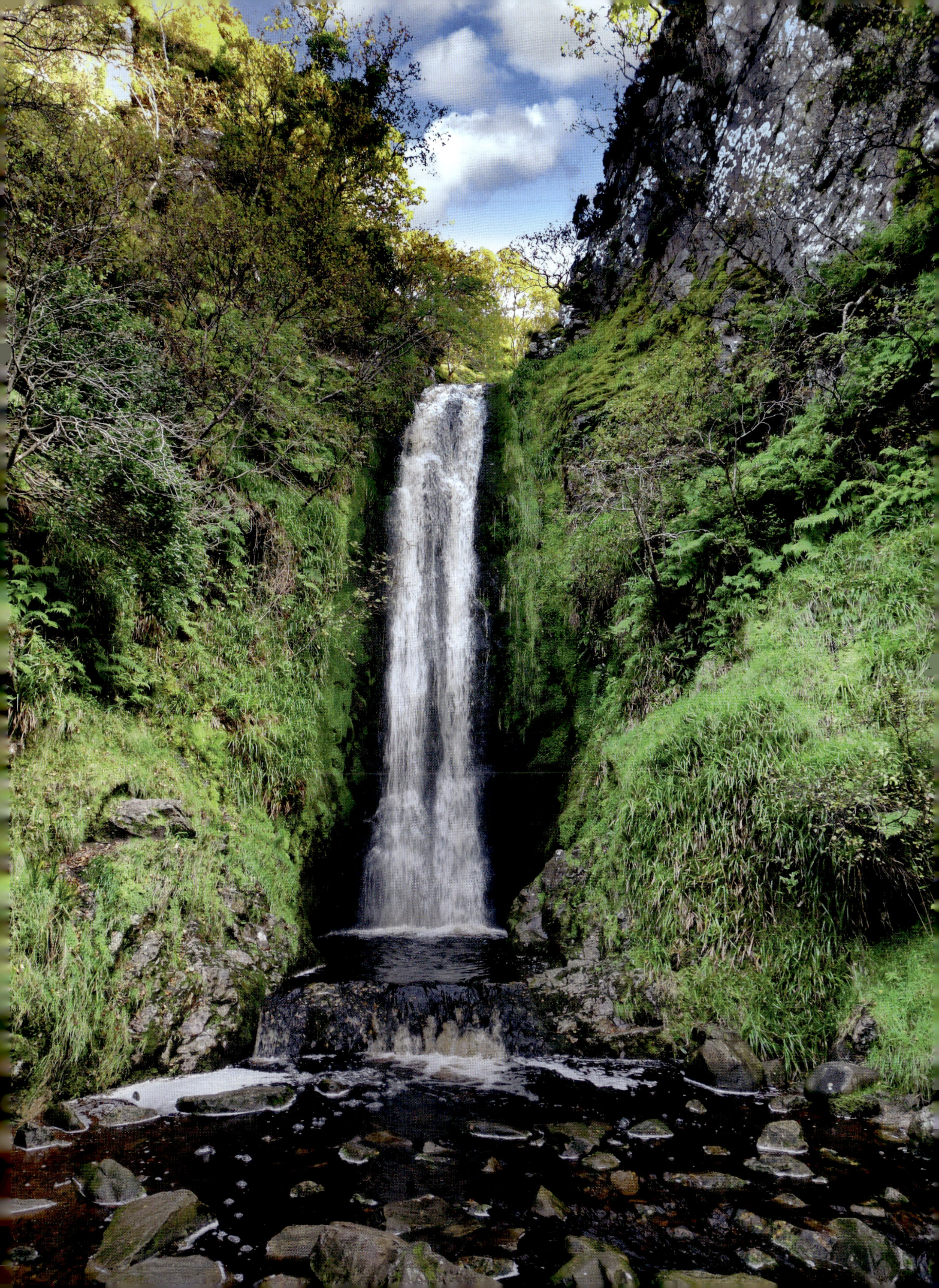

Opposite: Pollan Bay Beach stretches for three kilometres from Ballyliffin to Doagh Isle.

On the Buncrana road from Carndonagh lie two freshwater lakes, one on either side of the road: Lough Fad to the north and Lough Naminn to the south. The loughs are linked by a small stream that runs under the road. Lough Naminn has two small islands, one of which is accessible by a causeway. The remains of a crannóg can be found on Lough Fad, with ancient Irish rock art dating back to the Neolithic period on its shores.

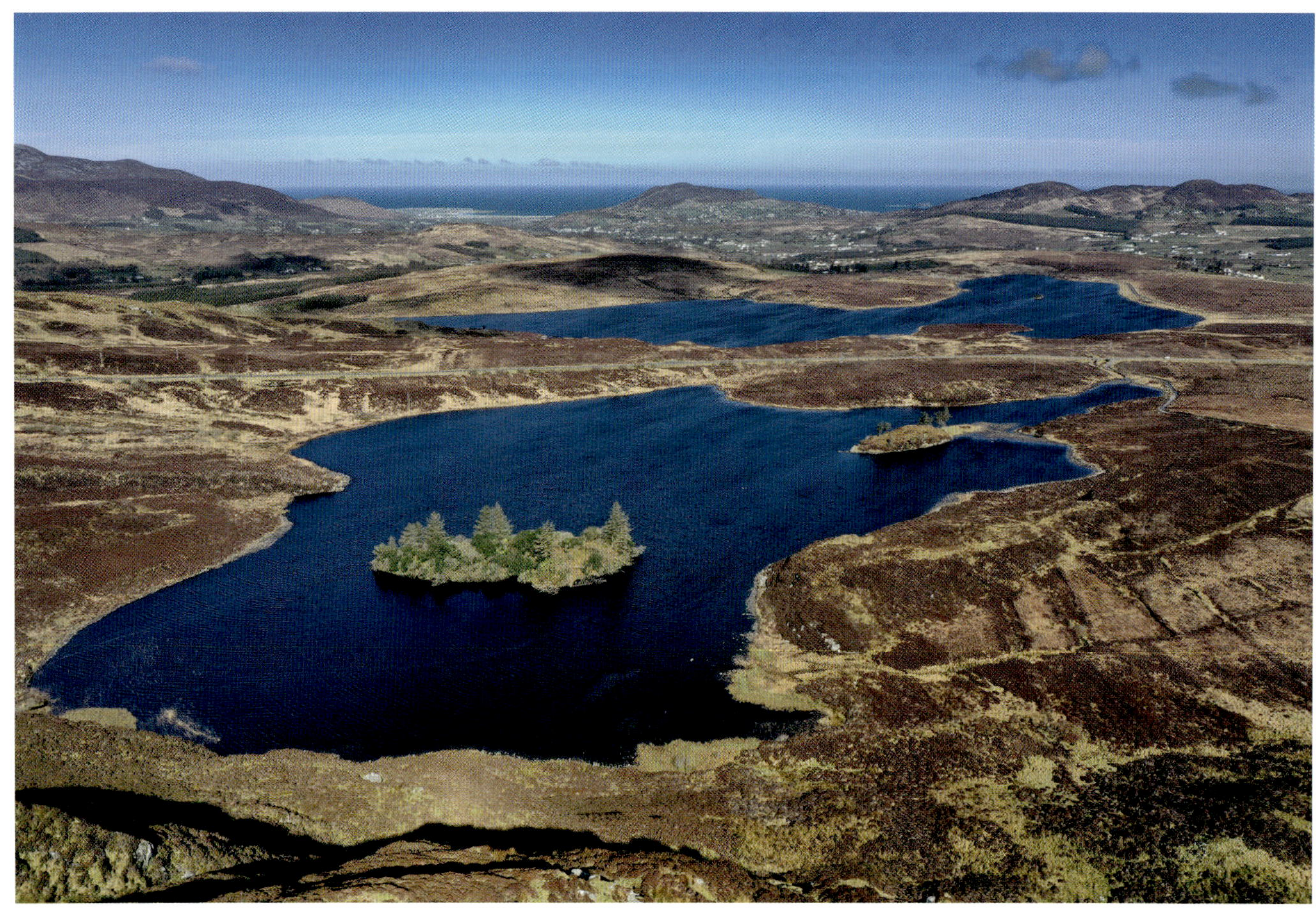

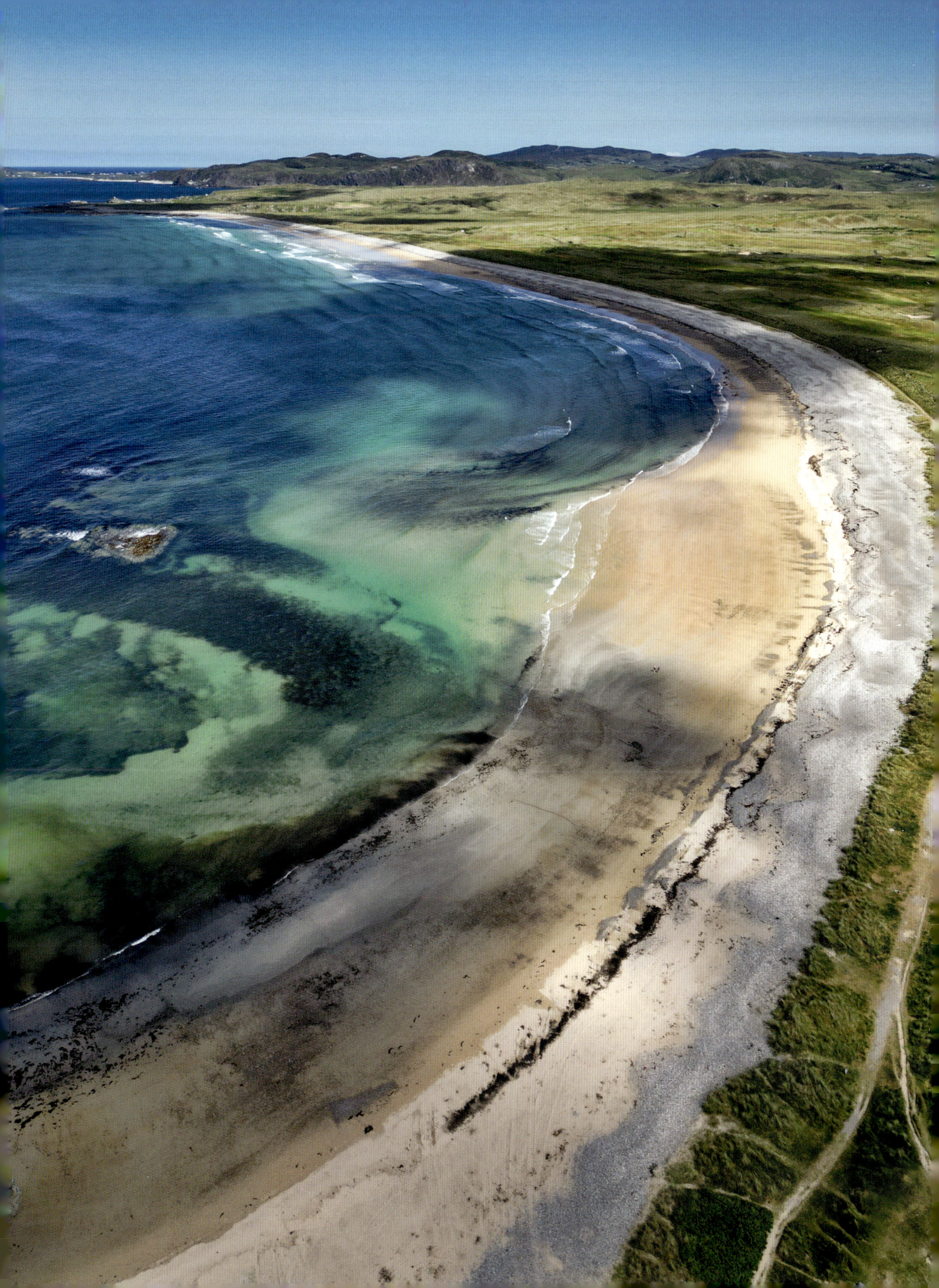

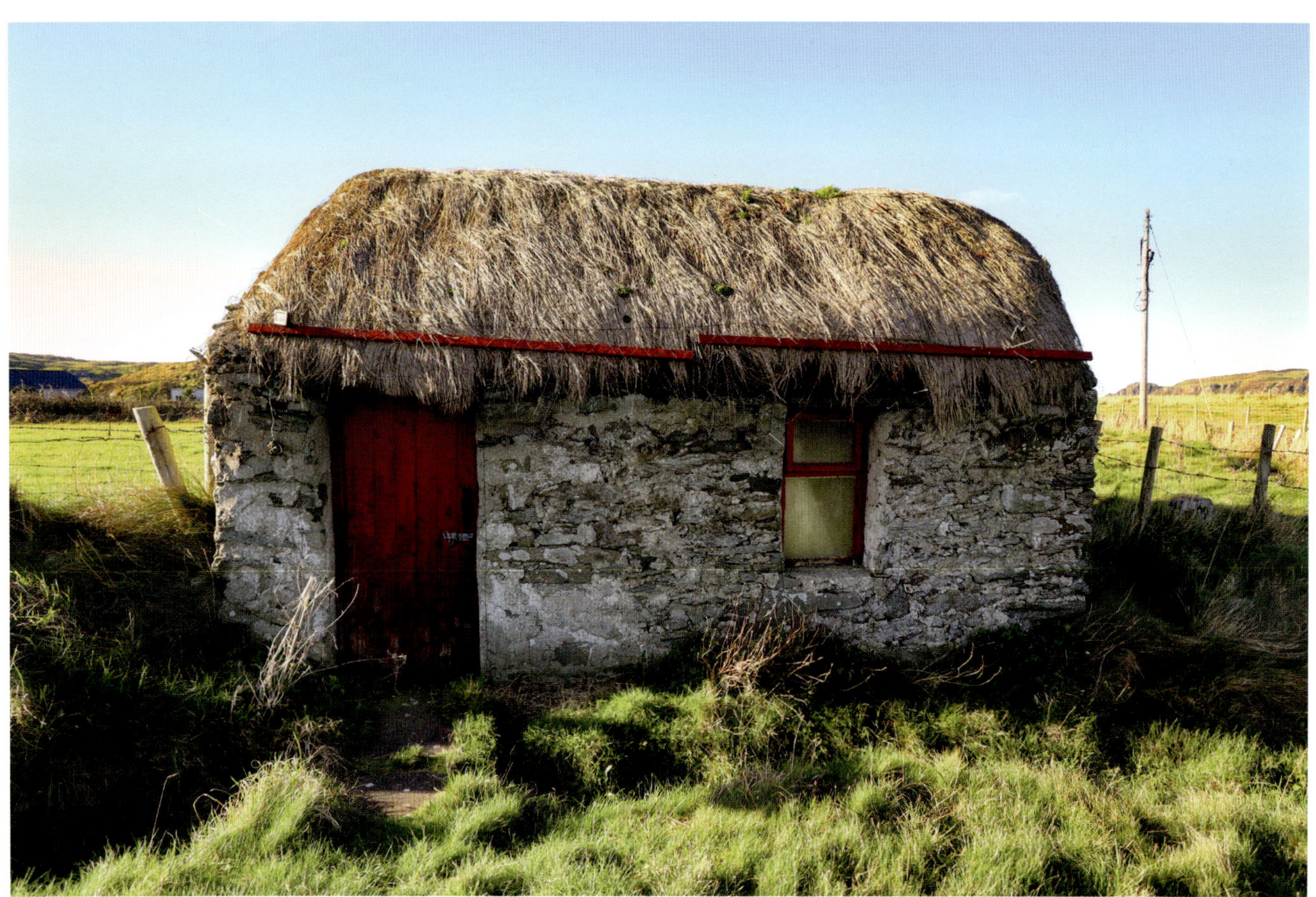

John Canny, born in Beltra on Doagh Isle, lived for a time in the American west. He was robbed of his hard-earned fortune on his return home. Back on Doagh, he dug a cave where he lived as a hermit. His neighbours, however, decided to intervene and built a small stone house for him on a site provided by local farmer Dan Gordon. Canny was persuaded to move into his new abode but, sadly, he died just six months later. The cottage has been preserved and Canny's memory lives on. The spot where he used to fish, near Carrickabraghy Castle, is known as Canny's Rocks, and there is also a well named after himl.

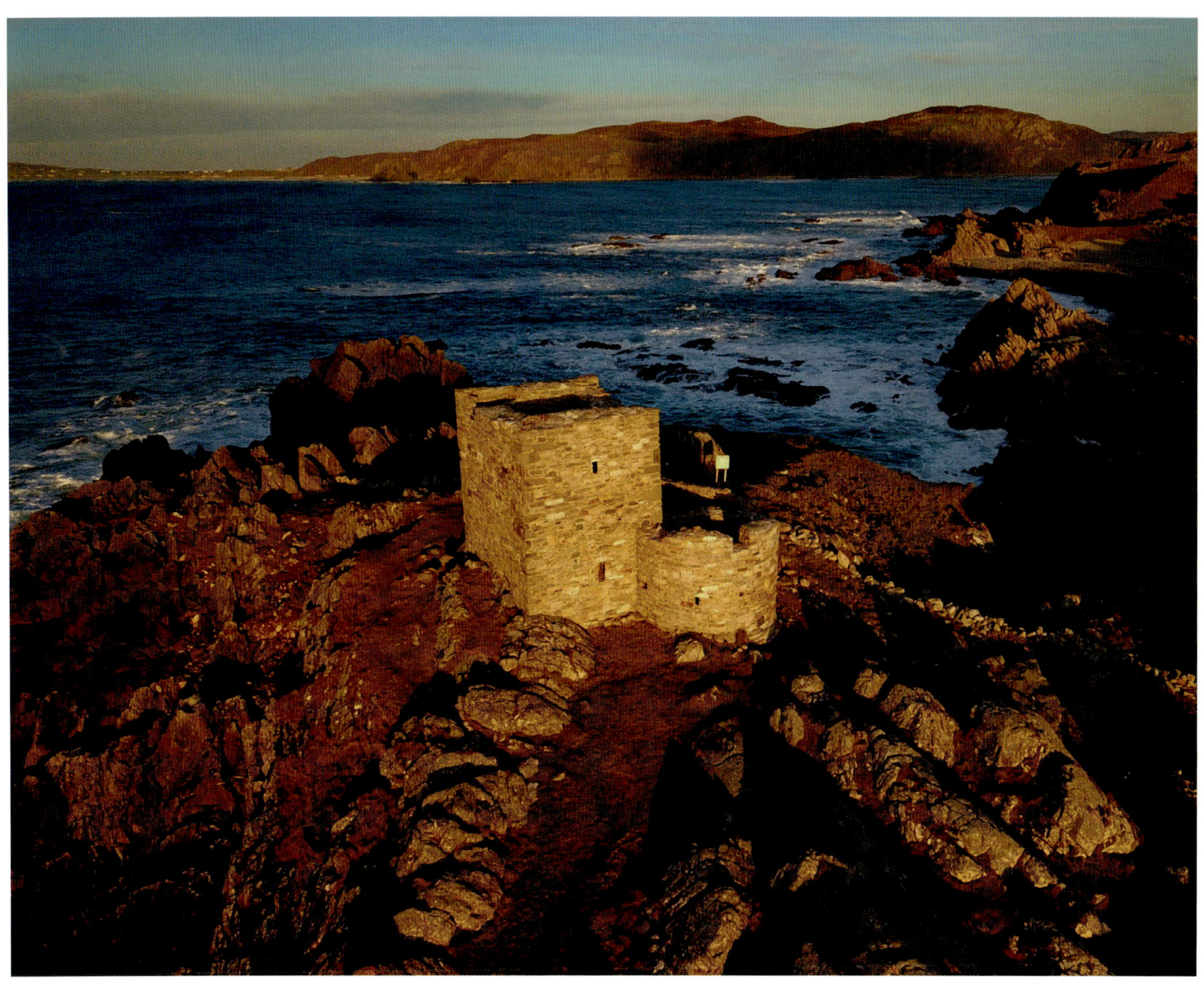

The ruins of Carrickabraghy Castle stand on Friar's Rock on the northern tip of Doagh Isle. It is one of four remaining Ó Dochartaigh strongholds in Inishowen, the others being at Burt, Inch and Buncrana. Built in 1540 by Phelemy Brasleigh Ó Dochartaigh during a brief period when the Doagh Ó Dochartaighs were chieftains of Inishowen, it was occupied by them until 1610. The Ó Dochartaigh clan claim descent from the legendary fifth-century high king Niall of the Nine Hostages, and were lords of Inishowen from *c.*1400 until the early 1600s. Doagh Isle was once an island but, over time, the channel silted up and it is now connected to the mainland.

Trawbreaga Bay (from the Irish 'Trá Bhréige' meaning 'False Strand') is on the western side of Malin Head. Doagh Strand (foreground) is an explorer's delight, with huge rock pools, caves and cliffs. On the other side is Five Finger Strand, which takes its name from five sea stacks at its northern end. This area is rich in biodiversity, attracting a variety of bird species. Swimming, unfortunately, is not permitted due to very dangerous undercurrents and rip tides.

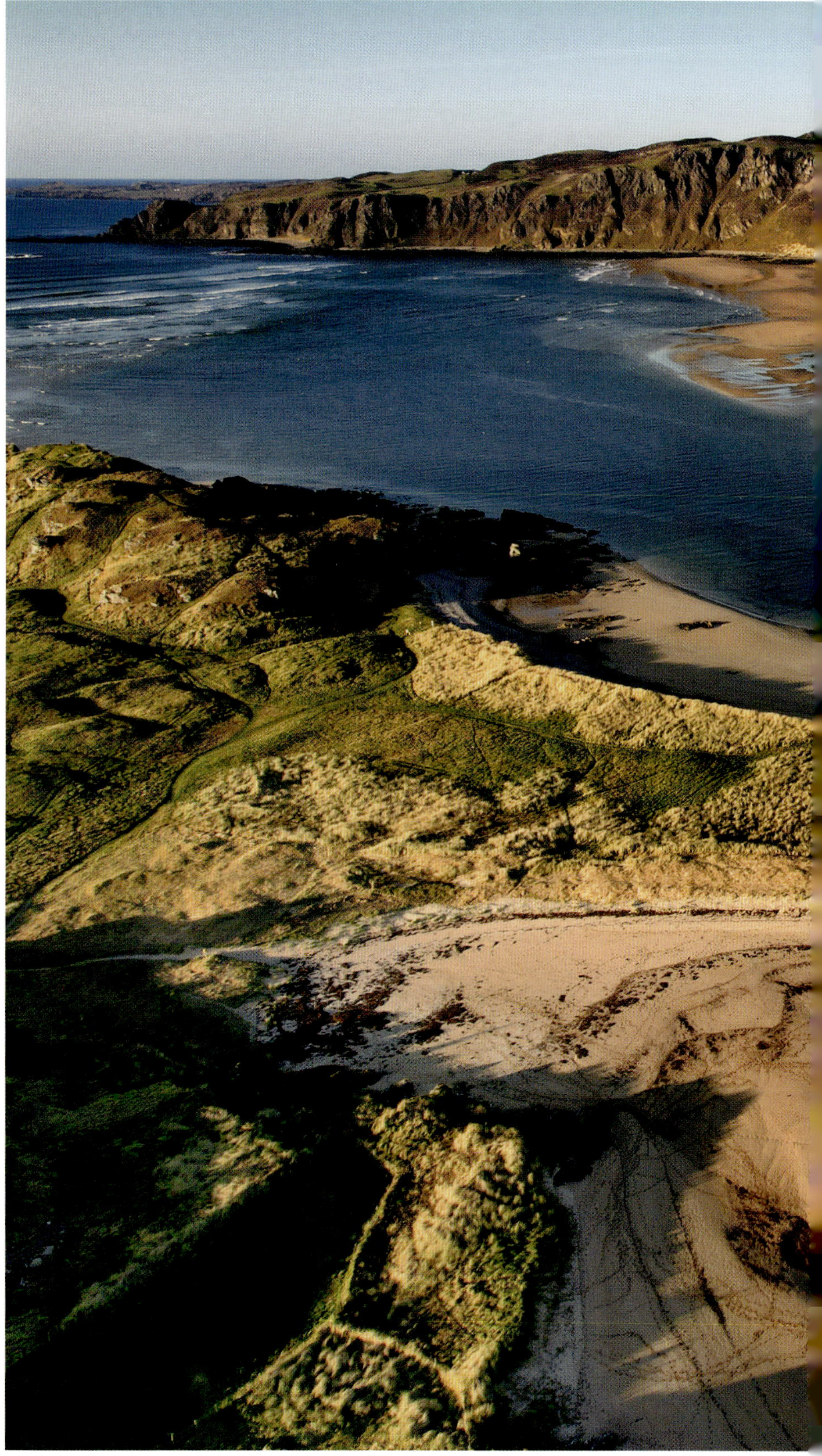

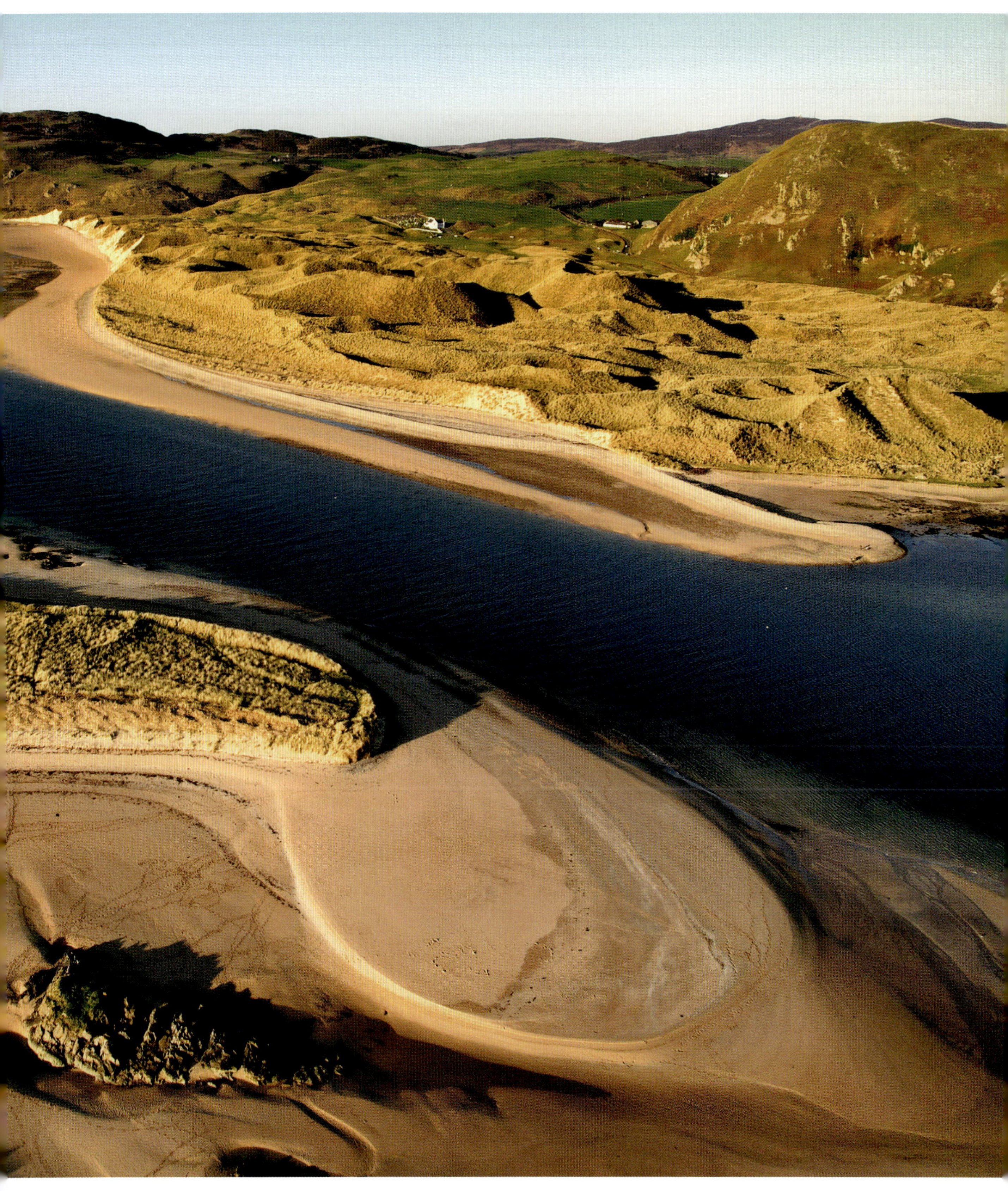

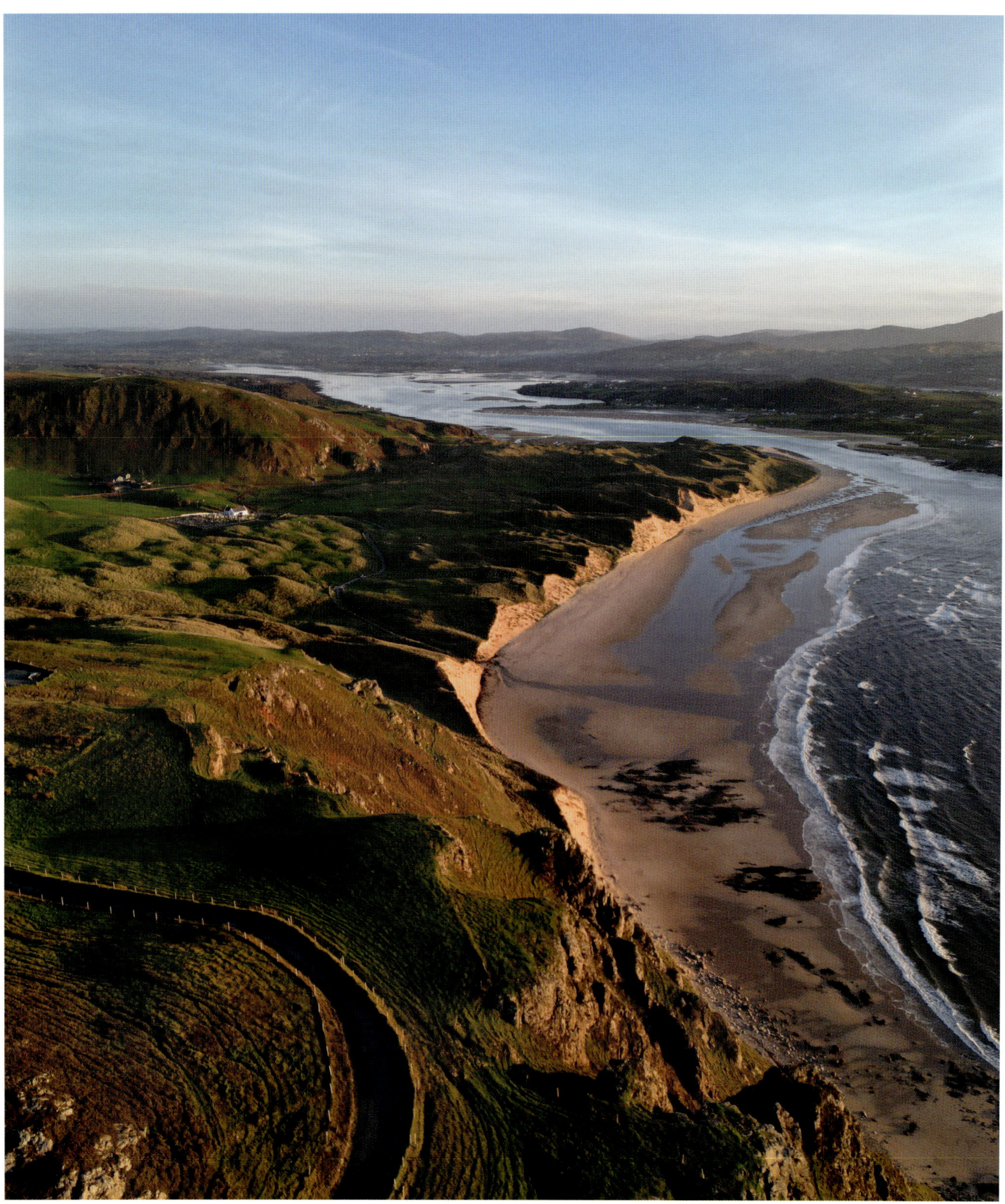

The secluded Five Finger Strand is nestled below the sheer cliffs of Knockamany Bens and backed by sand dunes which rise up to thirty metres (almost 100 feet) in height, reputedly amongst the highest marram grass dunes in Europe and five thousand years in the making. The dunes support a diverse array of plants and wildlife. As this is a tidal estuary, currents here are treacherous, so swimming is prohibited.

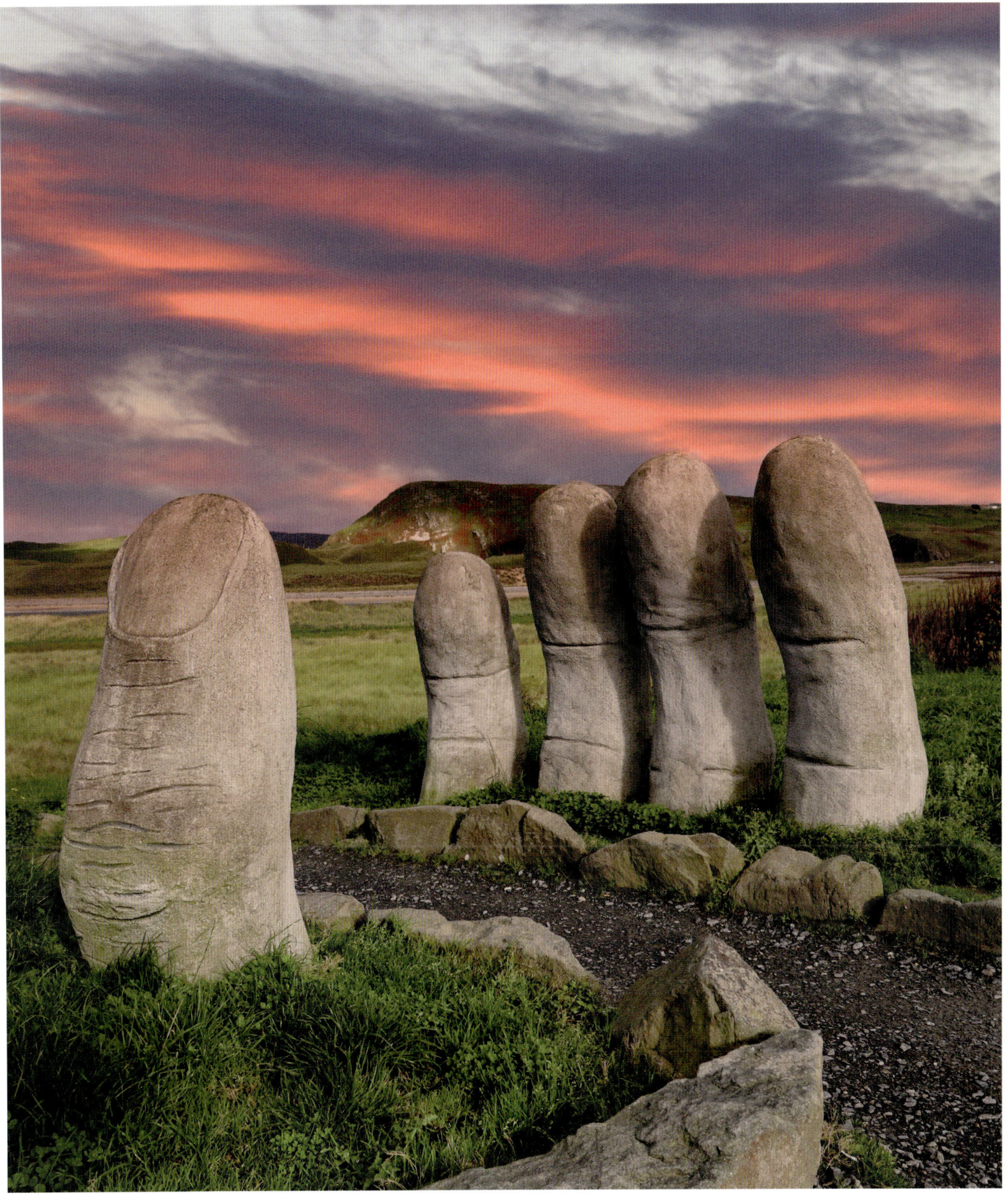

The Hand of Doagh, a scultpure created by artist Danny O'Donnell, is a poignant work of art, which represents all that is good about the human hand. According to the artist, it's the helping hand, the pat on the back, the friendly wave. It is situated in the car park opposite Doagh Famine Village, which traces the changing times of Ireland from the 1800s to the present day.

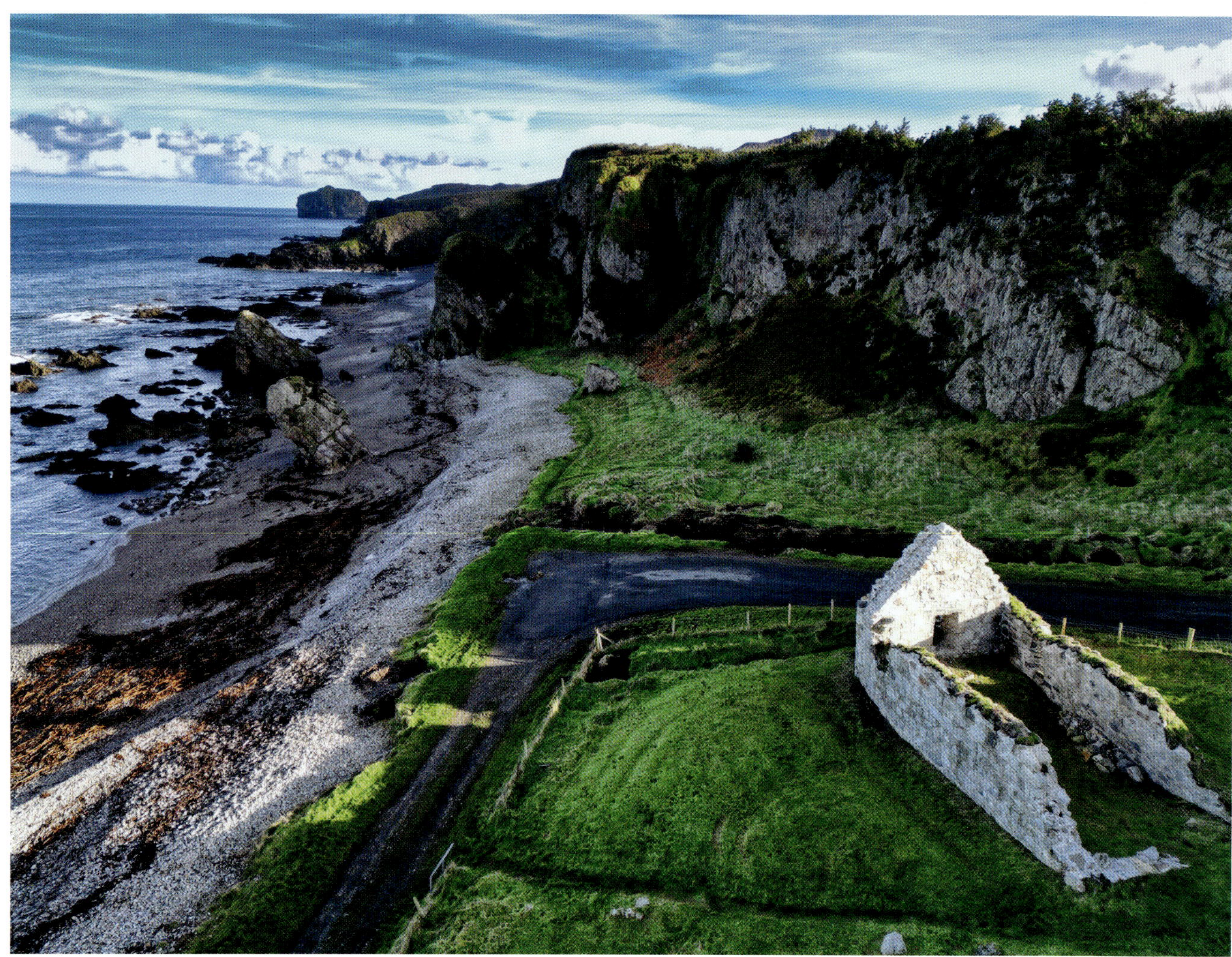

St Mahar's Church (also known as Gorman's Church). Once a place of pilgrimage, the ruins of this late medieval church, dating from the sixteenth century, are situated in the townland of Ballygorman, east of Portmore Pier. Nearby is a small cave carved into a cliff face, known as 'The Wee House of Malin', and also a small holy well. The pebble beach has fascinating sea stacks, including a 'wishing seat' within a natural cavern in the rock.

Opposite: The most northerly tip of Malin Head, and of Ireland, is known as Banba's Crown, named after the mythological patron goddess of Ireland. The area is renowned for its rugged, untamed coastal scenery but it is also rich in history and heritage. The signal tower was built in 1805 during the Napoleonic Wars to act as a coastguard, reporting via semaphore on ships passing along the busy transatlantic route. In 1902, the Marconi Company sent the first commercial message by wireless from Malin Head, to the SS *Lake Ontario*. Poignantly, on 2 April 1912, the station received a greetings message on behalf of the RMS *Titanic*.

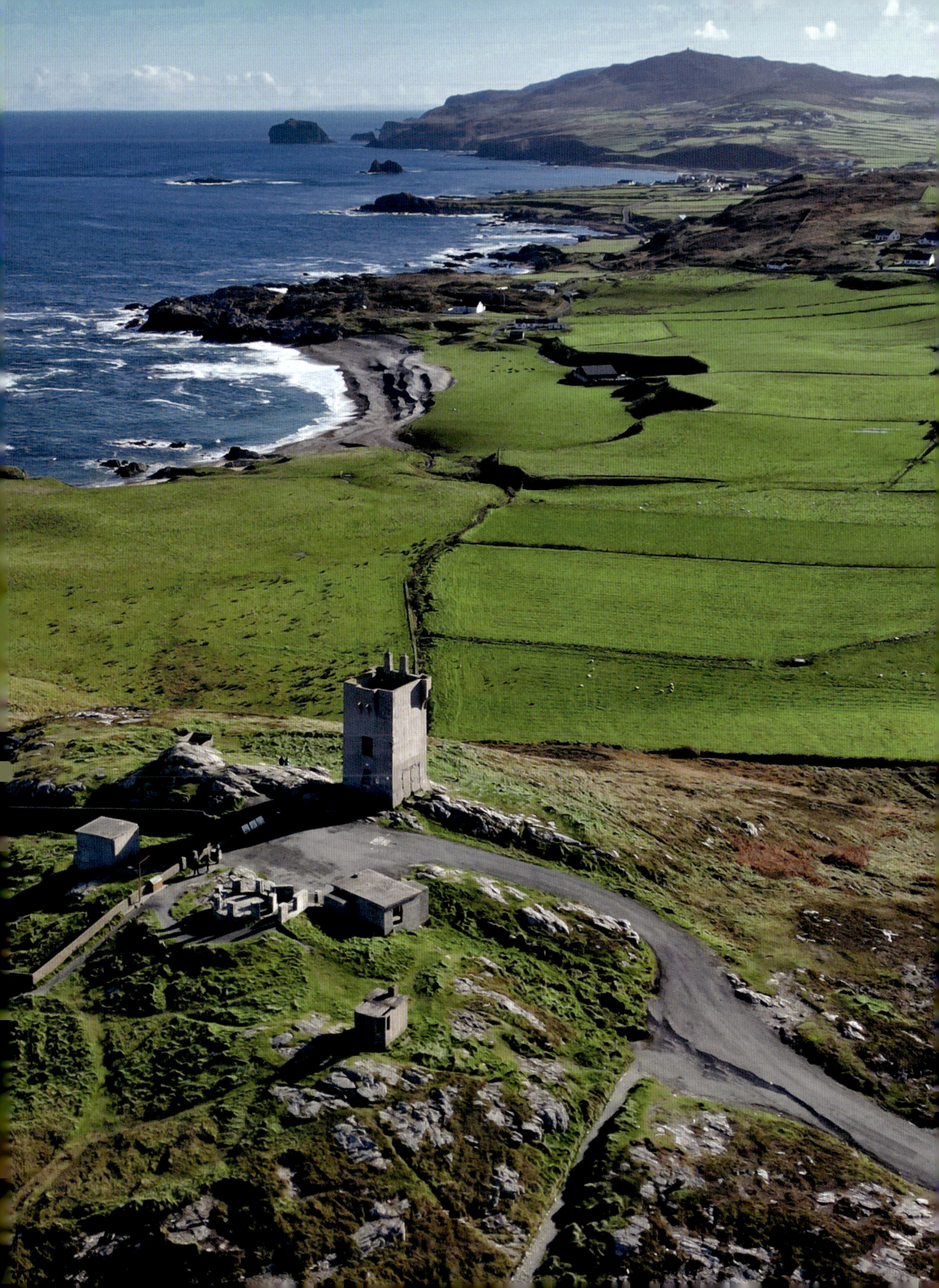

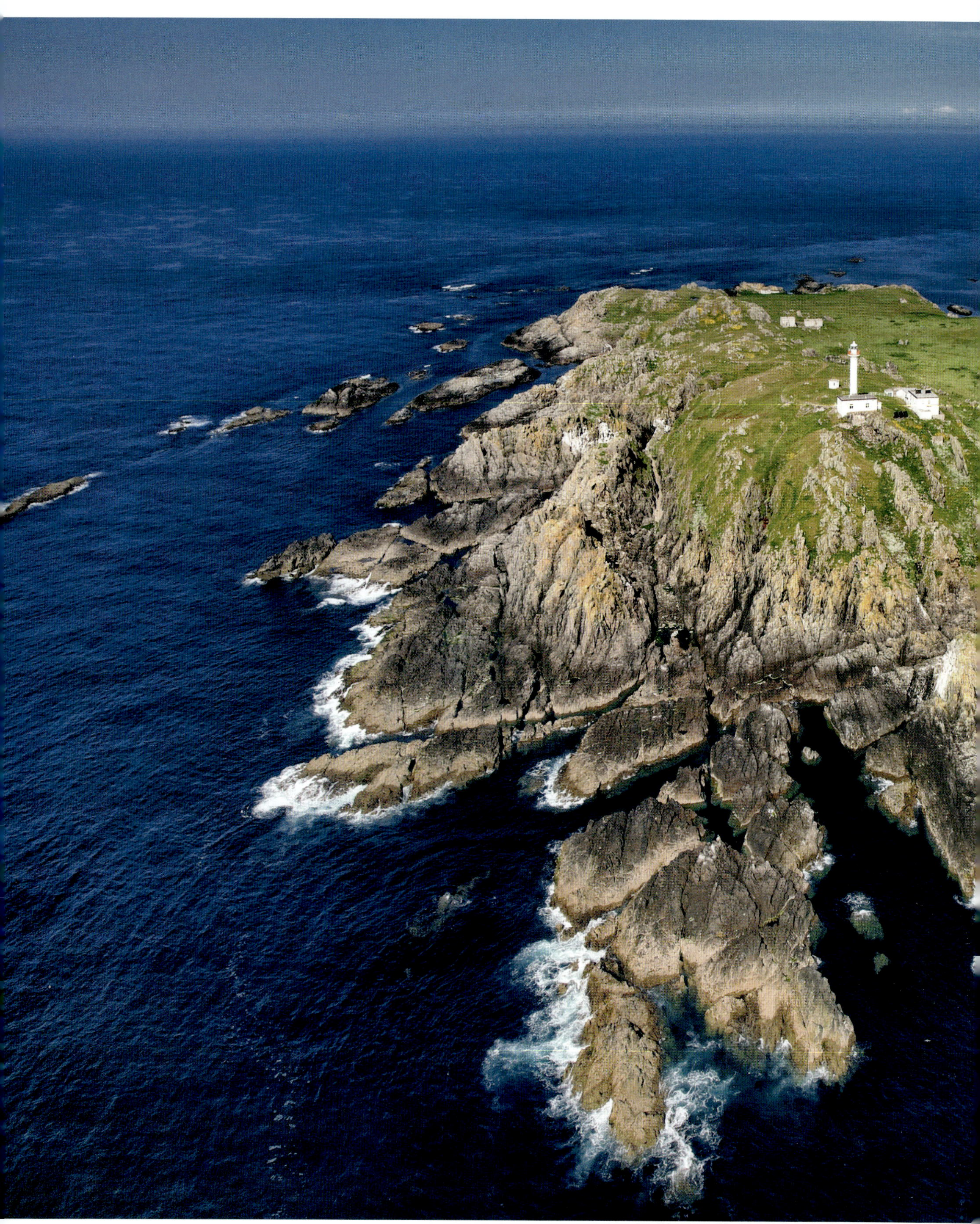

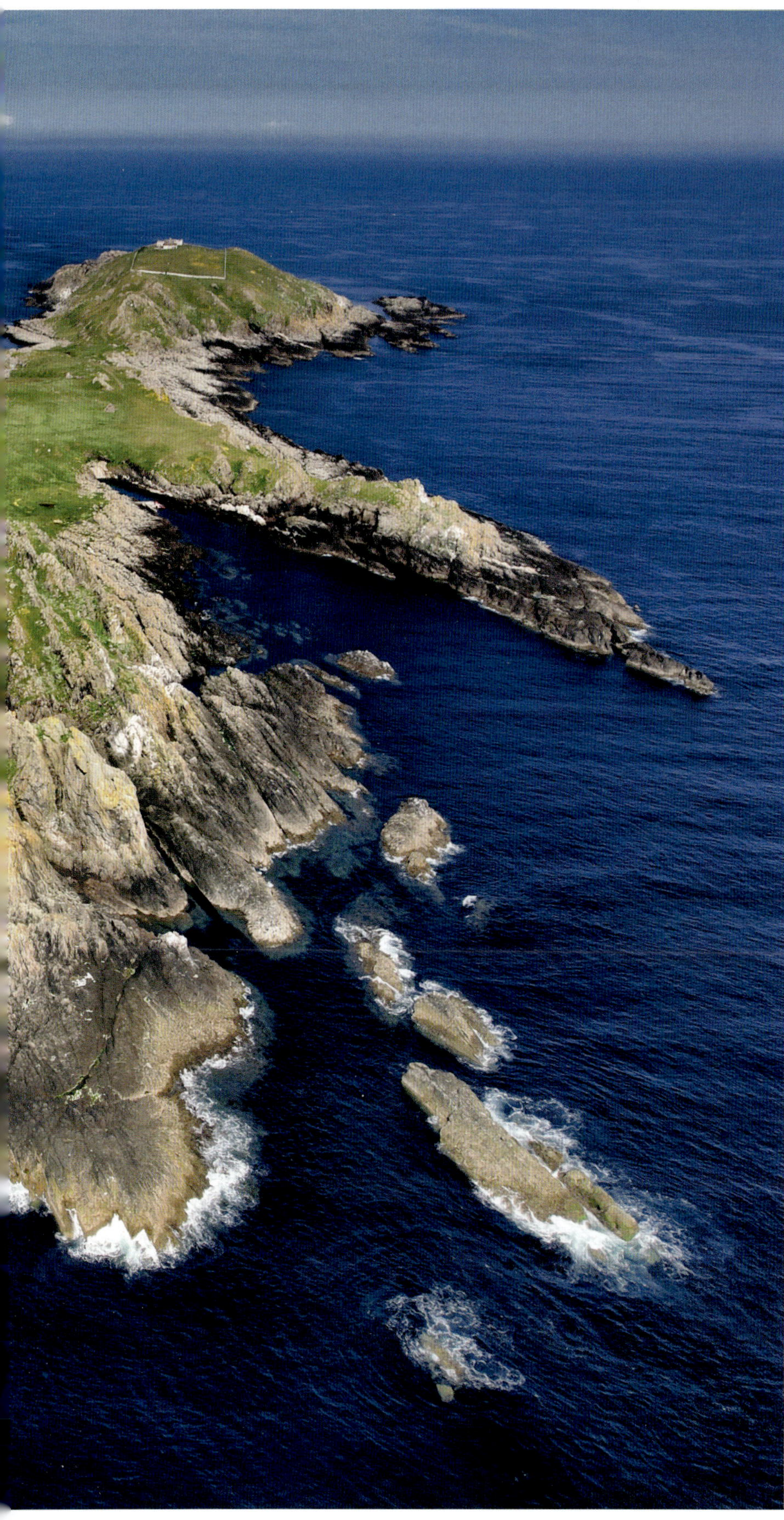

Inishtrahull, or 'Inis Trá Tholl', meaning 'Island of the Hollow/Empty Beach', is probably the most forgotten island off the coast of Donegal. Its thirty-four hectares lie ten kilometres northeast of Malin Head. It supported a thriving fishing community until about 1928. The lighthouse is the dominating feature of the island and was staffed until 1987. Today, Inishtrahull is uninhabited and has been designated a Special Area of Conservation. Boat trips to the island leave Bunagee Pier in Culdaff, passing by Ross Head and Malin Head. You may also get a chance to meet the local dolphins.

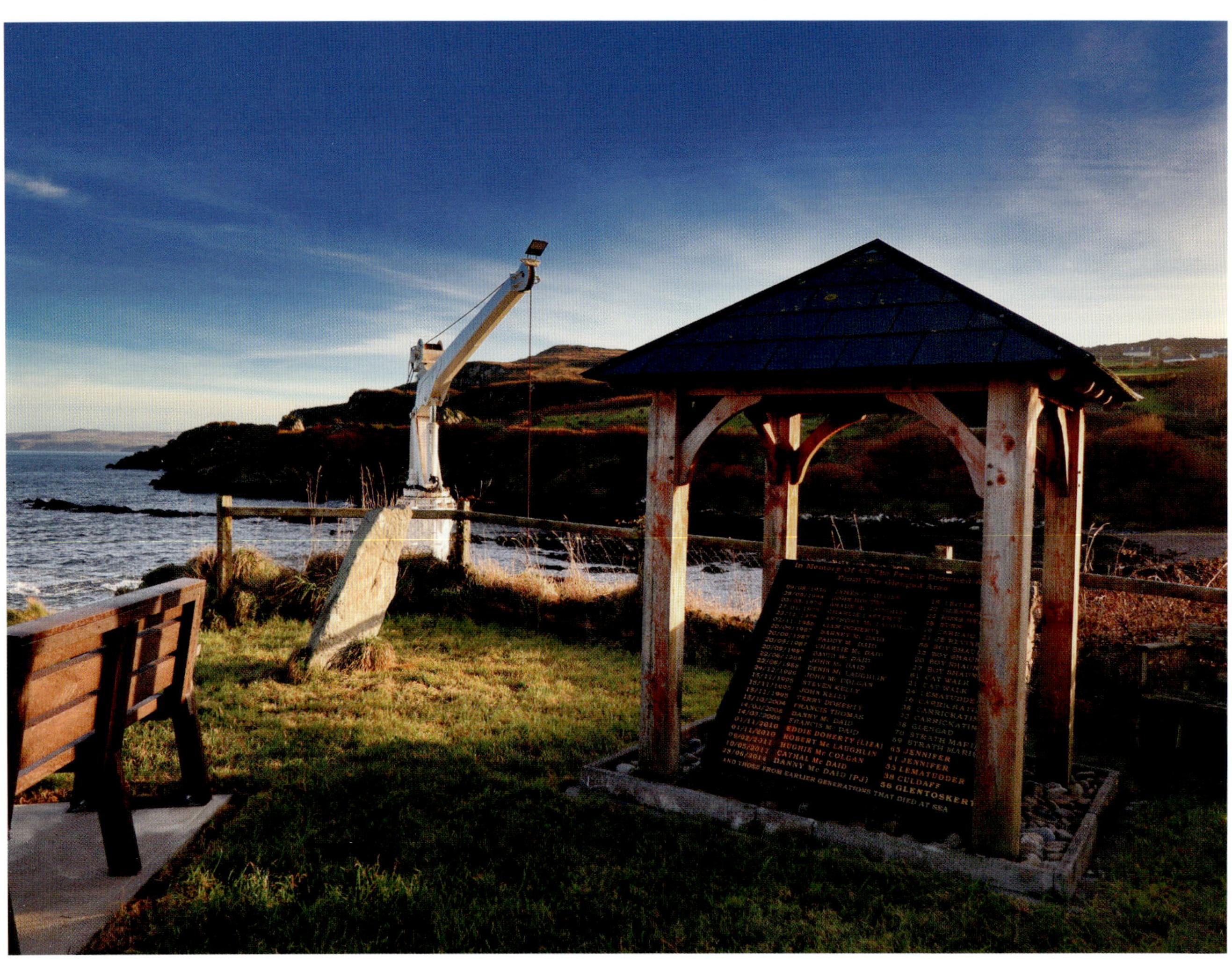

On a small raised promontory at Portaleen pier in Glengad, a memorial commemorates local fishermen who have lost their lives at sea. Beside it, a cross-inscribed standing stone marks Coolkill Burial Ground where, until the 1940s, stillborn babies or babies who died before being baptised were buried.

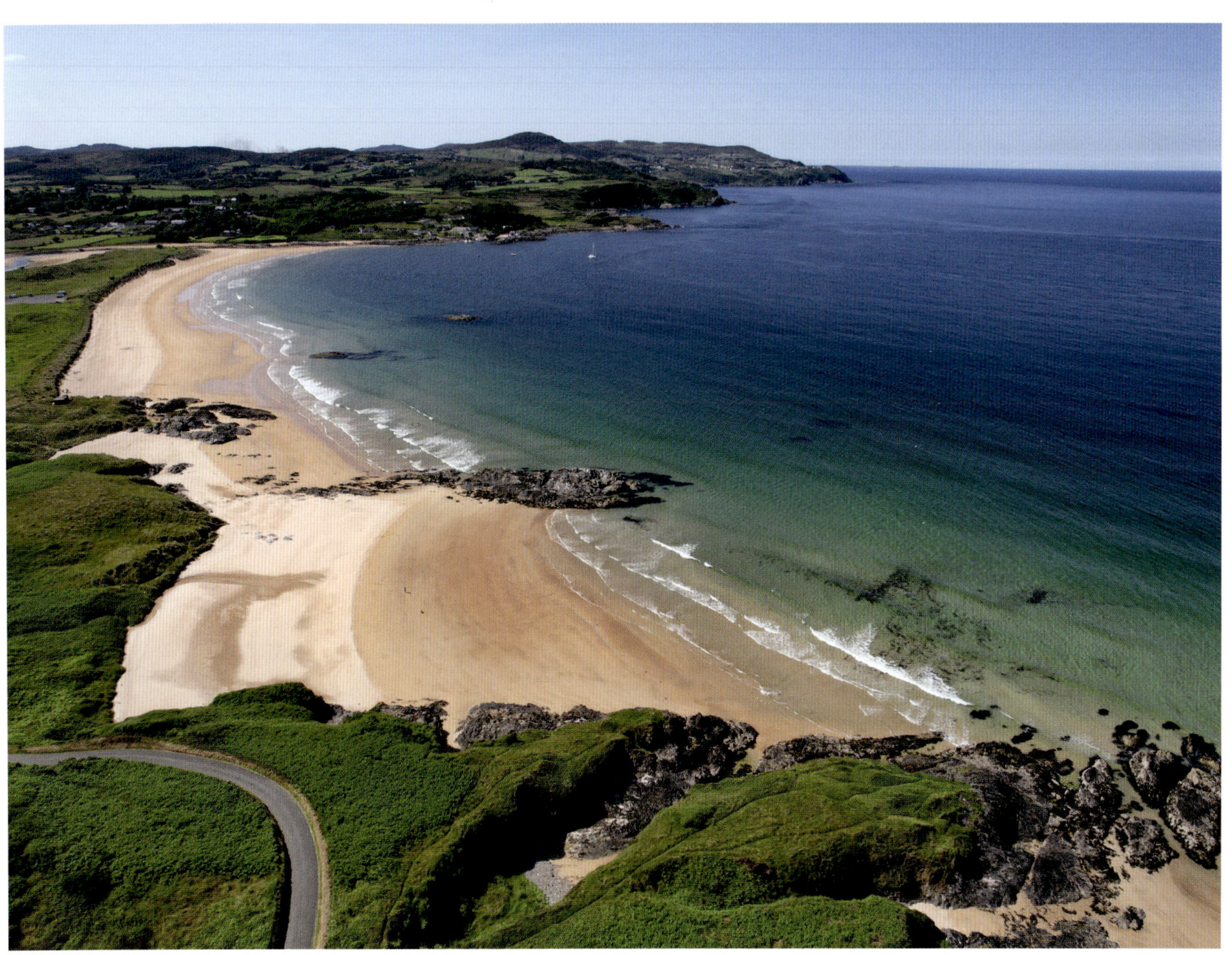

Rocky outcrops divide Culdaff Beach into two distinct areas, the 'small beach' and the 'big beach' (pictured). Surfing is best along the eastern shore in southwesterly winds, and is suitable for all skill levels. Bunagee, at the northern end of the beach, is a centre for angling and water sports. With its pristine sands and unique wildlife, the coastal habitats of Culdaff Beach have been designated a Special Area of Conservation. The spectacular coastal and mountain scenery draws hillwalkers, nature photographers, anglers and cyclists.

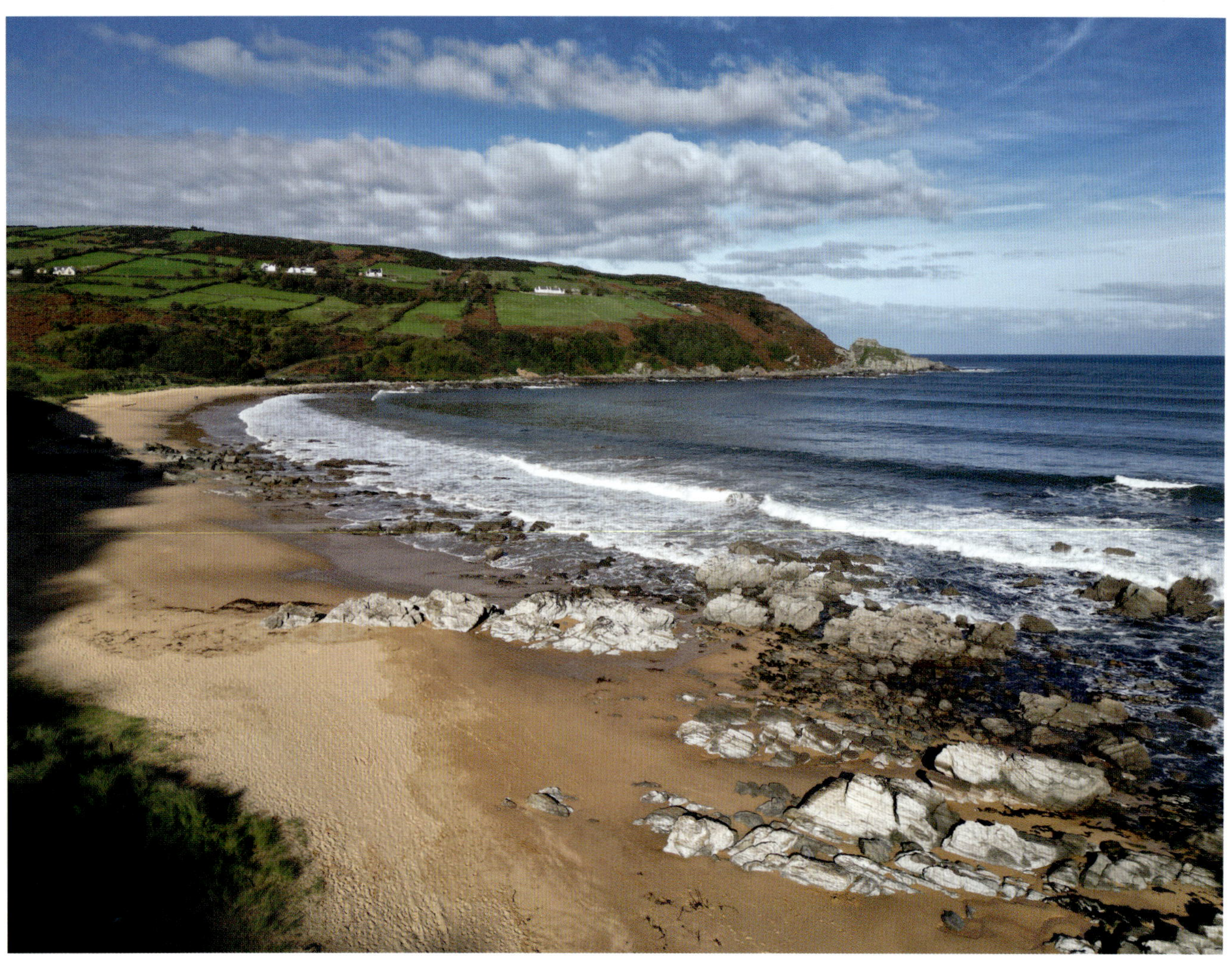

Kinnagoe Bay is on the east coast of the Inishowen Peninsula, seven kilometres from the fishing village of Greencastle. On 16 September 1588, a Spanish Armada vessel, *La Trinidad Valencera*, sank in the bay. The wreck lay undiscovered until February 1971 when divers from City of Derry Sub-Aqua Club made the exciting find.

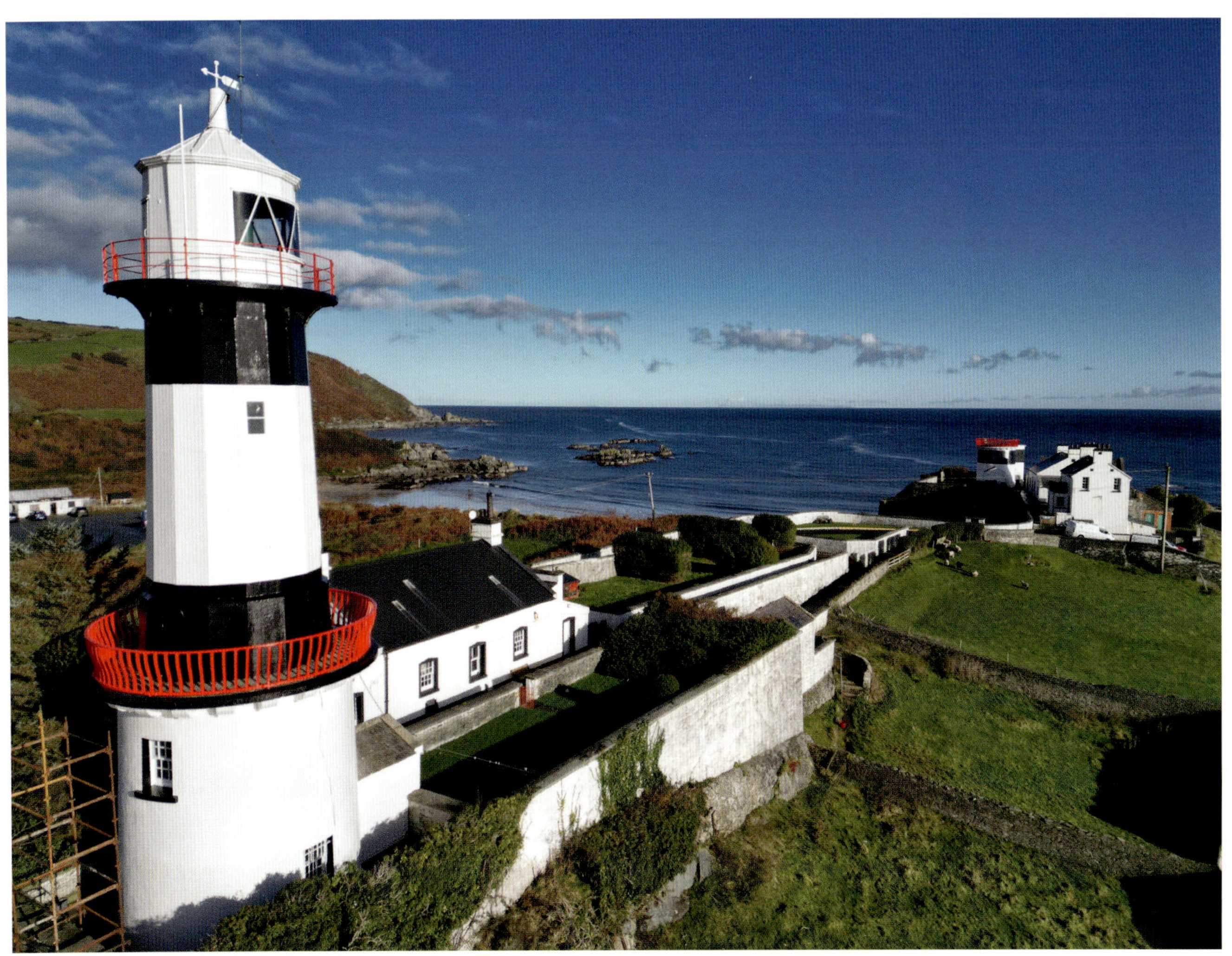

Stroove (Shroove) Lighthouse, also known as Inishowen Head Lighthouse, on Dunagree Point guides maritime traffic on the approach to Lough Foyle. Two lighthouses were built here in the 1830s. The front light was decommissioned in the 1950s, and the station was automated in 1979. St Colmcille, patron saint of emigrants, said his last farewell to his native land on Inishowen Head when he set out from his monastery at Derry to bring Christianity to the Scots *c.* AD 562.

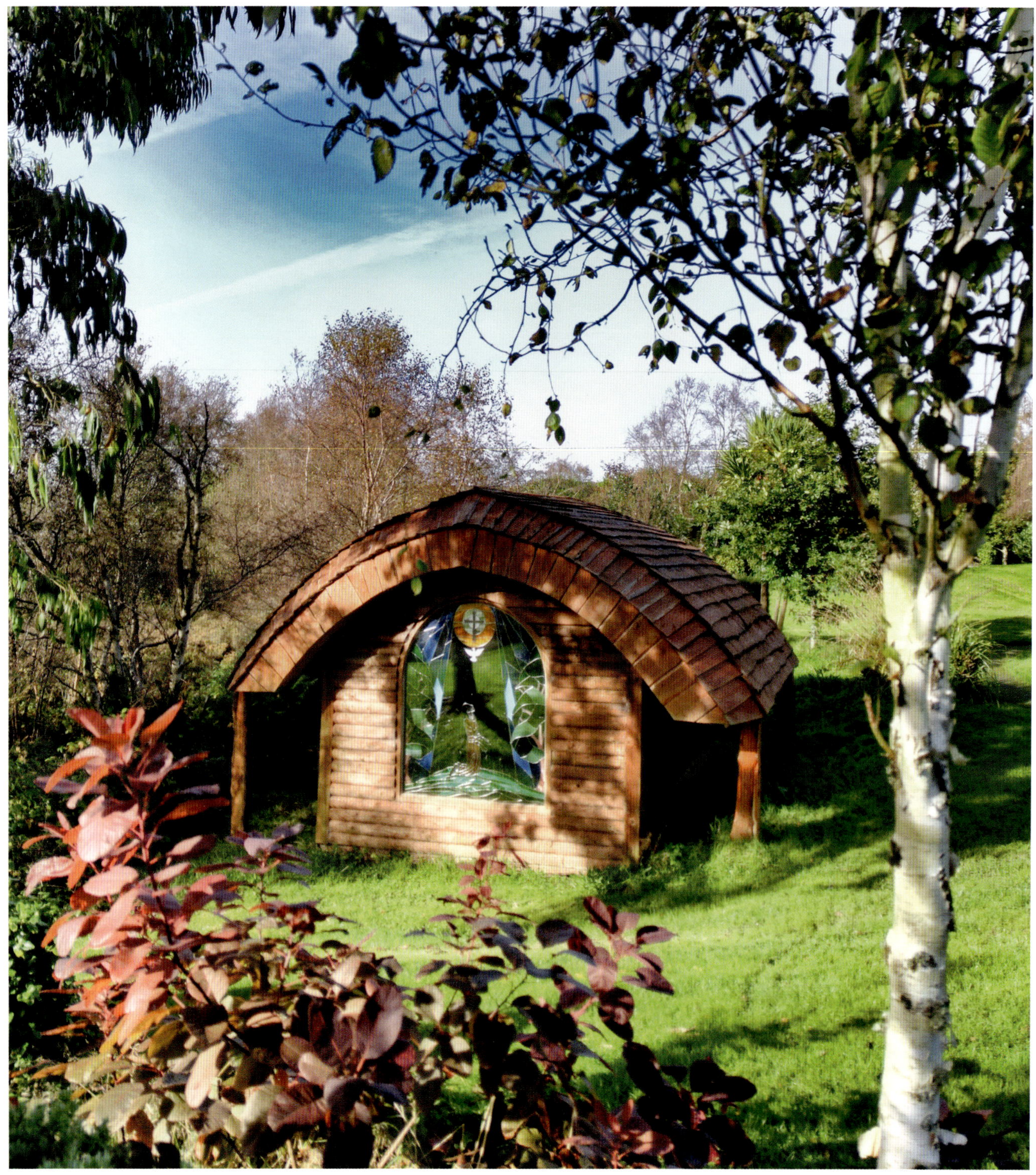

St Dymphna's Shelter in the Celtic Prayer Garden at the IOSAS Centre at Muff. The garden is a six-acre site designed in the shape of the island of Ireland and depicts the lives of the major saints of Ireland's Golden Age (the fifth to twelfth centuries). Winding pathways lead the visitor past representations of the Cross of Patrick, the Boat of Brendan, the Island of Columba and the Oratory of Canice. This hidden gem offers a sacred space to connect with nature and to nurture the spirit.

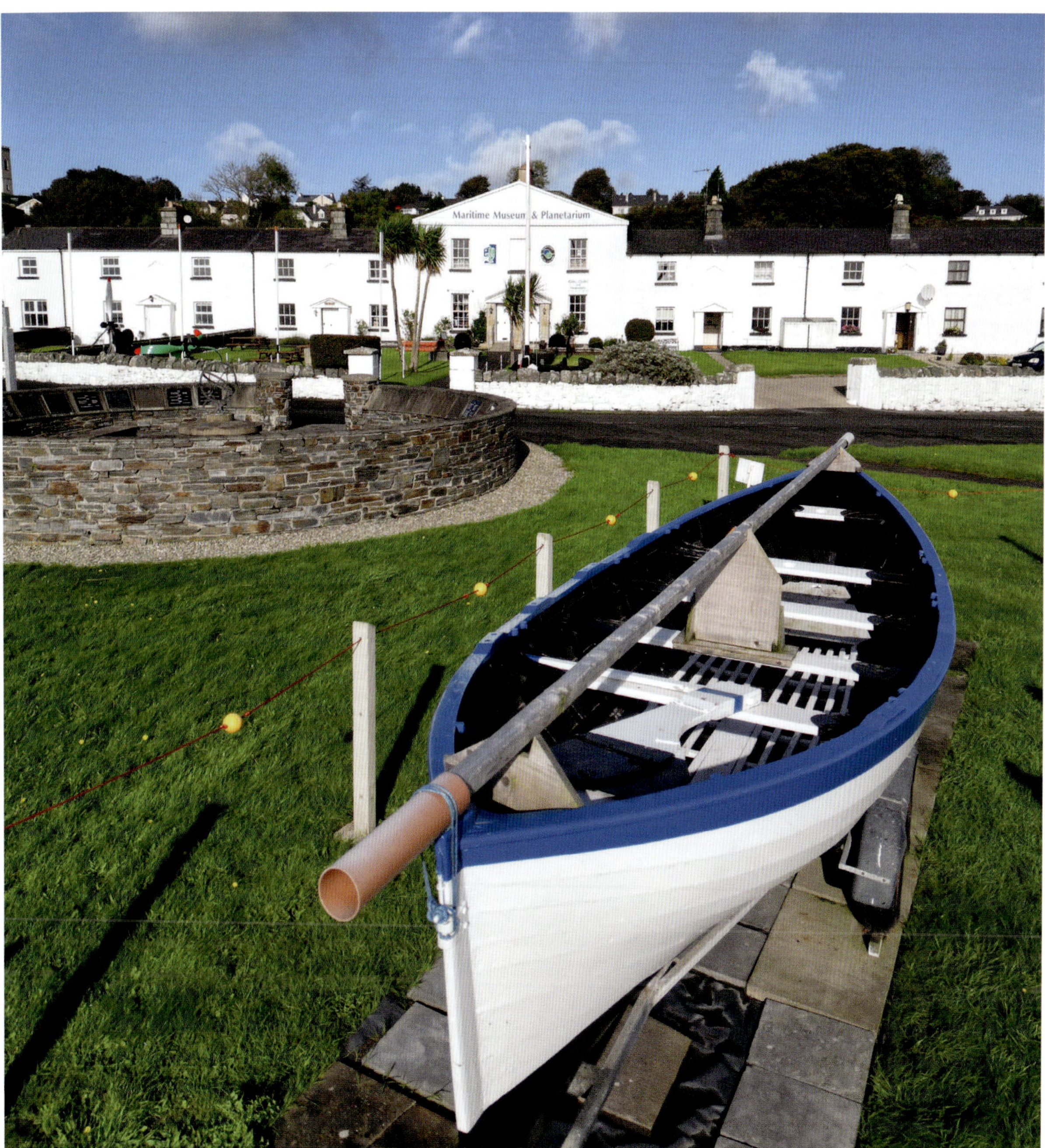

In Greencastle, the former coastguard station is now home to the Inishowen Maritime Museum & Planetarium, overlooking the harbour and the entrance to Lough Foyle.

Following page: Moville Shore Path Walk is a three-kilometre trail that begins at the Bath Green recreational area in Moville and follows the shoreline of Lough Foyle northeast towards Greencastle. Bishop Henry Montgomery (1847–1932) donated the area of shorefront to Donegal County Council in trust for the people of Moville as a recreation area. This easy walk passes elegant dwellings, quiet beaches, coves and a number of sites of historic interest. There are plenty of places to sit and rest along the way. Wildlife is abundant and the views in all directions, particularly across Lough Foyle to County Derry, are superb.

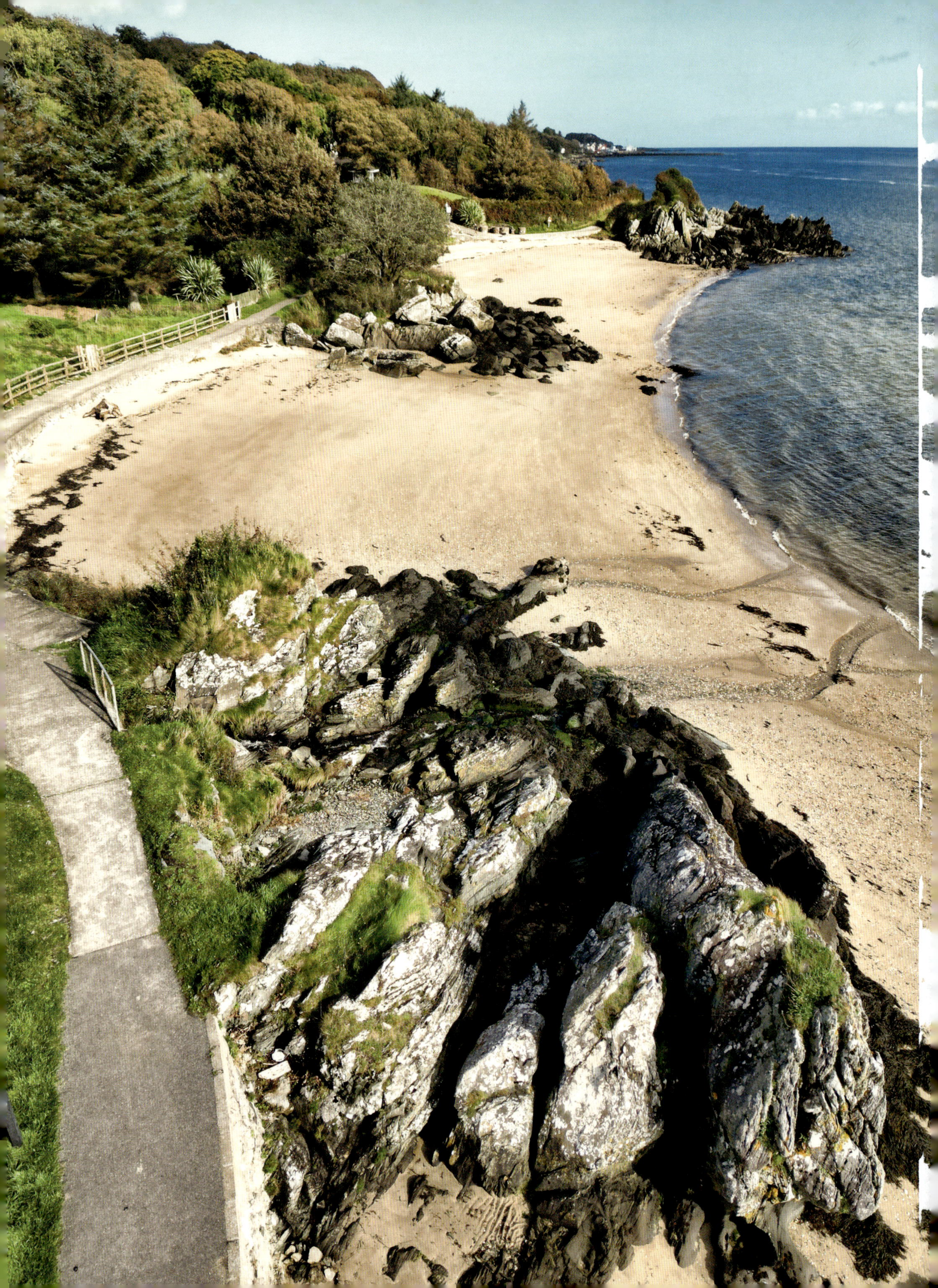